Away for the WEEKEND™

Great Getaways Less Than 250 Miles from LOS ANGELES

Michele Grimm and Tom Grimm

Photographs by Michele Grimm
and Tom Grimm
Maps by Richard Douglas

Clarkson N. Potter, Inc./Publishers
DISTRIBUTED BY CROWN PUBLISHERS, INC./NEW YORK

For Elizabeth Buckley
—Traveler Extraordinaire

Published by Clarkson N. Potter, Inc., One Park Avenue, New York, New York 10016, and simultaneously in Canada by General Publishing Company Limited

Away for the Weekend is a trademark of Clarkson N. Potter, Inc.
Manufactured in the United States of America
Designed by Dennis Grastorf

Library of Congress Cataloging in Publication Data
Grimm, Michele.
  Away for the weekend.
  Includes index.
  1. California, Southern—Description and travel—Tours.
2. Automobiles—Road guides—California, Southern.
3. Los Angeles Region (Calif.)—Description and travel—
Tours.   4. Automobiles—Road guides—California—Los
Angeles Region.   I. Grimm, Tom.   II. Title.
F867.G83 1984   917.94′90453   83-23796
ISBN 0-517-54940-9

10 9 8 7 6 5 4 3 2 1

First Edition

Contents

Map of Weekend Trips in Southern California   viii
Before You Go . . .   ix

NORTH COASTAL EXCURSIONS   1
Map of Weekend Trips   2
Hearst Castle and Quaint Coastal Towns   3
Clamming and Jamming at Pismo Beach   7
San Luis Obispo and the Gibraltar of the Pacific   12
Santa Barbara
    Part 1: On the Waterfront   19
    Part 2: Red Tile Tour to the Past   23
    Part 3: All Around the Town   29
Adventuring in Ventura and Anacapa   35
Seafaring Fun in Oxnard's Harbor and Port Hueneme   40

SOUTH COASTAL OUTINGS   45
Map of Weekend Trips   46
Catalina, the Island of Romance   47
Landlocked Cruise on the *Queen Mary* in Long Beach   52
Seaside Delights at Newport Beach and Balboa Island   58
Festive Times in Laguna Beach   64
Dana Point and San Juan Capistrano—for Boaters and History
    Buffs   69
Mickey Mouse and Many More Amusements in Anaheim and
    Buena Park   74
Marina, Mission, and Marines at Oceanside   81
Seaside Frolics and Flowers in Carlsbad and Environs   85
La Jolla and Del Mar: A Pair of Coastal Charmers   91
San Diego
    Part 1: Introducing California's Oldest City   96
    Part 2: The Southland's Most Enchanting Harbor   103
    Part 3: Balboa Park and Its World-Famous Zoo   108
    Part 4: Aquatic Action in Mission Bay Park   114
Escape to the Del and Coronado "Island"   119
South of the Border
    Part 1: Tijuana and Rosarito   123
    Part 2: Ensenada   128
"Thar She Blows!"—Watching the Annual Whale Parade   131

BACKCOUNTRY AND MOUNTAIN ADVENTURES   137
Map of Weekend Trips   138
Unsurpassed Yosemite—a National Park for All Seasons   139
In Search of the Giants in Sequoia and Kings Canyon National
    Parks   144
Alpine Retreat at Lake Arrowhead and Big Bear Lake   148
Escape to Old-Time Julian and Heavenly Palomar Mountain   153
Rambling Around Paso Robles   158
Flowers and Franciscans at Lompoc   163
History and Outdoor Adventure in Kern County and Isabella Lake   167
Danes, Wines, and Old West in Santa Ynez Valley   173
Happy Trails to Apple Valley and Silverwood Lake   178
Peaceful Pleasures of the Ojai Valley   181
Old-Fashioned Fun in Oak Glen and Redlands   186
Orange County's Canyon Country   191
Boats, Trains, and Planes in Perris Valley   195
Lazy Days at Lake Elsinore and Glen Ivy Hot Springs   199
Historic Riverside, the "Inn" Place   204
Fallbrook and Temecula for Antiques and a Taste of the Grape   208
Wild Animals and Wunnerful Music Near Escondido   214
Retreating to Rancho Santa Fe and Lake San Marcos   219

HIGH AND LOW DESERT DESTINATIONS   223
Map of Weekend Trips   224
The Delights of Death Valley   225
Beyond Barstow: Fun for All Ages Around Calico   229
Desert on Display at Joshua Tree National Monument   233
Sunning and Soaking at Desert Hot Springs   237
Palm Springs
    Part 1: Touring the Southland's Premier Resort   240
    Part 2: Cowboys, Indians, and Desert Lore   246
A Date in Indio and at the Salton Sea   251
Adventures in Anza-Borrego Desert State Park   256
Springtime Spectacular: Viewing the Wildflowers   261

Index   267

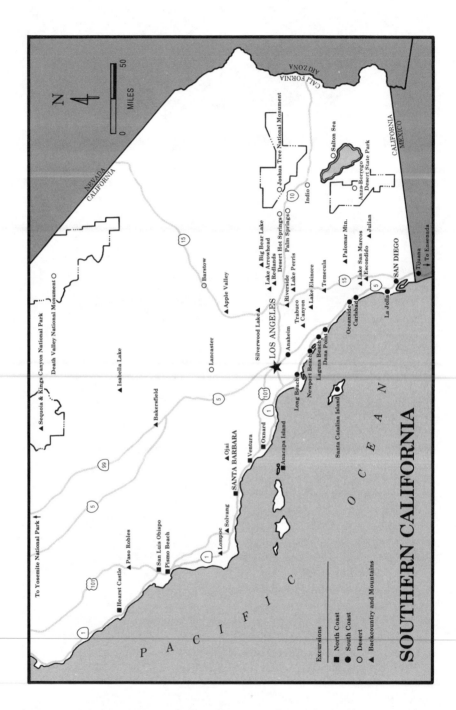

SOUTHERN CALIFORNIA

Excursions
- North Coast
- South Coast
- Desert
- Backcountry and Mountains

PACIFIC OCEAN

To Yosemite National Park
Hearst Castle
Paso Robles
San Luis Obispo
Pismo Beach
Lompoc
Solvang
SANTA BARBARA
Ojai
Ventura
Oxnard
Anacapa Island
Santa Catalina Island
Long Beach
Newport Beach
Laguna Beach
Dana Point
Oceanside
Carlsbad
La Jolla
SAN DIEGO
Tijuana
To Ensenada

Sequoia & Kings Canyon National Park
Death Valley National Monument
Isabella Lake
Bakersfield
Lancaster
Barstow
Apple Valley
Silverwood Lake
LOS ANGELES
Anaheim
Trabuco Canyon
Riverside
Lake Elsinore
Lake Perris
Temecula
Lake San Marcos
Escondido
Palomar Mtn.
Julian
Big Bear Lake
Lake Arrowhead
Redlands
Desert Hot Springs
Palm Springs
Indio
Joshua Tree National Monument
Salton Sea
Anza-Borrego Desert State Park

NEVADA
CALIFORNIA

CALIFORNIA
ARIZONA

CALIFORNIA
MEXICO

N

MILES
0   50

99
5
101
1
15
10

Before You Go . . .

Getting away for the weekend offers a wonderful tonic for body and soul, especially in Southern California, where there are so many delightful and diversified places to go. Astonishing as it seems, after only a short drive from Los Angeles you can be picnicking beside a backcountry lake, skiing down a snowy slope, basking beneath the desert sun, or strolling along the ocean shore. In fact, within a radius of 250 miles from the city's center is an array of natural and man-made attractions that will entice you on an outing every weekend of the year.

For the past decade we have been in pursuit of those pleasure-filled destinations as a vocation rather than a vacation, exploring Southern California as free-lance journalists for our regular "Trip of the Week" travel column in the *Los Angeles Times*. Now we are happy to gather and share our adventures and discoveries in a book that will guide you on 52 enjoyable excursions.

Reading our day-by-day itineraries, you'll see that the Southland, as the lower section of our oblong state is nicknamed, has something for everyone—nature lovers, history buffs, art connoisseurs, gourmet diners, mountain hikers, antique collectors, wine tasters, museum goers, tennis players, mission aficionados, flower fanciers, romantics, and more. Even armchair travelers will be tempted to leave home.

To make it easier for you to decide where to go, we've organized a selection of getaway weekends by their geographical location from the L.A. megalopolis: North Coastal Excursions, South Coastal Outings, Backcountry and Mountain Adventures, and High and Low Desert Destinations. You'll find the specific trips listed in the contents.

Every trip is planned as a two-day weekend—you can leave town on Friday afternoon or evening and return late Sunday. Some destinations that are more distant from Los Angeles or offer an abundance of attractions are better enjoyed on a longer, three- or four-day, holiday weekend.

Of course, you can adapt the trips to midweek travel as well, often avoiding the problems of overcrowding that can occur at popular spots on the weekends. And you can string two or three trips together to plan a complete vacation. Also, as you'll notice from our list of trips, three favorite Southern California cities—Palm Springs, Santa Barbara, and San Diego—deserve at least two, three, or four weekends for thorough exploration.

For almost every excursion we've first outlined what there is to see and do and then described each place and activity in more detail. Driving directions are included, but the essential information of any worthwhile travel guidebook—street addresses, telephone numbers, hours of operation, admission costs, and so forth—are given at the end of each weekend under "Sightseeing."

While describing a destination, we've also suggested where to spend the night and get a good meal, and the specifics of those places are given at the end of each trip under "Lodging" and "Dining." Wherever possible, we recommended only highly regarded resorts, hotels, or inns that are unique enough to make your weekend special; many are expensive, but worth it for their extra pleasures. If they are over your budget or booked up, check into one of the many motels that can usually be found in every area. For travelers with recreational vehicles (RVs) and folks who prefer to sleep out, we've also listed some public campsites under "Camping."

As to restaurants, those we've suggested are local or personal favorites that cover a wide range of tastes. Chain restaurants usually have not been included, because most travelers already know what they're like. Besides, much of the fun of a weekend getaway is treating yourself to some different dining experiences. Regarding the cost of a meal, the restaurants we've mentioned range from the big-splurge category to unexpectedly inexpensive. No menu prices are given, because they're always changing, but you can call the restaurant and ask about the current cost of a meal before making reservations. Also, many restaurants post their menus at the door, so you can check prices before being seated at a table.

For complete lists of restaurants and lodgings, as well as brochures and additional details about the local attractions, we have indicated the destination's chamber of commerce or visitors bureau under "For More Information" at the end of each trip. It's a good idea to contact them by telephone or letter before you leave, because most often their offices are closed on weekends. Also ask about annual events at your destination that may be of special interest or extra fun for your weekend or something to avoid if you'd rather not be part of the crowd. We've mentioned most well-known Southland celebrations and their usual dates in the trip descriptions or at the end under "Events."

Two of the weekend getaways actually feature a pair of seasonal events that are major attractions in Southern California—watching the grand parade of California gray whales that cruise along the coast in wintertime and viewing the spectacular wildflowers that bloom across the desert in the springtime. For these outings, rather than describing a specific itinerary, as with the other 50 weekends, we've listed all the ports where you can board whale-watching boats and given directions to the best places to find the flowers. When you decide where to go, look up a weekend trip that's in the same area and you'll find other attractions to enjoy, as well as recommended lodgings and places to eat.

Regarding the itineraries in this book, they are intended only as guidelines, because we know everyone's interests vary. Some people will spend hours viewing the exhibits in a museum, while others would rather lounge by the pool at their hotel. For each weekend we've included both the best-known and most offbeat attractions that make a place particularly interesting and enjoyable to visit. Pick a destination, read the trip description, note the sights and activities that entice you the most, then alter the itinerary to suit yourself.

After you decide where to go, be certain to map out your route. In fact, none of the excursions should be attempted without maps in hand. Once you leave Los Angeles via the freeways, we guide you along the most scenic routes—and while most highways in Southern California are well marked, you may inadvertently miss a turn or get on the wrong road without a map to keep track of where you're going.

While the maps in this book are useful for general directions to a destination, we recommend the outstanding maps of the Southern California Automobile Club, an AAA club that's renowned for its cartographic department. Unfortunately, the club's detailed freeway, city, and county road maps are available only to club members, but the membership fee is soon returned in a wide assortment of free maps and travel booklets, as well as other services to motorists, such as emergency road service and towing. The Automobile Club of Southern California has its headquarters at 2601 South Figueroa Street, Los Angeles 90007, and you'll find AAA district offices in many neighboring cities and outlying communities; look in the white pages of the telephone book for the nearest one.

Another of the Southland's major map makers is Thomas Bros. of Irvine; their detailed highway maps are sold in handy spiral bindings at many bookstores. Area maps also are available at most gas stations, while chambers of commerce and visitors bureaus usually have street maps covering their regions.

For each weekend trip we've indicated the round-trip mileage to give you an idea of the *total* amount of driving involved. The figure is not just the distance from Los Angeles to your destination and back again, but includes the driving to all attractions suggested in the weekend itinerary. Obviously, if you add or delete some sights, or choose alternate routes to the directions we've given, the mileage may be longer or shorter. By the way, our round-trip mileage measurement is made from the four-level interchange of five freeways in downtown Los Angeles, which is appropriately known as The Stack.

Also, in giving directions in this book, we usually refer to the freeways by their official route numbers rather than their common names. The reason is to avoid confusion for out-of-town readers, who may be misled by names such as the Pomona Freeway, which goes not only to Pomona but to Riverside as well. In addition, there may be more than one name for a freeway, or it may have one name but two different route numbers.

Also be aware that a freeway can be an Interstate, U.S., or California highway, and the sign shields with their identifying numbers are of different shapes. If you are unfamiliar with the Southern California freeway system, study the map and mark your route and road numbers before starting to drive; making sudden lane changes to another freeway or an exit is dangerous, both to yourself and to other motorists.

The freeway network makes it easy to escape from Los Angeles for the weekend—unless you get caught in rush-hour traffic. If you're a stranger to the area, ask local folks the usual traffic conditions for your exit route at the time you're intending to leave town. You'll discover that Southlanders discuss auto travel in terms of time rather than miles, but only mileage is indicated in our book, because we can't predict traffic delays or know your starting time or point of departure from the city.

If you'd like to get away for the weekend without driving, public transportation by bus and train is available to some of the destinations in this book. However, since Southern California is an auto-oriented society, we haven't included details for travel on Greyhound, Trailways, or Amtrak. Also, once you get to a destination, local bus transportation is often inadequate or even nonexistent, and it may be impossible to walk or to take a taxi to the various attractions. Some of the coastal cities are exceptions, however, and a rail trip on Amtrak is a pleasant alternative to driving north to Santa Barbara or south to San Diego. Their train depots are located near hotels, restaurants, and some major sights, and you can easily get around by foot or local bus. For train schedules and fares you can try calling Amtrak's toll-free number, (800) 872-7245, which often is busy, or inquire at any travel agency.

For out-of-town visitors without wheels, plenty of rental cars are available in Los Angeles, and you can even rent fully equipped motor homes. Many Southern Californians like vacationing in recreational vehicles, because they're more comfortable for family travel and help you cut back on the cost of accommodations and dining out. Get details and rates by contacting the Southland's major RV rental dealer, Altmans America, 1155 Baldwin Park Boulevard, Baldwin Park 91706; phone (213) 960-3853 or toll-free from outside California, (800) 258-6267. Even if you've never driven a motor home before, Altmans America gives renters a personal and professional checkout, as well as a detailed operational manual that's also available in foreign languages for overseas visitors.

Many county, state, and national parks with overnight camping sites offer RV hookups, which means you can connect up your vehicle's electricity and water, and sometimes its sewage disposal. Private campgrounds often are equipped for full hookup at each site, including those belonging to a nationwide chain, KOA, Kampgrounds of America.

To camp in Southern California's most popular state and national parks during the summer and other holiday seasons, you must make camping reservations through Ticketron, as we've noted in the ''Camping'' information following certain trips. The computerized reservations agency has outlets throughout the state; call (213) 642-3888 for locations in the Los Angeles area. You also can make camping reservations by mail to Ticketron, P.O. Box 26430, San Francisco 94126; call toll-free (800) 952-5580 for reservation forms. In addition to the full camping fee for the length of your stay, you'll pay a $2 reservation charge.

Fishing is a popular pastime in Southern California, and anyone 16 years or older must have a state fishing license before dropping a line in a river, a lake, or the ocean, unless you're fishing from a public pier in ocean or bay waters. For residents the annual license costs $6.25, plus $2.50 for a stamp if you're fishing in inland waters. Nonresidents can get a special 10-day license for $10. If you go on a sportfishing boat, special one-day ocean fishing licenses cost $2.

Before you begin reading about all the wonderful places to escape to for the weekend, here are a few final comments. If you have your heart set on staying in a specific hotel or other hostelry, make reservations well in advance of your visit. When you call or write, inquire about family plans (kids under a certain age often stay free with their parents) and discount rates for senior citizens, as well as weekend, vacation, or golf and tennis packages that are offered seasonally or year round at reduced rates. *The price quoted for the lodgings we've listed is minimum double rate at the time this book went to press.*

Of course, nothing ever stays the same, and this is true of the hotels, restaurants, and sightseeing attractions described in this guidebook. Prices and hours of operation are subject to change according to the economy and seasons. As for dining spots, their reputations and menus vary with the cooks and management. A restaurant we've suggested for French fare may since have switched to the latest rage, so-called California cuisine, featuring fresh locally grown ingredients presented with artistic simplicity. To avoid upsetting surprises—such as very high prices, a change in hours, or even finding that a place has gone out of business—call ahead before you go. Also, for future editions of this book, we'd appreciate hearing from you in care of the publisher regarding any corrections that should be made.

Now read on to find out about all the marvelous places in Southern California where you can get away for the weekend—or anytime. Happy travels!

North Coastal Excursions

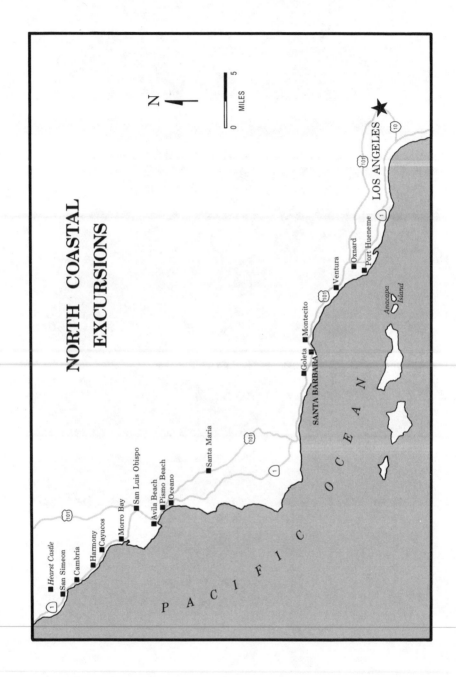

Overleaf: Santa Barbara County Courthouse

Hearst Castle and Quaint Coastal Towns

Imagine reading this "House for Sale" advertisement in the newspaper:

> Hilltop Castle. Historical mansion w/38 bedrooms, 31 baths. Exquisitely furnished. On 123 acres overlooking ocean. Features baronial dining room, plush movie theater, 2 libraries, 14 sitting rooms. Indoor/outdoor swimming pools, tennis courts, space for bowling alley. Guest houses w/46 rooms. Magnificent gardens, fountains, statuary. Original cost $50,000,000. Must see to believe.

What would it cost to buy the world-renowned home that William Randolph Hearst built at San Simeon? Almost everyone agrees it's a priceless piece of real estate, the most imposing private residence in California and indeed the nation.

Besides, it's not for sale. However, you're welcome to visit the late publisher's palace. Once you had to be an invited guest, but Hearst's opulent hideaway was given to the state in 1958, and guided tours are now conducted daily.

The newspaper and magazine magnate called his 100-room retreat La Casa Grande, but the public gave it another name—Hearst Castle. Visitors are awed by the mansion, which is set against the Santa Lucia Mountains on a 1,600-foot-high knoll overlooking Hearst's vast ranch and the Pacific Ocean.

Twin towers give the main building the appearance of a Spanish cathedral. The interior is like a museum, filled with furnishings and antiques that were collected all over the world and cost Hearst millions. The Persian rugs, Italian marble mantels, Flemish tapestries, and innumerable art treasures never fail to impress visitors at San Simeon, even those who have toured the great castles and palaces of Europe.

Outside there is more to see. Over a hundred acres are covered by gardens, terraces, pools, statuary, and a trio of palatial guesthouses. Before being deeded to the state, they were part of Hearst's mountain-to-seashore property, which exceeded a quarter of a million acres.

The Hearst San Simeon State Historical Monument will be the highlight of a weekend visit to a quartet of quaint coastal towns in San Luis Obispo County: San Simeon, Cambria, Cayucos, and Harmony. They're located along a scenic two-lane section of California 1 between Hearst's splendid estate and Morro Bay.

Although more than a million visitors a year make their way to the publisher's hilltop retreat, you'll still find plenty of peace and quiet in this exceptionally pretty and unspoiled part of the California coast. Beachcombing and picnicking at the ocean's edge are the perfect pastimes for such a mellow and memorable weekend.

Drive north from Los Angeles on U.S. 101 to San Luis Obispo, then continue north on California 1 to the Main Street exit for Cambria (say *kam-bree-ah*). Make this charming resort and retirement community your headquarters, since there are no accommodations at the historical monument. A popular place to stay is up a hill on Burton Drive at Cambria Pines Lodge, a complex of rustic cottages that opened in 1927. You'll also find two dozen other pleasant lodgings in the area, all convenient to Hearst Castle. Most are located near the shore along Moonstone Beach Drive, including San Simeon Pines Resort, where you can play on a 9-hole, par-3 golf course. Across the road, campers love the oceanfront sites at San Simeon Beach State Park.

In the morning, head a few miles north of Cambria to the place where William Randolph Hearst began construction of La Casa Grande in 1919. Even at the time of his death in 1951, at the age of 88, not everything in his elaborate building plans had been completed. Nevertheless, there is so much to view at his estate that four different tours are offered.

Tour 1 is recommended for first-time visitors. Your group will be guided through the elaborate gardens past marble statuary, fountains, and terraces to the lower level of the main building, La Casa Grande. Inside you'll be awed by the immense Assembly Room, where Hearst's many guests would gather with their host each evening before dinner. Overstuffed chairs contrast with exquisite tapestries covering the walls and Oriental rugs spanning the floors.

The adjoining Refectory, a baronial banquet area, was the publisher's favorite room. Imagine dining beneath a hand-carved ceiling of saints, with silken banners and monastery stalls lining the walls. The grand walnut table, adorned by antique silver, also was surprisingly set with paper napkins and bottles of catsup, mustard, and pickle relish!

Another featured room you'll see in the big house is the plush theater where the publisher played first-run movies for his guests. Today's visitors get to view some delightful home movies of Hearst and his famous friends.

Also on Tour 1 are the shimmering Neptune and Roman swimming pools, the latter one indoors and so large that two tennis courts were built on its roof. You'll be impressed by a visit to one of the three guesthouses, too.

There's much more to see, if you have time for another tour. The upper levels of La Casa Grande are displayed on Tour 2, which features Hearst's personal bedroom, two other extraordinary suites, both libraries, and the kitchen where meals for 50 or more guests were prepared.

Tour 3 shows you the guest wing of the castle and many works of art, another of the guesthouses, the gardens, and the pools. A fourth tour was added in 1982 for frequent visitors who want to explore even more of the fabulous estate. It focuses on the formal garden area and lower level of the largest guesthouse, including a recently discovered hidden terrace and the unfinished bowling alley.

You must leave your car at the monument's roadside parking area at San Simeon (just off California 1 and about eight miles north of Cambria) and board a bus for a narrated five-mile ride up the hill to the castle, where the two-hour tours begin. There is considerable walking, including 150 to 356 steps to climb, so wear comfortable shoes.

To reserve a place and avoid a long wait (sometimes overnight), get tour tickets in advance through Ticketron, reserving the specific tour, day, and departure time. Each day's remaining tour space is sold on a first-come, first-served basis at the monument's roadside visitors center beginning at 8 A.M.; no telephone reservations.

If you arrive early, or after your tour, drive a half mile from the monument's parking area to the oceanside hamlet of San Simeon. In the 1920s it was a busy port, receiving and warehousing the supplies and elaborate furnishings for Hearst's mansion. Drop into Sebastian's, a rustic general store built in 1852. It serves breakfast and lunch, or you can buy food and picnic in the shade of the surrounding eucalyptus trees. Just across from the store you'll find a free public fishing pier; bait and tackle are available, and no license is required. Between mid-May and mid-October you can depart on half-day or day-long deep-sea fishing trips from the San Simeon pier.

Besides visiting Hearst Castle, you'll enjoy exploring Cambria, a former whaling station, which also was a dairy center and sent daily shiploads of butter and cheese to San Francisco. Originally called Slabtown, because most buildings were constructed of roughhewn boards, it was officially given the Roman name for ancient Wales in 1869. A fire destroyed the original business section of Cambria 20 years later, but the town was rebuilt near Santa Rosa Creek and has since expanded along Main Street all the way to the coast highway. More recently sea-view homes have been built on the slopes of its pine-covered hills.

On Main Street in the newer section of town you'll find a few reminders of Cambria's past, including a century-old jail and the Santa Rosa schoolhouse, now home for an art gallery. Also look for the 1874 French-built lamp from the Point Piedras Blancas lighthouse, which formerly guided coastal cargo vessels.

You'll enjoy browsing in art galleries, antique shops, and gift stores, including one that features thousands of tin soldiers. Most are located along the lengthy, boomerang-shaped Main Street and Burton Drive. When you're hungry in the evening, join other visitors and townsfolk who fill up on home-cooked fare at the Brambles and Grey Fox dinner houses.

After exploring the town, cross the coast highway at the north end of Main Street and take the scenic ride along Moonstone Beach Drive, which parallels the shoreline. There's a turnout where you can beach-comb amid the ocean- and sun-bleached trunks of pine trees to collect colorful pebbles polished by the sea. Be on the lookout for the beach's namesake, milky-white moonstone. Keep your eyes open for otters frolicking in the surf and brown pelicans dive-bombing into the sea for their supper. Have a meal yourself in a nearby family restaurant, the Hamlet at Moonstone Gardens, next to a garden filled with 400 varieties of cacti and succulents. Follow the paths for a close look at the plants.

Moonstone Beach Drive loops back to California 1, which you can continue to follow south toward Cayucos, another historic coastal town. Five miles down the highway, turn left for a brief stop at tiny Harmony, population 18. The old buildings that once were used by a dairy cooperative now house gift shops, a pottery studio, a silversmith, and the town post office. Enjoy refreshments in the upstairs cafe, or time your visit for champagne brunch on Sunday or dinner in the Harmony Valley Inn.

About eight miles farther south on California 1, exit toward the ocean to Cayucos, an active seaport in the late 1800s. Sailing ships tied up at a long wharf to take on hides, beef, and cheeses brought from inland ranches. Today the town pier is occupied mostly by fishermen, while swimmers and surfers have fun at the adjacent public beach.

Look for the weather-beaten Cass House on Ocean Avenue, built by the town's founder in 1857 and currently an antique shop. More antiques and gifts will be found in the refurbished Way Station, a travelers' rest stop from the past century where you can still get a meal. Cayucos has several motels, in case you can't get accommodations closer to Hearst Castle.

Continue on Ocean Avenue to rejoin California 1 to San Luis Obispo, then pick up U.S. 101 south for the journey back to Los Angeles.

Round trip is about 508 miles.

San Simeon/Cambria Area Code: 805

SIGHTSEEING   *Hearst San Simeon State Historical Monument*, off California 1 (P.O. Box 8), San Simeon 93452, 927-4621. Choice of four two-hour tours given daily 8 A.M. to 5:30 P.M. in summer, 8:20 A.M. to 3:30 P.M. in winter. Departures every 10 to 30 minutes, depending on season. Each tour costs $7 adults, $3 children 6 through 12 years, ages 5 and under free if held on adult's lap aboard the tour bus. Advance reservations from Ticketron cost $1 extra per ticket. Flash photographs, tripods, and baby strollers not permitted. Wheelchairs accommodated on Tour 1 with 10 days' advance notice; call 927-4621.

LODGING   *Cambria Pines Lodge,* 2905 Burton Drive, Cambria 93428, 927-4200; $34. Cottages on 23 tree-shaded acres, indoor swimming pool and sauna. Also restaurant with entertainment and dancing. • *San Simeon Pines Resort,* Moonstone Beach Drive, San Simeon 93452, 927-4648; $34. Near beach amid cypress trees. Free par-3 golf. • *Fireside Inn by the Sea,* 6700 Moonstone Beach Drive, Cambria, 927–8661; $46. Fireplaces in rooms, close to beach. • *Cambria Shores Motel,* 6276 Moonstone Beach Drive, Cambria, 927-4107; $40. Ocean-view rooms.

CAMPING   *San Simeon State Beach,* 3 miles north of Cambria off California 1, 927-4509. 117 sites along beach, $3 per night; reserve through Ticketron. No hookups.

DINING   *The Brambles,* 4055 Burton Drive, Cambria, 927-4716. Delightful dinner house in century-old cottage with more recent Victorian-decorated additions to accommodate nightly crowds. Prime rib and fresh trout are favorites. Reservations necessary in summer. • *Grey Fox Inn,* 4095 Burton Drive, Cambria, 927–3305. Another popular dinner house in a family home, with dining on the terrace in summer. Try the fresh seafood. Also the place for Sunday brunch. • *Caffe Porta Via,* 2248 Main Street, Cambria, 927-8742. Italian fare for lunch and dinner. • *The Hamlet at Moonstone Gardens,* 1½ miles north of Cambria off California 1, 927-3859. Pleasant restaurant convenient to Hearst Castle, offering three daily meals; children's menu. Guests can tour adjacent cactus garden. • *Harmony Valley Inn,* 5 miles south of Cambria off California 1 in Harmony, 927-4205. Lunch and dinner in rear of renovated dairy creamery; also Sunday brunch. Restaurant and tiny town of Harmony closed Mondays and Tuesdays in winter.

FOR MORE INFORMATION   Contact the San Simeon Chamber of Commerce, P.O. 1, San Simeon 93452, 927-3500. Also the Cambria Chamber of Commerce, 767 Main Street (P.O. Box 134), Cambria 93428, 927-3624.

Clamming and Jamming at Pismo Beach

If you enjoy the coast, you'll love a getaway to two quiet beach-front towns that big development and large crowds continue to pass by. Pismo Beach and Avila Beach in San Luis Obispo County offer a wonderful assortment of surprises, in addition to an array of activities found at more bustling beach retreats: tennis, golf, horseback riding, fishing, and surfing.

First, there's the fun of digging your own clams or at least savoring clam chowder, like the kind that put Pismo Beach on the map. It's also the only place in the state where you can go for a Sunday drive on the beach itself. More adventurous motorists can even ride over the wind-swept sands in a dune buggy. A few miles north at Avila Beach is a fascinating deep-sea fishing port, where you can sip cocktails and dine on fresh seafood while the sun splashes color across the ocean at day's end. And in the tree-covered hills nearby, bubbling hot springs invite you to soak your cares away any time of the night or day.

Actually, it was a clam festival that brought fame to Pismo Beach and the area. Beginning with a New Year's Day clambake in 1945, Pismo's annual clam fest became the major event along the central California coast. However, because of voracious sea otters and an abundance of human clammers, the famous Pismo clams became rather scarce—and the festival ended with a final fling in 1977.

But the Pismo people missed their big midwinter bash and revived it three years later as a Mardi Gras featuring Dixieland jazz bands. Festival goers now are more likely to dig music than clams, so it's no wonder that one local wag calls it a jam festival! Even if you don't make its Mardi Gras in February, Pismo Beach is an enjoyable weekend destination any time of the year.

Although Pismo has a number of attractive ocean-view motels, make lodging reservations at the area's premier resort, San Luis Bay Inn, about six miles up the coast at Avila Beach. Built on a promontory that once was part of a Spanish land grant, the inn features spectacular views and spacious accommodations. Guests enjoy a championship 18-hole golf course with challenging play across a meandering river and tidal lagoon. There are miles of trails for jogging or hiking, tennis courts, and a heated swimming pool, too.

Get to the inn from Los Angeles by driving north on U.S. 101 almost to San Luis Obispo. Take the Avila Beach exit and follow Avila Road to the bay. Even if you don't stay at San Luis Bay Inn, at least make reservations for dinner in its gourmet restaurant, which is a favorite with the local folks. Many of the dishes are cooked at tableside, and you're presented with a wine list boasting 350 vintages. There's musical entertainment as well.

In the morning, take Front Street from Avila Road to the sandy Avila Beach strand, where you can sunbathe, barbecue, and picnic. It's marked by a 1,570-foot fishing pier, originally called Avila Wharf and built in 1887. Facing the beach are an assortment of places to eat and drink, including the popular Old Custom House Cafe. Photographs inside show the building when it was dedicated in 1926 as a customs office for coastal vessels.

During the 1920s many visitors arrived unannounced at night. They were Prohibition rumrunners, and the secluded central coast was a perfect port of entry. Today there's still plenty going on along Avila's water-front—in the daylight. Pirates Cove, a favorite landing spot for the clandestine booze boats, now is a popular beach for sunbathing sans suits. Most boat activity is around the third pier in the bay at Port San Luis, a protected harbor where deep-sea fishing vessels and pleasure craft bob at anchor. You'll see dozens of salmon trollers, gill netters, and albacore vessels, plus hundreds of sailboats and yachts awaiting weekend sailors. Year round you can catch rock cod and other ocean fish from Port San Luis Sportfishing boats that leave from the pier every morning.

Get there by following Avila Road along the shoreline and drive out to the end of the pier, where you'll also find a fish market and the Olde Port Inn restaurant. Enjoy a takeout seafood cocktail from the market, or walk upstairs to the restaurant bar for a bowl of clam chowder.

Later, by driving back east on Avila Road toward U.S. 101, you'll be tempted by two hot springs. The first is Sycamore Mineral Springs, which has been a spa and resort on and off since 1897. You can soak privately in deep tile tubs in the 1930s spa building or relax outside in redwood tubs constructed here and there on the woodsy hillside. Sycamore Mineral Springs is open 24 hours every day, but call in advance for reservations.

Down the road just before you reach U.S. 101 is Avila Hot Springs, discovered in 1907 while a well was being drilled for oil. At one time it was a regular stop for the Hollywood celebrities en route to San Simeon as guests of William Randolph Hearst. Now combined with an RV park, Avila Hot Springs has private tile tubs with adjustable temperature controls and an outdoor community tub maintained at 105 degrees. There's a freshwater swimming pool as well.

On Sunday, head south on U.S. 101 to Pismo Beach and exit on Hinds Avenue to reach the beach and public pier. Stroll out on the long wooden structure to watch surfers ride the waves alongside the pier's pilings. If you'd like to try your luck fishing from the pier, rods and bait are available there at Sheldon's Clam Stand. No license is required.

From the pier you'll also get a panorama of the Pismo coastline. To the north the rugged coast has coves and tide pools, while to the south stretch miles of flat and firm sandy shore where visitors are welcome to drive motor vehicles and ride horses. (There's a rental stable not far away in Oceano.) In fact, it's the only beach in California where you're allowed to drive your car. Go at low tide and keep to the 15 mph speed limit. This section of the coast is part of Pismo State Beach and also includes 850 acres of sand dunes that you can explore with a rented dune buggy or three-wheeled motorbike.

To drive on the beach and see the sand dunes, turn right off Hinds Avenue onto Cypress Street, which joins California 1 going south. If it's wintertime, pause to park on the road shoulder just past the Grover City city limits sign for a glimpse of the orange-and-black monarch butterflies resting on leaves of the eucalyptus trees. Usually they're in the area annually from December into March, during the insects' remarkable migration to escape the colder climes. Then continue south and turn right on Grand Avenue to the beach access auto ramp. Drive south on Pismo State Beach for a short ride on the sand and exit on the auto ramp at Pier Avenue in Oceano. Or drive farther on the beach to the sand dunes designated as a playground for off-road vehicles.

Digging for the famed Pismo clams is another favorite activity up and down the state beach park, which stretches for twelve miles from the city of Pismo Beach to the Santa Barbara County line. Clamming hasn't been very good lately, but determined clam diggers probably will be rewarded with some mouth-watering mollusks if you ask the local people where to search in the sand. At area sports and liquor stores you can rent clam forks for digging, get free tide charts, and also buy the required California fishing license.

The unique Pismo cannot be caught commercially, but it's still possible to order some delicious chowder in the local restaurants—made with clams from the East Coast. Try Pismo Fish & Chips, Inc., on Cypress Street, where there's often a line of seafood fanciers waiting to get in. Other popular Pismo places to go to for clam chowder and fish are Plessas Tavern, Trader Nick's, and D. W. Grovers (in adjacent Grover City).

For some old-fashioned fun on one night of your visit, reserve seats at the Great American Melodrama and Vaudeville Theater on Pacific Coast Highway (California 1) in Oceano. You'll be taken back to the Gay '90s era of stage entertainment when everyone in the audience boos the villain and cheers the hero of the old-time dramas. There are comedy and musical acts, too, and the family can enjoy it all while munching on popcorn, pretzels, and sandwiches.

You'll also be delighted with a Sunday-afternoon visit to the Good Old Days Museum, one man's lifetime collection of memorabilia that surpasses Grandmother's attic. From California 1, exit north on Hinds Avenue in Pismo Beach and go over the U.S. 101 freeway to 765 Price Canyon Road. Look left for a little sign to the museum, drive up the narrow road, and honk your horn. Dick Skeen will appear and show you his nostalgic collection of odds and ends—everything from an antisnoring device to snowshoes for horses—all displayed haphazardly in a rustic building. He'll also be happy to take you to the top floor of his house to see a collection of antique dolls, including one of the first talking dolls; call beforehand to make sure he's home.

When it's time for your return to Los Angeles, rejoin U.S. 101 and head south.

Round trip is about 420 miles.

Pismo Beach/Avila Beach Area Code: 805

SIGHTSEEING *San Luis Bay Golf Course,* San Luis Bay Drive (or P.O. Box 188), Avila Beach 93424, 595-2307. 18-hole, par-71 super-scenic course in an oak-lined canyon. Weekend greens fees $10 per person. • *Port San Luis Sportfishing,* Pier 3 (or P.O. Box 356), Avila Beach 93424, 595-7200. All-day rock cod fishing trips depart at 7 A.M. daily. Adults $20 weekends, $18 weekdays. • *Sycamore Mineral Springs,* 158 Avila Road (or Route 1, Box 158, San Luis Obispo 93401), 595-7302. Nature lovers delight in the 25 redwood hot tubs tucked among the trees; $12 minimum per hour per tub. Indoor mineral baths are $5 per person for an hour. Open 24 hours. • *Avila Hot Springs,* 150 Avila Road (or Route 1, Box 150, San Luis Obispo 93401), 595-2359. Open 10 A.M. to 10 P.M. daily. Private mineral bath, $4 per hour; massages and facials by appointment. Heated outdoor swimming pool, $3.50 all day, children $2.50. • *Livery Stables,* 1207 Silver Spur Place, Oceano 93445, 489-8100. Open daily with rental horses for beach rides; $7.50 per hour. • *Fun Rentals,* 1163 Strand Way, Oceano 93445, 481-6880. Open daily with dune buggies and three-wheel ATC motorbikes for beach rides; $15 to $20 per hour per vehicle. • *Great American Melodrama and Vaude-ville Theater,* 1863 Pacific Coast Highway (California 1), Oceano 93445, 489–2499. Evening shows Thursday through Sunday (also Wednesday April through December). $7 per seat for Friday and Saturday perform-ances, $1 less on other days. • *Good Old Days Museum,* 765 Price Can-yon Road, Pismo Beach 93449, 773-4400. Open 10 A.M. to 4 P.M. weekends only; call first. Adults $1, kids under 13 years 50 cents.

EVENTS *Pismo Beach Mardi Gras,* annual three-day weekend festival in late February featuring Dixieland jazz bands, costume ball, doo-dah parade, and clam chowder cook-off. Band names and tickets ($15 for all performances) available from Dixieland Mardi Gras, P.O. Box 3430, Pismo Beach 93449, or contact the Pismo Beach Chamber of Commerce (see below).

LODGING *San Luis Bay Inn,* Avila Road (or P.O. Box 188), Avila Beach 93424, 595-2333; $64. Former private hotel that's now a popular resort with 79 rooms overlooking ocean and golf course; two suites in-clude hot tubs. Lighted tennis courts and heated pool. Also excellent dining room (see below) and room service. • *Shore Cliff Lodge,* 2555 Price Street, Pismo Beach 93449, 773-4671; $48. Spectacular cliff-top location with Pacific views and spiral staircase to beach. Adjacent Shore Cliff Inn offers drinks and dining. • *Kon Tiki Inn,* 1621 Price Street, Pismo Beach, 773-4833; $40. Oceanfront rooms, plus penthouse suite with fireplace. Trader Nick's next door is popular for Sunday champagne brunch, daily meals, nighttime music and dancing. • *Sea Crest Motel,* 2241 Price Street, Pismo Beach, 773-4608; $44. Rooms with ocean view.

CAMPING *Pismo Beach State Park,* along California 1, 489-2684. Two camping areas available: Oceano, 82 sites (42 with hookups) south of Pismo Beach, and North Beach, 103 sites (no hookups) south of Grover City. All sites $6 per night. Popular on weekends and in summer; Ticketron reservations recommended. Also over 1,200 more campsites at private RV parks in the Pismo area.

DINING *San Luis Bay Inn* (see above). Delightful ocean-view dining room with gourmet dishes and excellent wine list; treat yourself to cherries jubilee for dessert. Open daily 7 A.M. to 10 P.M.; jackets for men suggested in the evening. ● *Olde Port Inn,* Pier 3, Avila Beach 93424, 595–2515. Fresh seafood, with a view of the fishing boats that bring it in. ● *Plessas Tavern,* 891 Price Street, Pismo Beach, 773-2060. Try baked clams on the half shell au gratin, a house specialty since 1921. Other seafood and also meat dishes served daily for lunch and dinner except Tuesdays; children's menu. ● *F. McLintock's Saloon and Dining House,* 750 Mattie Road, Shell Beach, 93449, 773-2488. Informal Western-theme dinner restaurant featuring oak pit barbecued steaks and ribs. Also, ranch-style buffet on Sundays. ● *D. W. Grover's,* 359 Grand Avenue, Grover City 93433, 489-1503. Lunch and dinner amid Victorian decoration; menu favorites are seafood, steak, and prime ribs.

FOR MORE INFORMATION Contact the Pismo Beach Chamber of Commerce, 581 Dolliver Street, Pismo Beach 93449, 773-4382.

San Luis Obispo and the Gibraltar of the Pacific

Motorists on the busy U.S. 101 freeway often slip into San Luis Obispo for gas, grub, or a good night's sleep because it's midway on the north-south run between Los Angeles and San Francisco. But travelers who linger awhile will discover that this attractive college town is much more than a convenient rest stop. San Luis Obispo is a wonderful weekend retreat, a friendly place where you can turn back the clock to California's early eras.

Nestled among verdant rolling hills at the foot of the Santa Lucia Mountains, this city is a real charmer. Its spick-and-span appearance reflects the pride of its residents, who want visitors to enjoy San Luis Obispo's many historical attractions, including an impressive Spanish mission, Victorian homes, and vintage businesses like the Ah Louis Store, which opened in 1874 and is still run by the founder's family.

Not far away, Mother Nature provides a spectacular attraction that also will be part of your SLO getaway, an immense volcanic outcropping that's called the Gibraltar of the Pacific. It's Morro Rock at picturesque Morro Bay, a busy fishing port and bustling summertime vacation spot.

Another area landmark, the garish Madonna Inn, is the place for you to sleep. You won't miss this sprawling hillside hostelry on the outskirts of San Luis Obispo, because everything in sight is painted a Pepto-Bismol pink. That's one reason the inn's become a must-see-it-to-believe-it tourist attraction. Some two million travelers pull in there every year, and you need to make reservations weeks in advance in order to spend the night. Each of the inn's 112 rooms has been designed and decorated at the whim of owner Alex Madonna, and guests agree that his tastes are definitely flamboyant, if not a bit bizarre.

Check into the Safari room, for instance, and you'll be surrounded by zebra stripes and leopard spots that cover everything from the wallpaper to the bedspreads. If a night in the jungle doesn't fit your fantasy, the Caveman room has an interior of rocks. Or select more restful quarters, such as the Old Mill room, which features a waterfall that turns on and off with the flick of a switch. For folks with claustrophobia, there's the enormous Austrian suite, which stretches 76 feet. Unless you reserve a room by name, guests take potluck on their quarters (depending on price range and beds requested), but it doesn't matter much because all the accommodations are far from ordinary.

Begin your getaway by driving north from Los Angeles on U.S. 101 and exiting on Madonna Road to the inn at the southern edge of San Luis Obispo. After checking in, have dinner in the Madonna Inn's dining room, which is extraordinarily decorated in a Christmas motif year round. With a menu featuring Australian lobster tail and French filet mignon, the food is superior to standard motel coffee shop fare, but don't be surprised when you're served pink toast!

On Saturday, see the sights of San Luis Obispo, guided by two brochures provided by the chamber of commerce. One describes the Path of History, a two-mile tour marked by a green line painted on the city's streets. Plan two hours to circle the route on foot (or 20 minutes by car), plus extra time to stop at any of the 19 points of interest along the way.

You also will have a delightful time strolling around the town on a self-guided tour of San Luis Obispo's vintage homes. A Heritage Homes pamphlet sketches the history of 38 houses you'll see on the eight-square-block walking route.

Begin your tours from the Madonna Inn by rejoining U.S. 101 north and taking the first exit, Marsh Street, to San Luis Obispo's downtown area. Turn left on Chorro Street to Mission Plaza, a delightful pedestrians-only area along San Luis Creek that's a lush and quiet oasis in the heart of town. It's the city's historical focal point, too.

As you'll soon observe, San Luis Obispo is a very peaceful place. However, a couple of hundred years ago it was quite a different story. When a Spanish expedition headed north from San Diego in search of Monterey Bay in 1769, they encountered numerous bears near the present town site. A hunting party cleared the way and brought back bear meat for the hungry soldiers, settlers, and local Indians.

Three years later the Spanish missionary Junipero Serra chose the scene of the hunt as the spot to erect Mission San Luis Obispo de Tolosa, fifth in his chain of Franciscan stations in California. It was named for a thirteenth-century French saint, the Bishop of Toulouse. Chumash Indians were recruited to build the adobe and thatched-roof mission, but their hostile brothers attacked it with flaming arrows on several occasions. As a result, the San Luis Obispo padres developed the fireproof tiles that became standard roofing material for all the Spanish missions in California.

Today the restored mission is the center of attention on Mission Plaza and serves as a parish church. Visit the original padres' residence, now a museum that portrays life in the state's early days. Also on Mission Plaza you'll find more Californiana—including Indian artifacts, glassware, papers, and pictures—in the San Luis Obispo County Historical Museum, once the city's Carnegie Library.

Another highlight is the Dallidet Adobe, built by a French vintner in 1853 after he arrived in the area to raise grapes. Its interior can be viewed on Sundays in summer only, but another old residence, the Murray Adobe on Mission Plaza, welcomes visitors year round. It was the early home of Englishman Walter Murray, a distinguished judge and journalist. For a brief return to contemporary times, enjoy the ongoing exhibits by local and visiting artists in the San Luis Obispo Art Center, across from the county museum at the edge of Mission Plaza.

Don't miss the Ah Louis Store, still operated by the same family that established it over a century ago to serve the 2,000 Chinese building railroad tunnels through the mountains nearby. Besides buying herbs and general merchandise, these itinerant laborers used the store as a bank and post office. Today it's a gift shop and state historical landmark.

Also on the Path of History route is another century-old store, Sinsheimer Bros., where you'll have fun browsing. Now called Granny's and noted for its iron-front facade, it's been re-created as a 1900s general store. You'll find everything from oil lamps to square nails to calico cloth. As in the old days, customers' money is sent to the cashier's booth via a change carrier on wires overhead.

Some of the town's other vintage buildings have been converted to pleasing shopping and dining spots. Built in 1906, the Golden State Creamery is just called the Creamery nowadays and houses nearly two dozen shops. Nearby on Higuera Street, a 1900s department store has become an arcade of 22 shops and is known as the Network. Downstairs is the informal Wine Street Inn, which features Swiss fondues. As home for 22,000 students at Cal Poly State University and Cuesta Community College, San Luis Obispo is host to a great variety of lively restaurants. At the Cigar Factory, where Pioneer cigars were made at the turn of the century, you can enjoy dinner and nightly entertainment. Other favorite downtown places for food and fun include Chocolate Soup, McLintock's Saloon, and Sebastian's.

Spend Sunday not far away in Morro Bay, where vacationers flock to picnic, swim, boat, fish, beachcomb, bird-watch, and play golf. Marked by the eons-old Morro Rock, the town has many other natural attractions that have been preserved for public enjoyment as state parks and beaches.

Head first to the 1,500-acre Morro Bay State Park at the south edge of that coastal town. Follow California 1 northwest from San Luis Obispo about 12 miles to the South Bay Boulevard exit and the park entrance. There the highway joins park roads that lead down to the bay and a small boat harbor where boats and bicycles can be rented for leisurely explorations. There also are nature trails to walk for close-up views of the park's extensive birdlife, which includes 250 species. Go to White Point and look north for a great blue heron rookery with nests high in the eucalyptus trees. Also stop at the park's Museum of Natural History to see its excellent displays about the area's birds and animals, as well as Morro Bay's earliest inhabitants, the Chumash Indians. If you have time, watch the films about local geology and oceanography.

Golfers can challenge the park's 18-hole public course, where you'll also find a driving range, pro shop, and clubhouse. Get a panoramic view of the bay and its landmark Morro Rock by following the park road that cuts through the golf course to an overlook on Black Mountain, the second of nine 50-million-year-old volcanic peaks that dot the landscape from the ocean's edge inland to San Luis Obispo.

From the observation point you'll also see the protective five-mile-long sandspit that separates Morro Bay from the Pacific. This isolated peninsula is part of the state park and the place to go for beachcombing. You can reach it by renting a small boat in the park harbor to cross the bay.

Spend some time strolling along the Embarcadero, the colorful harbor area where commercial and sportfishing boats tie up. Get there by taking Main Street into town from the park's northwest exit, then turn left on Pacific Street and go down to the waterfront. To try your luck catching rock cod, halibut, and other ocean fish, join a party-boat outing from Brebe's, Bob's, or Virg's sportfishing, all on the Embarcadero.

For other nautical fun, cruise aboard Tiger's Folly, a pseudo-paddlewheeler that makes relaxing harbor excursions from the Harbor Hut dock. The Embarcadero also is home for an aquarium with dozens of live marine specimens from local waters and some playful seals.

Ten restaurants line the waterfront as well, and all offer a feast of fresh seafood, including once-plentiful abalone, now an expensive treat. Try Rose's Landing, popular for value-priced early-bird specials and all-inclusive dinners.

Be sure to drive north on Embarcadero and cross the causeway to the dome-shaped sentinel, Morro Rock. The 576-foot-high outcropping was first noted by Portuguese explorer Juan Cabrillo when he sailed along the California coast in 1542. Long a navigational marker, it's now a state historic landmark and also serves as a preserve for the endangered peregrine falcons that nest on top. You're forbidden to climb the rock, but visitors can walk around part of its perimeter; watch out for high waves on the north side, which are unpredictable and dangerous.

Drive past a newer landmark, the PG & E power plant with its towering trio of candlestick smokestacks, and go about a mile north to Atascadero State Beach, where beachcombing, swimming, surf fishing, and skin diving are big attractions. Another section of sandy shoreline, Morro Strand State Beach, is two miles north and makes a pleasant place to picnic.

Or head 11 miles south of Morro Bay to explore rugged Montana de Oro State Park, a 10,000-acre wildlife preserve that once was part of a vast ranch. It lives up to its name as a ''mountain of gold'' every spring, when the wildflowers are in brilliant bloom. Get a guide map at park headquarters, which was the former landowner's turn-of-the-century home.

For your return trip to Los Angeles, follow California 1 back to San Luis Obispo and rejoin U.S. 101 south.

Round trip is about 442 miles.

San Luis Obispo/Morro Bay Area Code: 805

SIGHTSEEING   *Mission San Luis Obispo de Tolosa,* on Mission Plaza at Chorro and Monterey Streets, San Luis Obispo 93401, 543-6850. Museum and gardens open daily 9 A.M. to 4 P.M., to 5 P.M. in summer. Adults 50 cents, family rate $1. ● *San Luis Obispo County Historical Museum,* end of Mission Plaza, San Luis Obispo, 543-0638. Hours: 10 A.M. to noon and 1 to 4 P.M. Wednesday through Sunday. Free. ● *Murray Adobe,* on Mission Plaza. Private residence but opened to the public noon to 4 P.M. Monday, Wednesday, Friday. ● *San Luis Obispo Art Center,* opposite historical museum at end of Mission Plaza. Hours: noon to 5 P.M. daily except Monday. Free. ● *Dallidet Adobe,* 1185 Pacific Street, San Luis Obispo. 130-year-old home, a state historical landmark, open 1 to 4 P.M. Sunday in summer. ● *Ah Louis Store,* 800 Palm Street, San Luis Obispo. Open 1 to 5:30 P.M. daily except Sunday. ● *Granny's General Store* (Sinsheimer Bros.), 849 Monterey Street, San Luis Obispo, 543-7410. Authentic turn-of-the-century store. ● *Museum of*

Natural History, Morro Bay State Park, Morro Bay 93442, 772-2694. Hours: 10 A.M. to 5 P.M. daily. Adults 50 cents, kids 25 cents. ● *Morro Bay Golf Course,* Morro Bay State Park, Morro Bay, 772-2044. 18 holes, par 71. Greens fees $7.50 weekends, $6 weekdays. ● *Tiger's Folly,* Harbor Hut, 1205 Embarcadero, Morro Bay, 772-2255. 80-minute narrated cruises of the bay. 5 tours daily in summer season; weekends only from October through May. Adults $5, ages 5 to 12 $3. ● *Morro Bay Aquarium,* 595 Embarcadero, Morro Bay, 772-7647. Open from 9 A.M. to 8 P.M. weekends, to 6 P.M. weekdays. Adults 70 cents, children 35 cents.

EVENTS   *Mozart Festival,* San Luis Obispo's annual August musical celebration honoring the Austrian composer's birthday with recitals and orchestra concerts. Program and tickets available from Mozart Festival Association, P.O. Box 311, San Luis Obispo 93406. ● *Old-Time Country Fair* on the Fourth of July in San Luis Obispo's Mission Plaza. Arts and crafts, kids' contests, food, and old-fashioned fun in celebration of Independence Day. ● *California Challenge Fire Muster* brings 1,000 firemen to Morro Bay in mid-September for high jinks and high-spirited games to determine the best fire department in the state.

LODGING   *Madonna Inn,* 100 Madonna Road, San Luis Obispo 93401, 543-3000. Rates from $60 to $138. Reservations a must. Also dining room and coffee shop (see below). No credit cards. ● Alternate accommodations can be found at nearly 30 other motels in San Luis Obispo; ZIP code 93401. Two of the largest with full service, including retaurant: *Discovery Motor Inn,* 1800 Monterey Street, 544-8600, $50; *Royal Oak Motor Hotel,* 214 Madonna Road, 544-4410, $46. ● Or try *Heritage Inn,* 978 Olive Street, San Luis Obispo, 544-7440, a bed-and-breakfast with 8 antique-filled rooms in the heart of town; $47. ● Morro Bay (ZIP 93442) also has over two dozen other lodgings, mostly small motels. *The Breakers,* 780 Market Street, Morro Bay, 772-7317; $46. 25 rooms a block from the Embarcadero overlooking the ocean. Restaurant adjacent (see below). ● *Golden Tee Resort Lodge,* 19 Country Club Road, 772-7313; $35. Morro Bay's largest lodging, with 98 rooms. Scenic location at state park entrance across from the seaside golf course.

CAMPING   *Morro Bay State Park,* off California 1, south edge of Morro Bay, 772-2560. 135 tent and RV sites, $6 per night. ● *Atascadero State Beach Park,* off California 1, 3 miles north of Morro Bay, 772-8812. 104 beachfront sites, $5 per night. ● *Montana de Oro State Park,* via Pecho Road, 11 miles south of Morro Bay, 528-0513. 50 rustic sites, $3 per night.

DINING   *Madonna Inn* (see above). Surprisingly good food for high volume of tourist traffic from U.S. 101. Baked goods and desserts are fresh from the motel's own bakery. Have breakfast or lunch sitting on ice cream chairs at copper-top tables in the coffee shop, but reserve a booth for dinner in the gilded and pink Gold Rush dining room. Dinner served from 5:30 to 11 P.M. Dancing on weekends. Also a Wine Cellar cocktail lounge; don't miss seeing the surprising men's room that's adjacent. • *Wine Street Inn,* 774 Higuera Street (lower level of the Network), San Luis Obispo, 543-4488. Lunch (except Sundays) with salad bar and sandwiches; nightly dinner menu features seafood, too. • *Cigar Factory,* 726 Higuera Street, San Luis Obispo, 543-6900. Dine on teriyaki sirloin, lemon-marinated chicken breasts, and other specialties. Nightly entertainment and cocktails to the wee hours. • *Chocolate Soup,* 980 Morro Street, San Luis Obispo, 543-7229. Order the chocolate soup dessert. Vegetarian dishes, along with crepes, soups, salads, and specialty sandwiches. Lunch and dinner daily except Sunday. • *F. McLintock's Saloon,* 686 Higuera Street, San Luis Obispo, 541-0686. Old-time saloon with hearty Western dishes like beef stew and chili. Also seafood salads and daily specials. Open except Sunday from 11 A.M. to 8:30 P.M. (to 3 P.M. on Friday) • *Sebastian's,* Chorro Street at Monterey Street (Mission Plaza), San Luis Obispo, 544-5666. Overlooks mission; popular spot for Sunday champagne brunch and 4-to-7 P.M. happy hour with complimentary hors d'oeuvres. Also nice lunches and dinners daily. • *Apple Farm,* 2015 Monterey Street, San Luis Obispo, 544-6100. Home-style meals served daily. Try the old-fashioned pot roast and hot apple dumplings for dessert. • *1865,* 1865 Monterey Street (in Somerset Manor motel), San Luis Obispo, 544-1865. Loft dining amid hanging garden decor, with prime ribs the specialty. Open weekdays for lunch, nightly for dinner. • *Rose's Landing,* 725 Embarcadero, Morro Bay, 772-4441. Make reservations for lunch on weekends and holidays, and dinner daily. Seafood is super. • Other busy Embarcadero eateries with treats from the sea: *The Galley Restaurant,* at No. 899, 772-2806 (with a wonderful wine list); *The Anchorage,* No. 998, 772-2424; *Great American Fish Co.,* No. 1185, 772-4407; and *Harbor Hut,* No. 1205, 772-2255. • *Dorn's Original Breakers Cafe,* 801 Market Street, Morro Bay, 772-4415. Local favorite for breakfast, lunch, or dinner. Fresh seafood. • *Hungry Tiger,* 781 Market Street, Morro Bay, 772-7321. Better-than-average restaurant chain with oyster bar and piano entertainment. • *Dutch's Criddle House,* 2738 Main Street, Morro Bay, 772-8645. Worth driving two miles north of town (off California 1) for lunch, dinner, or Sunday brunch in a historic old home.

FOR MORE INFORMATION   Contact the San Luis Obispo Chamber of Commerce, 1039 Chorro Street, San Luis Obispo 93401, 543-1323. Open every day. Also open weekdays and weekends is the Morro Bay Chamber of Commerce, 385 Morro Bay Boulevard (or P.O. Box 876), Morro Bay 93442, 772-4467.

Santa Barbara
Part 1: On the Waterfront

Santa Barbara is one of Southern California's most-visited cities, and it's no wonder. Few places have such a cornucopia of attractions. Beauty, history, and activity are the main drawing cards, and you'll need at least three weekends to see the foremost sights and sample the city's other pleasures. Our trio of trips take you to Santa Barbara's wonderful waterfront, the historic downtown area, and the city's enchanting environs.

Santa Barbara celebrated its bicentennial in 1982, and even remnants of its first construction, a Spanish military outpost, have been preserved. It's a mission town, too, and when a devastating earthquake flattened the city's center in 1925, townsfolk began reconstruction with Spanish-style stucco and red tile roofs, which have come to symbolize Santa Barbara's lovely architecture. Extensive planting and constant care of the trees and flowers also have made the city a venerable garden. Add its picturesque location, sloping down from the Santa Ynez Mountains to palm-fringed beaches, as well as the agreeable Mediterranean-like weather, and you'll understand why visitors often say Santa Barbara is their favorite Southern California city.

One of the most stunning sections of coastline in the state also is one of the liveliest. You'll find activities for every age and interest along Santa Barbara's beautiful waterfront. A weekend there offers this seashore sampler: bicycling, visiting a zoo, roller skating, playing volleyball, fishing, enjoying an arts-and-crafts show, bird watching, sailboating, jogging, taking a shoreline cruise, and picnicking under lofty palm trees.

If you prefer less energetic alternatives, do some coastal sightseeing in your car or on foot, and pause to feast on fresh seafood at an ocean-view restaurant along the way. Santa Barbara's natural harbor enticed Spanish explorers to settle there two centuries ago, and you'll soon discover why the city's waterfront continues to captivate residents and visitors alike.

Begin your coastal weekend by driving north from Los Angeles on U.S. 101 to the exclusive residential community of Montecito at the eastern edge of Santa Barbara. Exit south on Olive Mill Road, follow it down to Channel Drive on the ocean, and check into Marriott's splendid Santa Barbara Biltmore. Surrounded by acres of lush landscaping, this rambling 1920s hostelry of 169 rooms and cottages gives guests a sense of well-being that today's travelers rarely experience away from home. It's a dignified yet friendly place—staying there makes you feel like a weekend guest at a country estate. As one of California's few elegant oceanfront resorts, the Biltmore is the place to stay (providing your budget can afford room rates that begin at $100).

If there's no room at the Biltmore, a number of other lodgings also face the waterfront, along Cabrillo Boulevard. One is the Sheraton Santa Barbara Hotel & Spa, headquarters for the White House staff and Washington press corps during President Ronald Reagan's visits to his ranch nearby. Just down the street is the somewhat smaller Santa Barbara Inn, location of a Don the Beachcomber restaurant that is popular for Sunday brunch. Closer to the boat harbor you'll find the West Beach Inn, operated by the owners of the well-known San Ysidro Ranch resort in Montecito. Or try El Patio or Ambassador by the Sea motels, also on Cabrillo Boulevard.

If you're staying at the Biltmore, relax at the hotel's secluded pool or private beach club before beginning your exploration along the waterfront in the morning. Head west on Channel Drive and follow the road inland around a cemetery to join Cabrillo Boulevard (California 225), then bear right into a parking area for the Andree Clark Bird Refuge, a winter home for flocks of migratory birds. Resident ducks always loiter around the shoreline of its peaceful lagoon, hoping for a handout, so bring some bread from breakfast. You can have a treat, too, by dining later at Penelope's, an elegant restaurant in the Victorian-style house that overlooks the big pond and its assortment of fine-feathered friends.

If you brought a bicycle or roller skates, the bird refuge is the place to embark on the four-mile bikeway that parallels Santa Barbara's scenic beachfront. You also can rent bikes or skates farther along West Cabrillo Boulevard at Beach Rentals.

Adjacent to the bird sanctuary you'll enjoy the fauna and flora at the Santa Barbara Zoological Gardens (formerly called A Child's Estate). Turn right at the zoo-entrance sign on Cabrillo Boulevard. About 500 animals are on view, everything from gibbons to golden eagles and llamas to sea lions. Kids especially like the farmyard area, where they can pet and feed sheep, goats, and other tame creatures. A miniature train ride is another favorite of the small fry. You'll find playground and picnic areas, too.

Returning to the coastal boulevard and continuing west, you pass along one of Santa Barbara's prettiest and most popular gathering spots, Palm Park. Come back here on Sunday, when it's the site of the city's year-round arts-and-crafts show. From 10 A.M. until dusk, local artists display and sell their paintings, drawings, graphics, sculpture, photographs, and crafts. Most Sunday afternoons you'll also find folk dancers frolicking in the park. On any day you can spread a picnic under the regal palm trees or take off your shoes and stroll along adjacent Cabrillo Beach. There are volleyball games, to watch or to join.

For outstanding ocean views and a panorama of the mountains that serve as the city's backdrop, head out to the end of a Santa Barbara landmark, Stearns Wharf. The owner of a local lumberyard, John P. Stearns, built the original wharf in 1872—then the longest deepwater pier between Los Angeles and San Francisco. It offered easy ocean access to the Santa Barbara area and helped that coastal city prosper. After serving passenger steamers, freighters, and fishing vessels in its early days, Stearns Wharf remained a focal point for the city's residents and visitors. Jutting 1,500 feet into the city's scenic harbor, it recently was reopened to the public after $5 million worth of restoration work. Now the newly restored wooden pier is home for a dozen shops and several eateries.

As in the past, visitors are welcome to walk, bicycle, or drive their cars on the wharf, a three-block extension of State Street, the city's main thoroughfare. You'll find free 90-minute parking spots, as well as optional valet parking for the Harbor Restaurant. Featuring fresh seafood and homemade pasta, this restaurant is the wharf's keystone for cuisine. Its harbor views are outstanding, too, especially from the indoor/outdoor bar upstairs.

More seafood specialties are on the menus at the Moby Dick Restaurant, while Char West serves English-style fish and chips and American mainstays like hamburgers and hot dogs. Or head to the end of the wharf and the Santa Barbara Shellfish Company to see and buy some of the local catch, including lobster, crab, and abalone in season. This fresh fish market has takeout seafood cocktails, too. If you want to try your own luck fishing from the pier (no license required), stop next door at J.P.'s Bait and Tackle to rent a rod.

Nautical types will like browsing in the Old Wharf Trading Company, which has the flavor of an 1800s ship chandlery. Its seafaring gifts include marine instruments, lamps, decorator items, clothing, and books. Look for more beach- and ocean-oriented items in a shop called The Devil and the Deep Blue Sea. At Nature's Own you'll find shells, rocks, fossils, and semiprecious stones for sale.

To see the varied works of many area artists and craftspersons, visit Galeria del Mar and the Elizabeth Fortner Gallery. Jewelry is featured at the Eastern Pacific Pearl and Mining Company, while Topside has sportswear and items with Santa Barbara slogans. Also on the pier, at Stearns Wharf Vintners, you can sample Santa Barbara County, California, and French wines. And there's the chance to learn about your future from palmist Madame Rosinka. Matriarch of a local gypsy family, the popular palm reader has been telling the fortunes of pier visitors for many years.

Continue west along Cabrillo Boulevard to another colorful area of the waterfront, Santa Barbara's yacht harbor, home port for 1,200 pleasure craft and commercial fishing boats. From the parking lot, walk out on the paved breakwater to see all the nautical activity. You can join in by renting a sailboat, powerboat, or rowboat from West Beach Marine Company or Santa Barbara Boat Rentals, both at the breakwater. Another choice is to let someone else be captain and join Santa Barbara Island Cruises for a tour of the waterfront. For more excitement, board one of the Sea Landing's vessels in the harbor for a coastal fishing trip, or a whale-watching cruise in winter.

Then climb the stairs to the John Dory restaurant on the breakwater, to relax with a drink and a seafood cocktail and watch the sun set over the colorful harbor. On Cabrillo Boulevard you'll find some more restaurants that offer ocean views, including the longtime favorite of locals and out-of-towners, Castagnola's Lobster House.

For your return to Los Angeles, rejoin U.S. 101 and head south.

Round trip is about 210 miles.

Santa Barbara Area Code: 805

SIGHTSEEING   *Santa Barbara Zoological Garden,* entrance from Ninos Drive at 1300 East Cabrillo Boulevard, Santa Barbara 93103, 962-6310. Hours: 10 A.M. to 5 P.M. daily, summer to 8 P.M. Adults $2.50, teens $1.50, children and senior citizens $1. ● *Stearns Wharf,* foot of State Street at the Santa Barbara Harbor, 962-0611, ext. 215. Shops and restaurants open daily. ● *Santa Barbara Island Cruises,* on the Breakwater, Santa Barbara Harbor, 967-4528. Two-hour waterfront excursions at 6 P.M. on Wednesday, Friday, and weekends from May through January; $12.50 per person. Full bar on board; drinks extra. ● *Sea Landing Sportfishing,* on the Breakwater, Santa Barbara Harbor, 963-3564. Half- to all-day ocean fishing trips; also twilight fishing excursions. ● *West Beach Marine Co.,* on the Breakwater, Santa Barbara Harbor, 963-5600. Open daily for boat rentals. Also, *Santa Barbara Boat Rentals,* on the Breakwater, Santa Barbara Harbor, 962-2826.

LODGING   *Marriott's Santa Barbara Biltmore,* 1260 Channel Drive, Montecito 93108, 969-2261; $110. Acclaimed oceanfront resort with beautiful grounds, including putting green. Splurge with a suite or garden cottage. Excellent restaurant (see below) and special Sunday brunch. ● *Sheraton Santa Barbara Hotel & Spa,* 1111 East Cabrillo Boulevard, Santa Barbara 93103, 963-0744; $69. Health spa facilities. ● *Santa Barbara Inn,* Cabrillo Boulevard at Milpas Street, Santa Barbara 93103, 966-2285; $68. Across street from the beach. Don the Beachcomber restaurant (see below) with Pacific panorama. ● *San Ysidro's West Beach Inn,* 306 West Cabrillo Boulevard, Santa Barbara 93101, 963-4277; $76. Overlooks Santa Barbara Harbor. Heated pool, saunas, and hot therapeutic pool. Tennis and horseback-riding privileges at San Ysidro Ranch resort in Montecito.

DINING   *La Marina Dining Room and Patio,* in Marriott's Santa Barbara Biltmore (see above). Gourmet cuisine served with continental flair; jackets required at dinner. Have lunch on the outdoor patio. Elegant and expensive Sunday brunch is worth the price. • *Penelope's,* 50 Los Patos Way (at the Andree Clark Bird Refuge), Santa Barbara, 969-0307. Dress up for a special evening of California cuisine in an 1872 home. Dinner nightly except Sunday and Monday; delightful greenhouse bar opens at 5:30 P.M. • *Harbor Restaurant,* Stearns Wharf (at the foot of State Street), Santa Barbara, 963-3311. Lunch and dinners of fresh seafood with homemade pasta. Or snack on steamed clams and shrimp in a bucket, with one of their premium wines. • *Castagnola's Lobster House,* 15 East Cabrillo Boulevard, Santa Barbara, 965-1174. Lunch and dinner daily. All seafood is on display for your selection; great clam chowder. • *John Dory,* on the Breakwater at the Santa Barbara Harbor, 966-4418. Casual second-story restaurant with best view of the boats. Super spot for a relaxing drink. *Don the Beachcomber,* in the Santa Barbara Inn (see above). Polynesian decor and cuisine, crazy rum drinks, and dazzling ocean view for lunch and dinner. Also Sunday champagne brunch with traditional and Polynesian dishes.

FOR MORE INFORMATION   Contact the Santa Barbara Chamber of Commerce, 1330 State Street (at Sola Street in Coast Federal Savings Building, or P.O. Box 299), Santa Barbara 93102, 965-3021. Open weekdays 8 A.M. to 5 P.M.

Santa Barbara Part 2: Red Tile Tour to the Past

Making a tour of a courthouse sounds like pretty dull stuff—unless you're touring the Santa Barbara County Courthouse. It's been called America's most beautiful public building. Santa Barbarans (or Barbarenos, as some folks say) taxed themselves $1.5 million to build the classic Spanish-Moorish structure in the 1920s. Today their courthouse is considered priceless.

It's just one of the joys of spending a weekend in downtown Santa Barbara exploring a host of historic sites, museums, antique shops, and art galleries. From ancient adobes to sidewalk cafes, a stroll around town presents a panorama of the city's past two centuries and its present unhurried life-style. Add to the mellow mood of your visit by staying in one of Santa Barbara's homey bed-and-breakfast inns. A half dozen B&Bs are convenient to the downtown area by foot, on bicycles borrowed from your innkeeper, or in just a few minutes' drive by car.

Reach Santa Barbara from Los Angeles by driving north on U.S. 101, and check into your bed-and-breakfast for the weekend. Guests often are greeted with a welcoming glass of wine; with advance arrangement at one B&B, the Old Yacht Club Inn, a gourmet meal will be waiting.

The next morning, after a leisurely breakfast at your home away from home, head to the downtown area, where it's easy to find your way around the historic heart of the city by following the Red Tile Walking Tour. Get a map from the visitors bureau at the chamber of commerce, then set your own pace for this mile-long self-guided excursion, which circles 12 blocks. Ask directions to El Paseo, an enchanting Spanish-style arcade off State Street, where you can begin your walking tour. El Paseo is adjacent to Casa de la Guerra, the original 1827 adobe home of the army commander in charge of the Spanish outpost at Santa Barbara. The commandant's impressive hacienda was once the social center for this part of California. You'll have fun browsing in the quaint cluster of shops and galleries that now surrounds the casa's Spanish-style courtyard. El Paseo also is a pleasant place to relax at the sidewalk cafe with midmorning refreshments or an alfresco lunch.

Across the street from El Paseo is the Plaza de la Guerra, which becomes a colorful outdoor marketplace during the city's annual Old Spanish Days Fiesta. California's earliest European residents always liked a good party, and the tradition is carried on in Santa Barbara every August. The five-day wingding features parades, rodeos and horse shows, street dances, a carnival, stage and musical shows, cookouts, and walking tours of historic sites.

Walk northeast along De la Guerra Street and cross Anacapa Street to tiny Presidio Avenue, the city's oldest street. There you'll find an 1840 adobe and Presidio Gardens, formerly parade grounds for the Spanish soldiers. Opposite, at the corner of De la Guerra and Santa Barbara streets, visit the treasure-filled Santa Barbara Historical Society Museum to see mementos of the city's Indian, Spanish, Mexican, and American heritage. Then follow Santa Barbara Street a block north and turn left on Canon Perdido Street to El Presidio de Santa Barbara State Historic Park. Here you can view excavations of the city's birthplace, the Spanish Presidio built in 1782, as well as El Cuartel, the original soldiers' barracks that once were part of that army fort, and the recently restored Padre's Quarters with its thick walls, dirt floor, and rawhide bed.

On the corner of Canon Perdido and Anacapa streets is the Lobero Theater, survivor of the 1925 earthquake that demolished much of the town center. It's still used for stage performances, and traditional Spanish and flamenco dancing is featured there during the annual fiesta.

Continue on the Red Tile Walking Tour by going two blocks northwest along Anacapa Street to the striking Santa Barbara County Courthouse.

Occupying an entire city block, the building and its lush gardens look more like a country castle than a government edifice. Turrets and towers rise above the red tile roof that crowns the building's bright white stucco exterior. There are curved staircases, graceful archways, and windows enhanced by balconies and iron grillwork.

Inside, the county's business goes on—in superior court rooms, judges' chambers, law library, county clerk's office, and hall of records—but many county offices have been moved to newer buildings nearby. The courthouse is a Southern California showplace, and visitors are welcome every day. Enter by the main archway beneath the clock tower on Anacapa Street and pick up the self-guiding leaflet that describes the building's unusual architecture, elaborate public rooms, and historical displays. The courthouse also offers Santa Barbara's best bird's-eye view of the city, ocean, and mountains, from atop a 70-foot observation tower. There's an elevator to this spectacular lookout, from which you can survey the other attractions of the historic city.

Taking Anapamu Street to State Street brings you to the imposing former post office that became the city's Museum of Art in 1941. Over the years it's been expanded to accommodate collections of Greek, Roman, and Egyptian antiquities, Oriental art and musical instruments, American and European paintings, and vintage dolls. Santa Barbara boasts dozens of art galleries, and several are clustered nearby in the attractive Spanish-tiled La Arcada, entered at 1114 State Street.

Across the street from La Arcada is the San Marcos Arcade, with another gallery, a few shops, and its major attraction, the Eleven 29 Restaurant, which is an excellent choice for lunch or dinner. Detouring from the Red Tile Tour, walk a block north on State Street toward Victoria Street and the spire that marks the grand Arlington Theater, a classic 1930s movie house that is now used for the performing arts.

Back on the Red Tile Tour route, you'll see that the pedestrian is king in downtown Santa Barbara, especially along a seven-block section of the main thoroughfare, State Street. It was redesigned and landscaped with greenery, fountains, and benches to encourage promenading. After detouring on Carrillo Street to see a fully restored adobe built in 1826, continue south on State Street back to your tour starting point at El Paseo. Ardent shoppers who still have the energy should cross the street to Piccadilly Square, a modern marketplace with a multitude of clothing boutiques and gift stores.

Downtown Santa Barbara is deserted on Sunday mornings, so it's a good time to relax at your bed-and-breakfast inn. Many restaurants, shops, and public attractions are open by noon, but save the afternoon between 2 and 4 P.M. to see two more historic homes and the types of transportation travelers used in Southern California before fast cars and freeways became part of the scene.

From downtown, drive southwest a few blocks to Castillo Street, turn left, and go under the freeway to Pershing Park and the Old Spanish Days Carriage Museum, where horse-drawn carts, carriages, and other vintage vehicles used by the area's early families and businesses have been restored and are on display. Every August they return to the streets in the fiesta parade; the rest of the year you can see them only at the museum on Sunday afternoons.

Inside this modern building are more than 40 shiny vehicles that seem to be waiting to be hitched to horses and loaded with passengers or cargo. Several are handsome black buggies, surreys, and hansom cabs. You'll also see an 1882 steam pumper fire engine that served in Los Angeles, as well as a mid-1800s funeral wagon complete with coffins. Look for the pioneer Conestoga wagons, early army wagons, and U.S. mail stages. There's an 1880s police paddy wagon, too. And don't miss the display of old and elegant saddles, worth $2 million.

Two blocks away you can visit two homes from the horse-and-buggy era, the Trussell-Winchester Adobe (1854) and the Fernald House (1878). Restored and maintained by the Santa Barbara Historical Society, both are open for escorted tours only on Sunday afternoons. From the carriage museum, walk or drive northwest on Castillo Street and turn left on West Montecito Street to the old adobe. Timbers in the house were salvaged from a side-wheeler, the *Winfield Scott,* wrecked off Anacapa Island in 1853.

The adobe was built by Captain Horatio Trussell, who came from Maine to California on the first steamboat to arrive in Santa Barbara. The cork oak tree in the front yard is an offshoot from acorns he brought with him. Later the house and property were bought by a local schoolteacher, Sara Winchester. Today the adobe is furnished with articles of the past century, including paintings, books, and china that belonged to the Trussell and Winchester families.

Walk behind the adobe to the Fernald House, a multigabled Victorian beauty that was moved here from its original site on Santa Barbara Street. On a tour of the 14-room mansion, you'll admire the carved staircase, doors, and wainscoting that was the exquisite work of a local cabinetmaker. The house was continuously occupied by Judge Fernald and his family for 80 years and has many original furnishings. The stained-glass window in the vestibule was given by the judge to his wife on their first wedding anniversary, in 1864.

Antique enthusiasts also will want to visit Brinkerhoff Avenue, a block of charming Victorian homes that now houses a wonderful assortment of antique shops. Head back on Castillo Street to Haley Street, then go right 2½ blocks to the residential avenue that was named for one of Santa Barbara's first physicians, Dr. S. B. Brinkerhoff. On both sides of the street you'll find antique items ranging from music boxes to teacups, and quilts to carrousel animals. At the top of the block on the West Cota cross street is one of the most beautiful homes, now Redwood Inn Antiques, with toys, paper goods, and oak items.

If you feel like an elegant ending to your weekend before heading home, make a reservation for dinner at the Talk of the Town, a block away from Brinkerhoff's antique row on Gutierrez Street. Or go up lower State Street for a much more informal finale at a Santa Barbara food-and-drink institution, Joe's Cafe.

When you're ready for the drive back to Los Angeles, rejoin the U.S. 101 freeway south.

Round trip is about 215 miles.

Santa Barbara Area Code: 805

SIGHTSEEING   *Santa Barbara County Courthouse,* 1120 Anacapa Street, Santa Barbara 93101, 966-1611, ext. 7600. Open weekends 9 A.M. to 5 P.M.; weekdays 8 A.M. to 5 P.M. Free. Also, free guided tours Fridays at 10:30 A.M. • *El Presidio de Santa Barbara State Historic Park,* 123 East Canon Perdido Street, Santa Barbara 93101, 966-9719. El Presidio archaeological site, Padre's Quarters, and El Cuartel (the barracks) interiors are open weekdays 9 A.M. to noon and 1 to 4 P.M. Free. • *Santa Barbara Historical Society Museum,* 136 East De la Guerra Street, Santa Barbara 93101, 966-1601. Open weekends 1 to 5 P.M.; weekdays (except Mondays) noon to 5 P.M. Free. • *Santa Barbara Museum of Art,* 1130 State Street, Santa Barbara 93101, 963-4364. Open Tuesday through Saturday 11 A.M. to 5 P.M.; Sundays noon to 5 P.M. Free. • *Old Spanish Days Carriage Museum,* 129 Castillo Street (at Pershing Park), Santa Barbara 93101, 962-2353. Open 2 to 4 P.M. Sundays only. Free. • *Trussell-Winchester Adobe* and *Fernald House,* 414 West Montecito Street, Santa Barbara 93101, 966-6639. Open 2 to 4 P.M. Sundays only. Admission to both houses: adults $1, children 12 years and under 25 cents. • *El Paseo,* can be entered from State, De la Guerra, and Anacapa streets, Santa Barbara, 965-0093. Stores open 10 A.M. to 5 P.M. Saturday; a few on Sunday mornings. Also restaurant and sidewalk cafe (see below). • *Brinkerhoff Avenue,* between Cota and Haley streets, Santa Barbara. The city's Antique Row, with most shops open every day except Monday from 11 A.M. to 5 P.M. • *Piccadilly Square,* 813 State Street, Santa Barbara 93101. Shops with clothes, handcrafts, and gifts usually open from 10 A.M. to 6 P.M. daily, except noon to 5 P.M. Sunday.

EVENTS   *Old Spanish Days Fiesta,* annual 5-day summer celebration of Santa Barbara's past starting first Wednesday in August. Historical and children's parades, variety shows, Spanish-style marketplace, and rodeo and horse show are highlights. Chamber of commerce has full schedule of events.

LODGING   Santa Barbara has a great variety of accommodations, including bed-and-breakfast inns that first appeared in 1980. Make reservations well in advance, because the number of B&B rooms is limited. Also ask the "house rules," which may include a two-night stay on weekends, full prepayment, restricted smoking, and age limitations on younger guests. ● *Old Yacht Club Inn,* 431 Corona del Mar, Santa Barbara 93103, 962-1277; $45–$65. Santa Barbara's first B&B, occupying a 1912 home that once served as a yacht club; 4 rooms, shared baths, full breakfast. Bicycles for guest use. Delicious dinners cooked by innkeeper with advance notice. ● *Glenborough Inn,* 1327 Bath Street, Santa Barbara 93101, 966-0589; $55–$100. B&B in 1906 home; 4 rooms, shared baths, breakfast served in bedrooms. Outdoor hot tub. Also 3 rooms and suite in 1880s cottage across the street. ● *Bath Street Inn,* 1720 Bath Street, Santa Barbara 93101, 682-9680; $45–$75. Three-story B&B, built in 1895; 5 rooms, private bath available. ● *Bayberry Inn,* 111 West Valerio Street, Santa Barbara 93101, 682-3199; $50–$70. B&B, former 1904 boarding school for girls and later a sorority house; 4 rooms, 2 with fireplaces. ● *Olive House,* 1604 Olive Street, Santa Barbara 93101, 962-4902; $45–$70. B&B in 1904 California Craftsman-style house; 6 rooms (4 with private bath), full breakfast. Also 3-room cottage with own kitchen and garden; $95. ● *The Parsonage,* 1600 Olive Street, Santa Barbara 93101, 962-9336; $55–$95. 1892 Victorian B&B, a former parsonage; 5 rooms and honeymoon suite. Full breakfast. ● *Blue Quail Inn,* 1720 Bath Street, Santa Barbara 93101, 687-2300; $45–$75. 8 antique-decorated rooms in house and cottages. ● *Hotel Upham,* 1404 De la Vina, Santa Barbara 93101, 962-0058; $49–$59, suites $79. Renovated old-fashioned hotel that's been welcoming guests since 1871; 45 rooms, continental breakfast included.

DINING   *El Paseo Garden Cafe,* 813 Anacapa Street in the heart of El Paseo, Santa Barbara, 962-2948. Very popular for meals and drinks at outdoor tables in the courtyard; served daily from 6:30 A.M. to 10 P.M. Champagne or margarita brunch on Sundays, and Latin music every weekend. ● *Eleven 29 Restaurant,* 1129 State Street in San Marcos Arcade, Santa Barbara, 963-7704. Restful spot for lunch or dinner, with an exhibition kitchen so you can watch all the tricks of the skillful cooks. Also, late-night entertainment. ● *Talk of the Town,* 123 Gutierrez, Santa Barbara, 966-4910. Continental dishes well prepared nightly for dinner and weekdays for lunch, except Mondays. Strict dinner dress code: dresses for ladies, coats and ties for men. ● *Joe's Cafe,* 512 State Street, Santa Barbara, 966-4638. Landmark eatery with big bar business too; known for steak, Italian food, and generous drinks.

FOR MORE INFORMATION   Contact the Santa Barbara Chamber of Commerce, 1330 State Street (at Sola Street in Coast Federal Savings Building, or P.O. Box 299), Santa Barbara 93102, 965-3021. Open weekdays 8 A.M. to 5 P.M. The chamber's Accommodations Directory includes listings of bed-and-breakfast inns.

Santa Barbara
Part 3: All Around the Town

While enjoying Santa Barbara's exciting waterfront and enchanting downtown, you'll undoubtedly discover that the city's pleasures extend to its beautiful environs, too. So plan a separate weekend for a scenic excursion in the Santa Ynez foothills and the Goleta and Carpinteria valleys, which add special appeal to the Santa Barbara area.

There's plenty to see and do as you meander over the back roads that skirt the boundary of Los Padres National Forest and look out on the Pacific Ocean. Along the way are all sorts of treats: Santa Barbara's queenly mission, a botanical garden with native California flora, high-spirited polo matches, greenhouses bursting with orchids, and much more.

A one-of-a-kind resort, San Ysidro Ranch, is a rural retreat in neighboring Montecito that's just right for your holiday headquarters. Located on 525 hill-slope acres nudging the national forest, it seems more a private estate than a public guest ranch. Peace and quiet are bywords at San Ysidro, where overnight guests have been welcomed since 1893. You'll be accommodated in one of the 18 white cottages, named after the trees, shrubs, and flowers that isolate each lodging from the others. Over the years a number of famous folks have found tranquillity here, including writers such as Somerset Maugham, Sinclair Lewis, John Steinbeck, and even Winston Churchill, who often worked on his book manuscripts on the open porch of Magnolia House. Actor Ronald Colman was co-owner of the ranch from 1935 to 1958, and it became a haunt of film stars like Katharine Hepburn, Rex Harrison, and David Niven. This was also the spot Jackie and Jack Kennedy chose for their honeymoon. Children are welcome at the ranch, and family pets can come along too. Many guests explore the foothills on horses rented from San Ysidro's stables. You'll find tennis courts and a heated swimming pool as well.

Begin your weekend by driving north from Los Angeles on U.S. 101 to

Montecito, the wealthy Santa Barbara suburb of impressive estates. Then take the San Ysidro Road exit toward the mountains and follow the discreet signs to the guest ranch. Most evenings there's entertainment in the old wine cellar, now a popular tavern called the Plow and Angel. Excellent meals are served above it in the dining room, which was a packing house in the early days when San Ysidro was a citrus ranch.

In the morning when you're ready for a picturesque excursion, go back to a foothill crossroad, California 192, and turn west toward Santa Barbara. It's called Valley Road, but the name changes several times as you follow the twists and turns of this state route to Mission Canyon Road, part of Santa Barbara's official Scenic Drive. Turn north toward the mountains to reach the Santa Barbara Botanic Garden, a horticulturists' haven devoted to California plant life. Amble along the easy-to-walk nature trails that lead you through various botanical areas, such as the meadows that are set ablaze with wildflowers in springtime. One blossom you'll easily recognize is the brilliant Golden Poppy, the state flower. Another section, bordering the creek that flows through Mission Canyon, features California's famed redwoods.

Artists, photographers, and others in search of botanic beauty are drawn to the 76-acre garden throughout the year, but many time their visits for specific blooming seasons. For instance, from February through April you'll see California lilacs in every shade of blue, while cacti, yuccas, and other desert plants show off their flowers best in early summer.

More of Mother Nature's handiwork is on display back down Mission Canyon Road at the Santa Barbara Museum of Natural History, almost hidden in the oak trees on Puesta del Sol Road. Housed in handsome 1920s Spanish-style buildings with red tile roofs are absorbing exhibits that range from marine life and minerals to bird life and botany. Especially fascinating is the preserved specimen of the endangered California condor that's suspended from the ceiling with its giant wings outstretched. There's a complete skeleton of a huge gray whale, too. Don't miss the California Indian Hall, with displays about the local Chumash tribes that greeted the first European explorers to the area. Watch one of the museum's planetarium shows if you have time, and take a peek at the seismograph to see how much the Santa Barbara area has been shaking lately.

An earthquake was responsible for the next attraction on your scenic itinerary: Mission Santa Barbara, an architectural beauty that's rightly called the Queen of the Missions. Founded in 1786 by Franciscan padres as the tenth in the chain of 21 California missions, its landmark twin towers and imposing stone facade were built after destructive temblors hit the area in 1812. Go down Mission Canyon Road and turn right on Laguna Street to this imposing mission, the fourth and final version erected on a magnificent site overlooking the city and the sea. The history and reconstructions of the mission, which still serves as a parish church, come to life in the exhibits and old photos you'll see on a self-guided tour. Also on view are an early-day padre's bedroom and a kitchen complete with vintage furniture and utensils. Mission crafts and tools used by the Indian neophytes are among the displays in other museum rooms.

Be sure to see the sanctuary, the garden patio, and the walled cemetery with graves of Santa Barbara's pioneer families. In front of the mission stands a pretty fountain that overflowed into a stone trough where Indian women did laundry. Cross the road to a pleasant park, where you'll find remains of the innovative aqueduct that brought an abundance of water down the canyon to the mission.

Close by the mission you're certain to enjoy a leisurely lunch in El Encanto Hotel, with wonderful views of Santa Barbara below. Or return for dinner when the city's lights are aglow. By the way, this delightful hotel, with 100 cottages in a lush garden setting, is the place to stay if you prefer town to the more remote San Ysidro Ranch. Follow the city's Scenic Drive along Alameda Padre Serra and go left on Lasuen Road to El Encanto. Where Lasuen Road rejoins the Scenic Drive, you'll come to one of the three campuses of the Brooks Institute of Photography, home for the Western States Museum of Photography. Even snapshot shooters will be intrigued by the museum's collection of photographic memorabilia from the early nineteenth century and its changing exhibits of photographs.

Continue east on the Scenic Drive back to Montecito and Olive Mill Road, turning south to Coast Village Road that parallels U.S. 101. A right turn will take you to the popular Olive Mill Bistro for dinner and an evening of entertainment. It adjoins the Montecito Inn, a historic hostelry that was recently renovated to its former glory and is another recommendation for your weekend lodging. Enjoying afternoon high tea with grand piano music in the inn's Garden Room has become a pleasant diversion for the local gentry and out-of-town visitors as well.

On Sunday, plan to survey beautiful orchids, homes, and horses in the neighboring Goleta and Carpinteria valleys. Goleta is west of Santa Barbara, and you can arrive there most quickly by following U.S. 101 through the city. A more leisurely idea is to join the Scenic Drive at Olive Mill Road and follow it west along Santa Barbara's pleasurable waterfront. A block after Stearns Wharf, be sure to turn inland on Chapala Street to reach Montecito Street and an unbelievable Moreton Bay fig tree, one of the largest in the nation. Planted as a seedling by a pioneer family in 1877, the tree now has a trunk circumference of 35 feet and branches that spread so far, someone figured they could shade over 10,000 people!

Continue west on Montecito Street, which becomes Cliff Drive and rejoins the Scenic Drive, eventually leading past resplendent homes in the rolling, wooded hills of the Hope Ranch residential area. The towering palms that line its main boulevard, Las Palmas Drive, were planted at the turn of the century.

Just beyond that luxurious community, leave the Scenic Drive route to take U.S. 101 west to Goleta. Exit south on Patterson Avenue and continue on Shoreline Drive, then go right on Orchid Drive. Turn left into the Santa Barbara Orchid Estate, where you'll encounter an amazing variety of orchids. Grower Paul Gripp caters to hobbyists seeking award-winning and exhibition-type plants. Since 1957 he and his staff have been breeding, propagating, and growing orchids of all types; their cymbidiums alone number over 950 varieties. A specialty is outdoor orchids that can live in coastal California. You're welcome to stroll on your own around this extensive nursery. Members of the staff will give you directions, or ask them for a brief tour. As a pretty remembrance of your visit, purchase a potted plant or just the orchid flowers.

If you adore old homes, return to U.S. 101 and continue west past the town of Goleta to the Los Carneros exit. Then go right to the fire station that marks the entrance road to the handsome and historic Stow House. To build this huge house back in 1872, lumber was unloaded from ships into the surf, then floated ashore and hauled a few miles inland to La Patera Ranch. That's where San Franciscan W. W. Stow had purchased over 1,000 acres of grazing land to create a showcase farm. Almond, walnut, and lemon trees eventually surrounded the impressive Stow House, which served as the family's home and farm headquarters for 95 years. Today it and the grounds have been preserved as a reminder of life in the area's early agricultural days.

You're welcome to tour the fully furnished home, a nearby blacksmith shop, and a 100-year-old storehouse that's now a museum of farm and household implements and carriages. A recent addition to the property is Goleta's turn-of-the-century railroad depot, which was moved to the site and refurbished.

If you fancy fine horses or want to feast your eyes on more orchids, head back east on U.S. 101 through Santa Barbara and Montecito to the Carpinteria Valley. Exit past Summerland at Santa Claus Lane, go under the freeway, then turn left on Via Real to Nidever Road and the polo field at Foothill Road. As home for the prestigious Santa Barbara Polo and Racquet Club, it's the site of many local matches and international tournaments of this thrilling sport on horseback.

Some of the players who come from around the world bring their ponies with them. You'll marvel at the superb horsemanship as the players signal their mounts to race across the field, make quick turns, and stop abruptly as they maneuver the ball to the goal. Games are played most weekends during a nine-month season, and you can watch from your car or the sidelines stadium.

This sheltered coastal area also is ideal for growing cut flowers and ornamental potted plants, so you'll see acre upon acre of flower fields and nursery greenhouses. Just north of the polo field visitors are welcome at a major orchid grower, Armacost and Royston. One look at the breathtaking array of delicate plants and you'll be eager to buy some. Prices range from $5 for a "bargain corner" cattleya to $1,000 for very rare varieties.

Before heading home, it's fun to have dinner at the Big Yellow House in Summerland. Follow Via Real west to this family-style restaurant in a nineteenth-century Victorian mansion. The familiar landmark for travelers along U.S. 101 is well known for its all-you-can-eat dinners and Sunday brunch.

Return to Los Angeles by taking U.S. 101 south.

Round trip is about 240 miles.

Santa Barbara Area Code: 805

SIGHTSEEING *Santa Barbara Botanic Garden,* 1212 Mission Canyon Road, Santa Barbara 93105, 682-4726. Open daily 8 A.M. to sunset. Free. Giuded tour 10:30 A.M. Thursdays. • *Santa Barbara Museum of Natural History,* 2559 Puesta del Sol Road (off Mission Canyon Road), Santa Barbara 93105, 682-4711. Open daily 9 A.M. to 5 P.M., except Sundays and holidays from 10 A.M. Free. Guided tour Sundays at 2 P.M. Planetarium shows twice daily; adults $1.50, children 12 years and under 75 cents. • *Santa Barbara Mission,* upper end of Laguna Street, Santa Barbara 93105, 682-4713. Open daily 9 A.M. to 5 P.M., except Sunday 1 to 5 P.M. Adults 50 cents, children under 16 years free. Self-guided tours of museum, garden, chapel, and cemetery. • *Western States Museum of Photography,* 1321 Alameda Padre Serra (on Jefferson campus of Brooks Institute of Photography), Santa Barbara 93103, 965-8664. Hours: 10 A.M. to 4 P.M. daily, except holidays. Free. • *Santa Barbara Orchid Estate,* 1250 Orchid Drive, Goleta 93111, 967-1284. Open daily 8 A.M. to 4:30 P.M., except Sunday 11 A.M. to 4 P.M. Free. • *Stow House,* 304 Los Carneros Road, Goleta 93017, 964-4407. Open weekends 2 to 4 P.M. (closed in January). Free, but donations appreciated. • *Santa Barbara Polo and Racquet Club,* 3375 Foothill Road (or P.O. Box 1200), Carpinteria 93013, 684-5819 (for recorded information about upcoming matches) or 684-6683. Trophy matches played Sundays at 1 and 3 P.M. from mid-March through December, weather permitting. Admission $3. Practice games Wednesday, Friday, and Saturday are free. • *Armacost and Royston,* 3376 Foothill Road (or P.O. Box 385), Carpinteria 93013, 684-5448. Hours: daily 8 A.M. to 4 P.M., except Saturday from 10 A.M. and Sunday from 12 noon. Free.

EVENTS *Santa Barbara International Orchid Show,* Earl Warren Showgrounds, U.S. 101 and Los Positas Road, Santa Barbara, 967-7153. Spectacular weekend event for orchid lovers every March. • *Santa Bar-*

bara National Horse and Flower Show, Earl Warren Showgrounds, Santa Barbara, 687-0766. Annually in mid-July, one of the top five national horse shows, plus a magnificent flower display.

LODGING   *San Ysidro Guest Ranch,* 900 San Ysidro Lane, Montecito 93108, 969-5046. Double rooms from $98; cottages from $119 (with fireplaces) to $239 (with private Jacuzzi). Outdoor activities include guided trail rides on horseback ($17.50). Also popular Plow and Angel bar and restaurant (see below). ● *El Encanto Hotel and Garden Villas,* 1900 Lasuen Road, Santa Barbara 93103, 965-5231; $70 (to $325 for villas). Classy French-style country inn overlooking city. Also favorite cocktail and dining spot (see below). ● *Montecito Inn,* 1295 Coast Village Road, Santa Barbara 93108, 969-7854; $70. Handsome 1920s hostelry restored to its original opulence and reopened in 1982. Complete health spa facilities. Guests may arrange a cruise aboard the inn's 65-foot yacht.

DINING   *Plow and Angel,* at San Ysidro Guest Ranch (see above). Candlelight dining in rustic ranch settting; jackets required for men. Specialties include breast of duck and local abalone. Also midday Sunday brunch, breakfast and lunch daily. Enjoy an after-dinner drink and entertainment in the intimate bar beneath the restaurant. ● *El Encanto,* in El Encanto Hotel and Garden Villas (see above). Savor California cuisine with a French influence (the sautéed squab with goose liver is a treat) outdoors on the terrace or in the hotel's exquisite dining room. Excellent and expensive menu; jackets suggested at dinner. At least have a cocktail on the terrace to enjoy the spectacular view or in the romantic lounge by the fireplace. ● *Olive Mill Bistro,* at the Montecito Inn (see above), 969-4900. The place to cap a gourmet dinner with musical entertainment and dancing; a Dixieland jazz band draws the Sunday-evening crowd. Continental and nouvelle cuisine; veal dishes are delectable. ● *The Big Yellow House,* 108 Pierpont Avenue, Summerland 93067, 969-4140. A family favorite for dinner and Sunday brunch. Menu changes daily, but fried chicken is a regular feature. Bountiful meal for a bargain price; kids 12 years and under pay according to their weight on an old-fashioned scale. Reservations advised on weekends.

FOR MORE INFORMATION   Contact the Santa Barbara Chamber of Commerce, 1330 State Street (at Sola Street in Coast Federal Savings Building, or P.O. Box 299), Santa Barbara 93102, 965-3021. Open weekdays 8 A.M. to 5 P.M.

Adventuring in Ventura and Anacapa

Scores of travelers rush through Ventura on the U.S. 101 freeway without realizing that the city is an ideal destination for a weekend escape. Hugging a peaceful crescent of the Pacific coast just 60 miles northwest of Los Angeles, it has marvelous beaches and a busy pleasure-boat harbor. From there you can embark on a sailing adventure to Anacapa Island, part of America's unique offshore national park.

A wonderful insight to early California history also is in store for visitors to Ventura, where the city's namesake—Mission San Buenaventura—celebrated its bicentennial in 1982. You even can view 3,500 years of history in one city block—an archaeological dig next to the mission has uncovered an aboriginal campsite that existed at the time the pharaohs were ruling Egypt.

To enjoy the beach, boating, and going back in time, drive north from Los Angeles on U.S. 101 to Ventura and exit toward the ocean on California Street, which takes you to the high-rise Holiday Inn, your weekend headquarters at the beach. After checking in, ride the elevator to the hotel's twelfth-floor lounge to watch the sun slip into the ocean. Have dinner that night in the rooftop revolving restaurant, then linger on for the evening's musical entertainment and dancing.

In the morning, walk along the oceanfront on the wide pedestrian Promenade, a modern "boardwalk" that leads to Surfer's Point, where you can watch acrobatic surfers ride the waves. Then stroll in the opposite direction to the Ventura Pier, one of the longest on the West Coast. Jutting into Pierpont Bay, the 1,700-foot pier originally was used by the railroad to transfer cargo to ships and now is a favorite hangout for fishermen. Walk to its end for an expansive view of the Pacific, or enjoy the ocean vista while having breakfast or feasting on a seafood lunch at the Pier Fish House. Charlie's Seaside Cafe near the Holiday Inn is another favorite spot for fish dishes accompanied by views of the beautiful bay. Also plan to join the sunbathers, swimmers, and picnickers on San Buenaventura State Beach, which flanks the pier and runs several miles south to Ventura Harbor.

Devote part of the day to exploring Ventura's pleasant downtown and viewing its historical sites. From the beach, walk or drive two blocks north on California Street and go left on Main Street to the archaeological dig that's just beyond the mission. The area was being razed for new buildings in 1973 when local archaeologists got the city to halt the bulldozers so they could excavate. Among their surprising discoveries were the original mission church foundations, which had been abandoned, foundations of the adobe quarters for the mission's Indian neophytes, a 2,300-year-old earth oven, and a fire hearth dating to 1600 B.C. You'll get an overview of the excavated site from an elevated platform at the north end of the dig. Continue up the steps to a water-filtration structure at the end of a seven-mile aqueduct that the Indians built in the 1790s to bring water to the mission. Later the tiny building served as Ventura's first city jail.

Artifacts recovered from the dig are displayed in the archaeological museum on the site. You'll see animal bones from the earth ovens, some of the 44,500 Indian trading beads that were found, Mexican ceramics, Chinese opium pipes, and early American glassware. Don't miss the two audiovisual programs in the museum's theater, which spotlight some of the prize finds and put three and a half millennia in perspective.

Cross the street to another treasure trove of yesteryear's relics, the handsome Ventura County Historical Museum. You'll learn more about the Indian, mission, and rancho periods, as well as the area's agricultural and oil-drilling activities. The excellent displays range from marine fossils to pioneer firearms.

Afterward, stroll a block down the street to Mission San Buenaventura. Ninth in California's chain of 21 Spanish missions, it was the last one founded by Father Junipero Serra before his death. You're welcome to explore the mission grounds and the church, where regular parish services are still held. Look for an ancient olive press in the courtyard garden.

A neighboring building on Main Street is the mission gift shop, which offers access to a small museum with more early-day articles. The collection features vestments of the Spanish padres, their European books, Chumash Indian baskets, a primitive confessional, and very rare wooden bells that once rang at the mission.

Outside, fountains bubble in Figueroa Plaza, a pedestrian mall that extends a block from the mission past the site of the city's former Chinatown to Santa Clara Street. There you'll find a renovated Victorian home, now Andy's Barbecue Heaven & Saloon, a local favorite for lunch or dinner. If you would rather picnic, choose a table beneath an immense century-old Moreton Bay fig tree in the adjacent Mission Park. You can buy food and refreshments in Peirano's Store. Built opposite the mission about 1874, it's the city's oldest brick structure and has been operated by the same family since the turn of the century.

Continue walking eastward on Main Street to share more of Ventura's history. Take a short detour north on Palm Street to the Old Town Livery, a blacksmith shop and stable dating from 1870 that's been restored with an assortment of gift shops and a deli. Farther along at California Street, turn left and head straight up the block to a Ventura landmark, the city hall. It's a classic beaux arts building that was erected in 1912 as the Ventura County Court House. Weekday visitors can go inside to admire its Italian marble staircase, wood paneling, and stained-glass domes. In front is a statue of Father Serra sculpted in 1936.

By walking or driving west on Main Street just past the California 33 junction to Ojai, you'll see another historical structure, the Ortega Adobe. This was the modest home of Emigdio Ortega, grandson of Captain Jose Ortega, who founded Santa Barbara. Built in 1857 near the Ventura River, half of the adobe was washed away in a flood, and an earthquake later cracked one wall. Now the old structure has been entirely restored and authentically refurnished, still covered by red tiles that Ortega bought from the padres after an earthquake knocked them off the roof of Mission San Buenaventura.

Much more extensive and impressive is the Olivas Adobe southeast of downtown Ventura. Reach it by joining U.S. 101 and driving south to the Harbor Boulevard exit. Continue south, skirting Ventura Harbor, then turn left on Olivas Park Drive and go past the golf course to the historic home. One of the largest and finest adobes anywhere, its sun-baked mud and straw-brick walls are two feet thick. It was build by Don Raimundo Olivas, a wealthy rancher who needed plenty of room to raise his 21 children. Much of the money for construction of the splendid hacienda, which includes a chapel, came from the cattle Olivas drove north during the gold rush to feed hungry miners. The adobe has been completely restored and is furnished with antiques donated by the area's pioneer families.

Built beside the Santa Clara River, the Olivas home has a pleasant garden and walled patio and was frequently the site of festive weddings. In the patio's southwest corner you'll see adobe bricks of the original house built there in 1837. Curved roof tiles were shaped from thick clay that was molded over the workers' thighs. Near the patio fountain are displays depicting more of the rancho's history.

On your way back to the Holiday Inn, dine at the Pierpont Inn off U.S. 101, one of Ventura's best hotels, and an alternate choice for weekend lodgings. Then get a good night's sleep, because you'll need to wake early for an adventurous day sailing the open seas and exploring Anacapa Island.

Anacapa, Santa Cruz, Santa Rosa, San Miguel, and Santa Barbara islands make up the nation's fortieth national park. These five of the eight islands in the Channel Islands chain off the Southern California coast were designated the Channel Islands National Park by Congress in March 1980. (Not included in the park are well-known Santa Catalina and two islands controlled by the U.S. Navy, San Clemente and San Nicolas.) For decades the rugged islands have been havens for a host of animals, seabirds, plants, and marine life, and they'll continue as nature sanctuaries with limited recreational use. Anacapa is the most accessible of this quintet of islands, which can be visited by public boat transportation, charter excursions, or private vessels.

The public trips begin at Ventura Harbor, headquarters for the Channel Islands National Park and the boat excursion company, Island Packers. Take Harbor Boulevard south and follow the signs that lead to Spinnaker Drive and the park's modern $2-million visitors center. From its observation tower you can glimpse the offshore islands and enjoy a panorama of the beautiful coast and harbor. In the main exhibit hall you'll see dioramas and maps of the islands, as well as illustrations and photographs of their animal and plant life. Well worth watching is a movie about the island chain that's shown in the auditorium. Kids especially enjoy the man-made tide pool with marine specimens they can touch.

Next door is the Anacapa boat departure dock, where you can board a modern diesel-powered vessel or go under full sail on a classic 82-foot schooner. The Island Packers Company captain and crew double as naturalists, describing the marine life and evolution of the Channel Islands as you sail to the island. En route you'll cross the busy Santa Barbara shipping lane and catch glimpses of ocean oil-well platforms. Watch for porpoises racing alongside your boat as well.

Anacapa is the nearest island to the mainland, just 11 miles south of Ventura, and the crossing takes about 90 minutes. Then you'll be ferried to shore in order to explore the island on foot. Actually composed of three islets that stretch almost five miles, Anacapa is distinguished at its eastern end by Arch Rock, an outcropping with an opening cut through it by the ocean waves.

The most popular West Coast nesting spot for the once-endangered brown pelicans, Anacapa also is a favorite rookery of Western gulls. Bring binoculars to study all the birdlife, including cormorants, black oyster catchers, and scoter ducks.

While aboard the boat and ashore on the island, be on the lookout for sea lions, harbor seals, and sharks. In wintertime Anacapa is an outstanding place to observe California gray whales during their annual migration between the Bering Sea and the lagoons of Baja California.

Most times the boat anchors in a cove on East Anacapa and then you climb 154 stairs to the rolling plateau of the cliff-rimmed island. You may be greeted by a park ranger, the island's sole resident. There's a small visitors center, but the best way to become acquainted with Anacapa is by picking up the descriptive booklet that guides you along a 1½-mile nature trail. You'll see a churchlike building that camouflages redwood tanks holding the island's freshwater supply, which had been targets for irresponsible boaters with high-powered rifles. Most important of the man-made structures on Anacapa is an automated lighthouse that includes a piercing foghorn.

After time to stroll around the island top and enjoy a picnic lunch, visitors reboard the boat to cruise around the island for another look at its marine life. Also, in late summer the water is usually warm and clear enough for passengers to go swimming and snorkeling before recrossing the channel.

By late afternoon you'll arrive back in Ventura Harbor, tired but happy. Then it's time to rejoin U.S. 101 south for the return trip to Los Angeles.

Round trip is about 144 miles.

Ventura Area Code: 805

SIGHTSEEING *Mission Archaeological Museum,* 113 East Main Street, Ventura 93001, 648-5823. Visitors center and dig open 10 A.M. to 4 P.M. daily except Mondays. Free. ● *Ventura County Historical Society Museum,* 100 East Main Street, Ventura 93001, 653-0323. Open daily except Mondays from 10 A.M. to 5 P.M. Free. ● *Mission San Buenaventura,* 211 East Main Street, Ventura 93001, 643-4318. Visitors welcome daily from 7 A.M. to 5 P.M. Enter mission museum through gift shop, 225 East Main Street. Hours 10 A.M. to 4 P.M. daily. Donation requested. ● *Ortega Adobe,* 100 West Main Street, Ventura 93001, 644-7421. Open daily 10 A.M. to 3 P.M. Free. ● *Olivas Adobe,* 4200 Olivas Park Drive, Ventura 93001, 644-7421. Grounds, gardens, and exhibits open daily 10 A.M. to 3 P.M., adobe open weekends only 10 A.M. to 4 P.M. Free. ● *Channel Islands National Park,* 1901 Spinnaker Drive, Ventura 93001, 644-8464. Visitors center open daily 8:30 A.M. to 5:30 P.M. Free. ● *Island Packers Cruises* to Anacapa Island, 1867 Spinnaker Drive (or P.O. Box 993), Ventura 93001, 642-1393 or 642-3370. All-day powerboat excursions depart year round on weekends and Monday and Friday at 8 or 9 A.M. Also Tuesday and Thursday trips in summer. Adult fare $24, children under 12 years $12. Bring along a Windbreaker or sweater, hat or scarf, and whatever you want to eat and drink en route and ashore; no refreshments are available aboard the motor vessels or on the island. Anacapa excursions on schooner sailing ships depart Friday, Saturday, and Sunday at 8:30 A.M. Per person fare $48.50, including lunch and a chance to help sail the ship. Make reservations well in advance for all these popular sea-and-land adventures.

LODGING *Holiday Inn,* 450 East Harbor Boulevard, Ventura 93001, 648-7731; $59. 225 rooms and suites at the beach; also revolving rooftop restaurant (see below). ● *Pierpont Inn,* 500 Sanjon Road, Ventura 93001, 643-6144; $48. Cottages available with fireplaces. Guests have tennis and racquetball privileges at nearby health club. Also, popular dining room (see below).

DINING *Top O' The Harbor* atop Holiday Inn (see above). Revolving twelfth-floor restaurant open daily for dinner from 5:30 P.M. Brunch on Sundays. Big Band music and dancing on Friday and Saturday nights. ● *Charlie's Seaside Cafe,* 362 California Street Mall, Ventura, 648-6688. Seafood specialties for lunch and dinner daily; also Sunday brunch. ● *The Pier Fish House,* on Ventura Pier at 688 East Harbor Boulevard, Ventura, 643-4825. Open for ocean-view meals from 9 A.M. to 9 P.M. weekends, from 11 A.M. weekdays. ● *Andy's Barbecue Heaven & Saloon,* 211 East Santa Clara Street, Ventura, 648-3011. Ribs, chicken, and steak are barbecued on live oak daily for lunch and dinner. Daily specials and children's menu; at dinner kids get to make their own ice-cream sundaes for dessert. ● *Pierpont Inn,* dining room in the Pierpont Inn (see above). Three meals daily; continental menu with seafood and prime ribs featured. Brunch on Sunday from 8 A.M. to 3 P.M. Dancing Thursday through Saturday, entertainment Monday through Wednesday.

FOR MORE INFORMATION   Contact the Ventura Visitor and Convention Bureau, 785 South Seaward Avenue, Ventura 93001, 648-2075. Visitors center open daily from 8:30 A.M. to 5 P.M. (from 10 A.M. weekends).

Seafaring Fun in Oxnard's Harbor and Port Hueneme

A New England fishing village may seem an apparition in agricultural Oxnard, but it's real enough. Wood saltbox buildings, a lighthouse, and fishing boats tied up to the pier are part of the nautical scenery you'll enjoy during a visit to Oxnard's pretty Channel Islands Harbor. This, one of the Southland's most pleasant harbors, offers boating, fishing, and shopping. You also find sandy beaches for sunbathing, a protected lagoon for swimming, green parks for picnicking, and plenty of ocean-fresh air. And it's home for a wonderful variety of restaurants, as well as deluxe accommodations on the waterfront. Make your weekend home at the Casa Sirena Marina Hotel in the heart of the harbor, and settle down for a relaxing time at the water's edge amid the boats and seabirds. You also can explore the neighboring harbor that hosts U.S. Navy ships and huge cargo vessels, Port Hueneme, and go inland to the historical sites of Oxnard.

Farming dominated the landscape at the turn of the century when four brothers by the name of Oxnard established a sugar beet business that put the city on the map. Soon after, Hollywood discovered the adjacent seashore, and movie idol Rudolph Valentino roamed across its sands in his 1921 classic *The Sheik*. Now Oxnard's official city boundaries extend to the ocean and include a pleasure-boat harbor that was dredged and dedicated in 1965.

A scenic way to reach Channel Islands Harbor in Ventura County is to drive west from Los Angeles on Interstate 10 to Santa Monica and pick up the Pacific Coast Highway, California 1. Follow it north along the shoreline past several state beaches and parks. The highway cuts inland beyond Point Mugu through some of the rich farmland that still surrounds Oxnard. Exit California 1 at Channel Islands Boulevard and follow it west through the ever-growing city to the harbor. Just past Fisherman's Wharf Village turn left on Peninsula Road to the Casa Sirena Marina Hotel. Many of its balconied rooms overlook boat slips, which are filled with 1,400 pleasure craft of all descriptions. For sunset cocktails, head to the hotel's popular rendezvous spot, the Lobster Trap Restaurant, then linger for a seafood feast or other dinner specialties, such as rack of lamb. End the evening enjoying the music and entertainment in the restaurant's Guadalajara Lounge, where you're also welcome to dance.

Your coastal weekend can be as leisurely or as active as you wish. The hotel has its own tennis courts, swimming pool, and Jacuzzis. You can rent a boat from Channel Islands Landing to go sailing for an hour or two or hop aboard a sportfishing vessel operated by CISCO (Channel Island Sportfishing Center—Oxnard) for a day with rod and reel on the open sea. To enjoy the harbor's unhurried pace, take a stroll along the boat docks and look for the old sailing-ship masts and lighthouse that mark Fisherman's Wharf at Channel Island Boulevard and Victoria Avenue. In the attractive shops of this mock New England village you'll find everything from handmade toys and gourmet kitchen gifts to the arts and crafts of Ventura artisans.

You'll be tempted by seafood here too. Fish and chips are served at Shipwreck Willie's Seafood Market, where catches of the day also are cleaned, cut up, and sold to takeout customers. Or you can dine and observe the dockside scene from well-known Castagnola's Restaurant, where some of its fresh seafood menu is displayed on an iced counter just inside the entrance. Behind Willie's you can watch the sea's bounty being unloaded from the fishing vessels, including spiny sea urchins with tasty eggs that are shipped to Japan. The wharf's lighthouse is really a storage house for ice, which is pumped underground through pneumatic hoses to the fishing boats that pull up to the pier.

Around the harbor are even more places to eat and drink while viewing the sleek sailboats and handsome yachts, such as Captain Jack's Seafood Cooker, farther south on Victoria Avenue. Across the channel on Bluefin Circle off Harbor Boulevard are a pair of other harbor-front restaurants, the Whale's Tail and Port Royal. Besides serving lunch and dinner, all three feature Sunday brunch and have nightly entertainment.

Just south of Channel Islands Harbor beyond Silver Strand County Beach is a neighboring boat basin you might also find fascinating. Despite being the home of the only deepwater harbor between Los Angeles and San Francisco, Port Hueneme isn't on the tip of many travelers' tongues. Perhaps that's because the place has such a funny-sounding name: *why-nee-me*. It's a Chumash Indian word meaning "halfway" or "resting place," referring to the midpoint on the canoe trips the Indians made between their coastal villages at Ventura and Mugu. During World War II Hueneme became a major port for shipping supplies to U.S. forces in the Pacific. It carries on a military role today as home of four Naval Construction Battalions, better known as the Seabees.

To get to the port from Channel Islands Harbor you have to skirt the naval base on a roundabout route. Go east on Channel Islands Boulevard to Ventura Road, then head south to Hueneme Road, and turn back west to the Hueneme harbor. You'll hear the foghorn from the lighthouse that was installed at the port entrance in 1941, when the harbor was being modernized. Its turn-of-the-century beacon was made in France and used in Hueneme's first lighthouse.

Prior to construction of a wharf in 1871, Ventura County's farmers shipped their crops by lightering them through the surf on small boats to seagoing vessels anchored offshore. Now you'll see huge navy and cargo ships that operate with ease from the deepwater harbor. Look for commercial carriers unloading bananas from Ecuador, cars from Japan, cattle from the Channel Islands, and supplies for the Southland's offshore oil rigs. Port Hueneme also boasts a half dozen deep-sea fishing boats ready to take eager anglers out in the ocean to try their luck. All-day fishing excursions with Port Hueneme Sportfishing depart from Dock 1.

On the way back to the Channel Islands Harbor, stop by the impressive Seabee Museum inside the navy base. From Ventura Road, turn left at Sunkist Street to enter the U.S. Naval Construction Battalion Center. Get a base pass from the gate guard before proceeding to the museum parking area. You can't miss the big gun-toting bee, symbol of the Seabees, that marks the entrance to this military museum, one of the most notable in the nation. On display are artifacts and souvenirs from Southeast Asia, the South Pacific, Antarctica, and other duty areas of the navy's Civil Engineer Corps. Religious masks, ceremonial swords, and hunting implements are among the memorabilia collected abroad by the Seabees. Don't miss the gallery that displays the uniforms and weapons of U.S. and foreign forces. Dioramas of the Seabees' major construction feats also are featured.

If you want to learn about local history and glimpse a little more of Oxnard, continue north on Ventura Boulevard to 5th Street and turn right (east) to Plaza Park, in the heart of town. At the corner with C Street is an outstanding example of the Grecian style of architecture with Ionic and Corinthian columns, the former city library, now the Carnegie Cultural

Arts Center. On its lower level you'll find the Historical Society Museum displays of vintage photographs and mementos of the area. Also look in the Plaza Gallery of Fine Arts, a showcase for local painters, sculptors, potters, and other artists. The upper floors feature changing exhibits, including artifacts gathered worldwide by amateur archaeologist H. H. Eastman, an Oxnard farmer and former city mayor. Works from the municipal art collection also are on view.

Go across the street to relax in pleasant Plaza Park and get a close-up view of an Oxnard landmark, the 72-year-old bandstand that resembles a Japanese pagoda. Then walk a block down 5th Street to see the Bank of A. Levy, noted for its Italian Revival style of architecture. Look up at the high-relief classical heads above the arched windows. It was French-born grain merchant Achille Levy who bought beet seed for the area's pioneer farmers over a century ago. That was the beginning of Oxnard's prosperity, which in turn encouraged Levy to open his family-owned bank.

When your visit to Channel Islands Harbor and environs is over, journey back to Los Angeles by taking California 1 north through Oxnard to join the inland freeway U.S. 101.

Round trip is about 136 miles.

Oxnard Area Code: 805

SIGHTSEEING *Channel Islands Landing,* 3821 Victoria Avenue, Oxnard 93030, 985-6059. Sailboat rentals. Open daily. ● *CISCO, Channel Islands Sportfishing Center—Oxnard,* 4151 South Victoria Avenue, Oxnard 93030, 985-8511 or (213) 457-9221. Deep-sea fishing; all-day and ¾-day boats. Open 24 hours daily. ● *Port Hueneme Sportfishing,* 310 West Hueneme Road, Port Hueneme 93041, 488-2212 or 488-4715. Deep-sea fishing. Open daily. ● *Seabee Museum,* Naval Construction Battalion Center, via Ventura Gate off Ventura Road, Port Hueneme 93041, 982-5163. Open from 9 A.M. Saturdays, 12:30 P.M. Sundays, and 8 A.M. weekdays to 4:30 P.M. Free. ● *Carnegie Cultural Arts Center,* 424 South C Street (at 5th Street), Oxnard 93030, 486-4311, ext. 710. Open 10 A.M. to 5 P.M. Tuesday through Saturday. Historical Society Museum and Plaza Gallery of Fine Arts open on the same days from 1 to 4:30 P.M. Free.

LODGING *Casa Sirena Marina Hotel,* 3605 Peninsula Road, Channel Islands Harbor, Oxnard 93030, 985-6311; $64. 274 rooms and suites; special weekend packages. Also popular restaurant (see below). ● *Casa Via Mar Inn,* 337 West Channel Islands Boulevard, Port Hueneme 93041, 984-6222; $51. One mile east of the Channel Islands Harbor at Patterson Road. 74 units, some with kitchens. Six tennis courts.

DINING   *Lobster Trap,* at Casa Sirena Marina Hotel (see above), 985-6361. Lunch and dinner daily; Sunday brunch. Musical entertainment at cocktail time and every evening. ● *Castagnola's,* 3910 West Channel Islands Boulevard (in Fisherman's Wharf village), Oxnard, 985-3922. Three meals daily and Sunday brunch. Blackboard lists fresh seafood specials. ● *Whale's Tail,* 3950 Bluefin Circle, Oxnard, 985-2511. Lunch and dinner daily, champagne brunch on Sundays. Fresh seafood and beef dishes. Upper deck area features shellfish bar, lounge, and entertainment. ● *Port Royal,* 3900 Bluefin Circle, Oxnard, 984-1919. Lunch and dinner daily and Sunday champagne brunch. Fresh seafood, steaks, and flaming desserts. ● *Captain Jack's Seafood Cooker,* 4151 South Victoria Avenue, Oxnard, 985-5200. Cozy bar and restaurant featuring mesquite charcoal broiling. Open daily for lunch and dinner; Sunday brunch.

FOR MORE INFORMATION   Contact the Oxnard Convention and Visitors Bureau, 532 Esplanade Drive, Oxnard 93030, 485-8833. Also Channel Islands Chamber of Commerce, 116 West Channel Islands Boulevard, Oxnard 93030, 985-2244.

South Coastal Outings

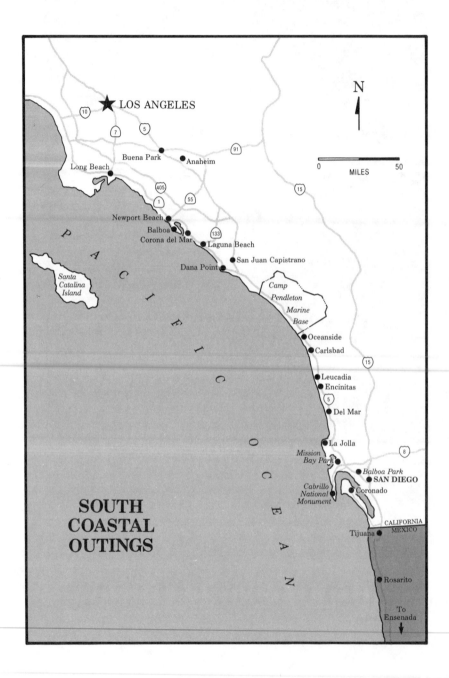

N

LOS ANGELES

⑩

⑦ ⑤

⑨①

Buena Park ●Anaheim

Long Beach ●

0   50
MILES

⑮

P
A
C
I
F
I
C

Newport Beach ●
Balboa ●
Corona del Mar ● ⑬③
Dana Point ● ●Laguna Beach
●San Juan Capistrano

Santa
Catalina
Island

Camp
Pendleton

Marine
Base

●Oceanside
●Carlsbad

O
C
E
A
N

⑮

●Leucadia
●Encinitas
⑤
●Del Mar

●La Jolla

Mission
Bay Park ●
⑧

Cabrillo
National
Monument ●

Balboa Park ●
●SAN DIEGO
●Coronado

SOUTH
COASTAL
OUTINGS

CALIFORNIA
MEXICO
Tijuana ●

●Rosarito

To
Ensenada
↓

Overleaf: Avalon, Santa Catalina Island

Catalina, the Island of Romance

Italy has its Isle of Capri, Greece its Mikonos, and Spain its Ibiza. California has Catalina. A weekend on Santa Catalina Island, as it's officially named, is a wonderful way to get off the mainland merry-go-round. Tensions of the big city fade away with the skyline as you cruise 22 miles across the ocean to tiny Avalon, the island's only town. As you ease into the pretty horseshoe-shaped harbor, Avalon almost seems to be a Hollywood set created for a 1940s movie. Many of the hotels, restaurants, and gift shops that line the bay and the hilly streets call to mind a resort town from an earlier era. Young boys come down to the pier with wagons to haul visitors' luggage to the hotels. Covering but one square mile and with only 2,030 year-round residents, Avalon is a small town in both size and flavor.

However, you won't be restless for something to do. Much of the action is along Crescent Avenue, a pedestrians-only street bordering the waterfront and Avalon's minuscule beach. Besides swimming and sunbathing, try your luck at fishing or go boating. Avalon also has tennis courts and a 9-hole golf course. Walking is the preferred way to explore this charming town, or you can rent a bicycle. And you can lope along some picturesque trails on horseback. There are a myriad of bus and boat tours of the island, which you can schedule at your own pace.

Settle in at one of the homey lodgings along the bay front, such as the 13-room Campo Bravo, where you can watch the colorful harbor scene from rocking chairs on the hotel's balcony. Also on Crescent Avenue in the heart of things are the Pavilion Lodge, Hotel Mac Rae, and Scari's Hotel. Catalina has two dozen other small hotels, nothing very fancy. Island dress is completely casual, so leave your elegant wear at home. Sometime during your carefree weekend, have a drink or dine on delicious seafood at two restaurants that include breathtaking views of the bay, Solomon's Landing and the Upstairs Place.

One reason so many people escape to Catalina is its weather. Even when haze from autos or the atmosphere settles over Los Angeles, chances are the island is bathed by sunlight and ocean breezes. No wonder that Avalon's population often swells to 6,000 on summer days. On holiday weekends the invasion of visitors sometimes tops 10,000. Despite the seasonal crowds, Santa Catalina Island may be the most unspoiled part of Los Angeles County. Most of its 76 square miles have been privately owned and preserved, notably by the man who made chewing gum so popular, William Wrigley, Jr. However, the Indians were here first (some Stone Age relics and more than 40 campsites have been discovered), and then European explorers claimed the island for the King of Spain in 1542. Pio Pico, the last Mexican governor of California, granted the land to its first American owner in 1846. Later, in the nineteenth century, brothers named Banning incorporated as the Santa Catalina Island Company and took possession. Wrigley's reign began in 1919, when he became the island company's major stockholder. The gum-making millionaire improved and promoted Avalon, but he kept most of the island off limits to the public, thus preserving its coastline and interior.

Fortunately, in 1975 a nonprofit foundation dedicated to continued protection of this land in its natural state gained title to 86 percent of the island. In exchange for a tax easement, the Santa Catalina Island Conservancy shares use of the land with Los Angeles County for conservation and recreation. Cars are allowed in Avalon but not encouraged anywhere; auto access to the interior is controlled by electric gates, and a key to open these barriers costs residents $80 a year.

Nevertheless, visitors can see much of the island on a variety of guided tours. If you want to view land that's changed little since Spanish times, don't miss the Inland Motor Tour. You'll visit Wrigley's El Rancho Escondido, where handsome Arabian horses are still raised and trained. And there's a pause for doughnuts and home-brewed cowpoke coffee at Old Eagle's Nest Stage Coach Stop, the same place early-day visitors had their refreshments. With luck you'll encounter some unexpected animals —wild boars and goats, mule deer, and even bison. About 400 buffalo roam around Catalina, a herd that originated in 1924, when the furry beasts were brought to the island by a movie crew. The half-day inland tour also takes you to isolated coves once frequented by pirates and smugglers and visits Catalina's mountaintop Airport-in-the-Sky.

Another way to enjoy Catalina is on a summer-season Around the Island Cruise that circles its 42-mile shoreline. You travel in a roomy 700-passenger excursion boat while listening to a taped narration about Catalina's unusual history and the sights along its rugged shore. This is an especially relaxing way to sightsee and get a suntan at the same time. Bring binoculars for a closer look at the island's many coves and beaches and the fishing boats and pleasure craft you'll pass at sea.

A shorter, 45-minute Coastal Cruise also sails from Avalon to give visitors an offshore look at the island. A summertime favorite is the Flying Fish Boat Tour offered in the evening. Powerful searchlights track schools of fish that skim across the water and sometimes even land in the excursion boat. You'll see some friendly seals as well.

Also in the summer, enjoy a Sunset Cruise aboard the *Phoenix,* a classic paddle-wheeler built in Wilmington, California, half a century ago. With drinks from the deck bar and live musical entertainment, it's not surprising that passengers are happily engaged in a songfest when their cocktail-hour coastal excursion boat returns to the dock in Avalon Bay.

The *Phoenix* is a glass-bottomed boat, and during the day you can board her or other smaller vessels for an underwater look into Catalina's crystal-clear waters. In summer, when the water is warmer, divers accompany these fascinating cruises to bring specimens of marine life to the boat's viewing windows for close-up inspection.

You have a choice of more tours on land too. The Scenic Terrace Drive takes you high above Avalon for a visit to Mount Ada, originally the residence of the William Wrigley, Jr., family. Now used as headquarters for University of Southern California's Institute of Marine and Coastal Studies, this hillside home still has its fine Victorian furnishings and lovely gardens. On the Skyline Drive tour you'll head 10 miles inland for a scenic look at the island's geography and native plant life. Some rare varieties you will see are Catalina ironwood, cherry and lilac trees, currant shrubs, and St. Catherine's Lace.

Visitors nostalgic for pre–World War II times should tour Catalina's landmark, the Casino, which Wrigley built for ballroom dancing, not gambling. The folks who attended dedication ceremonies in 1929 were thrilled by an immense motion picture theater, one of the first to be acoustically designed for the new "talkies." Samuel Goldwyn, Louis B. Mayer, Cecil B. De Mille, and other movie moguls used the casino's 1,200-seat theater to premier their latest sound films. And there was more. Above the theater is a dance floor unobstructed by support columns, which made it possible for as many as 3,000 dancers to swing to the sounds of the big bands. The Avalon Ballroom became well known when the music of Benny Goodman, Jan Garber, Kay Kyser, and other dance bands was broadcast across the nation from the Casino. After 50 years, the Casino continues to be Catalina's major entertainment center. Feature films are shown on weekends in winter, nightly in summer. And you can still hear some of the big bands, like the Jimmy Dorsey Orchestra, which are scheduled at least once a month from spring until fall. From the balcony that surrounds the building you'll get picture-perfect views of Avalon and its bay. The Casino also houses the Catalina Island Museum, with a large collection of Indian relics. And take a look in the Casino's gallery at the work of local artists.

If you want to explore even more of the island, get aboard the Two Harbors excursion boat that leaves from Avalon. You'll cruise along the coast of Catalina to a favorite spot of filmmakers, where you can swim at the beach, hike the trails, enjoy a picnic, or eat and drink at the Harbor Reef Restaurant.

Although you can fly by commuter plane or helicopter to Catalina, most visitors arrive by boat. Yachtsmen from everywhere tie up to buoys in Avalon's harbor, and daily cruise boats deposit passengers at the pier. Most popular are the 700-person vessels of Catalina Cruises that sail year round from the harbors at Long Beach and San Pedro. In the summer season you also can cruise to Catalina from Newport Beach.

To reach the boat terminal at Long Beach, take the Long Beach Free-way (California 7) south from Los Angeles to Long Beach. Exit at Golden Shore (Downtown) and follow the Catalina signs to the harbor parking lot. For departures from the Catalina boat terminal located under the Vincent Thomas Bridge in San Pedro, take the Harbor Freeway (California 111) south from Los Angeles, exit at Harbor Boulevard, and follow the Catalina signs.

Round trip to the Catalina boat-departure docks at San Pedro and Long Beach is about 48 miles. The cruise to the island takes about 1¾-hours.

Catalina Island Area Code: 213

PUBLIC TRANSPORTATION   Three companies offer boat service to Catalina Island from the mainland. Phone for departure times and reservations. ● *Catalina Cruises,* P.O. Box 1948, San Pedro 90733, 775-6111 or 832-4521 or (714) 527-7111. Year-round service on 700-passenger vessels to Avalon from Catalina Terminal at Pier 95 in San Pedro and Catalina Landing, 330 Golden Shore Boulevard, in downtown Long Beach. 1¾-hour crossing. Minimum 3 trips daily; June through September, service increases to at least 10 trips every day. Round-trip tickets $18.50 adults, $9.80 children 2 through 11 years, $1 kids under age 1. ● *Catalina Channel Express,* P.O. Box 1391, San Pedro 90733, 519-1212. Year-round daily service from Catalina Terminal in San Pedro to Avalon and Two Harbors. 60-passenger boat with airplane-type reclining seats, stewardess service, and cocktails. 1½ hour trip. Round trip $25 for adults, $15 children 2 through 11 years, $1 kids under age 2. ● *Catalina Passenger Service,* 400 Main Street, Balboa 92661, (714) 673-5245. From April through October only, daily service to Avalon from Balboa Pavilion in Newport Beach Harbor. 425-passenger boat makes crossing in 1½ hours, leaving Newport at 9 A.M. daily. Round trip $18 for adults, $9 for children 12 years and under.

Also, air service to Catalina is offered by two companies. ● *Allied Air Charter,* P.O. Box 1038, Avalon 90704, 510-1163 or 424-8545. Twin-engine 9-passenger planes from Long Beach Airport to Catalina's inland Airport-in-the-Sky. 15-minute flights, 1 round-trip daily. One-way fare $30; 30-minute ground transportation to Avalon included. ● *Helitrans,* toll-free (800) 262-1472. Daily flights in a 4-passenger jet helicopter from Catalina Terminal in San Pedro to Avalon's Pebbly Beach air base. Flights take 18 minutes, with several departures every hour. Adult round-trip tickets $70, children 12 years and under $50.

SIGHTSEEING   Catalina Sightseeing Tours, Santa Catalina Island Company, P.O. Box 737, Avalon 90704, 510-2500, operates most of the island's guided tours. Tickets and schedules are available at the Visitors

Information and Services Center in the lobby of Hotel Atwater, 123 Sumner Avenue, Avalon. • *Inland Motor Tour* departs daily at 9 A.M., returns by 1 P.M. Adults $11.50, children 5 through 11 years $5.50. • *Coastal Cruise,* a 45-minute boat tour, operates daily June through September. Adults $3.25, children $2. • *Flying Fish Boat Tour* goes evenings only June through September for 1 hour. Adults $4.75, children $2.25. • *Sunset Cruise,* a 2-hour cocktail cruise aboard an authentic paddle-wheeler, departs at 6 P.M. mid-May through mid-October. Tickets $15, including buffet and 1 drink; kids under age 5 free. • *Glass-Bottom Boat* tours operate year-round. 40-minute excursions. Adults $4, children $2.25. • *Scenic Terrace Drive* lasts 40 minutes and includes William Wrigley, Jr., home and grounds, mid-June through September; adults $4.50. Rest of the year, grounds only; adults $4. Children $2.25 all year. • *Skyline Drive* is a 1¾-hour inland bus tour, by reservation only. Adults $6, children $3. • *Casino Tour,* a 45-minute walking excursion, includes tram service to the bay-front landmark. Adults $3, children $2. • *Catalina Cruises* (see above) also operates two seasonal cruises besides its Long Beach/San Pedro-to-Avalon boat service. *Around the Island Cruise,* a 3-hour excursion, departs from Avalon daily except Sunday at 12:30 P.M., mid-June through September. Adults $9.50, children 2 through 11 years $5. • *Two Harbors Cruise,* a 5¾-hour outing, takes you to the isthmus, where there's time to picnic, swim, and loll on the beach. Departs Avalon daily at 12 noon mid-June through mid-September. Adults $9, children 2 to 11 years $4.50. • *Catalina Island Museum* in the Casino on the bay front, Avalon, 520-2414. Open Easter through October from 1 to 4 P.M. and 7 to 9 P.M. daily; rest of the year from 1 to 4 P.M. on weekends and holidays only. Free. • *Wrigley Memorial and Botanical Garden,* 1400 Avalon Canyon Road, Avalon, 510-2288. 38-acre garden with native plants. Open daily 8 A.M. to 5 P.M. Admission 50 cents, under 12 years free. 2 miles from town; hourly tram service in summer, $1 one way. • *Catalina Island Golf Course,* 100 Country Club Drive, Avalon, 510-0530. 9 holes, par 32. $5 weekends, $4 weekdays.

LODGING 2- or 3-night minimum stay required by some Avalon hotels on weekends and in summer season. Rates quoted below are for winter off-season; add $5 to $20 in other seasons. • *Campo Bravo,* 417 Crescent Avenue (or P.O. 767), Avalon 90704, 510-0035; $45. On the bay front in the center of town; 13 rooms. • *Scari's Hotel,* 111 Crescent Avenue (or P.O. Box 127), 510-0555; $45. Overlooking the bay; 34 rooms. Also restaurant (see below). • *Pavilion Lodge,* 513 Crescent Avenue (or P.O. 278), Avalon 90704, 599-1010; $50. 72 rooms across from bay-front beach. • *Hotel Mac Rae,* 409 Crescent Avenue (or P.O. Box 1517), Avalon 90704, 510-0246; $45. Across from bay-front beach and Pleasure Pier; 24 rooms.

CAMPING *Catalina Cove and Camp Agency,* P.O. Box 1566, Avalon

90704, 510-0303, handles reservations for Little Fisherman's Cove campsites at Two Harbors. For reservations at Avalon's Bird Park and other island campgrounds, contact Los Angeles Department of Parks and Recreation, P.O. Box 1133, Avalon 90704, 510-0688.

DINING   *El Galleon,* 411 Crescent Avenue, Avalon, 510-1188. Seafood and steaks for dinner; also lunch in summer. Closed January and February.   • *Flying Yachtsman,* 403 Crescent Avenue, Avalon, 510-9177. Seafood and salad bar. Lunch and dinner daily; dinner only in winter. • *Scari's Restaurant,* 111 Crescent Avenue, Avalon, 510-0031. Swordfish a specialty. Dinner nightly in season, weekends only in winter. • *The Upstairs Place,* 417 Crescent Avenue, Avalon, 510-0333. Charbroiled fish, clam chowder. • *Solomon's Landing,* in El Encanto Market Place, Marilla at Crescent Avenue, Avalon, 510-1474. Seafood and Mexican dishes. • *Harbor Reef Restaurant,* Two Harbors at the isthmus, 510-0303. Breakfast, lunch, and dinner; picnic boxes from the snack bar.

FOR MORE INFORMATION   Contact the Catalina Island Chamber of Commerce and Visitors Bureau, P.O. Box 217, Avalon 90704, 510-1520. Operates an easy-to-remember one-call-does-it-all number, "five-ten-fifteen-twenty," for lodging reservations and information about boat and air transportation and island tours. The office in Avalon is open daily on the green Pleasure Pier. Also contact Catalina Sightseeing Tours (see above).

Landlocked Cruise on the *Queen Mary* in Long Beach

Whether you're a sailor or a landlubber, you'll enjoy a nautical weekend "cruising" aboard the magnificent *Queen Mary*, once the world's largest ocean liner. This grande dame of luxury passenger ships crisscrossed the Atlantic 1,001 times before being retired and permanently berthed alongside Pier J at Long Beach in 1967. To step back into an unsurpassed era of elegance on the high seas, book one of the classy cabins that now make up the Queen Mary Hotel. Three decks of the ship are reserved for hotel guests, who have a choice of accommodations in 380 of the original first-class staterooms. You'll enjoy the same polished wood paneling, rose-tinted mirrors, and full-size baths that pleased passengers during the vessel's three decades of transatlantic service.

Besides living in luxury aboard the *Queen,* there will be time during your weekend "at sea" to tour the grand ship, dine in its excellent restaurants, and go ashore to enjoy some of the other attractions around the port and elsewhere in Long Beach. You'll want to go inside the adjacent aluminum dome to view Howard Hughes's famed flying boat, the mammoth *Spruce Goose,* as well as other airplane memorabilia. If you really feel like setting sail, embark on the harbor tour boat to cruise amid pleasure craft, oil tankers, container ships, and navy vessels in busy San Pedro Bay. On the opposite shore it's fun to wander in the harbor complex of shops, galleries, restaurants, and boat facilities at Shoreline Village. And inland you'll be intrigued by two nineteenth-century Spanish ranchos that are open to visitors.

To begin your weekend on the luxury liner, take Interstate 5 south from downtown Los Angeles and join the Long Beach Freeway (California 7) to the *Queen Mary* exit at the freeway's end. Then continue to the special hotel parking area. At curbside a doorman in ship's uniform will direct you to an outside elevator that lifts ovenight guests to A deck and the hotel registration desk. Settling in your cabin on A, B, or Main deck, you'll notice that some modern amenities—like plush carpeting, color television, and a direct-dial phone—have been added since the ship made her maiden voyage in 1936. Some rooms have even been outfitted with king-size beds. As in the *Queen Mary*'s oceangoing days, the cost of a cabin depends on its location. You'll pay the least for an inside room (no porthole) and the most for starboard accommodations with a view of the harbor. Suites of rooms also are available. One of the ship's restaurants and bars, the Capstan, is reserved exclusively for hotel guests, as is a private deck area for sunbathing.

Although the cost of a cabin on the *Queen Mary* doesn't include meals, you'll have as great a selection of food here as on any cruise ship. The tasty fare is prepared by European chefs and ranges from fish and chips to filet mignon. Especially popular is the Sunday champagne brunch in the beautiful Grand Salon, which recalls the bygone days of opulent dining at sea. A tuxedoed ensemble or harpist plays soothing music in the background as you choose from a tempting buffet of 70 dishes. There's even a captain's table, hosted by the *Queen Mary*'s current master, the very British John W. Gregory, who resides aboard ship with his dog, Happy.

One of the ocean liner's most famous passengers, Winston Churchill, also is remembered as one of its most enthusiastic eaters, so the *Queen Mary*'s gourmet restaurant has been named in his honor. Continental cuisine is served daily at lunch and dinner in Sir Winston's on the Sun deck. Fresh seafood delicacies and English specialties like prime ribs and Yorkshire pudding are served in the Promenade Cafe, stretching along the starboard Promenade deck. More intimate dining is offered evenings in the Promenade Dining Room. For quick meals to eat outside on the Sun deck, go to the Verandah Grill at the stern of the ship. And don't miss having a drink or dancing after hours in the attractive Art Deco observation lounge overlooking the bow.

Enjoy more of the *Queen Mary* by making a leisurely self-guiding tour of her decks, cabins, and public rooms, where huge photos and impressive exhibits recall the stately ship's heyday as a passenger liner and six years of service as a troop carrier during World War II. A day-long tour ticket is your passport to explore the 81,000-ton liner. With it you can go belowdecks to the gleaming engine room and even view one of the massive bronze propellers that helped make the *Queen Mary* the fastest liner afloat in the 1940s. Above, on A deck, you'll be able to compare the various original accommodations—first, tourist, and cabin—of the three-class ship and see the cramped quarters of soldiers when the *Queen Mary* was a troop ship. The captain's suite is open for inspection, too.

Exhibits on the Sun deck are equally fascinating and feature the hospital, beauty salon, chapel, first-class gym, and children's playroom. You're also welcome to visit the bridge and radio room. The kids especially like to watch the crewmen give daily demonstrations with the ship's sextant, ropes, engine works, and lifeboats. And you can see a model-ship builder engaged in his painstaking craft. For a fitting finale to your tour of the ship, have tea or coffee with the ship's officers at the Captain's Party in the Queen's Salon on Promenade deck. You'll be serenaded in style by the *Queen Mary*'s own orchestra, as well as a singing and dancing duo who present a musical medley from the '30s, '40s, and '50s.

It's easy to spend an entire day exploring the huge and historic ocean liner, but, as on any cruise, you'll also want to go ashore. Just beyond the ship's gangway is a mock-English village called Londontowne, where you can browse in the gift stores for souvenirs of your *Queen Mary* weekend. You won't want to miss the *Queen Mary*'s other neighbor, another novelty of transportation from a bygone era, which was put on public view for the first time in 1983. It's the *Spruce Goose,* conceived during World War II to carry troops and equipment over the oceans. As the world's largest plane, constructed entirely of wood and considered by many a $25-million fantasy, it flew only once, during a test run in Long Beach Harbor, and then was secluded nearby in a temperature-controlled hangar for 36 years. Now returned to the site of its historic flight, the *Spruce Goose* is the centerpiece of the Hughes Flying Boat Expo, an ongoing exhibit inside a huge shiny white dome. (Actually, its catchy nickname is a misnomer, because most of the wood used to construct the plane is birch.) The awesome aircraft is taller than an eight-story building and has a wingspan wider than a football field. You can ascend to the flight deck to view the cockpit and the instruments that controlled the eight engines needed to power the 400,000-ton behemoth. Also look inside the cavernous fuselage, designed to hold 750 soldiers and two tanks. Surrounding the *Spruce Goose* are multimedia shows and other displays that reveal some of the personal life and professional career of the plane's backer and builder, Howard Hughes, the only person ever to pilot the remarkable flying boat. You'll see his aviation trophies and clips from the Hollywood movies he made.

Set aside time on Sunday to visit Shoreline Village, which appears almost like a motion picture set just across the channel from the *Queen Mary* and *Spruce Goose*. A water-taxi service is planned to take visitors from Pier J to this new waterfront shopping and dining complex, which resembles a turn-of-the-century coastal village. Or you can take a short trip by car or shuttle bus on Shoreline Drive to reach this Victorian-looking attraction, neighbor to an aquatic park and boat-filled marina, two other handsome additions to Long Beach's redeveloped bay front. From the landscaped walkways you'll have expansive views of the downtown skyline and picturesque harbor. The four tropical-looking islands you see are cleverly diguised oil wells that have been named in memory of astronauts Grissom, Chaffee, White, and Freeman, who lost their lives in America's space program. A special reason for visiting Shoreline Village is to ride its vintage carrousel, a classic 1906 merry-go-round that takes you back to the days of oceanside amusement parks, like the former Long Beach Pike. Join the kids listening to the carrousel's happy music while galloping along on its 62 hand-carved horses, camels, giraffes, and rams.

Also make an inland excursion in your car to a pair of historic Spanish ranchos that have been restored and opened to the public in Long Beach. A few acres of two vast land grants, Rancho Los Alamitos and Rancho Los Cerritos, have been preserved with their adobe homes and gardens intact. They're sanctuaries from an earlier era when thousands of cattle, sheep, and horses grazed on the undeveloped land that's since become the L.A. megalopolis.

To reach them from Shoreline Village or the *Queen Mary,* drive back north on the Long Beach Freeway (California 7) and exit east on Del Amo Boulevard. Turn right on Long Beach Boulevard to San Antonio Drive, right again to Virginia Avenue, and another right to reach Rancho Los Cerritos. Surrounded by a private country club and golf course in a residential area, the rancho has been reduced to 5 of its original 27,000 acres and is now a national historic landmark. Tour the handsome two-story ranch house, made of adobe with redwood support beams shipped down the coast from Monterey. It was built in 1844 by Los Angeles merchant Jonathan Temple, who also developed one of California's first formal gardens. Look for some of the Italian cypress, black locust, and pomegranate trees he planted more than a century ago.

Head next to Rancho Los Alamitos. Go back to Long Beach Boulevard, turn right to the San Diego Freeway (Interstate 405) and follow it south about five miles to the Palo Verde Avenue exit. Continue south on Palo Verde past the guard gate and go up the hill to Bixby Hill Road and the rancho office. Volunteer guides take you back to yesteryear on a tour of the rambling ranch house, a complete blacksmith shop, and dairy and horse barns with equipment and displays. The adobe home was built over 175 years ago by the son of the Spanish land-grant holder, and eventually a series of owners renovated the house and expanded it to 19 rooms. Among the vintage furnishings is a wonderful 500-piece collection of American glassware. You'll also enjoy a walk in the extensive gardens. Some sections are formal, like the pathway of oleander, while others grow rather wild, including areas devoted to succulents and native California plants.

When your weekend shore excursions are over, return to Interstate 405 and go west to join the Harbor Freeway (Interstate 110/California 11) and head north to Los Angeles.

Round trip is about 68 miles.

Long Beach Area Code: 213

SIGHTSEEING   *Queen Mary Tour,* aboard the *Queen Mary,* Pier J (or P.O. Box 8), Long Beach 90801, 435-5671. Open daily 10 A.M. to 5 P.M. (to 4 P.M. on weekdays in winter). Self-guided tour; ticket includes tour map, brochure, and schedule of daily events for times and locations of engine room, lifeboat drill, navigation and knot-tying demonstrations. Restaurant hours and locations also are given. All-day adult tickets $6, children 5 to 12 years $4. Combination tickets for *Queen Mary* and *Spruce Goose* tours (see below) $8 adults, $5 children. Both tours free for Queen Mary Hotel guests. No charge to visit gift shops, lounge, and restaurants on Promenade deck. ● *Spruce Goose Tour,* in 12-story dome near stern of *Queen Mary* (see above), 435-5671. Open daily from 10 A.M. to 6 P.M. Self-guided tour of flying-boat exterior with peeks at interior; aviation experts on hand to answer your questions. Adult tickets $6, children 5 to 12 years $4. Free for Queen Mary Hotel guests. Combination tickets for *Spruce Goose/Queen Mary* tours also available (see above). The Hangar restaurant and gift shop located beneath plane's colossal tail. ● *Harbor Boat Tour,* departure dock near bow of *Queen Mary,* 547-0802. 90-minute narrated trip around Long Beach Harbor aboard a Catalina Cruises excursion boat. Departures at noon, 2, 4, and 6 P.M.; daily in summer, Thursday through Sunday rest of the year. Adults $6, children 5 through 11 years $3.75. ● *Shoreline Village,* off Shoreline Drive, Long Beach 90802, 590-8427. 40 specialty shops open daily where you can buy everything from kites to yachts; also 6 dining spots and antique carrousel (50 cents a ride). ● *Rancho Los Cerritos,* 4600 Virginia Road, Long Beach 90807, 424-9423. Open Wednesday through Sunday 1 to 5 P.M., except holidays. Free. ● *Rancho Los Alamitos,* 6400 Bixby Hill Road, Long Beacn 90815, 431-2511. Open Wednesday through Sunday from 1 to 5 P.M., except holidays. Free. 90-minute guided tours of adobe ranch house, barns, blacksmith shop, and gardens.

LODGING   *Queen Mary Hotel* (see above), 435-3511, or toll-free (800) 352-7883; $73 to $93. Also 8 elegant suites from $190 to $375. Ask about family plan and vacation packages. *Queen Mary* and *Spruce Goose* tours (see above) are gratis for hotel guests. Four restaurants (see below), one exclusively for hotel guests. ● *Hyatt Regency Long Beach,* Shoreline Drive at Pine Avenue, Long Beach 90802, 435-8291; $75. Grand 16-story hotel overlooking downtown bay front with its aquatic park, marina, and Shoreline Village. Opened in 1983 with 522 rooms and 20 suites, plus gourmet dining room with view of *Queen Mary.* ● *Queensway Bay Hilton,* 700 Queensway Drive, Long Beach 90801, 435-7676; $79. Half mile from *Queen Mary* on causeway to Pier J. 200 rooms with bay and marina views. Also tennis, jogging path, and restaurant (see below).

DINING   The *Queen Mary* (see above) offers a number of dining opportunities: *Sir Winston's,* Sun deck, gourmet fare for dinner nightly and lunch weekdays, with cocktail lounge and piano music most evenings; *Promenade Cafe,* Promenade deck, family dining daily for breakfast, lunch, and dinner, with seafood and cocktail bars; *Promenade Dining Room,* Promenade deck, dinner nightly with harbor views; *Verandah Grill,* Sun deck, hamburgers and other fast food daily; *Celebrity Room Bakery,* Sun deck, pastries, coffee, and soft drinks daily during tour hours; *Grand Salon,* R deck, for Sunday champagne brunch, with sittings at 11 A.M. and 1:30 P.M. (adults $14.50, children 10 years and under $7.50; reservations required); *Queen's Salon,* Promenade deck, for sandwich and salad bar at midday on weekends and daily in summer. ● *Adolph's,* Queensway Bay Hilton (see above), 437-5977. Seafood and steak specialties for lunch and dinner; also breakfast and weekend brunch, nightly entertainment and dancing. ● *Quiet Cannon,* 600 Queensway Drive, Long Beach, 436-2247. Lunch and dinner overlooking Queensway Bay; also Sunday brunch. ● *The Reef,* 880 Harbor Scenic Drive, Long Beach, 435-7096. Also at the water's edge. Lunch, dinner, and Sunday brunch amid nautical decor.

FOR MORE INFORMATION   Contact the Long Beach Area Convention and Visitors Council, 180 East Ocean Boulevard, Suite 150, Long Beach 90802, 436-3645.

Seaside Delights at Newport Beach and Balboa Island

One of the Southland's most attractive and affluent coastal communities, Newport Beach, has long been a glorious getaway. It began more than 75 years ago when the Pacific Electric Railroad's big red cars began whisking pleasure seekers and potential land buyers from Los Angeles to a beautiful stretch of beach in the neighboring county that was better known for its oranges and other agriculture. Since then Newport Beach has become Orange County's seaside showplace, where residents and visitors alike are drawn by a plethora of popular pastimes that include sailing, shopping, and dining.

Water dominates Newport life, beginning with several miles of ocean surf that lap onto a broad sandy beach extending southwest along a finger of land known as the Newport and Balboa Peninsula. At its end an inlet from the Pacific leads to Newport's boat-filled harbor, where palatial homes and cozy cottages cover eight odd-sized islands, including well-known Balboa. Inland the ocean tides have created an estuary, Upper Newport Bay, that is both a wildlife preserve and a picturesque setting for handsome homes clustered around its bluff-top perimeter. And south beyond the harbor inlet is a popular beach park and peaceful residential community, Corona del Mar, also within the boundaries of Newport Beach.

While this water-oriented resort area has been spared high-rise hotels along its beach, you can still enjoy ocean vistas and spectacular sunsets by checking into luxurious hilltop accommodations at the Newport Beach Marriott Hotel and Tennis Club or its exclusive neighbor overlooking Newport Bay, the Newporter. Either one can be reached easily from Los Angeles by driving south on Interstate 5 and California 55 toward Newport Beach and exiting on the partially completed Corona del Mar Freeway, California 73. After it merges with Bristol Street, turn right on Jamboree Road and head toward the ocean to the landmark Fashion Island and Newport Center shopping and business complexes. Turn left on Santa Barbara Drive to Newport Center Drive and the Marriott, or continue on Jamboree Boulevard and turn right to the Newporter.

These hotels offer enough temptations to make weekend escapes in themselves. Each has fine restaurants, lounges with entertainment, guest privileges at championship golf courses and tennis courts, and short shuttles to wonderful shopping in stores such as Neiman-Marcus and Bullock's Wilshire. But to really experience Newport Beach, you must get to the water. Drive down Jamboree Boulevard to Pacific Coast Highway, California 1, then turn right to reach Newport Boulevard going to the peninsula, which is flanked by the ocean and Newport Harbor.

Make your first stop Lido Marina Village, just beyond the overpass bridge that crosses the coast highway and a finger of Newport Bay. Turn left from Newport Boulevard on Via Lido to the attractive shopping village's parking structure, then stroll along red brick streets and pathways leading to dozens of boutiques and specialty shops. You'll find all kinds of treasures, from high-fashion clothes to rare coins and oil paintings to children's games. Along the village's waterfront, where boats bob in their slips and cruise in the bay, relax with a snack on the boardwalk or have lunch in the Warehouse Restaurant.

From Lido Marina Village, walk or drive southeast along Via Lido and veer right on Lafayette Avenue to a district known as Cannery Village. When fishing was a major industry in Newport Beach, the canneries here operated around the clock. Although they no longer exist, much of the original equipment can be seen in the Cannery Restaurant, a scenic place for drinks, a meal, or Sunday brunch. Another popular dining spot is Delaney's on the other side of the channel, where commercial fishing boats still tie up.

Between Lafayette Avenue and Newport Boulevard, explore the Cannery Village area from 22nd to 28th streets. Besides boat-related businesses, such as sail makers and marine-hardware dealers, you'll find a variety of gift shops and art galleries. This historic district, which is indicated by Cannery Village street signs, is the location of a gourmet dinner house, Le Saint Tropez.

Not much farther south along Newport Boulevard are more casual places to drink and dine that also are favorites of Newport Beach people. Woody's Wharf is on the bay and has its own dock to lure hungry and thirsty boaters. The Crab Cooker and the Old Spaghetti Factory always are crowded with seafarers and landlubbers.

For a look at the West Coast's only remaining dory fishing fleet, continue driving along the peninsula on Newport Boulevard—which becomes Balboa Boulevard—and turn right on 20th Street at the signs to Newport Pier and the business district. Park where you can, then walk to the north side of the pier to find colorful open wooden boats called dories.

Since 1891 Newport fishermen have been putting to sea in such boats every day before dawn. If you're early enough (about 9:30 A.M.), you can watch the returning fishermen roll their brightly painted vessels onto the beach. After setting up scales and cutting boards across the dories, they offer the day's catch for sale. Depending on the season, the dorymen bring in sea trout, red snapper, kingfish, flounder, crab, and lobster. Among the first customers at this unusual open-air fish market are the chefs from local restaurants.

You can do your own fishing, without a license, from the adjacent

Newport Pier, which juts into the Pacific. Rent a rod and reel from the tackle and bait shop at the foot of this 1940s wooden pier, which replaced one built in the previous century to offload supplies from coastal merchant vessels.

If you drive two miles farther along the peninsula and turn right at the signs to municipal parking lots on the beach, you'll spot the historic Balboa Pier, site of the first water-to-water aircraft flight in 1912. That's when Glenn Martin flew his seaplane from Balboa to Catalina Island, which was also the longest and fastest flight over water at the time. Walk back across Balboa Boulevard to the harbor and its 1906 Victorian-style landmark, the Balboa Pavilion. There you can board a harbor cruise boat, the *Pavilion Queen* or *Showboat,* for a narrated tour of Newport Bay. As home port for 10,000 pleasure boats of all descriptions, from rubber rafts to million-dollar yachts, the long and sheltered harbor is one of the busiest and most picturesque anywhere on the Pacific Coast. You'll also see some expensive waterfront homes, including those of the late John Wayne and "King" Gillette of safety-razor fame.

If you'd rather be at the helm when you cruise in the bay, small sailboats and skiffs with motors are moored near the Balboa Pavilion and can be rented by the hour or longer. Party sportfishing boats also sail from there for deep-sea fishing excursions that last half a day or longer. The same docks are the departure points for Newport's passenger service to Catalina Island in summer and whale-watching cruises in winter.

A must for all visitors is to sail across the harbor on one of California's few remaining ferryboats. The three-car ferries make the trip to and from Balboa Island in minutes. The quick toll trips have been operating since 1919, when the island's residents (who numbered just 26 back then) petitioned for ferry service. Once you're on Balboa, sidewalks along the bay front offer a good look at the handsome boats and a peek into the harborview homes. Take a leisurely stroll, or rent smooth-riding roller skates near the ferry landing for a more novel way to tour the island. Along Marine Avenue you'll find a number of gift stores and snack shops, including one that sells Balboa Island's own tasty invention, a frozen banana dipped in melted chocolate.

Of course, you should plan some time during the weekend to loll at the seashore. Join the sunbathers, swimmers, and surfers who fill up the four miles of white sand beaches stretching along the peninsula and also Corona del Mar State and City Beach just south across the harbor inlet. If it's midsummer, however, be warned that the population of Newport Beach multiplies into a traffic nightmare of 100,000 vacationers and residents; in the off-season months the scene is much more relaxing.

On Sunday if you prefer a peaceful alternative to Newport's seaside action, set your sights on a pair of delightful gardens nearby in Corona del Mar. From the Newport Beach Marriott or the Newporter hotels, take Jamboree Boulevard north to San Joaquin Hills Road and go east to Mac-

Arthur Boulevard. Cross the highway, where you'll see "Roger's" spelled in flowers on the corner, and look for the entrance sign to Roger's Gardens. This flower-filled nursery unabashedly bills itself as America's most beautiful garden center, and few visitors dispute that claim after strolling amid the stunning displays of more than 50,000 plants. You'll also discover that this seven-acre attraction is more than a botanical haven. Daily demonstrations give visitors step-by-step instructions for creating attractive hanging baskets, a Roger's Gardens specialty, and a professional "plant doctor" is on hand to offer advice for your ailing plants. You'll also find florists ready to make custom cut-flower arrangements, a library with all sorts of garden books, patio furniture and accessories in outdoor settings, and even antiques and artwork for other home decorating ideas.

After visiting Roger's Gardens, return to MacArthur Boulevard and continue south toward the ocean to the Coast Highway. Turn left and go 1½ blocks to Corona del Mar's other botanical showplace, Sherman Library and Gardens. Hidden by the inconspicuous blue-gray slat fence and covering an entire city block is one of the Southland's most beautiful floral sanctuaries. Turn right on Dahlia or Fernleaf Avenue to reach the free parking lot behind the gardens.

Over 850 botanical species grow in the immaculate two-acre compound, ranging from tropical and seasonal flowering plants to rare cacti and succulents. Be sure to enter the temperature-controlled conservatory, where you're surrounded by a world of greenery and flowers that includes orchids, staghorn ferns, carnivorous plants, and anthuriums. Elsewhere in the garden you'll find an enticing shop with flower books, plants, pots, and gifts for sale.

If you get hungry before ending your weekend at Newport Beach, enjoy a meal in one of the charming Corona del Mar restaurants located along the Coast Highway, such as Hemingway's or the Five Crowns. After dinner, go north on California 73 (MacArthur Boulevard), which becomes a freeway and intersects with California 55 to join Interstate 5 back to Los Angeles.

Round trip is about 110 miles.

Newport Beach Area Code: 714

SIGHTSEEING   *Pavilion Queen,* 400 Main Street at the Balboa Pavilion, Balboa 92661, 673-5245. Narrated cruises of Newport Bay on a double-deck excursion boat depart daily on the hour from 12 noon through 5 P.M. in summer and 2 or 3 times daily in winter. 45-minute trips cost adults $4, children 50 cents; 90-minute excursions are $6 adults, $1 children. ● *Newport Harbor Showboat Cruises,* operated by the Fun Zone Boat Company, 700 Edgewater Avenue, Balboa 92661,

673-0240. The *Showboat* departs from the foot of Washington Street, between the Balboa Pavilion and the peninsula ferryboat landing. 45-minute harbor excursions leave daily on the hour from 11 A.M. to 7 P.M. in summer, from noon to 4 P.M. in winter. Adults $4, children 5 through 12 years 50 cents. 90-minute bay cruises depart daily on the hour from 11 A.M. to 6 P.M. in summer, at 2 P.M. in winter. Adults $6, children $1. ● *Davey's Locker,* 400 Main Street, at the Balboa Pavilion 92661, 673-1434. Half-day sport-fishing trips depart daily at 6 A.M. and 12:30 P.M. year round, plus 5:30 P.M. twilight trips in summer. Adults $15, children 12 years and under $8. Also all-day and ¾-day deep-sea fishing excursions. Rental skiffs with outboards available for fishing or sightseeing in the harbor. ● *Balboa Ferry,* crosses Newport Bay from the end of Palm Street on the Balboa Peninsula to Agate Avenue on Balboa Island. Operates day and night during summer, early morning until midnight the rest of the year. Car and driver pay 75 cents, passengers and pedestrians 20 cents each way. ● *Corona del Mar State and City Beach,* off Ocean Boulevard, Corona del Mar 92625, 640-2156. Municipally operated beach park open daily from 8 A.M. to 10 P.M. Parking fee $3 in summer, $2 in winter. Volleyball nets, fire rings, and snack bar. ● *Roger's Gardens,* 2301 San Joaquin Hills Road, Corona del Mar 92625, 640-5800. Open daily from 9 A.M. to 6 P.M. Free. Hanging-basket demonstrations year round on weekends at 1 and 3 P.M., plus 11 A.M. on Saturday; also daily on weekdays in summer. ● *Sherman Library and Gardens,* 2647 East Coast Highway, Corona del Mar 92625, 673-2261. Open daily from 10:30 A.M. to 4 P.M. Adults $1, children 12 through 16 years 25 cents; free admission on Monday.

EVENTS   *Festival of Lights Boat Parade,* a grand parade of yachts and sailboats festooned with holiday lights and decorations, cruises around Newport Harbor's main waterways every night from 6:30 P.M. for one week prior to Christmas Eve.

LODGING   *The Newporter,* 1107 Jamboree Road, Newport Beach 92660, 644-1700; $100. Also weekend package: two nights for the price of one. Over 300 rooms and suites in a popular 26-acre resort that's undergone a $10 million renovation. 3-par, 9-hole golf course on the grounds, with an 18-hole championship course nearby. Also, guest privileges on 16 lighted courts at the adjacent John Wayne Tennis Club. Two excellent restaurants (see below). ● *Newport Beach Marriott Hotel and Tennis Club,* 900 Newport Center Drive at Fashion Island, Newport Beach 92660, 640-4000; $105. Also tennis and weekend packages. Over 375 rooms, most with ocean views. 10 lighted tennis courts with a resident pro. Golf privileges at nearby country clubs. Two fine restaurants (see below).

CAMPING *Newport Dunes Travel Trailer Park,* 1131 Back Bay Drive, off Jamboree Road, Newport Beach 92660, 644-0510. 195 RV sites; $20 per night with full hookup.

DINING *The Newporter* (see above). Enjoy a gourmet meal in the gardenlike *La Palme,* where dinner is served nightly except Sunday, lunch weekdays, and brunch on Sunday. A special treat is dinner in the *Wine Cellar,* with one seating for 32 guests each evening except Sunday and Monday. The 6-course menu of French cuisine changes weekly. Reservations required, as well as coats and ties for men. • *Newport Beach Marriott Hotel and Tennis Club* (see above). Famous for Sunday champagne brunch in its *Capriccio Cafe.* Also fine French cuisine in *Nicole's.* • *Warehouse Restaurant,* 3450 Via Oporto in Lido Marina Village, Newport Beach, 673-4700. International dishes and seafood served daily for lunch and dinner at the water's edge. Also Sunday brunch, patio dining, and entertaiment most evenings. • *Cannery Restaurant,* 3010 LaFayette Avenue in Cannery Village, Newport Beach, 675-5777. Seafood, steak, and fun along the water for lunch and dinner daily, plus Sunday brunch with musical entertainment. • *Delaney's,* 630 Lido Park Drive in Cannery Village, Newport Beach, 675-0100. A Newport favorite for Sunday brunch, plus fresh seafood for lunch and dinner daily. • *Le Saint Tropez,* 3012 Newport Boulevard, 673-7883. Dress up for a dinner of classic French haute cuisine served nightly except Monday. • *Woody's Wharf,* 2318 Newport Boulevard, Newport Beach, 675-0474. Informal local spot for food and drink at lunch and dinner with harbor views. Steak and seafood. • *The Crab Cooker,* 2200 Newport Boulevard, Newport Beach, 673-0100. Absolutely nothing fancy (the silverware is plastic!), but there's usually a line waiting for the broiled fresh fish, shellfish, and seafood chowder at this Newport institution. Lunch and dinner daily; no reservations. • *Old Spaghetti Factory,* 2110 Newport Boulevard, Newport Beach, 675-8654. Spaghetti served a dozen different ways. • *Hemingway's,* 2441 East Coast Highway, Corona del Mar, 673-0120. French country cuisine served with continental flair every night except Monday. Also Sunday brunch. • *Five Crowns,* 3801 East Coast Highway, Corona del Mar, 760-0331. Pleasant Old English atmosphere, with prime ribs the specialty. Dinner nightly plus brunch on Sundays. Also a popular piano bar.

FOR MORE INFORMATION Contact the Newport Beach Convention and Visitors Bureau, 1470 Jamboree Road, Newport Beach 92660, 644-8460. Also the Newport Harbor Area Chamber of Commerce, 1470 Jamboree Road, Newport Beach, 92660, 644-8211.

Festive Times in Laguna Beach

If you like art but aren't much for museums, you're going to love the summertime Pageant of the Masters in Laguna Beach, one of Southern California's prettiest coastal towns. Annually from mid-July through August, more than two dozen works of art are shown nightly to audiences comfortably seated in an outdoor amphitheater. You'll see works by Gauguin, Goya, Picasso, Monet, Delacroix, and many other famous artists. Instead of the original paintings, however, you'll be viewing remarkable reproductions—living pictures with real people posing as their canvas counterparts. Even if you don't see the pageant, you'll have fun visiting Laguna Beach during the concurrent art festival, which originated in 1932, when several local artists displayed their paintings on a fence near a beach. Since then the festival has grown to three separate sites, with nearly 500 Southland artists and craftsmen displaying their work.

Also luring visitors to the art colony is a creation by Mother Nature, several miles of beautiful sandy beach enclosed by high bluffs that create intimate coves for sunbathing and beachcombing. Other joys for Laguna Beach vacationers are a wide choice of accommodations—from homey bed-and-breakfasts to an oceanfront luxury hotel—and a variety of restaurants for every taste and pocketbook.

To discover all its many year-round pleasures and enjoy the art festivals and pageant, drive south from Los Angeles on Interstate 5 or 405 and exit south on California 133. This short freeway merges into Laguna Canyon Road and winds through some scenic ranchland before becoming Broadway Avenue and ending at the town's main thoroughfare, Coast Highway (California 1), which parallels the Pacific.

For accommodations on the beach, it's difficult to top Laguna's Surf & Sand Hotel, where all 160 deluxe rooms and suites overlook the ocean. Whether you stay there or not, don't miss a sunset drink or the continental fare in its Towers Restaurant, decorated in art deco style with mirrored ceilings that reflect the mesmerizing Pacific nine stories below. Also outstanding is the Surf & Sand's other restaurant, the Boardwalk, where a chalkboard tells you the flight numbers of the just-caught fish that are flown in daily from both coasts.

Another Laguna lodging with delightful guest rooms and excellent cuisine is Hotel San Maarten, just a block from the beach on Coast Highway. The courtyard swimming pool surrounded by tropical flowers and greenery is the West Indies setting for patio dining offered at Gauguin's.

Also steps from the ocean on Coast Highway is Laguna's first bed-and-breakfast, Eiler's Inn, a friendly 11-room hostelry where fellow travelers enjoy conversation by the soothing courtyard fountain during the late afternoon wine-and-cheese hour. Newer on Laguna's B&B scene and equally as enjoyable is the Carriage House, a colonial-style inn two blocks from Coast Highway toward the hills. Its six antique-decorated suites feature one or two bedrooms plus a sitting room and kitchen. Children and pets are welcome, too.

For a panorama of Laguna's stunning beach and cliff-rimmed coastline, head south a few blocks from the center of town to the bluff-top Laguna Village, a cluster of open-air shops with all kinds of art, crafts, and flowers. Every Sunday this parklike site on Coast Highway hosts an art fair.

An equally impressive view of the town that's built on gentle hills sloping down to the sea is from Heisler Park along Cliff Drive. Picnic on the grassy lawn while watching sailboats from Newport Beach and Dana Point race along the horizon. Or drink and dine with the same view at Las Brisas, a stylish Mexican seafood restaurant and cocktail spot that replaced the noted Victor Hugo Inn.

Next door, see what's current in the world of art by visiting the Laguna Beach Museum of Art, then stroll up and down the Coast Highway to find your favorite artworks in the dozens of Laguna art galleries. Tops in town is Vorpal Gallery, with Picasso and more of the masters. You'll find Lalique, Baccarat, and other fine crystal creations at Lippe/Waren. For Chinese art and antiques, Warren Imports is internationally known. Laguna boasts at least 20 antique shops, and Richard Yeakel has three stores of French, English, American, and nautical pieces from the fourteenth to eighteenth centuries.

Visitors also are treated to a cornucopia of gift shops, ranging from the landmark Pottery Shack to offbeat Chicken Little's. Village Fair, Forest Avenue, and Lumberyard malls are the town's trio of cozy shopping plazas.

Main Beach Park, Laguna's "Window on the Sea," draws not only sunbathers and swimmers but volleyball and basketball fans. Up in Heisler Park the older athletes prefer lawn bowling and horseshoes. And you'll find scores of nature lovers strolling through the flower-filled grounds.

However, even Laguna's pretty parks are hard pressed to best the personal garden of Hortense Miller. On a hillside overlooking the sea, she's covered 2½ acres around her home with more than 1,200 species of native and subtropical plants. In keeping with the art community's enjoyment of beauty, Miss Miller invites everyone to visit her private garden. Just call City Hall to arrange for a docent guide for Saturday morning or any weekday.

The Hortense Miller Garden is just one of the pleasant surprises for frequent or first-time visitors to this beach resort. Guided by an illustrated pamphlet of its historical homes, you also can go on a tour to view the enchanting exteriors of cottages and bungalows built as artists' studios, summer places, and dream homes in the 1920s.

For other activity, head to South Laguna for fishing off the pier at Aliso Beach Park or nine holes of golf on the Aliso Creek course in a scenic canyon. Adjacent is a quiet spot to spend the weekend, Aliso Creek Inn. Have Sunday brunch on the patio of its Ben Brown's Restaurant.

For good food and nighttime action, the place is the White House, Laguna's landmark roadhouse, opened in 1918. Adorned with Tiffany-type lamps, green plants, and photographs of Laguna Beach in its early days, the retaurant is popular for breakfast, lunch, and dinner. After 9:30 P.M. it's party time in the pub, with dancing to some of Orange County's best musical groups.

With its reputation well established in Corona del Mar, Hemingway's has pleased local folks and visitors by opening a tavern-by-the-sea restaurant in Laguna Beach. Other delightful dining spots are the funky Dizz As Is, expanded Tortilla Flats, and cozy Partners Bistro. And for sunsets over the Pacific at cocktail time, the Hotel Laguna's Pier 9 terrace is a memorable treat.

During the summer art festival, be certain to make reservations for dinner as well as for weekend lodgings. And be advised that the Pageant of the Masters is so popular that all of its 2,622 seats are sold out for weeks in advance for every performance. However, there's always a chance for latecomers to see the show. Pageant tickets that have been returned are sold first come, first served on the day of performance, beginning at noon at the Festival of the Arts ticket office, 650 Laguna Canyon Road. When those are gone, a waiting list is made for tickets returned later that day and resold an hour before the nightly 8:30 P.M. show.

The world-renowned pageant is worth the trouble for tickets, because you never see anything like it anywhere else. In costumes and makeup, volunteer townsfolk hold their breaths and positions in larger-than-life art re-creations that are surrounded by a huge picture frame. Clever lighting gives a painted look to the images on the stage; viewers often bring binoculars to confirm that the people in the pictures are real. Orchestra music and descriptive narration about each artist and his or her work are part of this one-of-a-kind pageant, which already has celebrated its fiftieth season. The show always climaxes with a 13-man depiction of Leonardo da Vinci's *Last Supper*.

The pageant's showplace, the six-acre Irvine Bowl on Laguna Canyon Road, also is the site of the celebrated Festival of Arts. There you can view and buy all sorts of arts and crafts, including watercolors, hand-blown glass, photographs, jewelry, serigraphs, wood carvings, ceramics, and leathercraft.

Other artisans exhibit and even make some of their works on the spot at the Sawdust Festival, just down the canyon road from the main festival grounds. You can watch them fashioning jewelry, blowing glass, and shaping pottery. There's musical entertainment, too, amid the artists' fanciful booths, which are set in a grove of eucalyptus. Other artists and craftsmen show and sell their creations at a third festival site, the Art-A-Fair, also on Laguna Canyon Road.

As you'll quickly discover, parking is a problem in this favorite Southland beach resort, so take the Laguna Beach Transit trams to reach the pageant and art festival grounds in Laguna Canyon. Any time of the year, have plenty of coins for the city's ubiquitous parking meters, because meter maids patrol daily, including Sundays and holidays; the cost for an overtime parking ticket is a stiff $12 fine and an unpleasant weekend memory.

Return to Los Angeles the way you came or take Coast Highway north. Round trip is about 110 miles.

Laguna Beach Area Code: 714

SIGHTSEEING *Laguna Beach Museum of Art,* 307 Cliff Drive, Laguna Beach 92651, 494-6531. Open 11:30 A.M. to 4:30 P.M. Tuesday through Sunday. Free. ● *Hortense Miller Garden,* c/o Recreation Department, City Hall, 505 Forest Avenue, Laguna Beach, 92651, 497-3311, ext. 201. Call in advance to arrange date and time to meet a free guide for 2-hour garden tour. Open daily except Saturday afternoon, Sunday, and Monday. ● *Historical Homes Tour Brochure,* c/o Department of Community Development, City Hall, Laguna Beach, 92651, 497-3311, ext. 229. Contact weekdays for free pamphlet. ● *Aliso Beach Park,* South Coast Highway, South Laguna 92677. Hours: 6 A.M. to 12 P.M.; $1 per vehicle. Free fishing from pier; also swimming and picnicking. ● *Aliso Creek Golf Course,* 31106 South Coast Highway, South Laguna 92677, 499-1919. 9-hole, 32-par course; $6 weekends, $4 weekdays. Adjacent to Aliso Creek Inn and Ben Brown's Restaurant (see below).

EVENTS *Festival of Arts,* Irvine Bowl, 650 Laguna Canyon Road, Laguna Beach, 92651, 494-1145. Open-air show of works by 160 artists and craftsmen, usually mid-July through August. Grounds open 10 A.M. to 11:30 P.M. daily. Adult admission $1. Special feature is *Pageant of the Masters,* a remarkable presentation of "living" artwork at 8:30 P.M. nightly. Tickets $6 to $20; order forms from Festival of Arts, P.O. Box 37, Laguna Beach 92652, or call 494-1147. Box office hours 10 A.M. to 9 P.M. ● *Sawdust Festival,* 935 Laguna Canyon Road (or P.O. Box 1234), Laguna Beach 92651, 494-3030. Over 200 artisans exhibit their works from 10 A.M. to 11 P.M., concurrent with the Festival of Arts. Adult admission $1. ● *Art-A-Fair Festival,* 113 Canyon Acres Drive at Laguna Canyon Road, Laguna Beach 92651, 494-5973. Creations of 120 artists and craftsmen on display from 10 A.M. to 10 P.M. (to 11 P.M. Friday and Saturday), also concurrent with the Festival of Arts. Adult admission $1.

LODGING   *Surf & Sand Hotel,* 1555 South Coast Highway, Laguna Beach 92651, 497-4477; $105. 9-story luxury hotel on beach front; also two excellent restaurants (see below). ● *Hotel San Maarten,* 696 South Coast Highway, Laguna Beach, 92651, 494-9436; $60 (except $90 on Friday and Saturday nights), continental breakfast included. Heated swimming pool, saunas; also gourmet restaurant (see below). ● *Aliso Creek Inn,* 31106 South Coast Highway (at Country Club Road), South Laguna 92677, 499-2271; $75. Secluded canyon location adjacent to golf course; also popular restaurant (see below). ● *Eiler's Inn,* 741 South Coast Highway, Laguna Beach 92651, 494-3004; $85, continental breakfast included. ● *Carriage House,* 1322 Catalina Street, Laguna Beach 92651, 494-8945; $60, continental breakfast included. ● *Vacation Village,* 647 South Coast Highway, Laguna Beach 92651, 494-8566; $50. Family favorite on the beach; 3-day minimum stay July through Labor Day.

DINING   *The Towers,* atop Surf & Sand Hotel (see above), 497-4477. Continental cuisine with ocean view; jackets for men after 6 P.M. Breakfast, lunch, dinner, and Sunday brunch. ● *The Boardwalk,* adjacent to Surf & Sand Hotel (see above), 494-8588. Fresh seafood specialties for dinner; also Sunday brunch. Dine amid antiques and Laguna memorabilia. Pleasant lounge with fireplace and piano player. ● *Las Brisas,* 361 Cliff Drive, Laguna Beach, 497-5434. Mexican-style seafood for lunch and dinner; also Sunday brunch. Outdoor dining in summer. Bar and patio are Laguna's meeting place; delicious hors d'oeuvres at happy hour. ● *Ben Brown's,* at Aliso Creek Inn (see above), 499-2663. Breakfast, lunch, dinner, and Sunday brunch. Music and dancing Wednesday through Saturday nights. Patio overlooks picturesque golf course. ● *Gauguin's,* in Hotel San Maarten (see above), 494-0162. Continental fare for lunch and dinner daily; also champagne brunch on Saturday and Sunday. Jazz Wednesday through Sunday evenings. ● *The White House,* 340 South Coast Highway, Laguna Beach, 494-8088. Diverse menu for all three meals. Nightly music and dancing (cover charge) in adjoining pub.

FOR MORE INFORMATION   Contact the Laguna Beach Chamber of Commerce, 357 Glenneyre Street (or P.O. Box 396), Laguna Beach 92651, 494-1018.

Dana Point and San Juan Capistrano— for Boaters and History Buffs

When square-rigged ships plied the California coast, their sailors all knew Bahia Capistrano. It was the major port between San Diego and Santa Barbara—a quiet cove surrounded by steep cliffs where ships anchored to load cowhides from the nearby mission at San Juan Capistrano. Nowadays the harbor has a new name and is much busier than a century and a half ago.

In the past decade men and machines have shaped it into a $20-million marina complex that's home for nearly 2,500 pleasure boats. With sailing, fishing, swimming, and other recreational activities, as well as restaurants and shops, Dana Point Harbor draws boaters and other visitors year round. It's also a picturesque place to headquarter when you want to see a neighboring Orange County attraction, the historic mission at San Juan Capistrano. For weekend lodgings you have the choice of a waterfront motel in the marina, a bed-and-breakfast inn along the coast, or an ocean-view campground in a state beach park.

To reach Dana Point Harbor from Los Angeles, drive south on Interstate 5 to the Pacific Coast Highway/California 1 off ramp. Follow California 1 north to Dana Point, then go left at the second stoplight onto Del Obispo Street, which leads to the harbor and the Marina Inn motel, overlooking the boat basin. Or turn left earlier along Del Prado to enter Doheny State Beach and its popular campground. If you opt for bed-and-breakfast at the coastal 1930s Capistrano Country Bay Inn, exit from the freeway off ramp to Doheny Park Road, turn left to Coast Highway, and go a mile south along Capistrano Beach.

Have dinner at the Quiet Cannon or Chart House, two restaurants that offer a panorama of Dana Point Harbor from atop 400-foot cliffs. There you can imagine sailors of the past century hurling hides down to the beach so they could be loaded onto the square-riggers. Get to either dramatic dining spot by returning to Coast Highway and going up the hill through Dana Point to the Street of the Green Lantern, a block beyond the scenic-lookout sign.

From the cliff top you'll spot a replica of the *Pilgrim,* a two-masted brig that came to the harbor in 1835. One of its crewmen was Richard Henry Dana, who later wrote about his seagoing adventures in the now-classic *Two Years Before the Mast.* In his book Dana described the peaceful cove as the only romantic place along the Califonia coast. Eventually it was named Dana Point in honor of the sailor-turned-author. Also in tribute, a handsome statue of Dana was erected at the harbor.

In the morning, get another view of the *Pilgrim* by following Del Obispo Street to the harbor's west end, where there's a county park with a small beach, swimming area, and picnic tables. From a short pier you can fish with drop lines and bait (sold in the pier shop) or rent a pedal boat to cruise around in the harbor basin and get a close look at the old-time sailing ship. Also go into the adjacent Orange County Marine Institute to see a gray-whale skeleton and some other oceanographic exhibits. Beyond the road's end and breakwater is a marine preserve where you'll be able to observe sea life in protected tide pools when the tide is out.

To watch all the sailboats parade by in the harbor's main channel, go back on Del Obispo Street and turn right on Island Way to the parking and picnic areas on Dana Drive. Along this scenic road paralleling the breakwater you'll also find Dana's bronze statue and a favorite seafood restaurant, Delaney's.

When you recross the jam-packed boat harbor on Island Way, turn right on Del Obispo to browse in some of the two dozen gift shops or have a drink in another of the waterfront restaurants located at Mariner's Village and Dana Wharf. If you'd rather not be a landlubber, rent a sailing sloop or a skiff with an outboard at Embarcadero Marina or head out to sea on a ¾-day fishing excursion with Dana Wharf Sportfishing. That same company will take you on a whale-watching excursion in wintertime during the annual California gray-whale migration.

The following day, leave beautiful Dana Point Harbor and return to Interstate 5 going north toward Los Angeles. Exit at the second off ramp, Ortega Highway/California 74, and turn left over the freeway into Orange County's first settlement and home of the "Jewel of the Missions."

As everyone knows, a hit song in the 1940s about the annual return of swallows to San Juan Capistrano's old Spanish mission brought the small and sleepy town worldwide recognition and a steady stream of visitors. In recent years Capistrano has become one of the area's fastest-growing communities, and the fertile fields that used to serve a smorgasbord of insects to the swallows now host housing tracts and shopping centers. However, a few of the birds continue to build their mud nests in the archways of the old mission, which is just two blocks west of the freeway at the corner of the Ortega Highway and Camino Capistrano. Lucky visitors occasionally spot a swallow or two, but you'll find plenty of other feathered friends, especially the white pigeons that coo for food in the mission courtyard. Also look for doves, finches, hummingbirds, and warblers.

Of course, Mission San Juan Capistrano is much more than a bird sanctuary. It's one of the state's most important historical and archaeological treasures. The Spanish outpost that Father Junipero Serra began in

1776 eventually became a self-sufficient settlement for its resident priests, soldiers, and Indians. You'll see the padres' living quarters, soldiers' barracks, an iron smelter, tallow vats, kitchens, and even the punishment room for unruly Indians. Thanks to ongoing excavations and renovations at the impressive mission, visitors really get an idea of what life was like in early-day California.

A highlight is the narrow chapel, thought to be the oldest building in the state. Look for the original Indian decorations and religious relics that have been preserved since the eighteenth century. And don't miss the ruins of the Great Stone Church, a magnificent sandstone structure that was toppled by an earthquake in 1812. Recently a $5-million replica has been constructed to serve as a visitors center and museum, as well as a place of worship for the mission's growing number of parishioners, who attend Sunday services and send their children to the mission school.

You're welcome to visit Mission San Juan Capistrano any day of the week, and admission includes a self-guided-tour brochure with a map of the grounds. Extra drama is provided when you rent a tape cassette unit with a recorded tour that includes music and special sound effects to relate the mission's past and present.

On Sunday afternoon you can discover more about the intriguing town by joining a walking tour of its old adobes led by members of the San Juan Capistrano Historical Society. You'll hear folklore as well as facts, including stories of bandits, buried treasure, and even ghosts. Tours start from the courtyard of El Peon Plaza, a cluster of shops across from the mission. The historical society also offers a free map and leaflet for a self-guided tour of the adobes. Pick up a copy at El Peon Plaza or the society's headquarters nearby on Los Rios Street in the O'Neill Museum, a restored century-old home that displays local memorabilia.

Down that same street is the Rios Adobe, which takes you back another century. It was built by the local Juaneno Indians in 1794 for Feliciano Rios, a Spanish soldier stationed at the mission. His descendants still live in the house. Also along Los Rios Street are two other adobes constructed of mud and straw bricks soon after the mission was established.

Just across the train tracks, look for the 1894 Santa Fe Railway station, built of handmade bricks and decorated with a cupola and red tile roof. Its interior has been attractively remodeled in railroad motif for a popular restaurant called the Capistrano Depot. Amtrak's sleek trains stop here several times daily on the Los Angeles–San Diego run. A block away on the town's main street, Camino Capistrano, you'll find more early buildings, including one that served as a stagecoach stop, courtroom, and jail. Today it's part of a well-known Mexican restaurant, El Adobe, another excellent choice for a meal.

If you have time after sightseeing and dining, as well as shopping in Capistrano's gift stores and galleries, drive eastward along the historic Ortega Highway for a relaxing soak in thermal waters before heading back to Los Angeles. Following a two-centuries-old trail past wilderness areas that have changed little since the days of the Spanish explorers, the rural road takes you through San Juan Canyon to the San Juan Forest Station at the western boundary of Cleveland National Forest. Go left there at the sign to San Juan Capistrano Hot Springs. The side road leads to the parking area for a bathing spot first enjoyed by the Indians and then families from the Spanish land-grant ranchos. After being closed for several decades, the San Juan hot springs reopened in 1982, this time with a dozen redwood bathing tubs scattered among the trees in a shady glen. The hot tubs, which have individual temperature controls for the purified mineral water, will accommodate four bathers comfortably and six in a pinch. They're open round the clock, but by reservation only. Bring your own food and drink.

When you're refreshed and ready for the return trip to Los Angeles, retrace your route to Interstate 5 and head north.

Round trip is about 160 miles.

Dana Point/San Juan Capistrano Area Code: 714

SIGHTSEEING   *Orange County Marine Institute,* 35502 Del Obispo Street, Dana Point Harbor 92629, 496-2274 or 831-3850. Open daily except Sunday from 10 A.M. to 3:30 P.M., with aquariums, touch-tide pool, and other marine exhibits. Free. • *Dana Wharf Sportfishing,* 34675 Golden Lantern, Dana Point Harbor 92629, 496-5794 or 831-1850. Daily ¾-day and longer open-party fishing trips. Adults $20, children 12 years and under $15. Also whale-watch cruises in winter. • *Embarcadero Marina,* Embarcadero Place, Dana Point Harbor 92629, 496-6177. Open daily for powerboat and sailboat rentals and lessons. • *Mission San Juan Capistrano,* Ortega Highway at Camino Capistrano, San Juan Capistrano 92675, 493-1111 or 493-1424. Open daily from 7 A.M. to 5 P.M. Adults $1, children under 12 years 50 cents. 40-minute tape-tour rentals $1 for one person, $1.50 for two. • *O'Neill Museum,* 31831 Los Rios Street, San Juan Capistrano 92675, 493-8444. Open weekends noon to 3 P.M. Donation appreciated. Restored 1880s home with local history exibits. Headquarters of San Juan Historical Society. For society-led one-hour walking tours of town, meet Sunday at 1 P.M. at El Peon Plaza, 26832 Ortega Highway, across from the mission. Adults $1, children 50 cents. • *San Juan Capistrano Hot Springs,* 35501 Ortega Highway (or P.O Box 58), San Juan Capistrano 92693, 493-8827. 13 miles east of the Capistrano mission at Hot Springs Canyon Road. Open 24 hours daily; call for a reservation. $6 per person, children under 12 years free.

EVENTS   *Festival of the Whales,* at Dana Point Harbor, 661-5177. Annual 3-weekend fest in February celebrating the California gray whale with talks, movies, and exhibits on marine wildlife and ocean lore. Whale-watch cruises depart every hour (see page 133). Also, a parade, military-ship visits, tide-pool tours, and entertainment. ● *Fiesta de las Golondrinas,* annual Swallows Day celebration in San Juan Capistrano. Week-long festival centering around March 19, traditionally the day when the swallows return from South America to the mission. Outstanding equestrian parade with bands and floats, pancake breakfast, barbecue, and contests.

LODGING *Marina Inn,* 34902 Del Obispo Street, Dana Point 92629, 496-1203; $54 summer, $49 winter. Only accommodations within Dana Point Harbor. Heated pool and redwood sauna. Walk to restaurants, shops, and boat docks for sportfishing and whale watching. ● *Capistrano Country Bay Inn,* 34862 Pacific Coast Highway, Capistrano Beach 92624, 496-6656 or California toll-free (800) 422-4404. $75 upstairs, $65 downstairs in summer ($5 less on weekdays), $65 and $55 in winter, including continental breakfast. 28-room bed-and-breakfast. Attractively renovated 1930s inn across from Hole-in-the-Fence beach on the coastal highway. Second-story rooms have ocean view. Intimate dinner house adjacent. ● Other lodgings in San Juan Capistrano are the *Mission Inn,* 493-1151, and *Capistrano Inn,* 493-5661.

CAMPING *Doheny State Beach,* 34320 Del Obispo Street, Dana Point 92629, 496-6171. 118 ocean-front sites, $6 per night; no hookups. Reserve through Ticketron well in advance. The park is very popular for swimming, fishing, surfing, and picnicking. Open for day use 6 A.M. to 10 P.M., $3 per vehicle.

DINING *Quiet Cannon,* 34334 Street of the Green Lantern, Dana Point, 496-9046. Open daily for lunch, dinner, and cocktails with spectacular harbor view. Seafood specialties. Also Sunday champagne brunch. ● *Chart House,* 34442 Street of the Green Lantern, Dana Point, 493-1183. Open daily from late afternoon for dinner only. Salad bar, seafood, and unbeatable harbor view. ● *Delaney's,* 25001 Dana Drive, Dana Point, 496-6195. Open daily for lunch and dinner at the harbor. Seafood and oyster bar. Also very popular for Sunday brunch. ● Other major restaurants in Dana Point Harbor are the *Jolly Roger,* with family fare for breakfast, lunch, and dinner; *Casa Maria,* with Mexican food for lunch and dinner; *Harpoon Henry's,* with prime ribs, seafood, and oyster bar for lunch and dinner; and *The Wind & Sea,* with steak and seafood, for dinner only. ● *Capistrano Depot,* 27601 Verdugo Street, San Juan Capistrano, 496-8181. Open daily for lunch and dinner. Pleasant dining in a renovated railroad depot that's now an Amtrak station. Varied meat and seafood menu. Cocktails served in vintage train cars. Entertainment evenings and Sunday afternoon. Reservations advised. ● *El Adobe,*

31891 Camino Capistrano, San Juan Capistrano, 493-1163. Open Monday through Saturday for lunch and dinner, Sunday for brunch. Mexican and continental fare with mariachi music in historic surroundings. • *L'Hirondelle,* 31631 Camino Capistrano, San Juan Capistrano, 661-0425. Dinner only Wednesday through Sunday. Excellent French cuisine in an intimate restaurant across from the mission.

FOR MORE INFORMATION   Contact the Dana Point Harbor Chamber of Commerce, 33621 Del Obispo Street, Dana Point 92629, 496-1555. Also, the San Juan Capistrano Chamber of Commerce, 31882 Camino Capistrano, San Juan Capistrano 92675, 493-4700.

Mickey Mouse and Many More Amusements in Anaheim and Buena Park

There's no debate that Orange County is a magnet for vacationers in Southern California, and most folks are drawn to a pair of neighboring cities that are host to a wonderful assortment of family amusements. Buena Park is home of the granddaddy of Southland theme parks, Knott's Berry Farm, already well known for its ghost town and family-style chicken dinners in the 1940s, a decade before Disneyland opened its gates six miles down the road in Anaheim.

Another old-time attraction is just across the street from Knott's, the California Alligator Farm, the state's first zoological attraction. Opening in Los Angeles to a fascinated public in 1907, what became one of the world's largest reptile collections was moved to Buena Park over three decades ago. Also from the animal world comes the latest enticement for visitors, handsome white Andalusian horses performing twice daily in spectacular shows at the Kingdom of the Dancing Stallions. That elegant indoor equine arena is opposite an ongoing favorite of Buena Park visitors, Movieland, a wax museum that brings 200 movie and TV stars almost to life in re-created Hollywood sets.

And that's not all you'll find in the shadow of the great Knott's Berry Farm and Disneyland amusement centers. Much less known but very enjoyable if you're nostalgic for earlier times and events are two privately run museums. Among a fascinating group of craft and collector shops known as Hobby City, you'll see a half-scale replica of the White House that houses the extraordinary Doll and Toy Museum. Inside you can spend hours admiring more than 2,000 rare and antique dolls and toys gathered from all over the globe. And not far away military buffs can relive the past by viewing memorabilia that ranges from uniforms to tanks in the Museum of World Wars, the largest privately owned military museum in the nation.

Before totaling up the abundance of attractions in Anaheim and Buena Park, add two more. Baseball and football fans flock to Anaheim Stadium, the 70,000-seat arena for home games of the California Angels and Los Angeles Rams. Also, the immense Anaheim Convention Center is host to all sorts of special events, from pop concerts to ice skating shows and the Ringling Brothers, Barnum and Bailey Circus.

With such an extensive menu of amusements, how do you see everything in a weekend? Obviously you can't, but some thoughtful planning will make the time you spend an enjoyable outing instead of an exhausting ordeal. Disneyland and Knott's Berry Farm *each* take a full day, perhaps even two, depending on the crowds, the weather, and how many are in your family group. Trying to tour both of these famed amusement parks in one weekend will tire your feet and exhaust your patience. For peace of mind, don't promise the kids Disneyland and Knott's on the same trip unless it's a three-day weekend or you're on a week's vacation. One good reason is that the berry farm alone offers 165 rides and other entertainment features. For another, on a holiday weekend or midsummer day, tens of thousands of visitors flock to Disneyland—and that means long waits in long lines.

Getting to Buena Park or Anaheim from Los Angeles is easy. Just drive south on Interstate 5, then take the Artesia Boulevard/Beach Boulevard (California 39) exit and follow the signs to Knott's Berry Farm or continue on Interstate 5 a few more miles to the Harbor Boulevard exit and follow the signs to Disneyland.

Although most auxiliary attractions are clustered around Knott's Berry Farm in Buena Park, Anaheim's Disneyland is the most popular destination, and that's where you'll find the majority of lodgings. More than 100 hotels encircle the Magic Kingdom, and their rates are competitive. Although more expensive than the mom-and-pop motels lining the access streets to Disneyland, the larger high-rise hotels offer greater comfort and amenities for a relaxing getaway. One advantage is that they have a choice of restaurants on the premises, so you don't have to go out to find a place to eat before or after your visit to the parks. In fact, the Disneyland Hotel offers eight dining spots, and so many delightful diversions that it could be a weekend destination in itself. This full-fledged resort even has a man-made marina with pedal boats and a white sand beach, not to mention three swimming pools scattered around its lush 60-acre grounds. It opened when Disneyland did in 1955 and has grown to a trio of towers with 1,120 rooms and suites. An international shopping bazaar called Seaports of the Pacific borders the marina, and twice nightly a dazzling show of dancing waters, colored lights, and music also entertains hotel guests. The kids get involved navigating remote-controlled miniature boats in the marina and small cars around an off-road raceway, plus testing their electronic-game skills in the hotel's fancy video game room.

While the Disneyland Hotel is considered "the official hotel of Disneyland" and is the only one connected directly to the Magic Kingdom by the park's monorail, several other major hotels are on Disneyland's perimeter and offer free shuttle service. These include the Grand Hotel, Hilton at the Park, Anaheim Marriott, and Sheraton-Anaheim. There also is shuttle transportation aboard the Fun Bus between the Disneyland Hotel and Knott's Berry Farm. If you make your headquarters in Buena Park to be closer to Knott's Berry Farm and its surrounding attractions, try the Buena Park Hotel or roomy Granada Royale Hometel, and use the Fun Bus shuttle if you also plan to visit Disneyland.

True to Walt Disney's desire, Disneyland is one of the happiest places on earth, and one visit is never enough. Many Southland residents return year after year to fall happily under the spell of the Magic Kingdom. Mickey Mouse and all the other familiar Disney characters are on hand to extend a happy welcome to visitors of every age, and there always are new attractions to draw families back to the beautiful 76-acre park. In 1983, for example, an all-New Fantasyland was unveiled. It's one of seven theme areas that transport you to another place and time with rides and automated attractions created with incomparable Disney cleverness and care.

Although Disneyland offers guided 2½-hour group tours to help you become acquainted with the park, it's not difficult to discover all the attractions on your own. Get a guide map at the entry gate, and agree with family members on a rendezvous spot in advance in case you get separated. Lost persons can be contacted at City Hall near the main entrance; lost children are cared for at the First Aid Center.

Entering Disneyland at the main ticket booths, a good idea for first-time visitors is to hop on the steam-powered train at the Town Square for a circle orientation tour of the park. Then disembark where you boarded and immerse yourself in the Magic Kingdom by strolling down Main Street, U.S.A., with its Penny Arcade and other delights of turn-of-the-century America. Not to be missed in the Opera House is the first of Disney's remarkable audio-animatronic displays, "Great Moments with Mr. Lincoln." At the park's hub, Central Plaza, the kids are drawn to Disneyland's enchanting symbol, Sleeping Beauty's Castle. Beyond its drawbridge their imaginations wander on Pinocchio's Daring Journey, Snow White's Scary Adventures, Peter Pan's Flight, and Mr. Toad's Wild Ride. And even adults enjoy a trip on Dumbo's Flying Elephants. Or board a bobsled for a white-knuckle ride in and around another Disney landmark, the snowcapped Matterhorn.

In Tomorrowland, where some of the "future" technology has become reality since the park opened in 1955, Space Mountain offers other thrills on an interplanetary rocket ride. Also spellbinding is the circle-vision cinema tour of America the Beautiful. Down-to-earth travel is on the opposite side of the park in Adventureland, where lifelike animals are seen on the exotic Jungle Cruise and birds serenade you with song in the Enchanted Tiki Room. Only a few steps away in Frontierland the perils of life in the Wild West come true on a runaway mine train at Big Thunder Mountain, and so do the old-time pleasures when you watch cancan dancing in Golden Horseshoe saloon.

Nearby is lively New Orleans Square, added after the park opened, when land was so limited that this theme area's most popular pair of attractions is mostly underground. You'll disappear into the Haunted Mansion and also cruise in a darkened grotto with the Pirates of the Caribbean. Then head to the adjacent woods, Bear Country, to join the jamboree of the mechanical bruins in a musical revue. Intermingled in all the theme areas are an assortment of shops with Mickey Mouse ears and other souvenirs and better-than-average gifts. And throughout the park you'll find two dozen restaurants and refreshment centers ready to provide nourishment and nonalcoholic drinks.

Adding to your enjoyment are the costumed Disney characters that cavort all over the Magic Kingdom, happily posing for pictures with young and old visitors alike. Musicians roam the grounds, band concerts and stage shows are featured daily, and there's always a colorful parade; summer evenings end with a grand fireworks display.

Disneyland also offers a variety of special services to keep guests happy. Lockers are available so you don't have to tote around sweaters or other clothes for the cooler evening hours or the souvenirs you're bound to purchase in the park. A baby-care center offers privacy for feeding and changing infants, while a kennel near the main gate provides day care for pets.

Best of all, Disneyland has done away with its books of coupons that were valid for specific attractions, and now the price of admission is an unlimited-use ticket to all activities (except the shooting galleries). If you decide to leave the park and want to return the same day, be certain to have your hand stamped at the exit gate or Disneyland Hotel monorail station.

For the most enjoyment on holiday weekends or in the summer months, begin your visit as soon as the park opens, because there are fewer people and waiting lines for the favorite attractions are shorter. Then return to your hotel for a leisurely lunch and an afternoon nap, and go back to Disneyland later in the afternoon, when it's cooler, and stay for the special evening shows, Flights of Fantasy parade and fireworks.

The same advice holds true for a visit to Knott's Berry Farm in Buena Park: arrive when the gates open, take a break from the crowd for a restful lunch (perhaps in the adjoining Buena Park Hotel), and return later in the afternoon. Covering 150 acres, the park is twice the size of Disneyland and also well known for its fun-filled attractions, thrill rides, entertaining shows, and gift shops.

Knott's Berry Farm may seem like a funny name for the Southland's second most popular amusement park, but that's how it began. Cordelia and Walter Knott had a roadside berry stand in rural Buena Park in the 1920s, and later they began serving fried chicken dinners in the family living room to passersby. Word of their delicious home-style meals spread, and so did the line of hungry customers. To keep the guests occupied during a three- to four-hour wait for Cordelia's chicken, Walter began to re-create an Old West ghost town. Today it's one of the four theme areas in the expanded complex, which includes Fiesta Village, the Roaring '20s Airfield, and Camp Snoopy.

The Ghost Town's steam train and stagecoach rides still delight children, but you're likely to find most of the kids lined up for a breathtaking trip on the Corkscrew double-loop roller coaster, 20-story-high Parachute Sky Jump, or other daring rides like Montezooma's Revenge. Also big draws are the musical variety shows staged around the park and the top-name entertainers who appear in Knott's 2,100-seat Good Time Theatre. Happily, all attractions at Knott's Berry Farm are included in the admission price. Of course, you'll have to pay extra for the old-fashioned chicken dinners that are still being served—and you'll still have to wait in line.

Unless you have time for an extended stay to enjoy the many other amusements listed in the "Sightseeing" section below, plan to come back for another weekend in Anaheim and Buena Park. Meanwhile, return to Los Angeles by joining Interstate 5 north.

Round trip is about 50 miles.

Anaheim/Buena Park Area Code: 714

SIGHTSEEING *Disneyland,* 1313 Harbor Boulevard, Anaheim 92803, 999-4565 or (213) 626-8605. Open daily from mid-June to mid-September from 9 A.M. to midnight, to 1 A.M. on Saturday. Rest of the year open weekends from 9 A.M. to 7 P.M., Wednesday through Friday from 10 A.M. to 6 P.M.; closed Monday and Tuesday except during Christmas and Easter vacations and on major holidays. Unlimited-use Passport ticket adults $12, children 12 through 17 years $10.50, 3 through 11 years $9. Parking $1. ● *Knott's Berry Farm,* 8039 Beach Boulevard, Buena Park 90620, 827-1776. Open daily from Memorial Day weekend through Labor Day from 9 A.M. to midnight, to 1 A.M. on Friday and Saturday. Rest of the year open from 10 A.M. to 6 P.M. Monday, Tuesday, and Friday, to 10 P.M. Saturday, to 9 A.M. Sunday; closed Wednesday and Thursday. Unlimited-use ticket adults $9.95, children 4 through 11 years $8.95, senior citizens $7. Free parking. • *Fun Bus,* 635-1390. Shuttle service between the Disneyland Hotel in Anaheim and Knott's Berry Farm in Buena Park departs from their entrances in summer every half hour from 8 A.M. to 12:30 A.M., in winter every hour from 9 A.M. to 10 P.M. Adults $1.75 each way, children $1. • *Movieland,* 7711 Beach Boulevard, Buena Park 90620, 522-1154 or (213) 583-8025. Open daily from June through Labor Day from 9 A.M. to 9 P.M., to 10 P.M. Friday and Saturday. Rest of the year open daily from 10 A.M. to 8 P.M., to 10 P.M. Friday and Saturday. Adults $7.50, children 4 through 11 years $4.50. • *Kingdom of the Dancing Stallions,* 7662 Beach Boulevard, Buena Park 92620, 546-4366 or (213) 546-4366. 45-minute musically choreographed performances daily at 2 and 8 P.M., Sunday at 2 and 5 P.M.; closed Monday September through March. Adults $6, senior citizens and children 3 through 12 years $4. • *California Alligator Farm,* 7671 La Palma Avenue, Buena Park 92620, 522-2615. Open daily from 10:30 A.M. to 5 P.M., to 8 P.M. in July and August. Alligator and snake shows alternate on the hour from 11 A.M. through 5 P.M. Adults $4.95, children 5 through 14 years $2.95. • *Hobby City Doll and Toy Museum,* 1238 South Beach Boulevard, Anaheim 90803, 527-2323. Open daily 10 A.M. to 5:30 P.M. Adults $1, children under 12 years 50 cents. • *Museum of World Wars,* 8700 Stanton Avenue, Buena Park 90620, 952-1776. Open daily except Monday from 10 A.M. to 7 P.M., Sunday from 12 noon. Adults $3, senior citizens and military $2, children 6 through 12 years $1. • *Anaheim Convention Center,* 800 West Katella Avenue, Anaheim 92803, 999-8950. Concerts, circus, and more; call for current events. • *Anaheim Stadium,* 2000 South State College Boulevard, Anaheim 92803. Arena for California Angels home baseball games mid-April through September; call 634-2000 for schedule and ticket info. Also home stadium for Los Angeles Rams football games from August through December; call 937-6767 for schedule and ticket info.

LODGING *Disneyland Hotel,* 1150 West Cerritos Avenue, Anaheim 92802, 778-6600 or toll-free (800) 323-1776; $86. 60-acre resort with 1,120 rooms in three tower buildings surrounding a man-made marina and mini-beach. Monorail transportation direct to the Magic Kingdom. Supervised youth program in summer. Also several restaurants (see below). • *Grand Hotel,* No. 1 Hotel Way, Anaheim 92802, 772-7777; $69 in summer, lower the rest of the year. 240 rooms adjacent to Disneyland with free shuttle to the Magic Kingdom. Also pleasant restaurant (see below) and dinner theater. • *Hilton at the Park,* 1855 South Harbor Boulevard, Anaheim 92802, 750-1811; $65. Towering 500-room hotel near Anaheim Convention Center; free two-block shuttle to Disneyland. Also novel family restaurant (see below). • *Anaheim Marriott Hotel,* 700 West Convention Way, Anaheim 92802, 750-8000; $84. Luxurious 750-room hotel near Anaheim Convention Center; free trolley to Disneyland. Indoor/outdoor swimming pool. Also elegant dining room (see below). • *Sheraton-Anaheim Hotel,* 1015 West Ball Road, Anaheim 92802, 778-1700; $70. English Tudor-style motel with 500 rooms close by Disneyland, with free shuttle to the Magic Kingdom. • *Granada Royale Hometel,* 7762 Beach Boulevard, Buena Park 90620, 739-5600; $75, with complimentary full breakfast and happy hour. Over 200 two-room suites with kitchen and bar opposite Knott's Berry Farm. Also, Le Bistro restaurant open for lunch and dinner. • *Buena Park Hotel,* 7675 Crescent Avenue, Buena Park, 90620, 995-1111 or California toll-free (800) 422-4444; $56. 10-story hotel with 320 rooms adjoining Knott's Berry Farm. Also, panoramic dining in penthouse restaurant.

DINING   *Shipyard Inn* in the Disneyland Hotel (see above). Tasty seafood for dinner nightly and lunch weekdays, overlooking the hotel's marina. Try the *Oak Room* for steaks and veal and *El Vaquero* for Mexican fare. • *JW's* in the Anaheim Marriott Hotel (see above). Acclaimed and expensive gourmet dining room featuring French cuisine, candlelight, and harp music. Dinner nightly except Sunday; make reservations and dress up. • *Crawdaddy* in the Grand Hotel (see above). French-Creole cooking for lunch and dinner daily amid New Orleans decor. Oyster bar, pecan pie, Dixieland jazz, and Sunday brunch too. • *Acapulco Mexican Restaurant,* 1410 South Harbor Boulevard, Anaheim, 956-7380. Mexican food and drink daily for breakfast, lunch, and dinner; also Sunday champagne brunch. • *Anthony's Pier 2,* 1640 South Harbor Boulevard, Anaheim, 774-0322. Seafood galore and bountiful salad bar for dinner daily. • *Overland Stage and Territorial Saloon,* in Hilton in the Park (see above), 750-3888. Lunch and dinner daily, including roast buffalo if you dare, in Old West surroundings. • *Hansa House Smorgasbord,* 1840 South Harbor Boulevard, Anaheim, 750-2411. Hearty Scandinavian fare offered buffet style daily for lunch and dinner at fixed price; also breakfast in summer. • *Knott's Berry Farm Chicken Dinner Restaurant* at Knott's Berry Farm (see above). The place for home-style fried chicken dinners and the boysenberry pie that began the Knott family fame. Open daily for breakfast, lunch, and dinner. Also *Knott's Berry Farm Steak House,* serving non–chicken lovers prime beef and seafood for lunch and dinner every day. • *Arnold's Farm House Restaurant,* 6601 Manchester Avenue, Buena Park, 521-9450. Family choice for cafeteria-style meals. Open daily except Monday for lunch and dinner.

FOR MORE INFORMATION   Contact the Anaheim Area Visitor and Convention Bureau, 800 West Katella Avenue (or P.O. Box 4270), Anaheim 92803, 999-8999. Also the Buena Park Visitor and Convention Bureau, 6696 Beach Boulevard (or P.O. Box 5308), Buena Park 90620, 994-1511.

Marina, Mission, and Marines at Oceanside

Oceanside is no secret to pleasure boaters. Midway between the marinas at Dana Point and San Diego, its attractive small craft harbor is a popular refreshment stop for weekend sailors playing along the coast in their sleek motor yachts or sailboats. Other travelers tend to pass by Oceanside, racing through town on Interstate 5 or aboard Amtrak's San Diegan trains, and that's a mistake. Spend a couple of days at this unheralded beach town and you'll be pleased by its unhurried pace, value-priced accommodations, and wonderful variety of attractions. Not to be missed is a visit to the "King of the Missions," San Luis Rey, and history as well as military buffs will be intrigued by a tour of Camp Pendleton, the nation's largest marine base.

To reach Oceanside and its harbor from Los Angeles, drive south on Interstate 5 and take the Oceanside Harbor Drive exit west toward the ocean. Settle in marina-view lodgings at Oceanside's harbor, where the scene is more reminiscent of Cape Cod than Southern California. Especially recommended is the Villa Marina Apartment-Motel, overlooking the ocean channel entrance.

The next day explore the peaceful harbor, where a lighthouse, sea gulls, attractive landscaping, and dock slips with nearly 800 boats give it the charm of a small port in New England. At quayside you can browse in gift shops and snack on fish and chips or other seafood in one of the nautically decorated restaurants. Climb to the lighthouse lookout for a good view of the harbor. A small beach along the breakwater jetty also has thatched-roof ramadas where you can picnic in the shade and watch all the boat and bird activity.

Besides being a haven for sailboaters and yachtsmen, Oceanside harbor is home for commercial craft that will take you into the ocean for a half day of sportfishing. If you're an avid fisherman or just an amateur angler hoping to hook a deep-sea specimen, board one of the Helgren's Sportfishing vessels for some fishing fun in the Pacific. Feeding in kelp beds not far from the harbor entrance, rock cod, mackerel, bonito, and barracuda are waiting for your bait. Rental rods and the required state fishing license are available when you check in at Helgren's departure dock.

South of the harbor, across the San Luis Rey River, you can join the surf fishermen, swimmers, surfers, and suntanners who enjoy life along Oceanside's three-mile-long city beach. Families also flock to the picnic tables, barbecue grills, and playground equipment scattered across the sand. A waterfront landmark is the public pier, once the longest on the Pacific coast. Storms have trimmed its 1,900-foot length almost by half, and the fate of the old wooden pier is uncertain. Walk barefoot along the shore to view this vintage beach structure, or stroll on the paved Strand bordering the sand. Facing the ocean is a long row of tourist cabins, simple lodgings from an earlier era, which you are advised to avoid in favor of Oceanside's newer motels. Inland are the Royal Scot and Marty's Valley Inn, also pleasant lodgings for the weekend.

After enjoying a lazy day at the marina and beach, plan to have dinner at Oceanside's top dining spot, Cafe Europa. This cozy chef-owned restaurant is known throughout northern San Diego County for its continental cuisine, including specialties like filet of beef Kempinski, duck with Cumberland sauce, rack of lamb, and Basque chicken. At the harbor, good meal choices are the Chart House for dinner and the Jolly Roger for Sunday brunch or tasty dishes and drinks anytime during the day or evening.

Unless you opt for another leisurely day at the ocean's edge, make Sunday the time to tour the nearby mission and adjacent marine base. Oceanside was incorporated in 1888, but the area was settled 90 years earlier with the founding of Mission San Luis Rey de Francia. Named for Louis IX, king of France in the thirteenth century, it later earned another regal title, "King of the Missions," by becoming the largest of all the missions in California. Get there from town by heading inland about four miles on Mission Avenue (California 76) and turning left at the entrance signs.

At one time Mission San Luis Rey's buildings covered six acres and served as home for as many as 3,000 Indians. Besides cultivating the countryside to grow grapes, olives, and oranges, the mission's Indians raised 27,000 head of cattle and almost an equal number of sheep. San Luis Rey was the eighteenth mission to be built, but geographically it is second in the famed California mission chain. It was founded in 1798 to fill the gap between the missions that were established earlier at San Diego and San Juan Capistrano. Some of the mission complex has been completely restored, and today it serves as a parish church and religious-retreat center.

Start your self-guided tour in the mission museum, which features artifacts used by the early Franciscan fathers, including an impressive collection of old Spanish vestments. Visit the padres' restored bedroom and library, where there's a gray robe that's typical of the type worn by these missionaries until the past century. In the sewing and tallow rooms you'll see how the Indians wove cloth from wool, cotton, and flax and boiled animal fat to make candles and soap. The adjoining kitchen rooms have utensils like those used in the mission period. A highlight is the mission church, which is still the site for religious services on Sunday. Its original adobe walls are six feet thick, and the interior has lofty beamed ceilings with decorations done by the Indians.

You exit through the cemetery, where hundreds of Indians are buried, and then the tour continues outside the mission walls. Look past a gate into the monastery garden to see the state's oldest pepper tree, brought from Peru in 1830. Across the driveway are the ruins of barracks of Spanish soldiers who were stationed at the mission. Beyond, through an ornate arch and down a tiled stairway, is the partially excavated outdoor *lavanderia,* where the Indian women washed clothes. Archaeological work continues to uncover more of the mission's past. A picnic area in front of San Luis Rey Mission is a pleasant spot to relax before continuing to neighboring Camp Pendleton.

If you really want to imagine what Southern California was like in the days of the Spanish missionaries, drive around Camp Joseph H. Pendleton to view the rugged coastal terrain, which has changed very little during the past two centuries. Most travelers speeding along the Interstate 5 freeway, which cuts through the base, catch only glimpses of the historic chaparral-covered land spreading from the ocean to the Santa Margarita Mountains. However, you're welcome to explore the 125,000-acre U.S. Marine training camp anytime during daylight hours. Despite modern facilities for a population of 45,000 marines and their families, much of the land appears as pristine as when Gaspar de Portola and his Spanish expedition camped there in 1796. You'll even see adobe structures built in the 1800s. Until the federal government bought the land for $4.25 million in 1942, it was the Rancho Santa Margarita, originally a huge Spanish land grant under custody of the Mission San Luis Rey padres. At one time the ranch was owned by Pio Pico, the last Mexican governor of California.

To reach Camp Pendleton from the mission, head back to town on Mission Avenue (California 76) and join Interstate 5 going north. Take the second exit, Harbor Drive/Camp Pendleton, to the Main Gate guard station. To enter as a visitor you need to show your driver's license and vehicle registration and sign in. An auto tour is outlined in a free guide, ''Land of Many Uses,'' that describes past and present uses of the sprawling base, including its vital role as an ecological preserve. Get a copy at the Main Gate entrance, and look for directional tour markers posted alongside the roads. These signs have an *O* and a *T* on top, representing the branding iron of Rancho Santa Margarita.

One points to the original adobe ranch house, now restored, that is the handsome private residence of the base commanding general. You'll also get exterior views of two adjacent historic structures. In 1810 mission Indians built a winery that later became the ranch house chapel, and the 1835 bunkhouse is now a museum where ranch artifacts and photos are kept. The chapel and the bunkhouse often are open to the public the last Sunday afternoon of every month; ask when you enter at the Main Gate. Another stop to make is at the outdoor LVT (Landing Vehicle Track) Museum, where every type of amphibious vehicle used by the marines since World War II is on display.

You'll see considerable military activity as you drive through the vast training center, but also keep your eyes open for wildlife. Most likely you'll spot soaring hawks and, with luck, a golden eagle or white-tailed kite, both endangered species. In winter Canadian geese stop here to feed. Coyotes, bobcats, and mule deer are other inhabitants, and beavers have been spotted building dams in Las Pulgas Creek. Even a small herd of buffalo roams in the foothills. Near the tour's end, look for a windmill and barn that are part of a Boy Scout camp surrounding a historical landmark, the vine-covered Las Flores Adobe. It was built in 1867 from the ruins of Asistencia de San Pedro, a way station along El Camino Real, the old Spanish road that connected the missions up and down the California coast.

Leave Camp Pendleton by exiting at Las Flores Gate and rejoining Interstate 5 north to Los Angeles. There are no food facilities on the base for visitors, so if you get hungry on the way home, exit inland on El Camino Real in San Clemente for outstanding Italian fare at Andreino's.

Round trip is about 183 miles.

Oceanside Area Code: 619

SIGHTSEEING   *Helgren's Sportfishing,* 315 Harbor Drive, Oceanside 92054, 722-2133. Daily outings on well-equipped boats with helpful mates and full galley. Adults $14. ● *Mission San Luis Rey,* 4050 Mission Avenue, San Luis Rey 92068, 757-3651. Open daily from 10 A.M. to 4 P.M., except Sundays from 12 noon. Adults $1, children 12 to 18 years 50 cents, 6 to 11 years 25 cents. ● *Camp Joseph H. Pendleton,* Joint Public Affairs Office, Marine Corps Base, Camp Pendleton 92055, 725-5566. Open daily during daylight hours for self-guided auto tours; get brochure with map at Main Gate. Free.

LODGING   *Villa Marina Apartment-Motel,* 2008 Harbor Drive North, Oceanside 92054, 722-1561 or toll-free (800) 422-4404; $50. One- and two-bedroom suites with full kitchens, separate living rooms with fireplaces, and patios with harbor or ocean views. Also Jacuzzi and saunas. Guest boat slips by reservation. ● *Royal Scott Motor Hotel,* 1680 Oceanside Boulevard, Oceanside 92054, 722-1821; $46. Also restaurant (see below). ● *Marty's Valley Inn,* 3240 East Mission Avenue, Oceanside 92054, 757-7700; $46. On highway to Mission San Luis Rey.

DINING   *Cafe Europa,* 1733 Hill Street, Oceanside, 433-5811. Lunch and dinner daily except Monday; no lunch on weekends. Closed Sundays in winter. Reservations suggested. ● *Chart House,* 314 Harbor Drive South, Oceanside, 722-1345. Dinner only, featuring steaks, seafood, and salad bar, overlooking Oceanside Harbor. ● *Jolly Roger,* 1900 Harbor

Drive North, Oceanside, 722-1831. Harbor-view dining daily from 7 A.M. Also entertainment nightly in summer. Fresh fish specialties. • *Christopher's,* in the Royal Scott Motor Hotel (see above), 722-8251. Breakfast, lunch, dinner, and Sunday brunch. Prime ribs, seafood, and salad bar. Call for reservations. • *Hungry Hunter,* 1221 Vista Way, Oceanside, 433-2633. Lunch and dinner daily; no lunch on weekends. Also entertainment. • *Andreino's,* 1925 South El Camino Real, San Clemente, (714) 492-9955. Attractive and popular family-run restaurant with pasta, veal, chicken, and seafood specialties. Open nightly for dinner; reservations advised.

FOR MORE INFORMATION   Contact the Oceanside Chamber of Commerce, 510 4th Street (or P.O. Box 1578), Oceanside 92054, 722-1534.

Seaside Frolics and Flowers in Carlsbad and Environs

Three neighboring coastal communities were rest stops for Los Angeles– San Diego drivers in prefreeway days, but now the traffic rushes past Carlsbad, Leucadia, and Encinitas on Interstate 5. However, by exploring along the old 101 coastal highway, you'll enjoy a relaxing weekend in this trio of beach towns. Although beginning to grow as fast as the rest of Southern California, they still retain the flavor and fun of earlier times. You'll also be treated to some of the most spectacular flower displays anywhere in the Southland.

As oceanfront cities go, Carlsbad is a sleeper. Called Agua Hedionda (Stinking Water) by early mission soldiers because of a foul-smelling lagoon, the site once was a Spanish rancho. Settlers arrived in 1881, when the railroad did. One was John Frazier, who dug a well and discovered its waters had properties similar to the mineral water in the famed Karlsbad health spa in Bohemia (now Czechoslovakia). A resort hotel was built, and health seekers came by train to take the waters and relax at the ocean's edge. Land development followed, and the new town was named Carlsbad. Mineral water no longer flows from Frazier's well, but vacationers keep coming because it's a wonderful place for sunbathing, swimming, surfing, and fishing. The beach is still a major Carlsbad attraction and now hosts two state parks. You'll find fire rings for oceanview barbecues and more than 200 sites for overnight camping.

Since its incorporation in 1954, Carlsbad's original 7½-square-mile size and 7,000 population both have quadrupled. From its original coastal site, the city has annexed land east of the freeway and now includes the well-known La Costa resort, featuring a health spa, golf courses totaling 27 holes, and two dozen tennis courts. The town also boasts Victorian homes, a wide range of antique shops, some excellent restaurants, and in the springtime lots of events for visitors. In early May, during Carlsbad's annual Spring Fair, eight blocks of the downtown area become an arts-and-crafts show and flea market with food booths, street entertainment, and lots of fun. Carlsbad's pride and joy is its public library, and in mid-May the Friends of Carlsbad Library hold a big book fair and party in Holiday Park. The same month there's an air show on the outskirts of town at McClellan-Palomar Airport. And look for a multicolored blanket of ranunculus flowers blooming in full force during May and June on the flower farms that flank old highway 101, now officially renamed San Diego County S21.

To reach Carlsbad from Los Angeles, drive south on Interstate 5. The Elm Avenue exit just beyond Oceanside takes you to downtown Carlsbad and lodgings overlooking the ocean, the Beach View Lodge or Beach Terrace Inn. If you feel like splurging and staying at La Costa Hotel and Spa, continue south on the freeway almost six miles more to the La Costa Avenue exit and head inland to El Camino Real and the entrance to that plush resort. There you have a grand choice of accommodations, with prices to match: hotel rooms, cottages, two- and three-bedroom villas, and even houses. Some guests come for the full-fledged spa program and never leave the resort. They're pampered with massages, herbal wraps, facials, manicures, body-toning exercises, whirlpools, saunas, and low-calorie gourmet meals. Even if you're not in the program, you can enjoy the spa facilities, as well as golf and tennis, for extra fees.

Reserve for Friday's dinner in one of La Costa's trio of grand restaurants. If you feel like candlelight, strolling violinists, and European cuisine, put on your best bib and tucker for an evening in the Continental After Dark dining room. Otherwise, try the Seville Room for Italian fare or the Steak House for prime beef. Have a nightcap in the lounge, where there's also music for dancing the night away.

In the morning, explore the town by heading back north on the freeway to Carlsbad and exiting toward the ocean on Elm Avenue. Go six blocks to the railroad tracks, where you'll see Rotary Park and the old Santa Fe train station, which has been restored as offices for the Carlsbad Chamber of Commerce. (The chamber folks advise everyone who wants to see the Carlsbad Caverns to go to New Mexico.) Beyond the tracks, turn right on Carlsbad Boulevard, the old coast highway, which is the main north-south street, and go past Grand Avenue to a town landmark, the Alt Karlsbad gift shop, a replica of a Hanseatic house built on the site of Frazier's well. Peer into the 400-foot shaft through a glass-covered opening at curbside. Better yet, go into the gift shop and be guided to an underground gallery for a closer look at the well and the owners' mini-museum of Carlsbad history. Salt water has invaded the well, so don't expect to sample the mineral water that put the town on the map. You'll enjoy the Alt Karlsbad's historical mementos and European handicrafts, however.

Cross the boulevard and go a block north to Beech Avenue and a city historical park, site of the restored Magee House, which was built over a century ago by a pioneer family. It's now headquarters for the Carlsbad Historical Society and occasionally open for tours. Look for the Magees' barn and carriage house, too. You'll also see the early St. Patrick's church, which later served as the town's city hall, jail, and public library. Nearby is another attractive 1890s building that is now a restaurant called Duck Soup. Other places to lunch, and many of Carlsbad's gift and antique shops, are nearby on Grand Avenue and State and Roosevelt streets. At the corner of Grand and Roosevelt is a complex of shops, the Old World Center, also home for a popular dinner house and Irish pub called Dooley McClusky's.

Back on Carlsbad Boulevard at Elm Avenue, don't miss the chance to have lunch, dinner, or Sunday brunch at the Twin Inns, a stately Victorian mansion that was built by a Carlsbad land promoter and later became a boardinghouse. For the past six decades it's been a popular restaurant and has become famous for all-you-can-eat-chicken dinners that bring you back to the good ol' days of family dining. Besides platters of pan-fried chicken, the reasonably priced meal includes corn fritters, potatoes and cream gravy, garden peas, biscuits and honey, salad, dessert, and a beverage. After you eat, cross the boulevard for a peek at another former residence, now the Royal Palms Motel, complete with its own wedding chapel and a Mexican restaurant, Fidel's Norte. Many episodes of the original *Zorro* television series were filmed on the grounds.

For some exercise after you eat, stroll along Elm Avenue to the beach or continue south on Carlsbad Boulevard until it turns to parallel the oceanfront and joins a bluff-top walkway overlooking the Pacific. A mile of the coastline below you is Carlsbad State Beach, a day-use park where the suntan set gather to swim, surf, and fish. For travelers with a tent or RV, three miles beyond is a longer stretch of sand, South Carlsbad State Beach, which has cliff-top campsites in sight of the ocean. On the way you'll pass the protected Aqua Hedionda Lagoon, where water skiing is the favorite pastime. Bird watchers should continue on to Batequitas Lagoon along La Costa Avenue at the city's southern limits or go back to the north end of town to Buena Vista Lagoon, a freshwater wildlife sanctuary that's home for 225 species of migrating waterfowl.

On Sunday continue south on Carlsbad Boulevard/S21 to Leucadia and neighboring Encinitas to visit several flower nurseries and gardens open to the public. As the growing center for potted and cut flowers that are shipped to florists all over the nation, those neighboring coastal communities have become Southern California's flower capital. If you're visiting in the springtime, look for a dazzling rainbow opposite South Carlsbad State Beach park where thousands of ranunculus grow in colorful rows in the Frazee flower fields. Continue south past La Costa Avenue to Leucadia and turn left on Leucadia Boulevard. Just before reaching the freeway, go right at the gas station onto Orpheus Avenue to Stubbs Fuchsia Nursery. You'll be awed by more than 30,000 flowering fuchsia plants, many in attractive hanging baskets. The owners of this wholesale nursery, Jill and Bob Meyer, invite visitors to buy fuchsias as well as view the spectacular display. You'll see more than 250 fuchsia varieties in every size, shape, and color. Also blossoming and popular in summer are New Guinea impatiens.

Head back to Leucadia Boulevard, go right to cross over the freeway, then turn left immediately on Piraeus Street to Weidner's Begonia Gardens at Normandy Road. Under a shady tent of screen mesh that filters the sunlight is an acre of begonias—20,000 plants in gorgeous full bloom. Annually from July to September, you can wander among the orderly rows to pick out plants for your own patio or garden. Digging forks, instructions, and carrying cartons are supplied, or bring your own pots and replant the begonias on the spot. The price for each begonia you dig up is only a few dollars, regardless of its variety, color, or size. This novel begonia garden was established in 1973, when Evelyn and Bob Weidner ''retired'' from the nursery business. Other plants have been added since then, including the popular fuchsias and impatiens and the treasured royal purple brunfelsia. Wear old walking shoes, because the garden grounds may be muddy. While parents are searching for the perfect plant to take home, the kids will be entertained by watching the Weidners' chickens, cow, horse, pig, sheep, goat, and other farm pets.

Return to the freeway and go south to the next exit, Encinitas Boulevard, then head inland a quarter mile to Quail Gardens Drive. It takes you to Quail Botanic Gardens, a county nature center with 30 acres of native, hybrid, and imported plants and trees. You're welcome to wander along five self-guided nature walks in this peaceful botanic preserve, which also serves as a bird and wildlife sanctuary. Rangers live on the grounds and will answer your questions, but most things are described in the seasonal calendar and tour leaflets that are available near the outdoor guest-registration book.

To glimpse what this area of Southern California coast was like before the twentieth century, take the Quail Gardens Nature Trail that starts on the unpaved walkway at the southwest corner of the parking lot. Numbered redwood stakes correspond to numbered descriptions in the tour leaflet. Besides a loop trail through the chaparral plant community, the area includes a pond where plants from other parts of California are displayed. Native birds and small animals rarely seen in other parts of the garden often come here, so walk quietly, because noise and other sudden movements scare them off. In addition to hummingbirds, doves, and the garden's namesake, California quail (seen late in the day), be on the lookout for cottontail rabbit, pocket gopher, long-tailed weasel, gray fox, and opossum. Along the trail you'll probaby smell black sage, a pungent bush used as seasoning or medicinal tea by early Californians, and also yerba santa, a shrub with aromatic leaves that were brewed for tea.

On the far side of the pond is a Torrey pine, a handsome tree that is now one of the world's rarest pines and is native only to this coastal area of the county and Santa Rosa Island. You'll see many kinds of cactus, including one with seedy fruits that taste like watermelon. It is called mission cactus because the Spanish missionaries first brought it to California. The other self-guided tours also will introduce you to a surprising variety of plants and trees. Look for the camphor tree, which was important as the source of moth-repelling camphor until synthetic mothballs were made. The bunya-bunya tree is nicknamed a monkey-puzzle tree because its sharp-tipped leaves would puzzle a monkey as to how to climb it safely. At certain times you'll see green cones which are as big as pineapples at the very top of this tree. Take a picnic lunch and drinks to enjoy at shaded tables; no refreshments are available in the botanic gardens.

You'll also enjoy a stroll through the gardens of the Self-Realization Fellowship, a religious retreat on a cliff overlooking the Pacific at the southern end of Encinitas. From Encinitas Boulevard, head south again on the coastal highway, S21. You can't miss the golden-domed towers, built by a sect from India in the 1930s. Members maintain a beautiful meditation garden inside the compound, and it's open to the public. If you decide to eat before the drive back to Los Angeles, you'll find a number of restaurants fronting the old coastal road. Going north on S21 you'll also discover art galleries and clusters of gift shops in Encinitas and Leucadia. Look for the Lumberyard, the Old Market, and Leucadia's weekend flea market. Then return to Los Angeles by rejoining Interstate 5 north.

Round trip is about 230 miles.

Carlsbad Area Code: 619

SIGHTSEEING *Alt Karlsbad,* 2802 Carlsbad Boulevard, Carlsbad 92008, 729-6912. Gift shop with museum of local memorabilia, open Tuesday through Saturday from 10 A.M. to 5 P.M., Sunday from 1 to 4:30 P.M. ● *Stubbs Fuchsia Nursery,* 737 Orpheus Avenue, Leucadia 92024, 753-1069. Open daily from 9 A.M. to 5 P.M. ● *Weidner's Begonia Gardens,* 695 Normandy Road, Leucadia 92024, 436-2194. Open 10 A.M. to 5 P.M. daily from mid-April to mid-September. ● *Quail Botanic Gardens,* 230 Quail Gardens Drive, Encinitas 92024, 436-3036 or 753-4432 (ranger). Open daily 8 A.M. to 5 P.M. (to 6 P.M. in summer.) Free admission; parking 50 cents. ● *Self-Realization Fellowship,* 215 K Street, Encinitas 92024, 753-1811. Gardens open daily except from Monday from 9 A.M. to 5 P.M. (from 11 A.M. Sunday). Free.

LODGING   *La Costa Hotel & Spa,* Costa Del Mar Road, Carlsbad 92008, 438-9111 or toll-free (800) 542-6200; $125, suites from $225. Also spa, golf, and tennis packages. Three fine restaurants. ● *Beach View Lodge,* 3180 Carlsbad Boulevard, Carlsbad 92008, 729-1151; $50. Across from Carlsbad State Beach. Whirlpool and sauna. Some rooms with gas fireplaces and kitchens. ● *Beach Terrace Inn,* 2775 Ocean Street, Carlsbad 92008, 729-5951; $71. On the beach. Rooms and suites with fireplaces and kitchens. ● *Royal Palms Motel,* 3001 Carlsbad Boulevard, Carlsbad 92008, 729-0971; $40. Tennis courts, Jacuzzi, access to beach. Also restaurant (see below).

CAMPING   *South Carlsbad State Beach,* off San Diego County S21/Carlsbad Boulevard, 3 miles south of Carlsbad, 438-3143. 226 sites, $5 per night; no hookups. Reserve through Ticketron. Also, *San Elijo State Beach,* south of Encinitas at Cardiff-by-the-Sea, 753-5091. 171 sites, $5 per night; no hookups.

DINING   *Twin Inns,* 2978 Carlsbad Boulevard, Carlsbad, 729-3131. Family-style feast featuring chicken served daily except Monday from 11:30 A.M. to 10 P.M. (Sunday brunch from 11 A.M.). ● *Dooley Mc-Cluskey's,* 640 Grand Avenue, Carlsbad, 434-3114. Seafood dinners daily from 5:30 P.M.; pub opens at 11 A.M. ● *Anchorage Fish Co.,* 3878 Carlsbad Boulevard, Carlsbad, 729-3170. Seafood specialties. Weekend brunch, dinner nightly, and lunch on weekdays. ● *Fidel's Norte,* 3001 Carlsbad Boulevard (at the Royal Palms Motel), Carlsbad, 729-4351. Mexican fare (try the tostada suprema) for lunch and dinner on weekends, lunch on weekdays. ● *Mariah's,* 37 Elm Avenue, Carlsbad, 729-6040. Informal dining in a converted home that's open daily for breakfast (dozens of omelettes), lunch, and family-style dinners. ● *Pegasus,* 1108 1st Street, Encinitas, 753-1770. Greek fare served for lunch and dinner daily except Monday. ● Also a restaurant row just south of Encinitas on old highway 101 (now S21) in Cardiff-by-the-Sea, including the *Triton* and *Chart House* (both on the beach and serving Sunday brunch) and *Fish House West.*

FOR MORE INFORMATION   Contact the Carlsbad Chamber of Commerce, Old Santa Fe Depot on Elm Avenue at the RR tracks (or P.O. Box 1605), Carlsbad 92008, 729-5924. Open weekdays 8:30 A.M. to 4:30 P.M. Also contact the Encinitas-Leucadia Chamber of Commerce, 930 1st Street, Encinitas 92024, 753-6041. Open weekdays.

La Jolla and Del Mar: A Pair of Coastal Charmers

As the most exclusive suburb of San Diego, La Jolla (*la hoy-ya*) is a residential community that displays an informal elegance. Known for a seven-mile coastline that's outstanding for surfing, swimming, and sunbathing, it's no wonder the attractive village also is a magnet for visitors. Ocean-view parks for picnics and tree-lined sidewalks for strolling—plus a wonderful variety of restaurants, art galleries, and shops—help make it a great getaway spot. Despite its upper-income status (just glance at the prices of homes pictured in real estate office windows), La Jolla isn't stuffy. In fact, the town has a very youthful and alive atmosphere, thanks in part to the students from the neighboring University of California San Diego campus.

During a weekend visit you'll find plenty more to enjoy on a side trip to Del Mar, another coastal charmer that's just 10 miles north of La Jolla. See the aquarium at the famed Scripps Institution of Oceanography, watch hang gliders and sailplanes soar from cliff tops along the beach, stroll among rare Torrey pines, and then relax on the beach. Once just a summer place, Del Mar overflows with visitors from June through mid-September because of three major Southland events: a national horse show, then the Southern California Exposition (San Diego's county fair), and finally Del Mar's renowned Thoroughbred racing season. But travelers have discovered that this mellow village makes a delightful diversion any time of the year.

Get to your weekend lodgings in La Jolla by driving south from Los Angeles on Interstate 5 to the La Jolla Village Drive exit. Go west along the edge of the UCSD campus and turn left on Torrey Pines Road to join La Jolla's main roadway, Prospect Street. Turn right on this curving thoroughfare, lined with shops and restaurants, and look for a La Jolla landmark, the classic 1926 Hotel La Valencia, conspicuous because of its pink tower with gilded top. Check in there or next door at another delightful lodging, the Village Hotel of La Jolla, a 23-room bed-and-breakfast.

As you'll discover while taking an evening stroll along Prospect Street, many shops and dining spots are clustered in pleasant complexes called McKellar Plaza, Coast Walk, and Prospect Mall. A local favorite if you're splurging for dinner is the Top of the Cove or dine in the Sky Room atop the Hotel Valencia. Or give up an ocean view to be part of the scene in the hotel's venerable Whaling Bar and Grill or Cafe La Rue. For musical entertainment with your meal or after-dinner drinks, join the jazz crowd at Chuck's Steak House. Or dress up to feast with a coastline panorama at Elario's, a rooftop restaurant at the Summer House Inn on La Jolla Shores Drive, then enjoy jazz music in its Crystal Room Lounge. Another street with recommended restaurants is La Jolla Boulevard between the 5600 and 6700 blocks, where you'll find informal dining and drinking spots like Bully's and Su Casa. They're south of the town center and not far from Windansea Beach, La Jolla's celebrated surfing area and a spectacular spot to watch the sun set.

With its curving park-studded coast and enticing shopping streets in the heart of town, La Jolla invites visitors to give up their cars for leisurely strolls to enjoy the scenery and shops, with pauses for refreshments at shaded sidewalk cafes. In the morning, go walking along Coast Boulevard. It leads to the La Jolla Cave and Shell Shop, where you can descend 133 steps through a 10-story tunnel to reach one of the seven caves carved by the ocean into La Jolla's sandstone cliffs. Topside again, enjoy more of the town's rugged coastal beauty by following an unpaved trail called Cliff Walk, where you'll get a bird's-eye view of La Jolla's caves and coves. Farther along Coast Boulevard are public parks with grassy expanses on the bluff top that welcome you to rest or picnic.

Some outstanding Pacific Ocean vistas also are offered from the La Jolla Museum of Contemporary Art on Prospect Street, where the main attraction is an excellent collection of post-1950 American art augmented by traveling exhibits. A dozen galleries along Prospect also will get your attention with avant garde, traditional, and Western artworks, as well as photography, fine crafts, and ancient arts. The galleries' free brochure called *Art in La Jolla* tells you where to find your favorites.

On Sunday, plan time to make a sightseeing drive to Del Mar. Turn left from Prospect onto Torrey Pines Road, then bear left on La Jolla Shores Drive to the Scripps Aquarium-Museum, part of the renowned oceanography institution, which is a graduate division of UCSD. Park on the street (two hours free) or weekends in the metered lots marked for aquarium visitors.

Just in front of the aquarium entrance is a man-made tide pool where you can easily see and photograph nearly two dozen live marine creatures. Preserved specimens of the same types are displayed in shadow boxes around the tide pool's perimeter to help you identify the living sea life. Inside the aquarium building, hundreds more live aquatic specimens are on view in 18 large tanks that duplicate various underwater habitats along the coasts of Southern California and Baja, Mexico. As you peer at this marvelous array of Pacific Ocean marine life and view the other exhibits about ocean geology and pollution, you'll understand why the aquarium at Scripps is considered one of the best in the nation. And there's extra fun Sunday and Wednesday afternoons at 11:30 P.M., when visitors can watch the fish being fed.

Continue north on La Jolla Shores Drive and turn left onto North Torrey Pines Road. Skirting the campus of the University of California San

Diego, drive north to Torrey Pines Scenic Drive, just beyond the famed Salk Institute for Biological Studies, then turn left and go to the very end until the road dissolves into an open area on the coastal cliff top. This is Torrey Pines City Park, a popular launch area for hang gliders. Walk to the ocean overlooks to watch the human butterflies make their dramatic takeoffs over the Pacific. This also is a glider port, and when the winds are strong enough you'll get to see the graceful sailplanes taking off and landing. Radio-controlled model airplanes often fill the skies here, too.

Returning to North Torrey Pines Road and continuing north, you'll pass Torrey Pines Golf Course, a championship 36-hole course that's open to the public. It's the site of the PGA's annual Andy Williams San Diego Open in January. After the highway descends to the ocean, turn left to the entrance of Torrey Pines State Reserve. This is California's only state park where picnics aren't permitted, smoking is forbidden, and dogs are unwelcome even if they're kept in the car. There's good reason for such strict regulations—the reserve is home for one of the world's rarest trees, the Torrey pine. This relic of the Ice Age is found in its native habitat in only two places in the world—isolated Santa Rosa Island, off the coast of Santa Barbara, and this windswept state reserve between La Jolla and Del Mar. After paying the park entry fee, drive up the steep hill to the main parking area, where you'll find a visitors center with a small museum. (In summer, when parking areas fill up, the entrance road is temporarily closed until some of the visitors leave.) The 1,000-acre reserve is a microcosm of what California looked like centuries ago. Foot trails lead to a variety of vegetation, including bent and gnarled Torrey pine trees clinging to eroded sandstone cliffs overlooking the ocean.

Be sure to view the natural-history displays in the visitors center, a former tourist lodge. You also can watch a brief slide show that introduces the park's trails. Two of the most popular are a marked nature path in Parry Grove and the almost-level Guy Fleming Trail. On either one you'll be surrounded by the *Pincus torreyana,* as the tree species is officially called. Named in 1850 for the American botanist Dr. John Torrey, the pine has flourished in the protected reserve and now numbers 10,000, including seedlings. Collecting pinecones is prohibited because their seeds are needed to assure survival of the species. Guided nature walks begin from the park museum Saturday and Sunday afternoons.

Drive back down to the park road and continue north on the highway, San Diego County S21, which becomes Camino Del Mar and brings you into the heart of the coastal village of Del Mar. The bluff-top town was founded in 1883, shortly before an impressive hotel, the Casa del Mar, was built to attract prospective land purchasers from Los Angeles and elsewhere. That hostelry burned down in 1890, about the time California's early land boom ended. Twenty years later Del Mar returned to prominence with the opening of the Stratford Inn, an expansive resort hotel in half-timbered Tudor style that overlooked the sand and surf.

Eventually renamed the Del Mar Hotel, it was a favorite of movie stars and other celebrities attending horse races at the Del Mar Turf Club, a Thoroughbred racecourse opened in 1937 by Bing Crosby and Pat O'Brien. The grand hotel has since been demolished, but a more modern one, also called the Stratford Inn, continues to welcome overnight guests. Don't confuse it with Stratford Square, a two-story mock-Tudor complex of art galleries, gift shops, boutiques, antique stores, and eateries at the corner of Camino Del Mar and 15th Street.

Slip into the town's easygoing mood by having refreshments or lunch beneath the patio unbrellas at Carlos & Annie's, a sidewalk cafe. Also at Stratford Square, be sure to browse in the Earth Song bookstore and adjacent Ocean Song Gallery of South American imports. Upstairs, you'll enjoy three unique shops, the Gift Horse, Plum Pudding, and La Mariposa, with its special section for kids. Also on the second floor, where you'll find the helpful chamber of commerce, view the vintage photographs that portray the town's past and see the collections of seashells and fossils found at Del Mar.

You'll discover more shops and restaurants along both sides of the four-lane Camino Del Mar, including a favorite of local folks, Bully's North. If you prefer to picnic, walk down 15th Street to Seagrove Park, overlooking the ocean. Just north is Del Mar's sandy city beach, popular for swimming, surfing, and sunbathing. Two restaurants nearby on Coast Boulevard overlook the sand—the Poseidon, which draws the barefoot beach crowd, and Jake's, where shirts and shoes definitely are required.

If your visit to Del Mar is the finale of your weekend and it's time to return to Los Angeles, continue north on Camino Del Mar/S21 past the racetrack and county fairgrounds and turn inland on Via de la Valle to join Interstate 5 north.

Round trip is about 270 miles.

La Jolla/Del Mar Area Code: 619

SIGHTSEEING   *La Jolla Cave and Shell Shop,* 1325 Coast Boulevard, La Jolla 92037, 454-6080. Open daily 10 A.M. to 6 P.M. in summer season, to 5 P.M. rest of the year. Entry to staircase to reach Sunny Jim Cave is 75 cents for adults, 50 cents for ages 3 to 16. ● *La Jolla Museum of Contemporary Art,* 700 Prospect Street, La Jolla 92037, 454-3541. Open weekends 12:30 to 5 P.M., weekdays except Tuesday from 10 A.M. to 5 P.M. Adults $3, students and senior citizens $2, children under 12 years $1. ● *Scripps Aquarium-Museum,* 8602 La Jolla Shores Drive, La Jolla 92037, 452-6933. Open every day from 9 A.M. to 5 P.M. Free; donations welcome. ● *Torrey Pines Municipal Golf Course,* 1480 North Torrey Pines Road, La Jolla 92037, 453-0380. Two 18-hole, par-72 courses. Greens fee $7 each course. ● *Torrey Pines State Reserve,* off

North Torrey Pines Road south of Del Mar (or P.O. Box 38, Carlsbad 92008), 755-2063. Open 9 A.M. to 8 P.M. April through September, to 5 P.M. rest of the year. Entry $3 per car; walkers and bicyclists free. Museum open weekends 11 A.M. to 5 P.M. Guided nature walks on weekends at 11:30 A.M. and 1:30 P.M.

EVENTS *Del Mar National Horse Show,* one of the largest in the nation, is held at the Del Mar Fairgrounds annually in May. Admission $3. Phone 755-1161 or 297-0338. • *Southern California Exposition,* old-fashioned county fair held annually at the Del Mar Fairgrounds from the third week in June through July 4. Phone 275-2705 or 755-6940. • *Del Mar Thoroughbred Club,* 44 days of horse racing at the Del Mar Fairgrounds track. Nine races daily except Tuesday from late July through early September. Post time 2 P.M. Grandstand admission $2.25, Clubhouse $4. Phone 299-1340 or 755-1141.

LODGING *Hotel La Valencia,* 1132 Prospect Street, La Jolla 92037, 454-0771; $90, suites from $135. Homey yet classy landmark hotel that sets the tone for a La Jolla visit. Guests gather in elegant lobby for the ocean views and relaxation in the heart of town. Heated pool, whirlpool, sauna, and exercise room. Also several impressive reataurants and the town's best-known bar (see below). • *Village Hotel of La Jolla,* 1110 Prospect Place, La Jolla 92037, 454-0133; $46 to $66, continental breakfast included. A renovated hotel that's now a hospitable 23-room bed-and-breakfast. Located in the heart of town half a block from the beach. Breakfast in your room or on the rooftop garden. • *Summer House Inn,* 7955 La Jolla Shores Drive, La Jolla 92037, 459-0261; $77. Roomy accommodations with balconies and views of ocean four blocks away. Also rooftop restaurant and lounge (see below). • *Del Mar Inn,* 720 Camino Del Mar, Del Mar 92014, 755-9765; $65 summer, $54 rest of year, including continental breakfast. English Tudor-looking hotel with many ocean-view rooms. • *Stratford Inn,* 710 Camino Del Mar, Del Mar 92014, 755-1501; $60 summer, $46 rest of year. Expanded hostelry with spacious rooms overlooking ocean. • *Rock Haus,* 410 15th Street, Del Mar 92014, 481-3764; $65 to $95, continental breakfast included. Two-night minimum weekend stay in season from Memorial Day to Labor Day. $10 less on weekdays except Friday in off-season. 8-room bed-and-breakfast in historic Del Mar home, one block from the heart of town. Two rooms with private bath, others share three baths. Complimentary afternoon wine selected from the wine cellar. No children or smoking.

DINING *Top of the Cove,* 1216 Prospect Street, La Jolla, 454-7779. Continental cuisine for lunch and dinner daily; also weekend brunch. Entertainment most nights. Reservations recommended, as are coats for men. • *Hotel La Valencia* (see above) has five dining areas and a well-known watering hole: 10th-floor *Sky Room* serves continental fare nightly except Sunday and buffet luncheons weekdays—all with majestic shoreline and ocean views. Coats and ties required. Reservations a must. *Whaling Bar and Grill* and *Cafe la Rue* offer same menu of prime ribs, steaks, and seafood with different decor. Lunch and dinner daily, with Sunday brunch in the Cafe. The Whaling Bar is a legendary rendezvous and drinking spot. *Mediterranean Room* and *Tropical Patio* also share menus and serve three meals daily. Buffet lunch and Sunday brunch in the Mediterranean Room; outdoor dining when weather permits. ● *Chuck's Steak House,* 1250 Prospect Street (in McKellar Plaza), La Jolla, 454-5325. Popular spot with soup and salad bar, choice beef and seafood for dinner daily. Jazz after 9 P.M. ● *Elario's,* 7955 La Jolla Shores Drive (atop Summer House Inn), La Jolla, 459-0541. Great for breakfast with a view, also Sunday brunch, lunch, and dinner. Dress up evenings for the fine French fare. Enjoy the jazz in the classy lounge after 9 P.M. ● *Bully's,* 5755 La Jolla Boulevard, La Jolla, 459-2768. Prime ribs and seafood for dinner nightly, salads and sandwiches for lunch weekdays only. ● *Su Casa Restaurant,* 6738 La Jolla Boulevard, La Jolla, 454-0369. Sonora-style Mexican dishes for lunch and dinner served daily with guitar and harp music in sixteenth-century-style hacienda; also fresh fish. ● *Carlos & Annie's,* 1454 Camino Del Mar (at Stratford Square), Del Mar, 755-4601. Open daily for breakfast, lunch, and dinner. Sidewalk dining. ● *Bully's North,* 1404 Camino Del Mar, Del Mar, 755-1660. Locals flock here for prime ribs and seafood nightly; lighter fare for lunch. ● *Poseidon,* 1670 Coast Boulevard, Del Mar, 755-9345. Very informal dining and drinks on the sand. A favorite for breakfast and musical groups in the evening. ● *Jake's Restaurant,* 1660 Coast Boulevard, Del Mar, 755-2002. On the beach, serving seafood and continental dishes for lunch and dinner; also Sunday brunch.

FOR MORE INFORMATION   Contact La Jolla Town Council, 1055 Wall Street, Suite 110 (or P.O. 1101), La Jolla 92037, 454-1444. Also, the Del Mar Chamber of Commerce, 1442 Camino Del Mar (in Stratford Square), Del Mar 92014, 755-4844.

San Diego
Part 1: Introducing California's Oldest City

Like a precious pendant at the end of a string of jewels, San Diego is the brilliant gem that seems to outshine all of the other sparkling cities along the Southland seacoast. It's attractions are so numerous and diverse—from historic to scenic to recreational—that you need several visits just to sample what San Diego has to offer.

We've planned four weekends to help you see the highlights. As the first landing point for European explorers along the West Coast and home for the state's first non-Indian settlement, San Diego makes early California history come alive. Return to the time of Spanish soldiers and Franciscan fathers by touring three well-preserved places—San Diego's mission, the presidio, and Old Town. These simple beginnings of what has become California's second largest city offer a delightful introduction to the 200-year-old town, along with the Victorian homes that abounded at the turn of the century and have been saved for the pleasure of future generations.

Plan another weekend to discover San Diego's wonderful waterfront of vintage ships, enticing shops, seafood restaurants, and resort hotels—all surrounding a picturesque bay that's home for countless pleasure craft, fishing boats, and naval ships. You'll need another weekend to thoroughly enjoy one of the nation's most impressive playgrounds, Balboa Park, home of the world-renowned San Diego Zoo. And for family fun and recreation or just do-nothing relaxation, Mission Bay Park and its famed Sea World make one more perfect getaway weekend in San Diego.

Get to San Diego from Los Angeles by driving south on Interstate 5, and set the mood for a yesteryear's weekend in California's oldest city by reserving a room in the 1887 Britt House, a charming bed-and-breakfast inn north of downtown at Fourth Avenue and Maple Street. Or check into the Cottage, a country-style bed-and-breakfast on Albatross Street, a quiet neighborhood cul-de-sac. You also can stay in the heart of the city at the authentically renovated Hotel San Diego, built in 1915 at Broadway and State Street. Another choice is to plant yourself nearby San Diego's original roots, the presidio and Old Town, with accommodations in a modern-style motel, the Padre Trail Inn on Taylor Street. Many other lodgings are close by on Hotel Circle in Mission Valley.

In the morning, begin following the city's Spanish trail by heading to the Mother of the Missions, San Diego de Alcala, the first of California's 21 missions. As the military and religious leaders of Spain's Sacred Expedition to Alta (upper) California in 1769, Gaspar de Portola and Father Junipero Serra established a presidio (fort) and a mission on a barren hill overlooking San Diego Bay. However, within five years a more reliable source of fresh water was needed, and the mission was moved to its present site, a few miles inland in Mission Valley. Reach it from Interstate 5 by joining Interstate 8 east for about six miles to the Mission Gorge Road exit. Turn left under the freeway and continue north to Twain Street, then go left again and follow the signs to the mission and its parking area on the right.

Surrounded by trees and flowers, this peaceful religious sanctuary now serves as an active parish church. It has been rebuilt and restored several times during the past two centuries. Especially fascinating is the sparse room of Father Serra, a remnant of the original mission. Note the rope bed, crosses, and candlesticks, as well as the adobe bricks under the whitewashed walls. At the front of the church, also look for the small statue of Father Serra that was carved in his homeland, the Spanish island of Mallorca. More statuary is in the foliage-filled garden, dominated by a campanario of bells. When hostile Indians destroyed the mission in 1775, they also killed Padre Luis Jayme, who became California's first Christian martyr and lies buried in the church sanctuary. Spend some time in the Luis Jayme Museum room, where artifacts from the early mission days are on display, including Father Serra's crucifix. Don't miss the photos of the mission before its restorations—in the mid-1800s the buildings were occupied by the U.S. Cavalry. Outdoors on the perimeter of a courtyard you'll see excavations by college archaeology students of the Indian workshops and monastery. Hear all about the mission's remarkable history by renting a tape recorder in the gift shop to guide you on a narrated tour through the buildings and grounds.

Afterward, return to Interstate 8 and go west to the Taylor Street exit, then cross the freeway toward Old Town. Follow the signs up the hill to Presidio Park, crowned by the Junipero Serra Museum. This imposing building was dedicated in 1929 as a memorial to the famed padre and often is mistaken by passersby as the San Diego mission. Civic leader George Marston donated it to the city, along with the park's 40 unspoiled acres where the first Spanish fort and mission were built.

You can view excavations in the park that have been made in search of the presidio ruins and objects that belonged to San Diego's settlers. Some of the unearthed artifacts are displayed in the museum, along with Father Serra mementos and examples of vintage Spanish furniture. Climb to the top of the tower to compare the sprawling city today with photos of the town taken from the hill in 1911.

As San Diego slowly grew, people moved from the presidio to the bottom of the hill and settled into what is now called Old Town. Since 1969, six square blocks of old San Diego have been preserved as a state historic park. To see some of the restored adobe structures of the 1800s, drive back down through Presidio Park to Old Town's free parking areas. A novel way to become acquainted with the Spanish-style village is to ride around it in a horse-drawn carriage that can be hired at the town plaza. You'll also enjoy strolling along Old Town's spacious streets, which are off limits to automobiles.

Intermingled with shops and restaurants are a dozen vintage buildings that re-create the setting of California life during the Mexican and early American periods. After Old Town was devastated by fire in 1872, San Diego was reestablished nearer the harbor in the present downtown, so the original town site was never obliterated by modern buildings. Park rangers reveal much of Old Town's history during their free and informative walking tours, which depart daily in the afternoon from the tree-shaded plaza. If you explore on your own, pick up a gratis guide map from any of the Old Town merchants or buy a guidebook at the park's visitors center. And be sure to go inside the small Historical Museum of Old California to view a detailed scale model of the entire town as it was in 1870.

Visit the 1830s Machado-Stewart Adobe to see the early San Diegans' simple living conditions. If you want to experience daily life in those early times, be there on Saturday morning to participate in the park's living-history programs, a favorite of families. With guidance from the rangers, children and their parents bake bread, prepare salsa, create candles, or make adobe bricks just as Old Town residents did 150 years ago.

Near the Machado-Stewart Adobe, peek into the town's first public schoolhouse, where replicas of the 16 flags that have flown over California are displayed. Pay a small fee to enter the handsomely furnished Casa de Estudillo, a grand adobe built in 1827 by the commander of the presidio. The ticket also admits you to the nearby Seeley Stables, a restored 1869 stage depot that features Western memorabilia and an impressive collection of horse-drawn vehicles. Included is a stagecoach Albert Seeley used on the stage line he ran to Los Angeles, a two-day trip in those days. Also watch the sound slide show that describes life in early San Diego.

Next door to the stables is Casa de Bandini, once Old Town's social center and now a Mexican restaurant with mariachi music. Have lunch there to enjoy more of the village's authentic flavor. You also can eat in the 1869 Casa de Pedrorena, a restaurant and bakery with a traditional adobe oven. At the edge of the plaza is the homesite of Pio Pico, California's last Mexican governor, now occupied by Bazaar del Mundo, an attractive complex of shops and popular restaurants. At Casa de Pico, join the line of old Town visitors waiting for a patio table, where you can relax with a refreshing margarita and nachos or a full Mexican meal.

Just outside the park boundary you'll find many more dining spots, shops, and historical sites within walking distance, including the Whaley House, which is thought to be the oldest two-story brick building in Southern California. This fine old home also has been a courthouse, store, theater, and church since being built in 1857, and it's believed to be haunted by ghosts. Several more of San Diego's vintage buildings have been preserved nearby in Heritage Park, but save them for the following day, when you also should make an auto tour of some wonderful Victorian homes in another part of town.

Meanwhile, spend the evening at the intimate Old Town Opera House, where historical dramas and comedies promise plenty of original entertainment. If you're looking for a convenient spot for a pre- or post-play dinner, a tasty choice is the Casa Vallarta Mexican restaurant on the top level of Old San Diego Square, a five-story complex of eateries and shops at the edge of the Old Town park.

Continue your tour of historic San Diego in the morning, starting with Sunday champagne brunch in a handsome Victorian house in Heritage

Park, just across from Old San Diego Square at the corner of Juan and Harney streets. This eight-acre park near the base of historic Presidio Hill was established in 1971 as a haven for endangered buildings that once were the city's pride but stood in the way of new development. Eventually a dozen or more architectural gems from Victorian times will be moved there and restored, serving not only as handsome reminders of the past but as offices, shops, and restaurants where visitors are always welcome.

Inspiration for the county park was a group of citizens who formed the Save Our Heritage Organization (SOHO) to move the Sherman-Gilbert House, an ornate 1887 structure that was going to be flattened by the wrecker's ball and replaced by a parking lot. On top of the house is a widow's walk for observing ships at sea, very common in New England seaport towns but now the only authentic widow's walk remaining in San Diego. You'll also admire the 1893 Burton House and the Busheyhead House, built in 1887. Another restored home is the 1896 Senlis Cottage, which houses the SOHO office and restoration library. The 1889 Temple Beth Israel, the first wooden synagogue in Southern California, has been moved to the park too.

Also built that same year is the Queen Anne–style Christian House, now converted to a period restaurant called Tiffany's, where Sunday brunch is served (as well as bargain-priced family-style dinners). After a relaxing repast, drive to another old section of the city to visit one of the finest and most unusual Victorian mansions on the West Coast, Villa Montezuma. From Heritage Park and the Old Town area, join Interstate 5 south past downtown to the Imperial Avenue exit. Turn left and go under the freeway to 20th Street, then turn left again and drive two blocks to the mansion, which dominates the corner at K and 20th Streets.

Villa Montezuma was constructed in 1887 and has been colorfully painted to represent the original color of its redwood exterior. The home's decoration inside and out is as eclectic as the man who had it built, Jesse Shepard, a composer, writer, and spiritualist medium. You'll discover his portrait in one of the building's exquisite stained-glass windows. The mansion has become a fascinating museum run by the San Diego Historical Society, with the second floor featuring an art gallery of changing exhibits.

While at Villa Montezuma, pick up a free booklet that describes and directs you to two dozen other historical homes and churches in the Golden Hill–Sherman Heights sections of southeast San Diego. First go east on K Street to 25th Street, then turn left and drive north 12 blocks to the hilltop park that overlooks the city and harbor. This section of town, called Golden Hill, is where many of San Diego's richest and most influential citizens lived at the turn of the century.

By driving up and down eleven streets, A through K streets, between 21st and 25th streets, you'll discover a variety of Victorian and other interesting homes. Some have been painstakingly restored, while others are in disrepair. All are private residences or have been converted to offices, and you can view them only from the outside. When it's time for your return to Los Angeles, rejoin Interstate 5 and drive north.

Round trip is about 288 miles.

San Diego Area Code: 619

SIGHTSEEING   *Mission San Diego de Alcala,* 10818 San Diego Mission Road, San Diego, 92108, 281-8449. Open daily 9 A.M. to 5 P.M. Admission $1, under 12 years free. 30-minute tape tour, $1. • *Junipero Serra Museum,* in Presidio Park at 2727 Presidio Drive, San Diego 92110, 297-3258. Open daily from 9 A.M. to 4:45 P.M. except Sunday from 12 noon. $1 donation, children free. • *Old Town San Diego State Historic Park,* with the Visitors Center at 2645 San Diego Avenue, San Diego 92110, 237-6770. Buildings open daily from 10 A.M. to 6 P.M., in winter to 5 P.M. Free parking and entry. Ranger-led walking tours daily at 2 P.M. Entry to Casa de Estudillo and Seeley Stables 50 cents for adults, 25 cents for senior citizens and ages 5 though 17. 20-minute carriage rides from 11 A.M. to 5 P.M. Wednesday through Sunday. Adults $2, children $1, family groups with up to 6 passengers $5. Living History Programs at Machado-Stewart Adobe 1st through 3rd Saturdays of every month at 10 and 11 A.M. by advance reservation; call park office. Donations accepted for materials. • *Whaley House,* 2482 San Diego Avenue, San Diego 92110, 298-2482. Open 10 A.M. to 4:30 P.M. Wednesday through Sunday. Adults $2, ages 12 to 16 $1, under 12 years 50 cents. • *Old Town Opera House,* 4040 Twiggs Street, San Diego 92110, 298-0082. 200-seat horseshoe-shaped theater presenting historical dramas and comedies Thursday through Saturday at 8 P.M., Sunday at 2 P.M. Evening shows $6.50 adults, $5.50 senior citizens and children 12 years and under. Sunday matinees $4.50 adults, $3.50 seniors and kids. Reserve by leaving your name and number of tickets on phone-answering machine; pick up tickets at the box office on the day of the show. • *Heritage Park,* Juan and Harney streets, San Diego 92110, 298-8845. Open daily. Victorian buildings with shops and restaurant (see below). • *Villa Montezuma,* 1925 K Street, San Diego 92102, 239-2211. Ornate 1887 Victorian mansion open from 1 to 4:30 P.M. Sunday and Tuesday through Friday. Museum and headquarters of the San Diego Historical Society. Free; donations welcome.

LODGING   *Britt House,* 406 Maple Street, San Diego 92103, 234-2926; $63 to $95, including breakfast. Classy 9-room bed-and-breakfast in 1887 Victorian home just east of Balboa Park. Enjoy welcoming wine, fresh fruit, the book-filled parlor, and a grand piano. Also a sauna. Reserve well in advance. ● *The Cottage*, 3829 Albatross Street, San Diego 92103, 299-1564; $40, including continental breakfast. Two-night minimum on weekends. Private cottage in a quiet neighborhood with living room, kitchen, bedroom, and bath furnished in turn-of-the-century style. ● *Hotel San Diego*, 339 West Broadway, San Diego 92101, 234-0221 or California toll-free (800) 522-1500; $45. A 70-year-old downtown hotel brought back to life with $2-million renovation of guest and public rooms that range from Early American to more modern design. Period lobby, antique-decorated Country Kitchen Restaurant, and funky Juke Box Lounge take you back to bygone times. ● *Padre Trail Inn*, 4200 Taylor Street, San Diego 92110, 297-3291; $48 summer, $38 rest of the year. Coffee shop on premises. Closest motel to Old Town and Presidio Park.

DINING   *Casa de Bandini*, 2660 Calhoun Street in Old Town, San Diego, 297–8211. Open daily for lunch and dinner. Enjoy Mexican fare amid foliage and fountains in the patio of this handsome 1829 hacienda and former hotel. Mariachi music too. ● *Casa de Pedrorena*, 2616 San Diego Avenue in Old Town, San Diego, 291-4231. Breakfast is offered daily at this Mexican bakery and coffee house in a historic adobe. Also, enchiladas, burritos, tacos, and other Mexican favorites are served for lunch and dinner in the courtyard. ● *Casa de Pico*, 2754 Calhoun Street in Old Town's Bazaar del Mundo, San Diego, 296-3267. Open daily for all meals, Mexican style. Favorite for huge fruit margaritas and mariachis in the courtyard. Other restaurants in this international marketplace of 17 shops are *Lino's* with Italian dishes and *Hamburguesa* with you know what (and omelette brunch on weekends). ● *Casa Vallarta*, 2467 Juan Street in Old Town's Old San Diego Square, San Diego, 260-8124. Open daily for lunch and dinner. Champagne brunch on weekends. Full Mexican menu and outstanding views of Old Town and all of San Diego. ● *Tiffany's*, 2470 Heritage Park Row, in Heritage Park by Old Town, 291-7275. 1889 Victorian home open daily except Monday for all-you-can-eat dinners served family style. Champagne brunch on Sunday.

FOR MORE INFORMATION   Contact the Old San Diego Chamber of Commerce, 2479 Juan Street, San Diego 92110, 291-4903. Also, San Diego Convention and Visitors Bureau, 1200 Third Avenue, Suite 824, San Diego 92101, 232-3101.

San Diego
Part 2: The Southland's
Most Enchanting Harbor

When Juan Rodriguez Cabrillo discovered California almost four and a half centuries ago, he couldn't have picked a prettier spot to drop anchor. Today's explorers will discover that beautiful San Diego Bay still holds all sorts of attractions for sailors and landlubbers alike. During a weekend there you'll enjoy cruising in the scenic harbor, touring historic ships that now are maritime museums, visiting aboard a naval vessel, shopping in a re-created waterfront village, and dining on fish that's fresh from the sea.

Spend a full day enjoying those nautical delights, which are conveniently clustered along picturesque Harbor Drive bordering downtown San Diego. Then reserve time the following day to follow part of San Diego's Scenic Drive around the bay to Cabrillo National Monument at the tip of Point Loma, the most southwesterly peninsula of the U.S. mainland.

Get to San Diego and its Embarcadero from Los Angeles by driving south on Interstate 5, exiting on Front Street (Civic Center) to Broadway, then turning right to Harbor Drive. Check into the Holiday Inn–Embarcadero, just across the street from the harbor, or headquarter around the bay in one of the hotels on Harbor or Shelter islands, man-made resort havens and home for hundreds of pleasure boats.

In the morning, the best way to become acquainted with San Diego's vast and enchanting bay is to admire it from the deck of a tour boat. Along the Embarcadero at Broadway Pier you'll find the veteran San Diego Harbor Excursion company, which has been conducting sightseeing cruises since 1916. An hour-long cruise is available, but take the more extensive two-hour excursion that covers 25 miles and sails as far as the channel entrance at Point Loma.

Look back at the city's sparkling skyline as you pull away from the dock. You'll be sailing among all kinds of vessels in this busy port, home to the nation's largest naval armada, a tuna fleet, and dozens of sportfishing boats. En route to Ballast Point, where Cabrillo is believed to have first landed in 1542, your excursion boat mingles with yachts and sailboats going to and from their marina slips at Harbor and Shelter islands. Along the west shoreline is the navy's submarine base, and in the center of the harbor you'll see North Island Naval Air Station. After reaching Ballast Point, your narrated cruise continues around North Island and underneath the graceful Coronado Bay Bridge for a glimpse of the old and elegant Hotel del Coronado. Circling back to the Broadway Pier, the boat passes warships and tuna canneries. Open sun decks offer the best views, but the harbor excursion boats also have glass-enclosed lounge areas. There are snack bars aboard, too.

At the pier before or after your cruise, you can inspect the *Glorietta*, a ferryboat that went out of service when the Coronado Bay Bridge opened more than a decade ago. Today the boat is a gift shop, and the kids can play sea captain with the ship's controls in the wheelhouse. On weekend afternoons at the Broadway Pier, you're also welcome to visit a military ship when the navy holds open house for the public on one or more of its impressive vessels.

Nearby are other waterfront attractions, three historic ships that are floating museums. You can't miss the towering three-masted *Star of India*, a magnificent square-rigger that's the oldest merchant ship afloat. Launched from England in 1863, she eventually circumnavigated the globe 21 times with cargo and passengers. Another ship of the Maritime Museum Association that can be boarded at dockside is the *Medea*, a steam-powered luxury yacht originally built for a Scottish gentleman at the turn of the century. An equally elegant vessel, the *Berkeley*, served six decades as a passenger ferry between San Francisco and Oakland. Hire a cassette recorder that directs you on an informative taped tour of all three vessels.

As San Diego is home port for the nation's largest tuna fleet, you'll probably find some of the expensive oceangoing tuna boats tied up along the seawall just north along the Embarcadero. Look for the deep-sea fishermen mending their huge nets. The tuna seiners are close by a San Diego landmark, Anthony's Fish Grotto, where local folks and visitors have been enjoying tasty seafood since 1946. You have a choice of takeout or table service, and you can eat on the patio overlooking the water.

For other seafood dining spots, walk south along the waterfront to the Harbor Seafood Mart at the foot of Market Street, just beyond the commercial wharf, where fishing boats unload their daily catches. You can sample more delicacies of the sea at restaurants in this modern harbor facility or buy fresh fish to take home.

Around the corner is an even newer addition to San Diego's wonderful waterfront, Seaport Village, an attractive assortment of shops and restaurants on the bay front. The 14-acre complex opened in 1980 on the site of the former San Diego–Coronado ferryboat landing. Look for the five-story replica of a vintage West Coast lighthouse, home for a cookie maker instead of the coast guard. A boardwalk leads to it and more than 60 other shops in a trio of plazas, where the architecture takes you back to early Monterey, Victorian San Francisco, and old Mexico.

Some shop specialties are as distinctive as the store's name, such as Wee Willie Winkie (candles), Southpaw Shop (left-handed items), and Freudian Slip (lingerie). You'll also find shops devoted to lollipops, soap items, wooden puzzles, magic, T-shirts, artwork, antiques, and much more.

If the kids get restless while you're browsing for gifts, head to the kite shop and then the lawn of breezy Embarcadero Marine Park, which extends from the village into the bay. For other family fun, take a musical spin on the Broadway Flying Horses carrousel, an original Coney Island merry-go-round. The colorful wooden animals you'll ride were carved by hand nearly 80 years ago.

With more than a dozen eating spots, you won't go hungry at Seaport Village, and it's an ideal place to end an enjoyable afternoon with a leisurely dinner. For excellent seafood and the best bay views, get a window table at the Harbor House. At Papagayo the specialty is Mexican seafood, while the Jolly Roger is a favorite for family fare. The San Diego Pier Company, a rustic restaurant built over the water, features fresh fish broiled over mesquite.

Return the next day to the Embarcadero at the Broadway Pier and join San Diego's Scenic Drive heading north on Harbor Drive. All you have to do is follow the birds—white sea gulls painted on blue-and-gold signs that are posted every quarter mile with directional arrows. Follow the route as it curves around the bay from the downtown harbor area to land's end at Point Loma. Visitors to that rugged promontory, which is crowned by one of California's oldest lighthouses, are presented with sweeping vistas of the Pacific Ocean and San Diego Bay from Cabrillo National Monument.

As you go north on Harbor Drive, look for the Teledyne Ryan buildings, where Charles Lindbergh had his famed *Spirit of St. Louis* built for the first transatlantic solo flight from New York to Paris. Beyond on the right is San Diego International Airport, originally named Lindbergh Field. You'll also spot the high-rise resort hotels on Harbor Island, a peninsula created with material dredged from the bay when the channel was deepened for naval vessels.

Some of the navy's training facilities flank the Scenic Drive before it turns south on Scott Street, past the sportfishing boat docks, and turns onto Shelter Island, a submerged shoal that was earth-filled and is connected to the mainland by a causeway. You'll pass the island's attractive hotels, restaurants, and marinas before reaching the huge Friendship Bell, a gift from San Diego's sister city, Yokohama, Japan.

The sea-gull signs lead you back across the causeway and onto Talbot and Canon streets to the high bluff road, California 209, that goes down the middle of the Point Loma peninsula to land's end. You'll pass through Fort Rosecrans military reservation and national cemetery before reaching one of the state's most visited parks, Cabrillo National Monument. It's named for the first European explorer to visit the West Coast, Juan

Cabrillo, a Portuguese-born mariner who claimed the land for the king of Spain.

Start at the visitors center, where there are exhibits and different programs about Cabrillo and Pacific Coast explorations. Pick up a free guide map before walking around the outside terrace for a panoramic view of the busy bay and San Diego from more than 400 feet above sea level. Illustrated signs help identify the navy ships and aircraft that pass by almost constantly.

Nearby, another viewpoint is dominated by a statue of Cabrillo. It was carved in Portugal for the 1939 international exposition held in San Francisco and placed at the monument later. On clear days you can see Tijuana and beyond to the mountains in Mexico from here.

Stroll up to the old 1854 lighthouse, which has been restored and authentically refurnished by the National Park Service. A tape recording describes what life was like for the keeper and his family who lived there nearly a century ago. The rangers give visitors free recipes for some of the things made during the time the lighthouse was occupied, like Scotch soda bread and bread-and-butter pickles.

Because this lighthouse is located on such a high point, its beacon was often shrouded by fog. A new one was built near water level in 1891, and the coast guard continues to use it. You can see the current Point Loma lighthouse from another overlook, which is crowded with sightseers during winter months when the gray whales pass by on their annual migration from the Arctic to Baja. A tape recording at this observation station describes the event.

For some exercise and a closer look at native vegetation, walk down the mile-long Bayside Trail. A nature-guide leaflet is available at the visitors center. Heed the rangers' advice and be careful on the sandstone cliffs. On the ocean side, marine life can be observed in protected tide pools, where the viewing is best during low winter tides. Watch your step on the slippery rocks.

When your weekend along San Diego's waterfront is over, return from Point Loma on California 209 and follow it north to join Interstate 5 back to Los Angeles.

Round trip is about 265 miles.

San Diego Area Code: 619

SIGHTSEEING *San Diego Harbor Excursion,* Broadway Pier at Harbor Drive (or P.O. Box 751), San Diego 92112, 234-1111. Two-hour cruises of San Diego Bay depart daily at 10 A.M. and 2 P.M. Adults $6.50, children 3 through 11 years $3.25. One-hour cruises depart 11 A.M., 1, 2:45, and 4:15 P.M. Adults $4.25, children $2.15. Also, summertime adults-only cocktail cruises from 7 to 9 P.M. on Friday and Saturday nights. ● *Naval Ship Open House,* Broadway Pier at Harbor Drive, San Diego, 235-3534. Visitors are welcome aboard one or more military ships most weekends from 1 to 4 P.M. Free. ● *Maritime Museum Association,* 1306 North Harbor Drive on the Embarcadero, San Diego 92101, 234-9153. Three historic ships open daily 9 A.M. to 8 P.M. Combined admission costs adults $3, senior citizens and children 12 through 17 years $2, kids 6 through 12 years 50 cents, and family groups $6. Self-guided 45-minute tour tape rental $1. ● *Seaport Village,* 849 West Harbor Drive at end of Pacific Highway, San Diego 92101, 235-4013. Most shops open from 10 A.M. to 9 P.M. daily, to 10 P.M. on Friday and Saturday. Vintage Broadway Horses Carrousel rides cost 50 cents. Also theme cafes and four restaurants (see below). ● *Cabrillo National Monument,* at end of California 209 on Point Loma (or P.O. Box 6175), San Diego 92106, 293-5450. Visitors center and museum open daily from 9 A.M. to 5:15 P.M., to 7:45 P.M. in summer. Free. Also films and slide shows. Viewpoint for California gray whale migration in winter. Historic Old Point Loma Lighthouse is open to monument visitors too. Also see "Events" below. ● *H&M Landing,* 2803 Emerson Street, San Diego 92106, 222-1144 or (213) 626-8005. Sportfishing trips in local and Baja waters. Also departure point for 62-foot sailing yawl, *Jada,* that makes 3-hour bay and ocean cruises daily at 1 P.M. Adults $25, children 5 to 12 years $15, including drinks and snacks. Call 234-4383.

EVENTS   *Cabrillo Festival* is a week-long commemoration of Cabrillo's discovery of the West Coast, held annually to coincide with the date of his arrival, September 28. Highlight is the reenactment of Cabrillo's landing staged at Shelter Island. Most events are free. Call 293-5450 for schedule and more information.

LODGING   *Holiday Inn–Embarcadero,* 1355 North Harbor Drive, San Diego 92101, 232-3861; $75. High-rise hotel at the waterfront; reserve a harbor-view room. Also home for Anthony's Harborside restaurant. ● *Sheraton Harbor Island Hotels—East & West,* 1380 Harbor Island Drive on Harbor Island, San Diego 92101, 291-2900; $90 summer, $100 winter, suites from $150. San Diego's largest hostelry, with 1,100 rooms and suites. Wonderful bay and marina views. Full-service resort with lighted tennis courts, swimming pools, putting green, and sauna. Departure point for a brigantine square-rigger, the *Rendezvous,* that makes daily harbor cruises. Also evening entertainment and exceptional restaurant (see below). ● *Shelter Island Marina Inn,* 2051 Shelter Island Drive, San Diego 92106, 222-0561; $60. Comfortable Polynesian-style waterfront hotel. Views of bay and small-boat marina. ● *Half Moon Inn,* 1901 Shelter Island Drive on Shelter Island, San Diego 92106, 224-3411; $90. Tropical-style lodgings overlooking bay and yacht harbor. Putting green, shuffleboard, and Jacuzzi. Also wonderful restaurant (see below).

DINING   *Anthony's Fish Grotto,* 1360 Harbor Drive on the Embarcadero, San Diego, 232-5103. Open daily except Tuesday from 11:30 P.M. to 8:30 P.M. Seafood only. Harbor views and outdoor dining. Also *Anthony's Star of the Sea Room* at the same location, 232-7408. Gourmet seafood dining room open nightly for dinner only. Fancy silver-cart service. Jacket and tie for men. Reservations a must. ● Harbor Seafood Mart, Harbor Lane at the end of Market Street, has three places to eat. *Saccio's Fish Factory,* 585 Harbor Lane, San Diego, 232-0151. Fresh fish and other seafood daily for lunch and dinner. ● *People's Fish Company,* 565 Harbor Lane, San Diego, 239-8788. Fish and chips and other deep-fried and grilled fish specialties; also fresh seafood market. ● *Anthony's Seafood Mart,* 555 Harbor Lane, San Diego, 232-2933. Open daily for seafood lunches and dinners at harbor-view tables or for takeout. Also retail fish market. ● Seaport Village, on Harbor Drive at the end of Pacific Highway, has numerous cafes with international dishes, plus four restaurants. ● *Harbor House,* 831 West Harbor Drive, San Diego, 232-1411. Fish specialties for lunch and dinner with bay-front views. Upstairs lounge has limited luncheon menu midday, music and dancing in the evening. Also Sunday brunch. ● *Papagayo,* 861 West Harbor Drive, San Diego, 232-7581. Seafood prepared Latino style for lunch and dinner. Wonderful water views. ● *San Diego Pier Company,* West Harbor Drive, San Diego, 239-3968. Fresh fish dishes daily for lunch and dinner in an informal restaurant built over the water. ● *Jolly Roger,* 807 West Harbor Drive, San Diego, 233-4300. Open daily, breakfast, lunch, and dinner. Family restaurant with American fare. ● *Sheppard's* in Sheraton Harbor Island Hotel–East (see above). Gourmet dining nightly in country French setting. Jackets for men. Reservations a must. ● *Humphrey's* in the Half Moon Inn on Shelter Island (see above), 224-3577. Serves all three meals daily, plus Sunday brunch. Outdoor dining at lunch and dinner with harbor view. Fresh seafood specialties. Also a local favorite for happy hour.

FOR MORE INFORMATION   Contact the San Diego Convention and Visitors Bureau, Suite 824, 1200 Third Avenue, San Diego 92101, 232-3101.

San Diego
Part 3: Balboa Park
and Its World-Famous Zoo

San Diego has a city park that puts most municipal playgrounds to shame. Not only is Balboa Park a 1,074-acre recreational and botanical haven, it's the city's art and culture center. You'll discover a cluster of eight museums and art galleries displaying everything from dinosaur bones and spacecraft to Russian icons and Rembrandts. Concerts and plays delight visitors, too, and so does the world-famous San Diego Zoo, which blends into the park's verdant scenery.

San Diego's foresighted citizens established City Park in 1868, when the town had but 2,300 residents. Later renamed Balboa Park for the discoverer of the Pacific Ocean, it annually attracts three million local and out-of-town visitors. For the most relaxing weekend there, plan to spend your first day at the zoo and then come back the next day to enjoy the park's many other attractions.

Get to San Diego from Los Angeles by driving south on Interstate 5. Stay downtown in one of the city's outstanding hotels, the Westgate, or at any other of the numerous lodgings that are convenient to the centrally located park, which can be reached from the freeway by following the Zoo-Museum signs.

Head for Balboa Park early Saturday morning to be there at 9 A.M. (8:30 A.M. in summer), when the gates open to the San Diego Zoo's collection of nearly 4,000 mammals, reptiles, and birds. Not only is the wildlife more active and fun to watch, the zoo is less crowded earlier in the day. One thing that surprises first-time visitors is that the zoo is a paradise for plant lovers, too. In fact, its flowers, shrubs, and trees are worth more money than all the animals. Zoo officials put the plant price tag at $42 million, but they say many of their botanical specimens are irreplaceable.

The lush landscape that helps make the 100-acre San Diego Zoo such an enjoyable place to visit includes everything from orchids to cacti to redwoods. You'll find a garden of bromeliads, a canyon filled with ferns, and even a banana grove. Over 25,000 species of plants grow throughout the zoo, beautifying the once scrub-covered terrain that existed when the zoo began in 1916. Some plants are practical as well as pretty—they're fed to the animals.

A comfortable way to admire both the flora and fauna is to take an orientation tour of the extensive, hilly zoo. Board one of the open-sided double-decker buses near the entrance gate and you'll be treated to a 40-minute trip with an entertaining guide who identifies and talks about the wildlife as you ride along. The tour briefly covers about 80 percent of the animal displays as the bus follows a few miles of winding roads down canyons and up to the mesas. Many of the zoo's inhabitants live in roomy enclosures that have no bars but are guarded by moats. Look for long-billed kiwis from New Zealand, huge hippos from Africa, wild Przewalski's horses from Mongolia, and cuddly koalas from Australia. Choose an outside seat in the tour bus if you want to take pictures.

Afterward go on foot to watch the gorillas, apes, and playful monkeys. In nearby cages is a colorful collection of parrots and other birds; be sure to go inside the two walk-through aviaries. Equally fascinating is the reptile house, where a main attraction is the Komodo dragon, the world's largest lizard.

A newer multilevel exhibit of Southeast Asian primates and birds involves visitors in the rain forest environment shared by playful orangutans and rare langur monkeys. In this Heart of the Zoo display you'll also see the acrobatic siamang apes and hundreds of beautiful feathered creatures, including red-billed blue magpies and hornbills.

For an exciting overview of the zoo, ride the Skyfari aerial tramway that cruises six stories above the ground. Its high-flying gondolas run from the reptile house near the Children's Zoo across the treetops to Horn and Hoof Plaza, where the buffalo roam.

The animal nursery is a highlight of the Children's Zoo, which is built to the scale of four-year-olds but enjoyed by all ages. Through the windows you'll see young apes that have been rejected by their mothers and are diapered and bottle-fed just like human babies. Kids also like the small farm animals they can pet and the live exhibit that shows chicken eggs being laid, incubated, and hatched.

Free animal shows are presented daily in an outdoor amphitheater. Sometimes sea lions are the stars, or the audience gets to meet a few of the zoo's more exotic feathered and furry residents, like an emu and a cheetah. Show times are posted at the Wegeforth Bowl, where the animals perform.

The Jungle Bazaar, one of the zoo's gift shops, is worth a stop because of its authentic artifacts imported from all over Africa. In addition, you'll also discover books, toys, and other gifts from around the world. Hungry visitors can snack at food stands throughout the zoo, or dine in the Golden Eagle restaurant. There's a weekend buffet service outdoors at the Lagoon Terrace, and picnickers will find shaded areas with tables.

Sunday is an ideal day to explore the rest of Balboa Park, which began to blossom earlier in this century when it was selected as the site for the 1915–1916 Panama-California Exposition, an international fair celebrating the opening of the Panama Canal. After the exposition was over, townsfolk decided to preserve some of the exhibits and the temporary buildings that were constructed with Spanish Colonial and Mayan Indian motifs. Later they also kept buildings from the 1935–1936 California-Pacific Exposition, another early world's fair staged at the park. Some of those original structures and subsequent ones have been lost to decay and fire, notably the Old Globe Theatre and Aero-Space Museum, which burned in 1978. San Diegans, who are justly proud of their municipal park and maintain an ongoing restoration and building program, reopened the aerospace museum and theater in new quarters just three years after the conflagrations.

The best way to enjoy Balboa Park's many attractions is by foot. Dress casually and wear comfortable shoes for strolling among the gardens, fountains, and lush landscaping and visiting the museums and art galleries. You'll find several of these along El Prado (the promenade), a narrow street with exhibit buildings from the 1915–1916 exposition. Look for the fancy 200-foot California Tower, housing a carillon that chimes melodiously every quarter hour.

Midway on El Prado, at the southeast corner of Plaza de Panama, stop in the House of Hospitality for a map of the park to help plan your outing. Adjacent is Balboa Park's only restaurant, Cafe Del Rey Moro, serving full meals and takeout picnic lunches. Snack bars around the park also offer refreshments, or bring your own picnic.

As you'll discover, the peaceful park is especially active on weekends. Every Sunday afternoon visitors gather in front of the Spreckels Organ Pavilion for an outdoor concert on the 3,400-pipe organ, a gift of the wealthy sugar family. Ask at the House of Hospitality about any special events or shows in the park at the time of your visit.

One of Balboa Park's most popular attractions is the Reuben H. Fleet Space Theater and Science Center on El Prado. Visitors are awed by spectacular audiovisual shows on a huge hemisphere-shaped screen. Kids also love the scientific exhibits they can touch and work.

Across the way there are dinosaurs, whales, birds, plants, reptiles, shells, and more to see in the Natural History Museum. Nearby you can explore the Spanish Village—small cottages, built for the 1935–1936 exposition—that now houses nearly two dozen studios for artists and craftsmen. Visitors are welcome to watch and buy.

Returning to El Prado, visit the Timken Art Gallery to see the works of old masters and early American artists, as well as Russian icons. More of the old masters, along with Asian art and a sculpture gallery, are next door at the outstanding San Diego Museum of Art.

Balboa Park is a haven for horticulturists. Even visitors without a green thumb are attracted by the 500 species of tropical and subtropical plants inside the Botanical Building. This immense greenhouse is the iron framework of a turn-of-the-century railroad station that has been covered with redwood lath. In front is a reflecting pool, the Lily Pond, once used as a swimming pool by World War II sailors recovering at the nearby naval hospital.

On the opposite side of El Prado, in the rebuilt Casa de Balboa, you'll find the Hall of Champions, which is filled with sports memorabilia and honors San Diego–area heroes such as boxer Archie Moore and swimmer Florence Chadwick. West on El Prado in a building called the House of Charm, the San Diego Art Institute displays and sells the work of local artists.

A few steps farther west, by the carillon tower, visit the Museum of Man, featuring Indian cultures of the Americas and an excellent exhibit about human birth, "The Wonder of Life." Behind the museum is the Simon Edison Centre for the Performing Arts, which includes the Old Globe Theatre, Cassius Carter Centre Stage, and the Festival Stage, an outdoor amphitheater. Check the playbills to see what's on during your visit. In summer this is the home of San Diego's acclaimed National Shakespeare Festival.

Stroll past the organ pavilion to Pan-American Plaza, stopping along the way at the House of Pacific Relations. Sunday afternoons on the lawn of this complex of cottages you can watch folk dances performed by various nationalities.

At the end of the plaza you'll see the Aerospace Historical Center, the refurbished 1935 Ford Building that's new quarters for the original fire-devastated Aero-Space Museum. All sorts of aircraft are on display, including a replica of Charles Lindbergh's *Spirit of St. Louis,* the plane that was built in San Diego for the first solo flight across the Atlantic. In addition, an international hall of fame honors heroes of aviation and space.

When your weekend is over, return to Los Angeles the way you arrived, via Interstate 5.

Round trip is about 254 miles.

San Diego Area Code: 619

SIGHTSEEING   *San Diego Zoo,* in Balboa Park via Park Boulevard and Zoo Drive, San Diego 92112, 234-3153. Open daily from 8:30 A.M. to 6 P.M. July through Labor Day, from 9 A.M. to 5 P.M. after Labor Day through October and March through June, and from 9 A.M. to 4 P.M. November through February. Adults $4.95, children 3 through 15 years $1.50. Combination tickets also available that include attractions with additional fees: guided bus tour, Skyfari ride, and Children's Zoo. Bus tour costs $2.25 for adults, $1.75 for children 3 through 15 years. Skyfari ride costs adults 75 cents one way, $1.25 round trip; children 50 cents one way, 75 cents round trip. Children's Zoo entry is 50 cents for everyone; under age 3 free. ● *Balboa Park,* via Park Boulevard to attractions along El Prado and near Pan-American Plaza. ● *House of Hospitality,* 239-0512. An information center open daily from 9 A.M. to 4 P.M. ● *Reuben H. Fleet Space Theater and Science Center,* 238-1168. Open daily from 9:45 A.M. until at least 9:30 P.M. (depending on evening programs). Adults $4.25, senior citizens, $2.75, children 5 through 15 years $2.50. ● *Natural History Museum,* 232-3821. Open 10 A.M. to 4:30 P.M. daily. Adults $2, children under 16 years free. No charge on Tuesday. ● *Spanish Village Art Center,* 233-9050. Most studios open daily from 11 A.M. to 4 P.M. Free. ● *Timken Art Gallery,* 239-5548. Open daily from 10 A.M. to 4:30 P.M. except Sunday from 1:30 P.M. Closed during September. Free. ● *San Diego Museum of Art,* 232-7931. Open daily except Monday from 10 A.M. to 5 P.M. Adults $2, senior citizens $1.50, students 13 through 18 years $1, children 6 through 12 years 50 cents. Free on Tuesday. ● *Botanical Building* open daily except Friday and holidays from 10 A.M. to 4:30 P.M. Free. ● *Hall of Champions,* 234-4542. Open daily from 10 A.M. to 4:30 P.M. except Sunday from noon. Adult donation $1, children 50 cents. ● *Museum of Man,* 239-2001. Open daily from 10 A.M. to 4:30 P.M. Adults $1.50, children 6 through 16 years 25 cents. Free on Wednesday. ● *Simon Edison Centre for the Performing Arts,*

239-2255. Plays usually presented year round in the evenings on at least one of the center's three stages: Old Globe Theatre, Cassius Carter Centre Stage, and the Festival Stage. Also weekend matinees. Call for current playbill and ticket information. ● *House of Pacific Relations,* 234-0739. Sunday afternoon open house March through October featuring native music and folk dancing. Free. ● *Aerospace Historical Center,* 234-8291. Open 10 A.M. to 4:30 P.M. daily. Adults $2.50, children 6 through 17 years $1. Free on Tuesday.

EVENTS *National Shakespeare Festival,* staged annually from mid-June to mid-September at the Simon Edison Centre for the Performing Arts in Balboa Park. Nightly performances except Monday. Call 239-2255.

LODGING *The Westgate,* 1055 Second Avenue at C Street, San Diego 92101, 238-1818; $94. Live in eighteenth-century European elegance in San Diego's award-winning downtown hotel. Persian carpets, antique furniture, gilt-framed paintings, and crystal chandeliers contribute to its classy atmosphere. View rooms on upper floors of this 20-story building. No swimming pool, but guests have privileges at private health club. Valet parking. Also intimate Plaza Bar and exquisite dining room (see below). ● See pages 101, 107, and 117 for alternate accommodations.

DINING *Golden Eagle Restaurant,* in the San Diego Zoo, Balboa Park, 231-1515. Open daily 9 A.M. to 3 P.M. (longer in summer) for breakfast and lunch. American fare. No reservations. ● *Cafe Del Rey Moro,* 1549 El Prado, in Balboa Park, San Diego 92101, 234-8511. Open daily for lunch and dinner except lunch only on Monday. Also Sunday champagne brunch. Reservations recommended. Fine food and cocktails indoors amid Spanish-Moorish decor or outdoors on the terraces. Also box lunches to take out for a picnic elsewhere in the park. ● *Fontainebleau Room* in the Westgate hotel (see above). Lunch and dinner daily except dinner only on Saturday. Fine French cuisine and white-glove service. Expensive, but a refreshing change from a day of snack food at the zoo or Balboa Park. Reservations recommended.

FOR MORE INFORMATION Contact the San Diego Zoo, 234-3153 or 231-1515. Also contact Balboa Park, 239-0512 or 236-5717. The San Diego Convention and Visitors Bureau is in Suite 824, 1200 Third Avenue, San Diego 92101, 232-3101.

San Diego
Part 4: Aquatic Action
in Mission Bay Park

What's so attractive about hundreds of acres of marsh and mud flats? Nothing. But add some determined townsfolk, nearly $60 million, 20 years for dredging and development—then you've got one of the West Coast's most beautiful aquatic parks and resort areas. San Diegans are rightly proud of their Mission Bay Park, less than 10 minutes from the downtown area. The former eyesore and mosquito breeding ground has become a popular getaway spot for day outings and more extensive holidays.

Spreading from Mission Beach on the ocean inland to Interstate 5, the 46,000-acre aquatic playground is perfect for water sports activities. You can swim, sail, water ski, wind surf, fish, and more. All types of boats can be rented—pedal, paddle, power, or sail—or bring your own (public launch ramps are free). There's even a stern-wheeler that makes evening cruises along the park's scenic waterways.

Mission Bay Park has land activities, too. You'll find miniature and par-58 executive golf courses, paths for biking, jogging, or walking, and numerous places to picnic. The park also is the location of Sea World, an aquatic wonderland that features three dozen exciting marine-life exhibits and shows, including Shamu the Whale and the one-of-a-kind Penguin Encounter.

To reach Mission Bay Park from Los Angeles, drive south to San Diego on Interstate 5. Exit west on Clairemont Drive/Mission Bay Drive and stop at the visitors information center to get a map and more details about the park's features and facilities, including lodging if you haven't made advance reservations.

Make your weekend headquarters in one of Mission Bay's six resort hotels, like the Vacation Village, Hyatt Islandia, or San Diego Hilton. Or settle down at a tent or RV site on the north shore at Campland on the Bay or the De Anza Harbor Resort. You'll enjoy a variety of restaurants and nightclubs at the park resorts, too. Since Mission Bay Park is San Diego's major recreation area, it's smart to reserve a room well in advance, especially in the summer months.

Plan to spend the first day of your weekend visiting Sea World, the 80-acre oceanarium that's considered one of the state's most popular tourist attractions, second only to Disneyland for family entertainment. It's in the heart of Mission Bay Park, marked by a revolving sightseeing tower. The biggest and best known of its half dozen marine shows stars Shamu, a two-ton trained killer whale, but a more recent addition to Sea World almost makes that amazing waterborne mammal play second fiddle. His show-biz competition hardly equals Shamu's total size and weight, and they're not even as intelligent. But who need smarts when you're born with an adorable face and all dressed up for a party. For a fascinating unrehearsed show, it's hard to beat a colony of comical penguins.

Until 1983 about the only place you could see these flightless birds was in their freezing native habitats south of the Antarctic Circle. Then the folks at Sea World spent $7 million to create Penguin Encounter, a little polar region in sunny San Diego that makes 300 penguins feel at home— all behind a 100-foot-long window so you can observe their unusual lifestyle. As far as the emperor, king, Adelie, and other penguin species are concerned, it's paradise.

Behind the glass, where the bacteria-free air is kept below freezing and fresh layers of crushed ice are blown over the polarlike compound, you'll see the birds toddle to the edge of an artificial ice shelf and dive into a deep, clear-water pool for a swim. Then they pop back onto shore to dine on fresh fish, court each other with a wing-flapping love dance, or take turns sitting on eggs in the nesting season. Television cameras can zoom in on any special action, such as an egg hatching or chick being fed by its parents, and bring you a close-up in the viewing gallery.

Ride the moving sidewalk to survey this Antarctic exhibit, then go to the upper observation level to study and enjoy all the penguins' activities. Illuminated illustrations help you identify the seven species on display; try to find the funny-looking rockhopper and macaroni penguins with their orange and yellow head feathers. You'll see another species on display outdoors, the temperate Humboldt penguin, an endangered species that lives along the coast of Chile and Peru. A third display area features Arctic birds of the alcid family—puffins, murres, and auklets—which are underwater swimmers like penguins but also can fly.

Penguin Encounter is but one of many exhibits and shows that put the marine bird and animal kingdoms in the spotlight at Sea World. Not to be missed is its superstar, Shamu, who shares his performing tank in an amphitheater with a pair of smaller killer whales, Namu and Kandu. Don't sit in the front rows unless you want a bath from the whales as they splash on command and with precision in a series of jumps and water ballets. Sometimes they even take their wet-suited trainers along for the ride.

The shows last about 20 minutes and are staggered throughout the day, so you'll have plenty of time to see them all, including one featuring bottle-nosed dolphins and a pilot whale and another with some entertaining sea lions and a walrus. An ongoing underwater performance by beluga (white) whales is highlighted by training sessions and ballets by graceful girls wearing scuba tanks. Animals are absent from two other shows where Japanese "ama" girls in traditional costumes dive for oysters bearing pearls, and computers choreograph fountains of water, colored lights, and music. In summer, musical stage shows also are presented several times during the day.

This lushly landscaped theme park also hosts a colorful collection of waterfowl, such as scarlet ibis, macaws, Caribbean flamingos, and harlequin ducks. Scattered around the grounds are all sorts of educational exhibits that are entertaining as well. Kids like to play with the anemones, sea stars, and other creatures in the shallow man-made tide pool. They can feed whiskered walruses and sleek sea lions and even pet some friendly dolphins. Also fascinating are the live shark exhibit and numerous aquariums filled with hundreds of exotic fish from all over the world.

Pace yourself during the day so the family doesn't get too tired. You'll find snack bars throughout Sea World, as well as a sit-down dining pavilion with cocktail service. For a change of pace and a more extensive menu, take the ground shuttle or skyride to the park's Atlantis restaurant, nearby on a cove of Mission Bay. If the kids need to let off steam, head to Sea World's Cap'n Kids' World, a fun-filled playground for ages 4 to 14. They'll love jumping on air mattresses, punching foam-filled bags, and wading through a sea of plastic balls. Many of the park's exhibits and shows have corporate sponsors, but all meet Sea World's high standards for education and entertainment. For a peek at its behind-the-scenes activities, including marine research projects, join a 90-minute guided tour of the park.

On Sunday, plan to relax at your resort hotel or elsewhere in the park. For sunbathing, swimming, and shore fishing, select any spot along Mission Bay's 27 miles of beaches. Boaters have designated areas for their particular craft, which means more fun and better water safety. A 1½-mile course is reserved for water skiers, with special pickup and landing areas. Powerboats can race over a marked 3-mile course without fear of running into sailboats, which keep to the western areas of the bay. Boats of all types are available for rent at Mission Bay's resorts and Seaforth Boat Rental in Quivira Basin. Deep-sea sportfishing boats leave daily from Islandia Sportfishing and Seaforth Sportfishing, also in Quivira Basin.

On one of the previous nights you'll enjoy sailing aboard a replica of an old-time riverboat that plies Mission Bay on a musical party cruise. A band plays on the second deck of the *Bahia Belle,* where there's a dance floor and cocktail lounge. The paddle-wheeler calls at the Bahia, Catamaran, and Vacation Village hotels on its hour-long excursions Friday and Saturday evenings (and nightly except Monday in July and August).

Exercise-minded visitors will appreciate the miles of scenic and level pathways in Mission Bay Park, which are ideal for jogging and bicycling. (Rental bikes are available at any of the resort hotels.) Golfers enjoy the 18-hole executive Mission Bay Golf Course at the north edge of the park, while fishermen find quiet bays and lure bass, perch, croaker, and flounder onto their hooks. The grassy areas along the bay shore are pleasant places to toss a Frisbee, fly a kite, or send a model airplane soaring into the sky.

When your relaxing weekend at San Diego's Mission Bay comes to an end, return to Los Angeles the way you came, via Interstate 5.

Round trip is about 240 miles.

San Diego Area Code: 619

SIGHTSEEING   *Sea World,* 1720 South Shores Road in Mission Bay off Sea World Drive, San Diego 92109, 222-6363 or 224-3562. Open daily from 9 A.M. to dusk. Adults $10.95, senior citizens and children 3 through 11 years $7.95, including all shows and exhibits. Also money-saving annual passes for frequent visitors. Guided tour, scenic skytower ride, and skyride to the Atlantis restaurant are extra. Free parking. • *Mission Bay Golf Course,* 2702 North Mission Bay Drive, San Diego 92109, 273-1221. Weekend greens fee $6, weekdays $5.50. • *Bahia Belle* stern-wheeler cruise boat departs hourly from 7:30 P.M. to 12:30 P.M. from Bahia Hotel (see below), with calls at Catamaran Hotel and Vacation Village. Adults $3.50, children under 14 years $2.50. • *Seaforth Boat Rentals,* 1641 Quivira Road, San Diego 92109, 223-1681. Sailboats, ski boats, rowboats, and runabouts by the hour, half day, or full day. • *Seaforth Sportfishing,* 1717 Quivira Road, San Diego 92109, 224-3383. Half-day deep-sea fishing departures daily at 6 A.M. and 12:30 P.M., plus twilight trips in summer at 6 P.M. Also whale-watching excursions in winter. • *Islandia Sportfishing,* 1551 West Mission Bay Drive, San Diego 92109, 222-1164. By the Hyatt Islandia (see below). Deep-sea fishing trips on same schedule as above. Also whale-watching cruises in winter.

LODGING   *Vacation Village Hotel,* 1404 West Vacation Road, San Diego 92109, 274-4630 or California toll-free (800) 274-4630; $76. Popular resort on Vacation Isle in the heart of Mission Bay with 450 cottage-style accommodations amid tropical landscaping. Tennis courts, 5 swimming pools, sandy beach, private marina with boat rentals, and fine restaurants (see below). A unique resort that's a favorite of families. • *Hyatt Islandia,* 1441 Quivira Road, San Diego 92109, 224-3541; $78. A towering 17-story hotel with 350 rooms and suites overlooking Mission Bay. Close to Sea World, Quivira Basin sportfishing docks, and Marina Village shops and restaurants. Also marina-view restaurant and lounge. • *San Diego Hilton,* 1775 East Mission Bay Drive, San Diego 92109, 276-4010; $88. Beach and tennis resort at east edge of Mission Bay with beach, boat, and bike rentals, popular night spot and restaurant (see below). • Other resort hotels on Mission Bay are *Bahia Resort Hotel,* 998

West Mission Bay Drive, San Diego 92109, 488-0551; *Catamaran Hotel*, 3999 Mission Boulevard, San Diego 92109, 488-1081; and *Dana Quality Inn*, 1710 West Mission Bay Drive, San Diego 92109, 222-6440.

CAMPING   *Campland on the Bay*, 2211 Pacific Beach Drive, San Diego 92109, 274-6260. 42 acres on Mission Bay with 728 sites, most with hookups. Boat and bike rentals. $12 to $18 for up to 5 persons June through September, $8 to $18 rest of the year. ● *De Anza Harbor Resort*, 2727 De Anza Road, San Diego 92109, 273-3211. 80 acres on mission Bay adjacent to golf course. 255 full-hookup sites. $19 to $23 for up to 4 persons June through September, $11 to $14 rest of the year.

DINING   *The Atlantis*, 2595 Ingraham Street, San Diego, 224-2434. Sea World's fancy restaurant, also reached by the skyride or free shuttle service from the park. Open daily for buffet and à la carte lunches, and dinners by candlelight, with Mission Bay views. Seafood specialties. Also Sunday brunch. ● *Bayview Retaurant* in Vacation Village Hotel (see above). Delightful dinner spot overlooking the water. Excellent continental menu plus fresh catch of the day. Entertainment and dancing in the adjoining Bay Lounge. ● *Casina Valadier*, 4445 Lamont Street, in Pacific Beach just north of Mission Bay, San Diego, 270-8650. Homemade pasta, veal dishes, and other outstanding Italian fare. Pleasant dining nightly except Sunday and Monday. Jackets required. Make reservations. ● *Tradewinds* in San Diego Hilton (see above). Dinner nightly amid nautical decor with windows on the bay. Seafood specialties. ● *Mercedes Room* in the Bahia Hotel (see above). Bay-view dining nightly nearby the restaurant's namesake, a 1902 Mercedes car. Beef and lobster specialties. Also Sunday brunch. ● *Salmon House*, 1970 Quivira Way in Marina Village, San Diego, 223-2234. Lunch and dinner daily featuring salmon and other seafood barbecued over a wood fire. Also prime ribs. Brunch on Sundays. ● *Windrose*, 1935 Quivira Way in Marina Village, San Diego, 223-2335. Varied menu for lunch and dinner daily, plus Sunday champagne brunch. Overlooking the marina. ● *Dos Amigos*, 1904 Quivira Way in Marina Village, San Diego, 223-8061. Mexican food and plenty of fun for lunch and dinner daily, champagne brunch on Sundays. Marina views from indoors or on the patio.

FOR MORE INFORMATION   Contact the Mission Bay Park Visitor Information Center, 2688 East Mission Bay Drive, San Diego 92109, 276-8200. Open daily 9 A.M. to dusk. Also, the San Diego Convention and Visitors Bureau, Suite 824, 1200 Third Avenue, San Diego 92101, 232-3101.

Escape to the Del and Coronado "Island"

A century ago, when Coronado was just a haven for small game, two wealthy visitors from the East Coast came to hunt rabbits. They left with the idea of building a splendid seaside resort that would attract investors to the undeveloped peninsula. Today the Hotel del Coronado is a remarkable reminder of the opulent hotels that once graced the West Coast and have since succumbed to fires and old age. And the peninsula is now a wealthy residential community and restful resort town that's perfect for a relaxing weekend.

Here you can escape the hustle and bustle of Los Angeles (or San Diego, for that matter). Although connected to the mainland by a graceful bridge, as well as a narrow neck of land called the Silver Strand, Coronado offers the quiet isolation of an island—and it's often called just that. With the blue Pacific on its front doorstep and handsome San Diego at the back, Coronado presents super-scenic views from any place along its shoreline (although the northwest end is a U.S. Naval Air Station and off limits to civilians). Besides discovering beautiful beaches and some pleasant places to dine and shop, you can play golf on a waterfront course, sail in pretty Glorietta Bay, and take a historical tour to view Coronado's charming homes.

To get to Coronado from Los Angeles, drive south on Interstate 5 to San Diego and follow the Coronado exit road, which leads across a soaring boomerang-shaped toll bridge to the peninsula. The $48-million bridge replaced the ferries that were the major route to Coronado until 1969. Continue from the blue San Diego–Coronado Bay Bridge to the main thoroughfare, Orange Avenue. Turn left and follow this attractive boulevard through the town shopping area to your weekend headquarters, the unmistakable Hotel del Coronado. You'll easily spot the red roof, turrets, cupolas, and Victorian gingerbread of this venerated hotel, which has been designated a city, state, and national landmark.

On Friday evening or Saturday morning, take time to explore the Hotel del Coronado, which is as much a museum as it is one of Southern California's best-known resorts. After all, not many hostelries in the state have been in business since 1888. And even fewer have retained a Victorian elegance while incorporating the modern amenities that today's travelers expect.

Two additions have been made to the hotel in recent years, but enter through the main entrance to the original building and you'll be taken back to the previous century. The busy lobby is of dark oak highlighted by a hand-cut Bavarian crystal chandelier. In one corner you'll see the original Otis birdcage elevator, which still services the hotel's five stories. Look around the Crown Room, praised by architects for its unsupported ceiling of Oregon sugar pine that was assembled with wooden pegs instead of nails. On Sunday return to this vast dining room to enjoy the Del's popular buffet brunch.

Although still very fashionable with the so-called smart set, the huge hostelry also caters to convention groups. For the most romantic weekend, be certain to reserve one of the original hotel rooms—unless you prefer more modern accommodations in the newer towers or pool buildings.

As you stroll around the hotel's extensive grounds, don't miss the flower-filled courtyard, a favorite setting for weddings. Overhead are the room balconies, which extend for a third of a mile around each floor. Outside the entrance to the Prince of Wales Grille, the Del's premium restaurant and a sophisticated choice for your first-night dinner, you'll see the last of the old fire wagons that guarded the immense all-wood building until room sprinklers were installed in 1913.

If it's unoccupied, peek into the ballroom, site of banquets for the 10 U.S. Presidents who have been guests at the hotel. In corridors on the basement level, walk along the Hall of History, where displays relate more of the hotel's enchanting past. Included here is a guest room with the original furnishings. For the most comprehensive tour of the hotel, rent a recorder at the lobby gift shop and take an audio tape tour narrated by the late actor Hans Conried.

Many well-to-do Easterners built winter homes on Coronado early in this century, and you'll enjoy seeing their varied architecture on a self-guided tour that can occupy several hours. Just follow the *Coronado Historical Tour Guide to Eighty-six Homes and Sites,* published by the Coronado Historical Association and available at the Victorian Corner shop in the Del.

One mansion not to miss was built in 1908 for sugar magnate John Spreckels and later occupied by newspaper-syndicate owner Ira Copley. The home is now the attractive Glorietta Bay Inn, just opposite the Hotel del Coronado and overlooking Glorietta Bay. If you can't get into the Del or prefer more intimate surroundings, you should stay here. At least peek into the lobby of this 100-room lodging, where a marble staircase with solid brass railings leads to the mansion's second-floor view rooms and suites.

Nearby at the Glorietta Bay Marina on Strand Way, rent a boat to sightsee, sail, or fish in big and beautiful San Diego Bay. Or just cruise quietly around pretty little Glorietta Bay in a self-powered paddleboat. At sunset enjoy wonderful views over the water with drinks and dinner at the Chart House restaurant, a Victorian-style boat house that once belonged to the Hotel del Coronado. Or walk around the corner to dine on seafood at the Brigantine. Other recommended restaurants nearby are La Avenida, Chez Loma, and Chu Dynasty.

On Sunday follow Glorietta Boulevard from the bay for a drive along the Coronado Municipal Golf Course, a lush 18-hole, par-72 course with shoreline scenery that can be distracting to your game. Also drive up Orange Avenue to its northern end, formerly the terminus for the ferryboats from San Diego and still a great spot for a panoramic view of that city's ever-growing skyline. The area is destined for condominium development, but access to its scenic shoreline is assured. You'll take the best photos on weekends, when all sorts of colorful pleasure craft are crisscrossing San Diego Bay. Nearby you can enjoy brunch or lunch at Bula's Pub and Eatery or the Mexican Village.

Midway on Orange Avenue in Spreckels Park, visit with area artists and craftsmen who display their work the first and third Sundays of every month during summer. (Another delight at the park is Sunday band concerts, beginning at 6 P.M., that take you back to pleasant summertime evenings of yesteryear.) Spend the remainder of your lazy day at the beach, browse in the cute shops along Orange Avenue, or play a few sets of tennis at the Del or on Coronado's public courts.

Return to Los Angeles via the bay bridge to rejoin Interstate 5 north. Or head south along the ocean on Silver Strand Boulevard, California 75, across a spit of land that was once laid with train tracks to bring building materials and then guests to the Del. It goes past the navy's amphibious base and a state beach park to Imperial Beach, where the road becomes Palm Avenue and meets Interstate 5.

Round trip is about 250 miles.

Coronado Area Code: 619

SIGHTSEEING   *San Diego–Coronado Bay Bridge,* round-trip toll collected incoming direction only; $1.20. • *Hotel del Coronado,* 1500 Orange Avenue, 435-6611. Visitors as well as hotel guests are welcome to take their own tour of this Victorian landmark; see the Hall of History on basement level at any time, as well as photo gallery outside the Del Deli. Enjoy it more with an audio tape tour obtained at the Lobby Shop from 8 A.M. to dusk; adults $2, students under age 18 and seniors over 65 $1. • *Coronado Touring,* 827 B Avenue, 435-5993. A guided one-hour eight-block stroll past oceanfront mansions, Victorian cottages, and quiet parks; $2.50 per person. Departs 11 A.M. Tuesday, Thursday, and Saturday from Glorietta Bay Inn opposite Hotel del Coronado. • *Coronado Golf Course,* off Glorietta Boulevard, 435-3121. Greens fee $6.50; make reservations. • *Glorietta Bay Marina,* 1715 Strand Way, 435-5203. Sailboat, outboard, and paddleboat rentals; closed Monday and Tuesday in

winter. ● *Coronado Tennis Center,* 1501 Glorietta Boulevard, 435-1616.
10 municipal courts available from 9:30 A.M. to 6 P.M. daily. Free.

LODGING   Coronado ZIP code: 92118 ● *Hotel del Coronado,* 1500
Orange Avenue, 435-6611. A very special resort with wide sandy beach,
seven tennis courts, heated swimming pools, health spa, excellent restaurants, shops. Rooms in original hotel are more interesting and less expensive than those in newer complex: $68 to $99 versus $99 to $140; lanais
and suites also available. Two-night minimum on weekends. ● *Glorietta
Bay Inn,* 1630 Glorietta Boulevard, 435-3101. Charming rooms and
suites in 1908 Edwardian mansion, with most accommodations in newer
guest wings; mansion rooms $58, others $48. ● *El Cordova Hotel,* 1351
Orange Avenue, 435-4131. Remodeled mansion near the Del, bay, and
beach; $40. ● *La Avenida Motel,* 1301 Orange Avenue, 435-3191. Pleas-
ant accommodations in central location; $45.

DINING   *Crown Room,* Hotel del Coronado (see above), 435-6611.
Magnificent main dining room of grand hotel. Eat here at least once. It's
worth standing in line for pricy Sunday brunch, served from 9 A.M. to 2
P.M.; no reservations. Early Dinner Special served from 5 to 6:45 P.M. is
a Del bargain: choice of three entrees, soup or salad, dessert, and drink
for about $10. *Prince of Wales Grille,* Hotel del Coronado (see above),
435-6611. Roast beef and other British fare is served with style in hotel's
gourmet dining room; dinner only. Wake up with a continental breakfast
in the *Lobby Bar.* ● *La Avenida Restaurant,* 1301 Orange Avenue,
435-6262. Favorite of local folks for four decades; also noted for murals
by Mexican artist. Opens daily at 8 A.M. for tasty family fare in its coffee
shop and dining rooms; try Jack's romaine salad. ● *Bula's Pub and Eatery,* 170 Orange Avenue, 435-4466. Informal place with patio for lunch,
dinner, and excellent Sunday brunch. Diverse menu includes calamari,
ratatouille, and chicken Marsala; Pavlova is a fruit-and-meringue dessert
treat. ● *Mexican Village Restaurant,* 120 Orange Avenue, 435-1822.
Busy daily for lunch and dinner, evening entertainment; Mexican pizza is
special. ● *Chez Loma,* 1132 Loma Avenue, 435-0661. When you want to
splurge on fine French food for lunch or dinner (except Mondays); in
Victorian home. ● *The Brigantine,* 1333 Orange Avenue, 435-4166. Casual spot for fresh swordfish and other seafood; dinner nightly, lunch
weekdays. ● *Chu Dynasty,* 1033 B Avenue, 435-5300. Excellent Man-
darin fare for lunch (except Sundays) and dinner. ● *Chart House,* 1701
Strand Way, 435-0155. Steak and seafood with Glorietta Bay views; dinner only.

FOR MORE INFORMATION   Contact the Coronado Chamber of
Commerce, 720 Orange Avenue (or P.O. Box 396), Coronado 92118,
435-9260. Open weekdays 10 A.M. to 5 P.M.

South of the Border
Part 1: Tijuana and Rosarito

Margaritas and mariachis—for some people those are reason enough to spend a weekend in Mexico. But there's much more to savor south of the border than exotic cocktails and exciting music. Delicious food, bargain shopping, first-class accommodations, friendly people, and a different life-style are just a few of the other enticements. And for anyone in the Los Angeles area, a Mexican weekend doesn't take much effort or planning. Just drive south a couple of hours on the freeway to the Mexican state of Baja California, where you'll discover a trio of favorite tourist destinations: Tijuana, Rosarito, and Ensenada.

U.S. citizens don't need a passport or tourist card to enter northern Baja, just some identification such as a driver's license. Also, U.S. dollars can be spent legally in Baja without being exchanged for Mexican pesos. And don't worry about a language barrier, because many of the Mexicans you'll meet speak English.

Unless you're going on a three-day holiday, plan a weekend just for Tijuana, Baja's biggest city, and Rosarito, the popular Pacific beach town that's only a 25-minute drive beyond. Save Ensenada for another time (see "South of the Border, Part 2").

Drive south from Los Angeles on Interstate 5 past San Diego to the U.S.-Mexico border. Border officials won't stop you until the return trip, when you reenter the U.S. Just before or beyond the border, pause at one of the special insurance offices to buy Mexican auto insurance for the length of your stay; U.S. policies aren't valid here if you have an accident.

Follow the *Centro* signs from the border to downtown Tijuana (locals say *tee-wah-nah*) and drive down the main thoroughfare, Avenida Revolucion. Turn left on Calle 7 (7th Street) to the guarded parking lot at the Fronton Palacio and join the enthusiastic spectators who gather there nightly except Thursdays to watch and bet on the ancient Basque ball game, jai alai (*hi-lie*). In the same building is TiaJuana Tilly's, a popular drinking and eating spot where you can enjoy a dinner of barbecued ribs, the house specialty, or choose from a full menu of Mexican dishes. For quieter dining, leave the jai alai palace and walk across Avenida Revolucion to Pedrins, where the seafoods of Mexico are featured.

After spending the night in one of Tijuana's better lodgings, such as the Hotel Lucerna, El Presidente, or El Conquistador, return downtown to Avenida Revolucion to browse or buy in the many shops that are filled with imported as well as Mexican goods.

The once-raucous border town, now with a population exceeding one million, has acquired some big-city refinements in the past few years, and previous visitors especially will be surprised by the new look of Tijuana's main street. After all utility wires were put underground, nine blocks of Avenida Revolucion were attractively repaved with bricks. Its sidewalks were doubled in width and planted with trees, and now even sport an open-air cafe. To make pedestrians feel even more welcome, parking is banned and local buses and taxis are prohibited.

Stroll along the beautified avenue between Calles 1 and 9 (1st and 9th streets) for Mexican handicrafts and foreign items at reasonable prices, and also seek out its alleylike shopping arcades. Be certain to bargain in the souvenir stores, but remember in the boutiques and better shops that prices are fixed. Don't be confused by dollar signs on price tags; if the amount is preceded by "M.N.$," the price is in Mexican pesos.

For quality Mexican-made goods, visit the Tolan folk art shop across from the jai alai building and the three government-sponsored craft stores—Fonart, Cariem, Artesanias—that also are along Avenida Revolucion. Next door to Tolan you can watch glass-blowing artisans at work at the Inco shop and factory. The street hosts a number of restaurants, too, including one in the Hotel Caesar, where it is claimed the Caesar salad originated.

Go a few blocks east from Avenida Revolucion to reach another main boulevard, Paseo de Los Heroes, and a newer shopping destination, Plaza Rio Tijuana, a huge, covered complex of over 100 stores in the city's reclaimed riverbed. You'll find bargains in both the small shops and major department stores like Dorian's and Comercial Mexicana. Also tempting in Plaza Rio Tijuana is the Suzett Bakery and Pastry Shop, where you can watch bakers create 300 varieties of breads, pies, cakes, and specialties like tasty filled *tortas*. If you're ready for lunch, enjoy some fine Mexican fare at the award-winning Restaurant Las Espuelas in the shopping center.

Or drive south on Paseo de Los Heroes to have a midday meal at the city's new landmark, the Tijuana Cultural Center. You'll easily spot its immense eight-story sphere, which houses an Omnitheater where a spectacular panoramic film presentation, *El Pueblo del Sol* (*City of the Sun*), describes the history of Mexico and shows the nation's vast contrasts—from ancient temples to ultramodern cities. Time your visit for the 2 P.M. show, which is narrated in English. You'll also want to wander through the center's spacious museum to view masterpieces of Mexican arts and crafts that span 3,500 years. In the restaurant you can dine on native dishes from around the country. With luck you may be there when a folkloric show is being presented on the open-air stage. Inquire at the center's ticket booth.

Among Tijuana's longtime attractions are sporting events that take place at the Agua Caliente racetrack, three miles from downtown. Try your luck betting on Thoroughbred horses, a favorite activity of foreign visitors every weekend. (Greyhound racing dogs compete in the same arena most weekday evenings.)

When you're ready to leave Tijuana on Saturday, follow the Ensenada Toll Road (*Cuota*) signs through town to the four-lane highway that leads south to the beach at Rosarito. After passing through the first toll station, take the first Rosarito exit and enter the north end of town.

Don't expect a Puerto Vallarta or other fancy beach retreat like those on the Mexican mainland. Rosarito hugs a two-mile section of the old Tijuana-Ensenada highway, where roadside stands greet you with bamboo baskets, brightly painted pottery, and even saddle horses for hire.

Celebrate your arrival with a $1 margarita on the patio of El Rancho Restaurant. The local vaqueros sometimes ride up for refreshments after their Sunday rodeos, and folk dancers also liven up the weekend there.

Continuing south on Rosarito's main street, you'll see the Quinta del Mar, an extensive resort with hotel rooms and vacation time-share *casas*. Whether an overnight guest or not, you're welcome at the resort's La Masia Restaurant and the ocean-view Beachcomber Bar. Be sure to browse in the shops that flank the resort entrance. Don't miss La Casa del Arte y la Madera (House of Gifts and Decor), jam-packed with handicrafts from all over Mexico. Opposite is the ever-busy Calimax supermarket, a good place to buy picnic and camping supplies, as well as Kahlua, tequila, and other Mexican liquor to bring home. (One quart per adult is allowed duty-free by U.S. Customs.)

About a mile farther south you'll see the arched entrance to the town's landmark, the Rosarito Beach Hotel, built in the 1920s. Once a hideaway for Hollywood folk and international celebrities like Prince Aly Khan, the 76-room resort draws guests from everywhere and is popular with families.

Wander through the lobby, hallways, and public rooms to view the immense murals and other artwork that contribute to the hotel's character. Look up for the hand-painted ceiling beams and go to the main dining room to see the framed images of six Aztec gods created with colorful wool yarn on a base of beeswax. In this Aztec Room, which overlooks the swimming pool, you can enjoy a Saturday-evening dinner buffet with such Baja specialties as quail and fresh fish. Just in front of the hotel you'll also be tempted by a colorful variety of gifts in the shopping arcade.

On Sunday, relax at your resort hotel or throw down a towel and sunbathe anywhere along Rosarito's beaches—all are public. At lunchtime, drive about 12 miles south of Rosarito on the old Ensenada highway to see more of the beautifully rugged Baja coast and to reach the fishing village of Puerto Nuevo (Newport) for a feast of fresh lobster. There's no road sign to the village; look for it on the right about two miles beyond Las Gaviotas resort development.

Originally the fishermen's families served lobster to visitors in their homes at the kitchen table, but several have built restaurants and now live above them. You'll spot one of the largest and nicest just off the highway, Restaurant Nuevo Ortega's. As at the two other Ortega restaurants in the village, which are run by his father and a brother, David Ortega and wife, Gloria, offer lobster dinners at unbeatable prices. A small one costs $4.50, medium $8, large $9.75, but you'd better be really hungry before ordering a *giantica* lobster at $16 to $20.

When you're ready to return to Los Angeles, continue a mile south to the Ensenada toll-road entrance at Cantamar and head north to Tijuana. If you've always wanted to see a bullfight, arrive there by midafternoon for an exciting *corrida* in Tijuana's downtown bullring, El Toreo. From May to September, you can watch this traditional Sunday entertainment at the bullring-by-the sea, Plaza de Monumental, which you'll see from the toll road near the Playas de Tijuana beach area, on your way north from Rosarito.

Afterward, follow the directional signs to San Diego, but prepare for a delay at the border for the customary check by U.S. immigration officials. Then continue north on Interstate 5 to Los Angeles. *Ole!*

Round trip is about 310 miles.

Tijuana/Rosarito Area Code: 706

SIGHTSEEING   *Tijuana Cultural Center* (Centro Cultural Fonapas), Paseo de Los Heroes, Tijuana, 684-1111. Museum open 11 A.M. to 8 P.M. weekends, to 7 P.M. weekdays. Admission 40 cents. Omnitheater with wraparound movie of Mexico shown in English at 2 P.M. daily; also 3:30 P.M. weekends. Spanish narration at 5, 6:30, and 8 P.M. daily. Admission $2.40 per person. Restaurant open 11 A.M. to 8 P.M. daily. Buffet lunch $4.50 ● For quality handicrafts from all over Mexico, visit *Fonart,* Avenida Revolucion 1020, *Cariem,* Avenida Revolucion 918-D, *Artesanias,* Avenida Revolucion 635, and *Tolan Arte de Mexico,* Avenida Revolucion 1111. ● In Rosarito, look for more colorful Mexican crafts at *La Casa de Arte y La Madera* at the north end of the Quinta del Mar shopping arcade. ● These are Tijuana's spectator sports: *Jai alai,* fast-paced action in the Basque ball court at 8 P.M. Friday through Wednesday in the Fronton Palacio on Avenida Revolucion at Calle 7, with parimutuel betting. ● *Horse racing,* 11 races every Saturday and Sunday at Agua Caliente Racetrack off Boulevard Agua Caliente, post time 1:15 P.M. (noon in winter). ● *Dog racing,* greyhounds run at Agua Caliente Racetrack at 8 P.M. every day except Tuesday in summer and at 7:30 P.M. Wednesday through Sunday in winter. ● *Bullfights,* Mexico's top matadors perform Sunday afternoons at 4 P.M. in El Toreo bullring downtown from mid-May to mid-July, then in Plaza Monumental bullring-by-the-sea to mid-September.

LODGING *Hotel Lucerna,* Paseo de los Héroes and Avenida Rodriguez, Tijuana, 684-0117; $32. Modern 6-story hotel, nearest to Rio Tijuana shopping center and downtown shopping area. ● *Hotel El Conquistador,* Boulevard Agua Caliente 700, Tijuana, 686-4801; $35. Pleasant twin-story motel with colonial architecture; opposite Tijuana Country Club and near Agua Caliente Racetrack. ● *El Presidente Hotel,* Boulevard Agua Caliente 1, Tijuana, 686-5000; $33. Older high-rise hotel adjacent to country club and near racetrack. ● *Rosarito Beach Hotel,* Highway 1 (Boulevard Benito Juarez), Rosarito, 612-1106; $40. Rosarito's landmark lodging is the beach town's center of activity and entertainment. Unfancy, and a favorite Baja resort; make weekend and holiday reservations well in advance. Parcourse fitness circuit around the hotel grounds. ● *Quinta del Mar Resort Hotel,* Highway 1 (Boulevard Benito Juarez), Rosarito, 612-1300; $34, one-bedroom house $59. Rosarito's other major hostelry, where reservations also should be made well in advance.

DINING *TiaJuana Tilly's,* in Frontón Palacio on Avenida Revolución, Tijuana, 685-6024. Barbecued ribs are a specialty in this happy hangout at the jai alai palace. Popular with the youthful drinking crowd. ● *El Reno,* on Calle 8, catty-corner from the jai alai palace, Tijuana, 685-9210. Elegant dining amid 1930s decor with music and dancing. Varied menu featuring steak and seafood favorites, and a few surprises like eels. ● *Boccaccio's Nueva Marianna,* Boulevard Agua Caliente 2500, Tijuana, 686-2266. Gourmet Mexican and Italian cuisine. ● *Victor's,* Avenida Sanches Taboada opposite the Rio Tijuana shopping center by the Calimax supermarket, 688-3823. Long known for its impressive and filling buffet, offered daily from noon to 5 P.M.; try the swordfish or *carne asada* at dinner. ● *Carnitas Uruapan,* Boulevard Agua Caliente just east of racetrack, Tijuana, 686-1681. Chunks of pork (*carnitas*) cook in sauce-filled caldrons outside this old-style restaurant and then are served by the plate or pound at long tables. Mariachi serenades accompany the good food and fun. ● *Restaurant Nuevo Ortega's,* Puerto Nuevo off Highway 1 south of Rosarito, no phone. Fresh local lobster at bargain prices; don't miss this taste treat in a tiny fishing village. ● *El Nido Steak House,* Highway 1, Rosarito, no phone. It's hard to top the *carne asada* or regular steaks cooked over a mesquite wood fire; try the fried cheese for an appetizer. ● *El Rancho Restaurant,* Highway 1, Rosarito, no phone. Inexpensive margaritas and informal patio dining with Mexican specialties and even good hamburgers.

FOR MORE INFORMATION Contact the Tourism Department for Baja California, 348 West Market Street, Suite 404, San Diego 92101, 299-8518, or toll-free (800) 522-1516 (outside San Diego).

South of the Border
Part 2: Ensenada

You'll love spending a weekend in the relaxed fishing port of Ensenada, just 70 miles south of the U.S.-Mexico border on the photogenic west coast of Baja California. Visitors agree that it's much more "Mexican" in appearance and flavor than Tijuana, although Ensenada is far from being a sleepy little village. As the peninsula's main seaport, it's grown to be Baja's third largest city. Ensenada boasts Mexico's major Pacific Coast fish cannery, as well the nation's biggest winery—Bodegas de Santo Tomas.

In recent years, Ensenada also has become an increasingly popular resort town. One reason is that it's now a bona fide cruise port. Twice weekly the S.S. *Azure Seas* sails with a shipload of holidaymakers into Bahia de Todos Santos (Bay of All Saints), Ensenada's enormous natural harbor. Since 1980 the gleaming white cruise vessel has been making regular three-night and four-night party trips from Los Angeles to Ensenada. Cruise passengers have about 24 hours in port, enough time to explore Ensenada's myriad of shops, savor just-caught seafood in the first-class restaurants or at street stands, and down a margarita in the town's most notorious cantina, Hussong's.

But if you want to absorb more of the beauty and excitement of Baja, go by car and spend the weekend at one of Ensenada's resort hotels. The drive south along the sheer cliffs and sandy beaches of Baja's picturesque Pacific coast is worth the trip itself.

Get to Ensenada from Los Angeles by taking Interstate 5 to San Diego and continuing to the international border. Pause to purchase Mexican auto insurance at one of the special offices; U.S. policies aren't valid in case of an accident. Also, if you plan to stay longer than three days or to extend your trip beyond Ensenada, be sure to carry a Mexican tourist card. Get one at the border *migración* office or later at the first road checkpoint, 12 miles south of Ensenada; you'll need proof of citizenship, such as a passport or birth certificate. Then follow the Ensenada toll road (*Cuota*) signs to bypass Tijuana and join the four-lane highway (No. 1-D) that takes you directly to Ensenada. Small tolls are collected at three booths en route.

In the heart of town you'll find several attractive motels along Avenida Lopez Mateos, including El Cid and Mision Santa Isabel. A few blocks beyond is the popular San Nicolas Resort Hotel, Ensenada's largest lodging. Another pleasant resort, Estero Beach Hotel, is on the bay front six miles south of downtown Ensenada. There are several campgrounds and trailer parks, too.

Mexicans like to eat late, so you'll probably arrive in time for dinner on Friday. Ensenada is known for seafood, but restaurants feature Mexican, American, and international dishes as well. Favorites of frequent visitors are the French cuisine and Mexican fare at El Rey Sol Restaurant, an Ensenada landmark on Avenida Lopez Mateos for almost four decades. Among its specialties is abalone. Seafood aficionados also like Casamar, Cosmo's, and Alfonso's, a trio of sidewalk restaurants located along the bay on Avenida Macheros just off Boulevard Costero.

The fish market at the foot of Avenida Macheros bustles with activity every morning when Ensenada's housewives and restaurant chefs bargain for seafood fresh off the commercial fishing boats. Ensenada's immense bay has abundant fish, and you can try your luck aboard sportfishing boats that make daily excursions for bottom-fish varieties or deep-sea specimens. Sign up at Fritz's, Gordo's, or one of the other sportfishing offices located along Avenida Lopez Mateos.

Several blocks south, at the end of Boulevard Costero (also known as Boulevard Lazaro Cardenas), you'll find sandy public beaches for sunbathing or swimming in the bay. Horses also can be rented there for a scenic saddle ride along the water's edge.

Be sure to make the 20-mile drive to the bay's western tip on Punta Banda peninsula to see La Bufadora. Mother Nature created this age-old blowhole that spouts roaring geysers of seawater with each ocean wave. Don't forget your camera.

Back in town you can admire man's handiwork inside the Hotel Riviera del Pacifico, a 1930s bay-front casino and resort that has been renovated as the city's cultural, arts, and convention center. The original hand-painted wooden ceilings and other adornments date from earlier times, when the elegant hotel was a haunt of Hollywood film stars and heavyweight boxing champ Jack Dempsey was its honorary manager.

Ensenada is a super place for shopping, and one shop not to miss is Fonart, the government-run store that's behind the cultural center, just beyond the dip in the road across the Ensenada riverbed. The museumlike shop is filled with original arts and crafts from all over Mexico, and prices are reasonable. Many other stores also specialize in Mexican wares, including pottery, ceramics, jewelry, furniture, leather goods, and clothing. But you'll also find a surprising array of imported products—French perfumes, Swiss watches, European fashions, and more—competitive with or below U.S. prices. The supermarkets offer good buys in Mexican-made liquors and liqueurs, like coffee-flavored Kahlua and the well-known Santo Tomas wines. (For U.S. citizens, up to $400 of whatever you buy in Mexico can be brought back to the U.S. without paying customs duty.)

Stroll along the main shopping streets, Avenida Lopez Mateos and Avenida Ruiz. Prices are fixed in the shops, but you can bargain with street vendors and at a few small street stalls. U.S. currency is accepted everywhere, although prices usually are given in Mexican pesos. The peso amount is indicated with a dollar sign too, but should be preceded by the initials "M.N." to indicate Mexican currency.

Return to Los Angeles via the same toll road to the border at Tijuana and rejoin Interstate 5 going north.

Round trip is about 395 miles.

If you'd rather visit Ensenada aboard a comfortable cruise ship, book a cabin on the S.S. *Azure Seas,* which sails south of the border from Pier 93-A at San Pedro. Take the Harbor Freeway (Interstate 110/California 11) south to Harbor Boulevard and the port area.

The weekend cruise leaves Los Angeles Friday evening at 7:45 P.M. and returns at 8 A.M. Monday morning. (Allow up to three hours for disembarkation while all the baggage is put ashore and as many as 800 passengers clear U.S. Immigration and Customs.) Whether you're on the three-night weekend cruise or four-night midweek trip, the ship docks at 10 A.M. in Ensenada and sails again about the same time one day later. (On the longer cruise the ship also includes San Diego as a port of call.)

At sea you'll enjoy stage shows, music and dancing, movies, a captain's cocktail party, gambling in the casino, many more cruise activities, and plenty to eat. Cruise costs depend on the location and size of your cabin. Rates per person, double occupancy, range from $350 to $520 for the weekend cruise, $400 to $555 for the weekday sailing. Fares include all meals aboard ship; guided shore excursions are optional. Port taxes and shipboard tips also are extra.

Book passage through a travel agent or by calling toll-free (800) 327-5780 or 327-0271. For more details about the Los Angeles-Ensenada cruise, contact Western Cruise Lines, 140 West 6th Street, San Pedro 90731, (213) 548-8411.

Ensenada Area Code: 706

SIGHTSEEING   *Hussong's Cantina,* 118 Avenida Ruiz. An Ensenada watering hole and Baja institution that's frequently jam-packed, noisy, and lots of fun—especially after a few margaritas or cervezas. At least drop in to say you've been there. ● *Bodegas de Santo Tomas,* 666 Avenida Miramar, Ensenada, 678-2509 or 674-0836. Guided half-hour tours of the downtown Ensenada winery at 11 A.M. and 3 P.M. Monday through Saturday. $1.50 per person, including wine tasting.

LODGING   *San Nicolas Resort Hotel,* Avenida Lopez Mateos at Avenida Guadalupe, Ensenada, 674-0814; $58. Modern motor inn with coffee shop, dining room, and discothèque. ● *Estero Beach Hotel Resort,* 6 miles south of Ensenada via Highway 1 to resort's side road, 676-1001;

$42. Waterfront complex with beach, tennis courts, restaurant; a favorite of families. • *El Cid Hotel,* 993 Avenida Lopez Mateos, Ensenada, 678-2401; $40. Small Mexican-Colonial style hotel in the heart of town. • *Mision Santa Isabel Hotel,* Avenida Lopez Mateos at Avenida Castillo, Ensenada, 678-3616; $34. Attractive small hotel in town center.

CAMPING *Estero Beach Trailer Park,* adjacent to Estero Beach Hotel Resort (see above), 676-1001. 76 sites with hookups, use of resort facilities. • *Campo Play Ensenada RV Park,* Boulevard Lazaro Cardenas at Calle Delante, 678-1818. 90 sites across from beach, some hookups.

DINING *El Rey Sol Restaurant,* Avenida Lopez Mateos at Avenida Blancarte, 678-1733. Open 7:30 A.M. to 11 P.M. Top Mexican and continental cuisine, with fresh vegetables, fruit, and poultry from the restaurant's ranches. Its own bakery makes mouthwatering French pastries. • *Casamar,* fresh seafood (mariscos) restaurants at two bayfront locations: Boulevard Costero at Avenida Blancarte, 674-0417, and Avenida Macheros at Boulevard Costero, 678-2540. Lunch and dinner daily. • *Alfonso's,* Avenida Macheros at Boulevard Costero, 674-0570. Bar and restaurant with Italian and seafood specialties for lunch and dinner. • *Cosmo's,* Avenida Macheros at Boulevard Costero. Breakfast, plus seafood, steak, and Mexican fare for lunch and dinner. • *Enrique's,* Highway 1-D, 1½ miles north of town, 678-2461. Well-known chef-owned restaurant open 8 A.M. to 11:30 P.M. Seafood, lobster, and steak.

FOR MORE INFORMATION Tourist Bureau, 1350 Avenida Lopez Mateos, 678-2411. Office is next to Fonart store. • Also, for advance information, call the Tourism Department for Baja California headquarters in San Diego, 299-8518, or toll-free (800) 522-1516 (outside San Diego).

"Thar She Blows!"— Watching the Annual Whale Parade

If you want a glimpse of California's official state mammal, look to the Pacific Ocean. The annual parade of California gray whales along the Southland coast runs from mid-December to April. This remarkable voyage, the longest known migration of any mammal in the world, is monitored by a flotilla of whale-watching boats, and you're welcome to climb aboard. It's a wonderful treat to include in one of your weekend getaways to the coast in the wintertime.

During the boats' 2- to 3½-hour outings at sea, you're almost certain to spot some of the marathon travelers, which are estimated to number as many as 13,000. And there's a good chance you'll see whales spouting, fluking, and, with luck, even breeching—when they propel their multi-ton bodies out of the water. In winter you'll find these immense yet graceful cetaceans swimming south from the Bering Sea to their breeding and calving grounds in Baja's quiet lagoons, and in early spring they're guiding their newborn offspring back north to the Alaskan waters.

Starting in late December, whale-watching vessels depart every weekend and some weekdays from Ventura, Oxnard, Marina del Rey, San Pedro, Long Beach, Redondo Beach, Newport Beach, Dana Point, Oceanside, and San Diego. Later in the season, when the grays are making their return trip, boats also leave from Santa Barbara to look for the baby whales and their mothers. The whale-watching trips end by early March, when most of the north-bound leviathans have passed the Southland's shores.

Be certain to dress warmly for the ocean excursions by bringing a heavy coat and hat or scarf. You'll get better views and pictures by taking along binoculars and a telephoto lens. Most vessels sell refreshments, or pack your own snacks.

For extra excitement, board one of the San Diego-based sportfishing boats that head south to the quiet lagoons of Baja, Mexico, and be the first on your block to pet a whale. Gray whales are surprisingly relaxed in the calving grounds, and some of them, nicknamed "friendlies," seem to enjoy it when human visitors reach out to pet their barnacled backs. Details of those eight-day natural-history voyages to Baja follow, but first is a port-by-port summary of the shorter morning and afternoon whale-watching excursions from Southern California harbors.

Boat capacities vary, so be sure to make reservations. Also call to confirm departure times and get directions to the dock; unless otherwise indicated, the area code is 213. Adult fares average about $8; children usually sail at reduced rates. Prices of more costly trips will be noted.

SAN PEDRO: Four companies offer whale-watch cruises from L.A.'s harbor at San Pedro. Ports O'Call Sportfishing at Berth 79 has 100-passenger boats leaving once each morning and afternoon on weekdays and six times daily on weekends. Phone 547-9916.

Also at Ports O'Call Village at Berth 76, Buccaneer Cruises' 49-passenger Swift heads to sea in search of gray whales two times a day on weekends only. Phone 548-1085.

Not far away, Skipper's 22nd Street Landing at 141 West 22nd Street operates whale trips every weekday morning and afternoon and three times daily on Saturdays and Sundays. Weekday excursions on the 125-passenger boats cost less than the weekend trips. Phone 832-8304.

Also sailing from San Pedro, from Berth 95-96, are the triple-deck ferryboats that sometimes abandon their regular runs to Catalina Island in order to take up to 525 passengers on gray whale excursions. The spacious boats are more comfortable than the smaller sportfishing vessels that are used for most of the whale-watch cruises, and their 25-foot-high top decks offer excellent vantage points for spotting whales.

A novel attraction of the Catalina Cruises' boats are underwater microphones that broadcast the sounds of whales, porpoises, and other ocean life. Also, a representative from L.A.'s Cabrillo Marine Museum is aboard to give a commentary about the gray whale.

The boats go out every weekend morning and afternoon and also make trips some weekday mornings in January, February, and March. Call 832-4521 or (714) 527-2111 for exact sailing dates and departure times; tickets can be purchased in advance through Ticketron.

LONG BEACH: Ticketron also can book you aboard whale-watching boats operating from Long Beach Harbor. Queen's Wharf Sportfishing at Berth 55 off Pico Avenue has a morning and an afternoon departure every day. On weekends you'll pay more to board the 80- to 120-passenger vessels. Phone 432-8993.

MARINA DEL REY: Captain Frenchy sails his 49-passenger boat in search of cetaceans every morning and afternoon. The three-hour trips depart from dock 52 in Fisherman's Village on Fiji Way. Phone 822-3625.

REDONDO BEACH: Every weekday and weekend in both morning and afternoon, the 145-passenger *Voyager* leaves Redondo Sportfishing pier at 233 North Harbor Drive in Kings Harbor to seek the oceangoing gray whales. Phone 372-2111.

NEWPORT BEACH: Whale watchers also can embark from the Balboa Pavilion at 400 North Main Street in Newport Beach. You can board the 100-passenger *Western Pride,* operated by Davey's Locker, for morning or afternoon trips seven days a week. Phone (714) 673-1434. Or set sail in the morning on weekdays and in the morning and afternoon on weekends with Catalina Passenger Service's 300-passenger *Catalina Holiday.* Phone (714) 673-5245.

DANA POINT: From the Dana Wharf Sportfishing pier at 34675 Golden Lantern in Dana Harbor, whale-viewing vessels head to sea three times every day. On weekends in February during Dana Point's annual Festival of Whales, the boats depart hourly from 8 A.M. to 4 P.M. Phone (714) 496-5794.

OCEANSIDE: Helgren's Sportfishing at 315 South Harbor Drive in Oceanside Harbor boards whale watchers on its 15- to 120-passenger boats every day in the morning and afternoon. Senior citizens and teenagers get reduced rates. Phone (619) 722-2133.

SAN DIEGO: You'll find five embarkation points in San Diego for gray whale excursions. H&M Landing's boats depart from Municipal

Pier at Emerson and Scott streets, between Harbor and Shelter islands, every day in the morning and afternoon and also three times daily on weekends. Phone (619) 222-1144.

Fisherman's Landing sets sail on the same schedule from a neighboring dock. Phone (619) 222-0391.

Both H&M Landing and Fisherman's Landing run longer day trips to the Coronado Islands to view whales and other sealife. Boats with 15 to 40 passengers leave Municipal Pier Wednesday through Sunday mornings for the seven-hour outings.

Fisherman's Landing's fares are $28 for all ages, and $7 more buys a champagne brunch aboard ship; food also can be purchased from the galley. Tickets for H&M Landing's all-day excursion to the offshore islands are $25 for adults, $20 for juniors. Bring a picnic or buy food on board. Call the numbers above for more details and reservations.

Also from Municipal Pier, Point Loma Sportfishing's Sundown cruises with up to 90 passengers in search of whales. Departures are weekday afternoons and three times daily on weekends. Phone (619) 223-1627.

From San Diego's Mission Bay you can board Islandia Sportfishing vessels three times daily at 1551 West Mission Bay Drive. Phone (619) 222-1164.

Also in Mission Bay, Seaforth Sportfishing at 1717 Quivira Road goes forth from Quivira Basin with whale watchers every afternoon and also twice in the morning on Saturdays and Sundays. For reservations to board the 118- to 150-passenger boats, call (619) 224-3383.

VENTURA: North of Los Angeles you can sail from Ventura Harbor aboard Island Packers' boats to look for whales in the Santa Barbara Channel. The three-hour trips depart early morning and early afternoon on Friday, Saturday, and Sunday from Island Packers' new docks at the end of Spinnaker Drive. Fares are $12 for adults, half price for children 12 years or less. Call (805) 642-1393 or (805) 642-3370.

For extra adventure, join an Island Packers' all-day excursion from Ventura to Anacapa Island with whale watching along the way. There are departures daily at 9 A.M. to explore Anacapa, one of the five islands that are part of Channel Islands National Park. Bring a picnic lunch to eat when you go ashore. Adult tickets cost $24, children half price.

For $13 per person more you can make a special whale cruise aboard an 82-foot sailing ship. You'll enjoy a thrilling motorless sail (winds permitting) to Anacapa to look for whales and visit the island. Call the Island Packers' numbers above for more information and reservations.

OXNARD: Cisco Sportfishing also takes whale watchers from Oxnard's Channel Islands Harbor out to Anacapa but doesn't land on the island. Boats depart from 4151 South Victoria Avenue every day in the morning and also in the afternoon on Saturday, Sunday, and holidays. Phone 457-9221 or (805) 985-8511.

SANTA BARBARA: Beginning in early February, Sea Landing's *Con-*

dor sails from the Breakwater of Santa Barbara's boat harbor to seek out gray whales on their home-bound journey. You can join the ocean excursion three times daily on Tuesdays, Thursdays, and weekends. Fares are $12.50 for adults, $8 for kids 12 years and under. Phone (805) 963-3564.

In addition to the listed trips, L.A.'s Cabrillo Marine Museum in San Pedro can make reservations for you on boats that feature a naturalist or tour guide. Call (213) 832-2676 or 832-4444 weekdays from 9 to 12. On most whale-watching trips the boat captain gives a brief background about the gray whales and their migration and announces to passengers where to look when whales have been spotted.

While whale watching anywhere along the Southern California coast makes an enjoyable wintertime outing, you can experience the added thrills of close-up encounters with the leviathans in the Baja lagoons where they go to give birth. You'll sail south from San Diego on a sportfishing boat to San Ignacio or Scammon's Lagoon to mingle with the gray whales that have completed their annual swim from the Bering Sea. Everywhere you look there seems to be activity. Salt water shoots skyward with a roar when these warm-blooded mammals come to the surface to refill their lungs with air. Huge tail flukes flash above the water as the whales prepare to dive. And when they're playful, the blubbery beasts erupt from the water and then fall back with a resounding splash.

To encourage the "friendlies" to come close enough for you to pet them, small skiffs with only a few passengers are lowered from the main boat to slowly cruise the lagoon. With patience and luck, a whale or two will get curious and surface alongside. Watch out for the spray if one decides to take a breath!

At night you'll sleep in a cozy cabin or berth aboard the mother ship. The vessel's cooks dish up hearty meals, and there are plenty of snacks for hungry seafarers. After dinner the naturalists on board give illustrated talks and discuss the next day's events.

En route to the lagoon you'll stop at some of Baja's rarely visited islands and go ashore with the naturalists to explore the unspoiled wilderness. On Todos Santos, San Martin, San Benitos, and Cedros islands you see a rich array of animal and bird life, including elephant seals and blue-footed boobies. The naturalists will identify dozens of little-known plants and flowers, too.

These trips operate through March, until most of the gray whales have headed back to their summer feeding grounds in the Arctic. Cost of the eight-day Baja whale adventure is about $960.

For more details and to make reservations for these increasingly popular nature excursions, contact H&M Landing at (619) 222-1144, or write to that sportfishing company at 2803 Emerson Street, San Diego 92106.

Backcountry and
Mountain Adventures

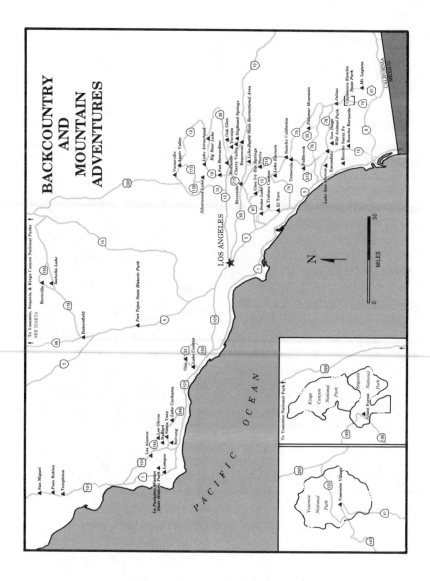

BACKCOUNTRY AND MOUNTAIN ADVENTURES

Overleaf: Sequoia National Park

Unsurpassed Yosemite— a National Park for All Seasons

Even the first visitors to the glacier-carved valley in the central section of the Sierra Nevada were awed by its uniqueness and beauty. The year was 1851, and a group of soldiers was in search of some troublesome Indians. The militiamen failed to capture the tribe, but they returned with glowing descriptions of the valley's natural wonders.

The search party also named the valley with the Indians' word for grizzly bear, *u-zu-ma-te,* which eventually evolved into *Yosemite (yo-sem-it-tee).* Yosemite Valley—with its unsurpassed scenery of massive granite monoliths, thundering waterfalls, alpine meadows, and handsome forests—was given protection by a special bill signed by President Abraham Lincoln in 1864.

Today the valley is the focal point of one of America's most scenic national treasures. Every year more than 2.6 million visitors enjoy nature's handiwork in the 1,200 square miles of Yosemite National Park. It's a wondrous place to visit in any season.

For the most enjoyment, plan a three-day weekend in the park and headquarter in Yosemite Valley at the renowned (and expensive) Ahwahnee, one of the West's grand hotels from a bygone era. Built in 1927, the Ahwahnee's stone-and-wood exterior matches the grandeur of its surroundings, all of which can be viewed through floor-to-ceiling windows in the imposing public rooms and from some of the guest-room balconies.

If the price of a room or suite in this historic hostelry is more than your budget can bear, at least make reservations for a meal in the Ahwahnee's Main Dining Room, where the tables are laid with fine linen, crystal, silver, and the hotel's exclusive china, and the food is excellent. Men must wear coats at dinner; ties are preferred as well.

The hotel is managed by a longtime concessionaire, Yosemite Park and Curry Co., which also provides most visitor services and all accommodations in the park, including the two other places where you can stay in Yosemite Valley, the modern Yosemite Lodge and more modest Curry Village. There are campgrounds, too, operated by the National Park Service.

To reach beautiful Yosemite from Los Angeles, go north on Interstate 5 to join California 99 and continue to Fresno. Then follow California 41 north to the park's southern entrance. A few miles beyond the entry station you'll be surprised by an expanse of green grass, the 9-hole golf course that's part of Yosemite's classic Victorian resort, the charming Wawona Hotel. This modernized lodge has hosted park visitors for over 100 years and is the perfect place to spend your first night in Yosemite after the long drive from Los Angeles. It's also an ideal alternative choice for accommodations for the entire weekend if you want to avoid the hustle and bustle of Yosemite Valley, 27 miles away. At least visit the hotel for dinner in its turn-of-the-century dining room.

In the morning, go back south from the Wawona on California 41 and take the nearby side road that leads to a parking lot for the Mariposa Grove of rare giant sequoias. Follow the footpaths to this group of 500 magnificent trees, some of them over 200 feet tall. Yosemite's oldest sequoia, nicknamed the Grizzly Giant, dates from about 800 B.C. You'll need 20 friends with outstretched arms to encircle its massive trunk. The much-photographed tunnel tree, with a hole large enough for cars to drive through, fell over from the weight of snow in 1969.

Also close by the Wawona Hotel, enjoy the living history program offered in a mini-village of restored buildings called the Pioneer Yosemite History Center, then continue north through the park on California 41 to reach Yosemite Valley. Along the way, detour on the Glacier Point side road that leads to an outstanding panorama of the High Sierra and Yosemite Valley. Back on California 41, just after you emerge from the long Wawona tunnel, there's another excellent view of the picturesque valley.

As the road descends, it's easy to spot Yosemite's grand granite sentinel, El Capitan. To your right is famed Bridalveil Fall, created by melted Sierra snow that plunges 620 feet to reach the Merced River coursing through the valley. For a closer look, you can park and follow the footpath that leads to the base of this breathtaking waterfall. The road finally brings you to Yosemite Village, site of the Ahwahnee Hotel and other lodgings, as well as restaurants, stores, and park headquarters.

Summer, of course, is the peak time for vacationers, and most congregate in the valley's seven-square-mile area. To handle the crowds, and keep the scenic roads from resembling a freeway at rush hour, visitors with vehicles are asked to park and use Yosemite's free shuttle bus service instead. In fact, the roads to some points of interest in Yosemite Valley are off limits to all vehicles except the shuttle buses. You also can get around to see the sights by hiking, bicycling, and horseback riding.

Once you're settled in your lodgings or campground, stop at the visitors center to view exhibits that explain Yosemite's natural features. Subjects and times of walks and talks offered by park rangers also are posted. Among the publications at the center that will make your visit more worthwhile is *Trails of Yosemite Valley,* which outlines short and long hikes.

Trails, and shuttle buses, will take you to Mirror Lake for excellent views of Yosemite's granite monoliths, including awesome Half Dome. And you can hike or ride a shuttle bus to Yosemite Falls, one of the world's highest waterfalls. The total 2,425-foot drop is divided into three sections, and there's a path to the base of the lower fall, which itself is twice the height of Niagara Falls. These and the park's other well-known falls—Bridalveil, Vernal, Ribbon, and Nevada—give their peak performances in May and June, although the water show continues into July and August.

A wonderful way to relax and get acquainted with Yosemite at the beginning of your visit is to take the narrated two-hour bus tour of Yosemite Valley. And if there's a full moon, board one of the open-air trams for a romantic evening tour of the valley.

If you arrived by an alternate route or didn't stop to sightsee in the park on your way to Yosemite Valley, be sure to plan time during the weekend to take one of the half-day guided bus tours to Glacier Point or the Mariposa Grove or the all-day tour to both. Or leave early on the return trip to Los Angeles and visit both attractions in your own vehicle.

If you're in no rush to go home and want to see more of Yosemite, cross the Sierra Nevada Mountains on the Tioga Road, California 120, the only east-west highway through the park. (In winter this mountaintop highway is closed by snow.) You can stop for refreshments at Tuolumne Meadows before the scenic highway reaches 9,945-foot Tioga Pass, the highest automobile pass in the state. The road descends to Lee Vining and meets U.S. 395, which you follow south through the Owens Valley to join California 14 across the Mojave Desert. Then pick up Interstate 5 back to Los Angeles.

Round trip is about 710 miles.

If you want to enjoy this most popular park without the usual swarm of sightseers, plan your trip to Yosemite during the winter, spring, or fall. Each season has its own special appeal. In autumn the alpine weather is especially pleasant, and the trees are putting on a colorful show as Jack Frost turns the leaves to red, russet, and gold. Come springtime, the mountain meadows bloom with wildflowers and resemble pretty patchwork quilts that only Mother Nature can create.

Winter may be the best time of all for a trip to Yosemite. Snow makes this protected wilderness extra spectacular, and like the park's waterfalls, the number of park visitors slows to a trickle. Besides its pristine appearance and uncrowded conditions, Yosemite offers all sorts of activities in the winter season. You can go ice skating on an outdoor rink within sight of Half Dome and strap on snowshoes for nature walks with the park rangers. Other options include scenic tours via bus, tractor-tread snowcat, or cross-country skis, as well as downhill skiing and snow camping.

For many visitors, the snow-covered scenery is enough enticement for a winter weekend in Yosemite. Snow plows keep the main park roads open, but carry tire chains because of changeable weather conditions. And be sure to have clothing that's appropriate for the season, including a warm hat, gloves, and boots.

You'll find the park's ski center at Badger Pass, 23 miles from the

Yosemite Valley lodging area. The easiest way to reach it is by boarding the free ski buses. Rental skis, boots, and poles are available at the slopes, and there's a ski school if you want to improve your downhill skills.

Badger Pass also is the place to view the High Sierra during an overland tour aboard a snowcat. It's exciting and inexpensive to take this unusual outing to the mountain ridge. Snowshoes can be rented if you decide to sightsee on foot.

Instructors at Yosemite Mountaineering School at Curry Village in the valley will give you cross-country skiing instruction. All-day classes and guided ski excursions start at the Mountain Shop, where Nordic ski gear also can be rented.

Park rangers lead free tours on skis and snowshoes in Yosemite Valley, at Badger Pass, and in the Mariposa Grove of giant sequoias. Days and details are posted at the visitors center. Road and weather conditions permitting, bus tours will show you the best-known of the park's natural wonders in Yosemite Valley, including towering El Capitan and Bridalveil Fall.

In wintertime, reserve a cozy room in the Ahwahnee Hotel, Yosemite Lodge, or Curry Village, which are open year round; the Wawona Hotel is closed from December through March. At least one campground in Yosemite Valley also is open for wintertime visitors on a first come, first served basis. You can dine at the Ahwahnee or in the restaurant at Yosemite Lodge.

For the best route to the park in wintertime, head north from Los Angeles on Interstate 5 to join California 99 and continue through the San Joaquin Valley to Merced. Then follow California 140 northeast into Yosemite Valley.

Yosemite Area Code: 209

SIGHTSEEING   *Park Entry Permit,* $3 per vehicle. ● *Yosemite Valley Bus Tour,* 2 hours, at least twice daily year round, $8; also during periods of the full moon in summer. *Glacier Point Bus Tour,* 4 hours, twice daily June through November, $13.50. *Mariposa Grove Bus Tour* to the giant sequoias, 4 hours, once daily year round, $12.25. *Glacier Point and Mariposa Grove Bus Tour,* all-day tour once daily June through November, $18.50. All bus tours are operated by Yosemite Transportation System (YTS) from the Ahwahnee Hotel, Yosemite Lodge, and Curry Village in Yosemite Valley, 372-1240. ● *Saddle Horses,* daily guided 2-hour ($12.50), half-day ($18), and all-day ($29) trail rides except in winter, 373-4171. Stables are located in Yosemite Valley, at Wawona and Tuolumne Meadows. ● *Bicycles* can be rented by the hour ($1.50) or day ($7) in Yosemite Valley at Yosemite Lodge and Curry Village. ●

Badger Pass Ski Area, open daily Thanksgiving to mid-April for down-hill skiing (adult all-day lift pass $13.75, children $8), snowcat tours ($3.50 per person), 372-4691. • *Yosemite Ice Rink,* outdoor ice skating at Curry Village in Yosemite Valley. Open daily from Thanksgiving to mid-March; 2-hour sessions ($2.25 adults, $2 children), skate rentals (75 cents).

LODGING   All accommodations within the park are operated by a concessionaire, Yosemite Park & Curry Co., Yosemite National Park 95389, 373-4171. Make reservations well in advance, especially in summer and on holiday weekends. • The *Ahwahnee,* a distinctive hotel with outstanding views in Yosemite Valley, $95. Most elegant place to stay in the park. Some cottages adjoin main building. Nightly entertainment Tuesday through Saturday. • *Yosemite Lodge,* more informal lodging in motel-type rooms or modest cabins, $45 lodge, $24 cabin. Most lodge rooms have balcony or patio with Yosemite Valley views. • *Curry Village,* large (600 units) and rustic accommodations in Yosemite Valley in hotel-type rooms ($45), cabins ($24), and tent cabins ($16). • *Housekeeping Camp,* canvas-covered cabins in Yosemite Valley, $16. Almost like living outdoors; communal bath. Open mid-April through September. • *Wawona Hotel,* attractive century-old hotel near southern entrance to park, $21. Golf course. Open April through Thanksgiving weekend.

CAMPING   All campgrounds operated by the National Park Service, Yosemite National Park 95389, 372-4605. Make reservations for Yosemite Valley campsites (except walk-in camps) through Ticketron from May through September; first come, first served at other times of year and at all other camps. Yosemite Valley has 5 drive-in RV and tent campgrounds, $4 per night, no hookups. *Lower Pines* is open all year. *Wawona,* near park's southern entrance, also open year round, $3 per night.

DINING   Meal service in the park is available at the hotels and lodges, all operated by the Yosemite Park and Curry Co. Grocery stores in Yosemite Valley and at Wawona have picnic and camp supplies. • *Main Dining Room at the Ahwahnee* (see above) serves park's finest fare. Breakfast menu features eggs Benedict, while seafood salad is a nice choice for lunch. Entrees at dinner (reservations required) include roast duckling à l'orange. • *Mountain Room Broiler,* one of three dining spots at the Yosemite Lodge (see above). Steak and lobster place with mammoth rock-climbing murals and view of Yosemite Falls, open only for dinner from May through October. • *Four Seasons Restaurant,* also in Yosemite Lodge, breakfast and dinner daily with step-above-coffee-shop fare that includes filet mignon. • *Yosemite Lodge Cafeteria,* open for breakfast, lunch, and dinner. • *Cafeteria at Curry Village* (see above), good for moderate-priced breakfasts and dinners from April to mid-October. • *Dining Room at Wawona Hotel* (see above), buffet lunch is especially popular; reservations required for dinner. Open from early spring to mid-October.

FOR MORE INFORMATION   Contact the Superintendent, Box 577, Yosemite National Park, CA 95389, 372-4461.

In Search of the Giants in Sequoia and Kings Canyon National Parks

What towers 272 feet, weighs about 625 tons, and is at least 2,500 years old? It's the largest living thing on earth, a giant sequoia. You can view this immense tree, nicknamed General Sherman, not far from Los Angeles in Sequoia National Park.

A weekend in Sequoia and neighboring Kings Canyon National Park makes a wonderful outing away from the noisy metropolis. While relaxing in the quiet woods, you'll also be treated to sparkling waterfalls, beautiful rivers and lakes, lush mountain meadows, dramatic granite-walled canyons, and caves with fascinating marble formations. You're certain to see fleet-footed deer and other wildlife.

Sequoia was established in 1890 as America's second national park in order to protect its rare trees, the few giant sequoias that survived the last ice age and are found only along the western slope of the Sierra Nevada range. It adjoins Kings Canyon National Park, where you'll see other towering beauties like one called General Grant, a huge sequoia that's the nation's official Christmas tree.

Together these parks cover 1,324 square miles of America's most magnificent wilderness, crowned by Mount Whitney, the highest point in the U.S. south of Alaska. Of course, the majestic giant sequoias—close relatives of the soaring coastal redwoods—are the big attractions. You'll find them in two major groves, Giant Forest and Grant Grove, which are 32 miles apart but connected by a scenic and twisting mountain road named the Generals Highway.

To reach Sequoia and Kings Canyon National Parks from Los Angeles, take Interstate 5 north and join California 99 through Bakersfield to the

California 198 exit. Follow that road past Visalia to Sequoia's Ash Mountain entrance and the final zigzag section to Giant Forest.

If you don't enjoy mountain driving or are traveling in a RV, the longer but easier alternative route is to continue on California 99 to Fresno (or exit near Tulare onto California 63 going north), then turn east on California 180 to reach Kings Canyon's Big Stump entrance and Grant Grove.

Except for the park-service-operated campgrounds, all facilities for visitors—accommodations, dining rooms and cocktail lounges, grocery markets, gift shops, gas stations, and bus services—are provided under government contract by Sequoia and Kings Canyon Hospitality Services. Lodgings range from very rustic cabins with wood-burning stoves and communal bath facilities to more modern motel rooms with private showers. Make your headquarters at Sequoia's Giant Forest Lodge, which has the greatest choice of accommodations in either park. Camping is on a first come, first served basis except at the most popular campground, Lodgepole near Giant Forest, which you reserve through Ticketron.

You won't go hungry in the parks, but the food is far from gourmet fare. Most meals are served cafeteria or buffet style, and there's limited menu service at a couple of coffee shops and snack bars. The nicest place to eat is the dining room of Giant Forest Lodge, where you'll also find a cocktail lounge. To savor more of the fresh air and mountain scenery during your visit, shop for groceries at the village markets and picnic under the trees.

Ask at the park entry stations or visitors centers for maps and trail guides to help plan your weekend. The *Sequoia Bark,* a free park newspaper, lists daily activities. You can join guided bus excursions, follow rangers on nature hikes, walk the self-guided nature trails, and go sightseeing on saddle horses, too. Also attend the illustrated talks presented by park rangers in the evening.

On Saturday, head first to Giant Forest to see the General Sherman Tree, which measures 103 feet around its massive trunk. Also look for the Auto Log, a fallen tree wide enough to drive your car on. You can drive through another fallen giant, the Tunnel Log. A trail leads to Tharps Log, named for a cattleman who lived in the tree's burned-out trunk.

After seeing the sequoias, follow an old mountain road from Giant Forest to Crystal Cave. This marble cavern of marvelous stalactites and stalagmites is the only one of 90 caves in the parks open to the public. Rangers lead guided tours (except Wednesdays and Thursdays) in summer only.

On Sunday, drive along the Generals Highway to Grant Grove, where you'll discover more memorable sequoias like the Fallen Monarch, a hollow log once used as a tavern, living quarters, and even a stable. Nearby is the world's second largest sequoia, General Grant, which stretches 267 feet into the sky and has a trunk 40 feet thick.

If it's summer, continue north on California 180 to Kings Canyon and the rugged Cedar Grove area bordering the south fork of the Kings River. There's terrific backcountry scenery along the hiking and horse trails, as well as a four-mile unpaved nature route for motor vehicles.

If you'd rather not drive in the park, bus tours of the sequoia groves and other nature sights leave daily in the summer from Giant Forest Lodge. There are short early-morning and late-afternoon tours in Giant Forest, and an all-day outing to Grant Grove, Kings River Canyon, and Cedar Grove. Make reservations at the lodge or with Sequoia and Kings Canyon Hospitality Service.

The parks are open in winter, too, but be sure to carry tire chains. Some roads are subject to closure by snow, including the Generals Highway from Lodgepole in Giant Forest north to Grant Grove. Your best bet is to settle in at the lodge in Sequoia's Giant Forest, the parks' center of activity in wintertime and the most convenient to Los Angeles. Be sure to book well in advance for accommodations during the Christmas holidays, when both of these alpine parks are a winter wonderland and a big hit with families.

The snow-covered sequoias resemble huge candelabra and are a remarkable sight. Rangers will lead you to the big trees on snowshoes or cross-country skis, or follow the trails on your own. For more wintertime fun, there's downhill skiing at the Wolverton Ski Bowl a few miles north of Giant Forest, as well as snow play areas where the kids can frolic on sleds, saucers, and inner tubes.

When your weekend is over, leave the park via California 198 or 180 to rejoin California 99 and Interstate 5 for the drive south to Los Angeles.

Round trip is about 480 miles.

Note: You also can reach Sequoia and Kings Canyon National Parks by public transportation from mid-May through mid-September. Fly, train, or bus to Fresno from Los Angeles and connect with the special daily bus to Grant Grove and Giant Forest.

Sequoia/Kings Canyon Area Code: 209

SIGHTSEEING   *Park entry permit* $2 per vehicle; valid for multiple entries and exits in both parks. ● *Guided bus tours* of the parks daily from mid-May to mid-September, 565-3373. Two-hour tours of Sequoia depart 7:45 A.M. and 5:45 P.M. from Giant Forest Lodge; $5 per person. All-day tour of both parks departs 10 A.M. from Giant Forest Lodge; $12.50 per person. ● *Crystal Cave,* one-hour tours, Friday through Tuesday from mid-June to early September. Adults $1, under 16 years free. ● *Guided walks and campfire programs.* Times and places for ranger-led activities are listed at visitors centers at Lodgepole (Giant Forest) and Grant Grove and in free park newspaper, the *Sequoia Bark.* ● *Saddle horses* can be rented for trail rides in summertime from corrals at Grant

Grove, Cedar Grove, and Wolverton near Giant Forest. ● *Cross-country skiing,* Sequoia Ski Touring Center, Giant Forest Village, Sequoia National Park 93262, 565-3308. Open 8 A.M. to 5 P.M. daily, November through April. Rentals, lessons, and tours. ● *Wolverton Ski Bowl,* north of Giant Forest, Sequoia National Park, 565-3381. Ideal for novice downhill skiers; 3 rope tows, rentals, ski school, snack bar. Open weekends and holidays from Thanksgiving to April.

LODGING   *Giant Forest Lodge,* Giant Forest Village, Sequoia National Park 93262, 565-3373. Largest park lodging, with 243 motel, cottage, and very rustic cabin units; $19 basic to $48 best. Open all year. ● *Grant Grove Lodge,* Grant Grove Village, Kings Canyon National Park 93633, 335-2314. 52 rustic cottage and cabin rooms; $22 basic to $38 best. Open early May to late October. ● *Cedar Grove Lodge,* on Kings River in Cedar Grove, Kings Canyon National Park 93262, 565-3373. 18 modern motel rooms, $35. Open mid-May to September. Three lodgings above operated by park concessionaire, Sequoia and Kings Canyon Hospitality Service. ● *Wilsonia Lodge,* near Grant Grove Village, Box 808, Kings Canyon National Park 93633, 335-2310. 20 cabin and motel units, $36. Open all year. ● Other accommodation available just outside park boundaries in Three Rivers, en route from Los Angeles on California 198.

CAMPING   Parks have 14 campgrounds with four open year round, 565-3341. All sites $5 per night. In Sequoia, largest is *Lodgepole,* with 250 tent and RV sites; reserve through Ticketron. In Kings Canyon, *Azalea* is largest, with 116 sites. Camping (except for Lodgepole) is on first come, first served basis.

DINING   *Dining room in Giant Forest Lodge* (see above) overlooks Round Meadow. Breakfast and dinner only. Best food in the parks but served buffet style; also cocktail lounge. Open mid-May to mid-October. ● *Cafeteria in Giant Forest Village* offers breakfast, lunch, and dinner year round. ● *Coffee shop in Grant Grove Village,* with cocktail lounge adjacent. 3 daily meals available from mid-May to mid-October. ● *Snack bar in Cedar Grove Village* serves lunch and light snacks during summer. ● *Wilsonia Lodge* (see above) operates a year-round coffee shop. ● *Stony Creek Lodge,* midway between Giant Grove and Grant Grove villages, offers coffee-shop fare from mid-May to October.

FOR MORE INFORMATION   Contact Sequoia and Kings Canyon National Parks, Three Rivers, CA 93271, 565-3341.

Alpine Retreat at Lake Arrowhead and Big Bear Lake

Los Angeles is blessed with a convenient alpine retreat, the San Bernardino Mountains. If you're eager for a complete change from the maddening megalopolis, pack some casual clothes and outdoor gear for the short drive to a pair of mountain lakes. Tucked away in the mile-high evergreen forests are two informal year-round resorts, Lake Arrowhead and Big Bear Lake.

Crisp air, mountain scenery, friendly local folks, and all sorts of activities promise a delightful weekend. The resort villages are especially attractive when dressed with snow, but the family will have a wonderful time even when there's not enough of the white stuff for kids to pack snowballs or sled down a hill. (In wintertime, be sure to contact the California Highway Patrol to see if tire chains are required.)

Part of the scenic sojourn to Lake Arrowhead and Big Bear Lake is a ride along the Rim of the World Drive, which zigzags up and along the mountainside. Reach it from Los Angeles by driving east on Interstate 10 (the San Bernardino Freeway), then exiting north toward San Bernardino/Barstow on Interstate 215. Follow the freeway direction for Highland Avenue/Mountain Resorts, California 18 and 30. Then take the Crestline/Lake Arrowhead exit, Waterman Avenue, which is California 18.

The roadside flora changes from palms to chaparral to pines as the highway ascends into the San Bernardino National Forest. The original road was constructed by Mormons hauling timber from the mountains to build a new settlement at San Bernardino in the mid-1800s. The improved route you're driving was carved from the mountainside in 1915, with some portions later widened to four lanes for a less harrowing trip.

Pause at the turnouts for some inspiring aerial views over the cloud tops, far above the smog that's frequently trapped in the basin below. Continue on Rim of the World Drive until you meet California 173 and turn left to Lake Arrowhead.

Some previous visitors will be surprised to discover that the original 1920s resort village has disappeared. In 1979 it was destroyed by fire—on purpose. The village owners decided the place was too small and shabby-looking, so they offered the area's firemen a chance for some training and let them burn it down.

From the ashes has risen a new and larger village that opened for business in 1981. It now features 40 shops, several restaurants, and other facilities for mountain residents and visitors. Part of the two-level, 38-acre complex is the Arrowhead Hilton Lodge at the lake's edge, a pretty spot to spend the first night of your weekend getaway. Have dinner in the hotel's gourmet Beau Rivage restaurant, then enjoy the musical entertainment and go dancing at Rodney's, also in the Hilton.

On Saturday you can board the *Arrowhead Queen,* a paddle-wheeler that takes you on a 45-minute tour of the man-made lake (weather permitting) from a nearby dock at Lake Arrowhead Marina. There you also can rent a motorboat for sightseeing or fishing and let the kids challenge each other in the round bumper boats. More fun is in store for all ages at the village roller skating rink, which has a panorama of the lake.

Look for the spire-topped pavilion, a village landmark and the only building spared in the planned conflagration. Glenn Miller, Tommy Dorsey, and other big bands played there a half century ago, when the pavilion was a dance hall. Today it's home for a variety of shops where you'll find leather goods, needlework, jewelry, kitchenware, artwork, and more.

When activity or the alpine air makes you thirsty or hungry, stop in one of the several village restaurants that also dish up views of the lake. Families enjoy the Swiss-German food and decor at Heidi's. Chantecler is another good choice for lunch.

Afterward, drive on narrow roads around the lake to see the varied architecture of Arrowhead's many vacation homes and residences, including some of French Normandy and Norman English design. Head east from the village on California 173; just after you cross the dam is a nice lookout over the lake. Continue on the state highway, then turn left to go west on North Bay Road, which winds among the trees and attractive homes. Eventually it joins California 189 at Blue Jay, another mountain community that is undergoing redevelopment.

From there go south on Daley Canyon Road to rejoin California 18, then head east again along Rim of the World Drive through Running Springs to Big Bear Lake, where you should have reserved accommodations for Saturday night. There's a wide choice of family-run lodges with kitchen units, as well as vacation cabins and modern condominium units scattered among the fragrant pine trees that surround the seven-mile-long lake.

If it's late afternoon, turn north off California 18 on Alden Road and go to the Lighthouse at lakeside to enjoy the sunset view and cocktails. Then cross the road for a dinner of continental fare at the Harbor House. Or head to the Snow Summit ski area for dinner at the T. J. Summit and Co. Restaurant, which also is a popular spot for brunch on Sunday morning.

You'll find plenty to do in this mountain valley, which is best known as Southern California's ski center. From Thanksgiving to Easter, thousands of skiers flock to Big Bear when Mother Nature and snow-making equipment turn the steep slopes into a winter playground at the Snow Summit,

Goldmine, and Snow Forest ski areas. In the other seasons you can enjoy boating, hiking, horseback riding, golfing, fishing, camping, and much more.

On Sunday, choose your favorites from a host of activities that are easily reached from California 18, the south-shore highway that runs through the village of Big Bear Lake and is its main street, Big Bear Boulevard. Side roads take you to several marinas where craft can be rented for fishing, sightseeing, or water sports. Skim across the blue water on Jet-skis or a wind surfer, or fly above it by donning a parachute and going for a parasailing ride. Less adventurous visitors can cruise around the lake aboard the *Sierra,* an excursion boat that sails from Pine Knot Landing.

If you want to try your luck catching lake trout, bluegill, or bass, the marinas also have tackle, bait, and the necessary state fishing license. Or go to a private trout farm, Alpine Lake, where you pay only for what you hook and no license is required.

Also off Big Bear Boulevard are a trio of stables with rental horses that will take you on a scenic trail ride through the trees. Nearby one of the stables you'll spot the Alpine Slide, a snowless bobsled thrill ride that twists down the mountainside.

For a special treat, hop aboard the scenic ski ride that carries you up a mountain to an altitude of over 8,100 feet. Follow signs to the Snow Summit ski area and cruise quietly above the tree tops on a mile-long ride up the slope. At the end of the open-air trip by chair lift, you'll find some spectacular views and peaceful spots to picnic.

A few miles east, at the Goldmine ski area, you can play on the much-improved public golf course, an official nine holes after its gopher holes were filled in recently. The kids will be fascinated by a black bear, timber wolf, and other local mountain wildlife on display in the adjacent Moon-ridge Animal Park, a free county-run zoo.

For more family fun, there's skating at the Big Bear Roller Rink on Lakeview Drive. A short drive east of it is a tennis ranch with plenty of courts and a pro to improve your game.

Visit the U.S. Forest Service ranger station on the north shore of Big Bear Lake and ask for the Gold Fever Trail tour map of historic Holcomb Valley, where gold was discovered in 1860. If you decide to explore this old mining area, figure two to three hours to make the rugged trip over dirt roads. The rangers have hiking and camping information, too.

To get an exciting aerial view of this picturesque area, take a 30-minute scenic flight from Big Bear Airport with Mountain Air Service.

When your weekend in the mountains is over, drive east on California 18 to join one of the state's designated scenic highways, California 38. The road twists and turns as it descends through the forest and Barton Flats to Redlands, where you pick up Interstate 10 heading west to Los Angeles.

Round trip is about 210 miles.

Lake Arrowhead/Big Bear Lake Area Code: 714

SIGHTSEEING   *Lake Arrowhead Marina,* Lake Arrowhead Village, 337-2553. 60-passenger paddle-wheeler *Arrowhead Queen* departs hourly on 45-minute cruises from noon to 3 P.M. daily; weekends only in winter. Adults $4, children 4 to 12 years $2.50. Also canoe, bumper boat, rowboat, motorboat, and water ski rentals. ● *Lake Arrowhead Village Roller Skating Rink,* 337-8316. 2-hour afternoon and evening sessions daily; $2.50 per session including skates. ● *Snow Summit,* Big Bear Lake, 866-4621 or 866-5766. Open daily from 7:30 A.M. to 10 P.M. from mid-November to mid-April. 6 double chair lifts, 2 quad chairs, and a rope tow; daily lift pass $17.50. Lighted for night skiing. Summertime scenic ski lift ride weekends only from 10 A.M. to 4 P.M.; adults $3, children $1.50 for round-trip ticket. ● *Goldmine Ski Area,* Big Bear Lake, 585-2518. Open daily from 8 A.M. to 4 P.M. from mid-November to mid-April. 5 double chair lifts, 2 rope tows; daily lift pass $18. ● *Goldmine Golf Course,* Clubview Drive, Big Bear Lake, 585-8002. 9 holes, $7.50 weekends, $5.50 weekdays; open daily May through September. ● *Moonridge Animal Park,* Moonridge Road, Big Bear Lake. Open 8 A.M. to 4 P.M. daily, closed in winter. Free. ● *Pine Knot Landing,* end of Pine Knot Avenue, Big Bear Lake, 866-2628. One of 8 marinas on Big Bear Lake. Open April to mid-November from sunrise to sunset; canoe, rowboat, motorboat, powerboat, sailboat, pontoon boat rentals. Also, 40-passenger *Sierra* makes 90-minute cruises of Big Bear Lake from April to November. Adults $4, children age 5 to 12 $3. ● *Alpine Lake,* 440 Catalina Road, Big Bear Lake, 866-4532. Private trout farm open March to November; pay only for your catch. ● *Big Bear Roller Rink,* 40679 Lakeview Drive, Big Bear Lake, 866-3535. $3.75, including skates. ● *Big Bear Tennis Ranch,* end of Erwin Ranch Road, Big Bear City, 585-3133. 15 tennis courts; adult tennis camp on weekends during spring and autumn, children's tennis camp in summer. ● *Mountain Air Service,* Big Bear Airport, Big Bear City, 585-2511. 30-minute scenic flights for up to three passengers, $30, up to five, $40.

EVENTS   *Oktoberfest,* from mid-September to late October. For seven autumn weekends, Big Bear Lake is the place to go for oompah bands, bratwurst, and beer. Everyone joins in sing-alongs, dancing, yodeling, and log-sawing contests. Call the Big Bear Lake Valley Chamber of Commerce, 866-4601. ● *Old Miners' Days,* late July. Colorful week-long celebration of the Big Bear area's early days. Burro races highlight the summertime high jinks, which include pie-eating contests and "whiskerino" contests, dances, parades, and barbecues. Call 866-4601.

LODGING   *Arrowhead Hilton Lodge,* Lake Arrowhead Village, 336-1511. New 175-room motor lodge nestled at lakeside among the pines; guests welcome at private health club; $65. ● *Tree Top Lodge,* ½ mile from lake on Rainbow Drive, Lake Arrowhead, 337-3659. Pleasant motel in forest setting, open June to October; $50. ● *Escape Ski & Racquet Club,* 41935 Switzerland Drive, Big Bear Lake, 866-7504. 75 townhouses with kitchens, fireplaces, and patios at base of Snow Summit ski area; $65 weekends, $55 weekdays; except $100 weekends, $85 weekdays during ski season, mid-November to mid-April. ● *Marina Riviera Motel,* 40770 Lakeview Drive, Big Bear Lake, 866-7545. Super location in town on lakefront; $35. *Robinhood Inn & Lodge,* Lakeview Drive at Pine Knot Avenue, Big Bear Lake, 866-4643. In town, a few steps to lake; $35. No children under age 10. ● *Frontier Lodge,* 40472 Big Bear Boulevard, Big Bear Lake, 866-5888. Cottages with kitchens almost on lake, ½ mile west of town, $35. ● *Krausmeier Haus Bavarian Village,* 1351 Midway Boulevard, Big Bear City, 585-2886. Lodge and cottages in alpine meadow 6 miles from Big Bear Lake; $35.

CAMPING   Five U.S. Forest Service campgrounds are near Big Bear Lake; Grout Bay is the only one at lakeside. Most are $5 per night (no hookups) and closed in winter. Contact ranger station on North Shore, 866-3437.

DINING   *Beau Rivage,* gourmet dining room featuring French fare in Arrowhead Hilton Lodge (see above), 336-1511. ● Chantecler, Lake Arrowhead Village, 336-2151. Elegant restaurant at lakeside serving lunch and dinner by reservation only; especially popular for Sunday brunch. ● *Heidi's,* Lake Arrowhead Village, 336-2141. Fun for family-style dining daily from 6 A.M. to 9 P.M. ● *Sportsman Restaurant,* 2 miles from Lake Arrowhead Village on Hook Creek Road in Cedar Glen, 337-9036. American and Chinese dishes for lunch and dinner, plus children's plates; reservations advised. ● *The Royal Oak,* 2 miles from Lake Arrowhead Village on State Highway 189 in Blue Jay, 337-6018. English pub decor with prime ribs, veal dishes, seafood specialties for lunch and dinner; reservations advised. ● *T. J. Summit and Co. Restaurant,* base of Snow Summit ski area, Big Bear Lake, 866-3337. Delightful inexpensive in-spot for lunch, dinner, and weekend brunch; ski movies featured in upstairs lounge. ● *Lighthouse,* end of Alden Road, Big Bear Lake. Indoor-outdoor watering hole with best views of lake. Across the road is the *Harbor House,* another local favorite serving dinner from 5 P.M., also Sunday brunch; 866-5771 for reservations. ● *Captain's Anchorage,* Big Bear Boulevard at Moonridge Road, Big Bear Lake, 866-3997. Rustic dinner house specializing in steak and seafood. ● Always popular and dishing up German and American fare for breakfast, lunch, and dinner are *Old Country Kitchen,* 41226 Big Bear Boulevard, 866-5600, and *Log Cabin,* 39976 Big Bear Boulevard, 866-2639, both Big Bear Lake.

FOR MORE INFORMATION Contact Lake Arrowhead Village, P.O. Box 640, Lake Arrowhead 92352, 337-2533; and Lake Arrowhead Resorts Chamber of Commerce, at Fire Station No. 1 on State Highway 173 (or P.O. Box 155), Lake Arrowhead 92352, 337-3715. ● Also, Big Bear Lake Valley Chamber of Commerce, 40641 Lakeview Drive (or P.O. Box 2860), Big Bear Lake 92315, 866-5652. Open weekdays 9 A.M. to 5 P.M., Saturday 10 A.M. to 4 P.M.; closed Sundays. Also, 24-hour telephone accommodations service, 866-4601.

Escape to Old-Time Julian and Heavenly Palomar Mountain

When you yearn for some peace and quiet and a breath of fresh air, head to San Diego County's mountainous backcountry. In the scenic area between the Pacific Coast and the Colorado Desert you'll find plenty to entice you, including a century-old mining town that makes a quaint headquarters for your weekend escape.

Tucked in the foothills at the edge of Cleveland National Forest, the six-square-block village of Julian has old-fashioned lodgings, good places to eat, all sorts of gift shops, and a museum of pioneer memorabilia. Another drawing card is an annual fall harvest festival, when friendly townsfolk bake up mouth-watering apple pies and put on a crafts show for visitors.

Any time of the year you'll also have fun touring Julian's only remaining gold mine, going to a country dinner theater, and viewing Mother Nature's handiwork nearby in Cuyamaca Rancho State Park, a restful area of pine forests and oak groves. On the way home you'll be delighted by the fabled Dudley's Bakery at Santa Ysabel, as well as a charming Indian mission. And a mile high in the sky at Palomar Observatory you're welcome to view the world's largest telescope.

Start your excursion from Los Angeles by driving south on Interstate 5 and heading east just beyond Oceanside on California 78. You'll see a mixture of suburban housing developments and rural ranch life before the road leads to Julian, your weekend hideaway in the hills.

The town was created when miners rushed there to stake claims during a gold strike in 1870. Its oldest lodging is still taking guests, but reserve well in advance for a room in the Julian Hotel. Opened in 1887 as the

Robinson Hotel by a freed slave from Georgia, Albert Robinson, the 14-room inn still retains its Victorian flavor. Guests relaxing on the front porch and playing the piano in the parlor are reminiscent of travelers in earlier times. You'll slumber in four-poster beds and find the facilities down the hall. Or treat yourself to the private honeymoon cottage, with its own bath and a fireplace.

Visitors can opt for other lodgings in secluded cabins and European-style rooms (no bath) three miles from town in the rustic Pine Hills Lodge, built in 1912. If you arrive in time on Friday, go there for the barbecue dinner theater and enjoy a musical or comedy starring local performers. (The popular country-style meal and show also are offered on Saturday evenings at the lodge.)

Julian is a place to park your car and explore on foot. At Washington and Fourth streets is a former brewery building that's now the Julian Memorial Museum, jammed with local nostalgic items of the past century. On the hill behind you'll spot Julian's unusual library, a one-room schoolhouse built in 1888 and moved to town from nearby Witch Creek. Go a block to Main Street and stroll down the row of false-front buildings. Drop into the Julian Drug Store, circa 1886, and settle down at the old marble-topped fountain for a brown cow or sarsaparilla.

Then drive up the hill at C Street to the Eagle Mine, where you'll learn about Julian's gold rush days. In the past century the mine has yielded $3.5 million in gold, and it is still producing. During a tour that goes 1,000 feet into the cool dark tunnels, you'll get an insight into the mining process and be entertained with tales of early-day prospecting.

More productive today are the orchards that surround the town and fill roadside stands with apples and pears in the autumn. You can order homemade hot apple pie any time of the year at the Julian Cafe No. 2, successor to the town's oldest eatery. A number of restaurants have opened in recent years, all with quaint decor that complements the village's vintage look. Enjoy lunch at Romano's Dodge House, Rongbranch Cafe, Casa de Coronado, or the venerable roadside cafe west of town, Tom's Chicken Shack.

Julian's quaintness has caught on with refugees from the city who like this rural area's informal life-style, and some have opened shops for transient guests and local folks alike. Several are clustered in the K.O. Corral on B Street, including Julian Gem Traders, where you'll find a cache of semiprecious stones. The Julian Cider Mill on Main Street, which boasts 40 kinds of honey and other tasty treats, is a good place to refresh yourself with freshly pressed apple cider before embarking on an afternoon outing to Cuyamaca Rancho State Park.

To enter this attractive 26,000-acre park, drive about 10 miles south of Julian on California 79. Look for signs and a side road that lead to Stonewall Mine and an excellent mining exhibit in an old prospector's cabin. Nearby the entrance to Paso Picacho campground, visit the Interpretive

Center to learn about the animals, flowers, and geology that you'll see in this natural preserve.

A self-guided nature trail begins in the adjacent picnic area. For unsurpassed vistas on a clear day, hike the three-mile trail to Cuyamaca Peak, where you can see the ocean, the desert, and Mexico. A little farther along California 79, turn left to visit the interesting Indian Museum in an old stone ranch house near park headquarters.

Unless you decide to camp at Cuyamaca Rancho State Park or at William Heise County Park, close by Pine Hills, return to Julian to spend the night. On Sunday morning, head to the Pine Hills Lodge for the Bloody Mary Brunch, an all-you-can-eat buffet. Or drive west on California 78/79 for fresh pastries and coffee at Dudley's Bakery in Santa Ysabel. Located at a crossroads that seems to be in the middle of nowhere, this two-decade-old baking institution sells 21 kinds of oven-fresh bread to a clientele that comes from all over San Diego County. Few people ever pass Dudley's without going in to smell the wonderful bakery aromas and buy a loaf or two to take home.

Afterward, head north on California 79 about two miles to lovely Mission Santa Ysabel, founded in 1818 as an *asistencia,* or branch, of the mother mission in San Diego. It continues to serve the Indians of ten reservations, and visitors are welcome in the reconstructed church and its museum. Look for the religious murals painted by the Indians, and learn about stories of the lost treasure of Santa Ysabel and the mystery of its stolen bells. Also visit the Indian burial grounds.

Continue north and turn west on California 76 toward Lake Henshaw. Just past that popular fishing spot, turn right on San Diego County Road S7, East Grade Road, and follow it up to the summit road junction on Palomar Mountain. (In winter the mountain can become a white wonderland, and tire chains may be required; check with the highway patrol or the county road department.) Then go right on S6, the Highway to the Stars, which leads through some spectacular forest scenery to the famed Palomar Observatory.

An immense silver dome houses its 200-inch Hale telescope, the world's largest optical apparatus for peeking into the heavens. You can view the 530-ton instrument from a glassed-in gallery, but actual observations are not possible. The telescope is restricted to scientific researchers, who use it at night to make photographs of the stars in our solar system and beyond. Its huge mirror, about two feet thick, was cast of Pyrex glass in 1935, but grinding and polishing the mirror to perfection took 11 years. Since then scientists have been able to see a sextillion (1,000,000,-000,000,000,000,000) miles into space! For comparison, our moon is less than 240,000 miles away.

Owned and operated by Pasadena's California Institute of Technology since 1948, the observatory was built over 12 stories high in order to house the 55-foot-long telescope. An astronomer taking pictures actually rides the telescope as it follows the star being photographed, which may be nearly one billion light years away. Scientists at Palomar spent seven years making a photographic map of the entire sky as seen in the Northern Hemisphere. Pamphlets in the viewing gallery describe other feats of the telescope. Stop first at the adjacent astronomical museum for a description of the telescope, samples of pictures taken with it, and a look at a life-size replica of the enormous mirror.

Flanking the Palomar Mountain post office at the summit road junction are a store and restaurant, where you can get picnic supplies, snacks, and vegetarian meals. Both are run by a half dozen members of the Spiritual World Society of the Costa Mesa-based Yoga Center of California. Mother's Kitchen features homemade soups and breads, Mexican dishes, salads, sandwiches, ice cream, and fresh-baked pies. Beer and wines are available, too.

West from the summit road junction at the end of S7 is the entrance to Palomar Mountain State Park, a peaceful retreat for campers, picnickers, and hikers. Another attraction is Doane Pond, which is stocked with trout and open to fishing all year.

Return to S6 and descend that steep, switchback route through the dense forest to California 76. Then go west past hillside orchards of oranges and avocados to join Interstate 15 and head north to pick up California 60 (Pomona Freeway) back to Los Angeles.

Round trip is about 360 miles.

Julian/Palomar Mountain Area Code: 619

SIGHTSEEING　*Julian Memorial Museum,* Washington Street at Fourth Street, Julian, 765-0227. Open 9 A.M. to 5 P.M. weekends and holidays only. Admission free but donations appreciated. ● *Eagle Mine,* eastward at the top of C Street, Julian, 765-0036. Open daily 8 A.M. to 4 P.M. One-hour escorted tours that are informative and fun. Adults $6, children 15 years and under $3. ● *Cuyamaca Rancho State Park,* along California 79 about 10 miles south of Julian (P.O. Box 618, Julian 92036), 765-0755. The state highway runs through this forested park; there's a $2 per vehicle day-use fee to visit the park's interpretive center, Indian museum, and picnic areas. Also camping (see below). ● *Mission Santa Ysabel,* on California 79 (P.O. Box 128), Santa Ysabel 92070, 765-0810. Open daily from 7 A.M. to dusk. Admission free. ● *Palomar Observatory,* at northern end of San Diego County Road S6 atop Palomar Mountain, 742-3476. Viewing gallery in dome open daily 9 A.M. to 4:30 P.M. Admission free. ● *Palomar Mountain State Park,* western end of San Diego County road S7/State Park Road, Palomar Mountain 92060, 742-3462. $2 per vehicle day-use fee. Also camping (see below).

EVENTS *Fall Harvest and Apple Days Celebration* is held in the Julian Town Hall every weekend in October; craft show upstairs, apple pie sold downstairs. Craft shows and pie sales continue on weekends throughout November.

LODGING *Julian Hotel,* 2032 Main Street, Julian 92036, 765-0201. Cozy turn-of-the-century hotel with 14 rooms; $45 on Friday and Saturday, $34 from Sunday through Thursday. Also honeymoon cottage for $70 or $55. ● *Pine Hills Lodge,* 2960 La Posada Way (3 miles southeast of town), Julian 92036, 765-1100. 12 rustic cabins in woodsy setting with private baths and patios, some fireplaces; $45 to $85 Friday and Saturday, $40 to $50 other days. Continental breakfast included (except Sundays). Also, 5 rooms with shared bath in main building built of logs; $40, Friday, Saturday, and holidays only. Lodge dining room is popular for dinner, a dinner theater, and Sunday brunch (see below). ● Julian area has other modest accommodations, including 3 bed-and-breakfast inns; contact the Julian Chamber of Commerce (see below).

CAMPING *Cuyamaca Rancho State Park* (see above). Paso Picacho Campground has 85 tent and RV sites, Green Valley Falls 81 sites; $6 per night, no hookups. ● *William Heise County Park,* one mile west of Julian on California 78/79 to Pine Hills Road, then two miles south to Frisius Road and two more miles east, 565-3600 (San Diego County Parks information). 83 all-year tent and RV sites in a forest of oaks and pines; $5 per night, no hookups. ● *Palomar Mountain State Park* (see above). 31 tent and RV sites at Doane Valley Campground; $6 per night, no hookups.

DINING *Pine Hills Lodge* (see above). Enjoyable barbecue dinner theater Friday and Saturday nights with buffet of BBQ ribs and prime ribs preceding musical or comedy show; $17.50 per person. Seating for 72; reservations suggested. Also, hearty dinners served nightly except Monday and Tuesday in country-style dining room. Sunday Bloody Mary brunch from 10 A.M. to 2 P.M.; all you can eat and drink for $6.75; children half price. ● *Julian Cafe No. 2,* 2112 Main Street, Julian, 765-9932. Local favorite for breakfast, lunch, and dinner, or just a piece of apple pie. Whole apple pies to go, $4.50. Open every day. ● *Romano's Dodge House,* 2718 B Street, Julian, 765-1003. Italian fare for lunch and dinner; boasting Julian's only full bar. Open daily, except Tuesday and Wednesday, with guitar player or violinist on weekend nights. ● *Rongbranch Cafe,* 2722 Washington Street, Julian, 765-9929. Open daily for all three meals; sandwich specialties. ● *Casa de Coronado,* 2128 4th Street (behind Town Hall), Julian, 765-9926. Mexican menu for lunch and early dinner daily except Tuesday; late afternoon closing on Sunday. ● *Tom's Chicken Shack,* on California 78/79 at Wynola Road, 3 miles west of Julian, 765-0443. Well-known cafe serving its namesake and other American fare for lunch and dinner. Closed Tuesday and Wednesday. • *Dudley's Bakery,* at California 78 and 79 junction, Santa Ysabel 92070, 765-0488. Nearly two dozen types of freshly baked bread to take out, or savor pastries and other bakery treats in the adjoining restaurant. Open daily except Monday and Tuesday. • *Mother's Kitchen,* at junction of San Diego County roads S6 and S7, Palomar Mountain 92060, 742-3496. Restaurant (and store) with vegetarian menu and snacks open weekends from 8:30 A.M. to 6 P.M., weekdays 10:30 A.M. to 5 P.M. except Tuesday.

FOR MORE INFORMATION   Contact the Julian Chamber of Commerce, P.O. Box 413, Julian 92036, 765-1857. The town map includes a list of accommodations.

Rambling Around Paso Robles

Pity the travelers who rush along U.S. 101 between Los Angeles and San Francisco. They don't have time to discover the delights that often can be found just off the freeway. Exit at Paso Robles, for instance, and you'll find an array of pleasant surprises to fill a weekend.

Named by the Spanish missionaries for a pass through the thick oaks, this pastoral place is now adorned with almond trees that were planted on the rolling hills that surround the town. They bring not only a bountiful crop of tasty nuts, but a stream of visitors in late February and early March, when the trees paint the hillsides with their beautiful pink and white blossoms.

Any month of the year is a fine time to ramble around Paso Robles, which planted its roots along the El Camino Real stagecoach route, then became a well-known hot springs resort, and now is the hub for this scenic agricultural area in northern San Luis Obispo County. In addition to all the almonds, you'll see walnut, pistachio, and apple orchards, grain fields, and grape vineyards.

Winery tours and tastings are among the activities you'll enjoy in the Paso Robles countryside. To keep out-of-towners happy and around for a while, the chamber of commerce has compiled a list of 113 things to do. Save most of them for another time, but be sure to visit Mission San Miguel, a rural sanctuary that hasn't changed very much during the past two centuries. A leisurely circle excursion also will take you to a delightful doll museum and some historical adobes. And don't miss the perfect Sunday drive, a bucolic back-road route through the Santa Lucia Mountains to the ocean.

You'll need an early start from Los Angeles to reach Paso Robles by nightfall. Take U.S. 101 north to the California 46 East (Fresno/ Bakersfield) exit, but go west under the freeway on 24th Street to check in at the Black Oak Motor Lodge, Paso Robles's major motel. For more home-style accommodations, exit six miles sooner on Vineyard Drive at Templeton and stay at the Country House Inn, a five-room bed-and-breakfast inn that was built when the town was established in 1886.

In the morning, begin a lazy day of touring by heading seven miles north of Paso Robles to Mission San Miguel Arcangel. Along the way, leave U.S. 101 at Wellsona Road to visit Helen Moe's Antique Doll Museum. Her intriguing collection of nearly 1,000 dolls includes a wooden one that belonged to the son of Henry VII and dates to 1540. Especially fascinating are the miniature furnishings of bygone days that decorate a large dollhouse. Helen and her husband, Emerson, also operate a gift shop and a family-style restaurant, the Almond Country Inn. It's a pleasant place to have breakfast before continuing on U.S. 101 to the San Miguel exit. There you'll be greeted by a campanile of bells and a rural scene reminiscent of the days when Franciscan fathers from Spain founded the mission in 1797. San Miguel is one of only four missions in the famed chain that are still run as parish churches by the brown-robed padres.

Enter the mission through its courtyard, now a cactus garden, and pick up a self-guided-tour leaflet in the gift shop. In St. Michael's Room you'll see a sixteenth-century wood carving that depicts the mission's patron saint overpowering the devil. Other rooms—including the friars' sleeping quarters and dining room and a kitchen with its original beehive oven— are filled with artifacts and prestatehood history. A highlight is the long, narrow, and unusually adorned church sanctuary, with adobe walls almost six feet thick. Its remarkably well preserved decorations were painted in the early 1800s by the Indian neophytes, directed by Spanish artist Esteban Munras. Unique to this mission is the all-seeing eye of God represented above the altar.

Alongside the church you can view the cemetery, burial site for hundreds of Indians as well as the William Reed family, who purchased San Miguel after all the California missions were secularized by Mexico in the mid-1800s. The family was murdered at the mission by bandits. One of Reed's partners was Petronillo Rios, who built a family home nearby on the north-south stagecoach road that later was paved and became the original Highway 101. Today Rios's hacienda has been restored and is open as a museum.

Backtrack to the San Miguel exit from U.S. 101 and follow the signs to reach the Rios-Caledonia Adobe and gift shop, which are just down the road from the mission. During its lifetime this rustic residence also served as a stagecoach stop, hotel and tavern, schoolhouse, mattress factory, tailor shop, and a 1920s tourist attraction. Volunteers known as the

Friends of the Adobe restored the structure in the past decade and usually are on hand to answer questions and show you around. They also have a craft guild and run a gift shop to sell their work—homemade quilts, embroidered and crocheted items, dolls, and more—to support continuing restoration.

After your visit, head back north on Mission Street past the mission grounds and go into the town of San Miguel, which boomed during World War II, when there were 45,000 soldiers at neighboring Camp Roberts. Nowadays about the only place to find food or drink in the quiet community is at the Park Garage Restaurant and Saloon on 14th Street.

Top off your easygoing day with a tour and wine tasting at the award-winning Estrella River Winery, and savor some back-road scenery along the way. From San Miguel go east on 14th Street, which crosses the wide Salinas riverbed and turns south to become River Road. Turn left to head east on Estrella Road at the sign with a black-and-white cow, then go right on Airport Road until you see the white fence that surrounds the 1878 Estrella Adobe Church. This state historic landmark is open only occasionally, for weddings, but you can park on the road shoulder and explore its old pioneer cemetery.

Continue south past the Paso Robles municipal airport to busy California 46 and turn left to go east about four miles to the roadside vineyards of the Estrella winery. Slow down for the left-hand entrance, marked only by a small Tasting Room sign. Drive past rows of grapevines to the hill-top winery, where you can climb an observation tower for a better view of the impressive vineyards before taking a tour and tasting the wine. Grapes from the very first harvest in 1977 produced two gold medal winners, and Estrella River vintages now are sold in Europe and Asia as well as locally.

Return to California 46, heading back west toward Paso Robles for dinner at Joshua's, a century-old church that's been converted into a charming restaurant. It's a town favorite, specializing in barbecued spare-ribs, fresh seafood, and steak. A combo plays Saturday and a few other nights, so you can dance, too. Another popular place for dinner is the Iron Horse in Templeton.

The following day, continue your unrushed auto touring by heading into the close-by coastal mountains to visit three small, family-run wine-ries, and then proceed to the Pacific Ocean on a former horse-and-buggy lane, picturesque Santa Rosa Road. That meandering country road meets the coast highway at Cambria, just eight miles from the state's most-visited historical monument, Hearst Castle.

From Paso Robles, go south on U.S. 101 and exit west on Vineyard Drive at Templeton into the Santa Lucia foothills, one of the county's main wine-making regions. After about three miles you'll see the large white buildings of Pesenti Winery and some of its 100-acre vineyard, mostly planted with Zinfandel grapes. Pesenti's red wine was an early favorite with Basque shepherds from the San Joaquin Valley. Three generations of the Pesenti family have been making wine since their winery was established in 1934. You might meet some of them in the tasting room or while walking around on a self-guided tour. In October visitors are welcome to watch all the activity during the annual grape harvest.

Also visit the neighboring Las Tablas Winery, about 200 yards up the street on Winery Road. Its small tasting room is inside an old redwood wine vat. Until 1976 Las Tablas was called the Rotta Winery, named for a family of Swiss descent that produced wines for 70 years. They bought the land that was the county's first vineyard, planted with grapes by a Frenchman in 1865.

Continue on Vineyard Drive to California 46 and momentarily follow that modern highway west to York Mountain Road. Turn right and drive along the narrow, twisting road under arches of moss-covered trees to the York Mountain Winery, founded by the York family over a century ago. New Yorker Max Goldman purchased the property in 1970, eventually replanted 100 acres of grapes, and now produces more than a dozen different kinds of wine. You can sample some of them in the restored, hand-made-brick winery building.

Return to California 46 and continue west a couple of miles before turning right onto Cypress Mountain Road, a quiet, rural two-lane road. The narrow pavement curls along 2,232-foot Black Mountain and becomes Santa Rosa Road before it slowly descends and follows the stream bed of Santa Rosa Creek. The road is flanked by trees and pretty meadows interspersed with barns, lazy cows, and occasional fleet-footed deer. It leads you to Marquart Park, an idyllic spot for a picnic, and then continues through a wooded hollow to the main street of the growing coastal community of Cambria.

If you didn't pack a picnic, this attractive town is a good place to eat before beginning the return trip to Los Angeles, or make Cambria your base for an extended weekend; see the itinerary for visiting Hearst Castle and nearby coastal towns (page 3).

For the journey back to Los Angeles, go south on California 1 to rejoin U.S. 101 at San Luis Obispo.

Round trip is about 490 miles.

Paso Robles Area Code: 805

SIGHTSEEING *Helen Moe's Antique Doll Museum,* U.S. 101 at Wellsona Road (or Route 2, Box 332), Paso Robles 93446, 238-2740. Open daily 9:30 A.M. to 5:30 P.M., except Sundays from 12:30 P.M.-Admission: $3 per couple, $2 single, 50 cents for ages 5 to 12. Also gift shop and restaurant (see below). ● *Mission San Miguel Arcangel,* 801 Mission Street, San Miguel 93451, 467-3256. Open daily 10 A.M. to 5

P.M. Admission donation: 50 cents per person, $1 per family. • *Rios-Caledonia Adobe,* end of Mission Street at U.S. 101, San Miguel 93451, 467-3357. Open weekends and Fridays 10 A.M. to 4 P.M. Free. At other times you can walk around the signposted grounds. • *Estrella River Winery,* 6 miles east of Paso Robles off California 46 (or Shandon Star Route, P.O. Box 96), Paso Robles 93446, 238-6300. Open for tours and tasting every day from 10 A.M. to 5 P.M. Free. • *Pesenti Winery,* 2900 Vineyard Drive, Templeton 93465, 434-1030. Open daily for tours and tasting 8 A.M. to 6 P.M., except Sunday from 9 A.M. Free. • *Las Tablas Winery,* 3 miles west of Templeton on Winery Road (or P.O. Box 697), Templeton 93465, 434-1389. Open daily for tasting from 9 A.M. to 6 P.M., except Sunday from 10 A.M. to 5 P.M. Free. • *York Mountain Winery,* 10 miles west of Templeton on York Mountain Road (or Route 2, Box 191), Templeton 93456, 238-3925. Open daily for tasting from 10 A.M. to 5 P.M. Free.

EVENTS   *San Luis County Fair,* Paso Robles Fairgrounds, off U.S. 101 at 24th Street. Annual mid-August wingding with rodeo, horse show, livestock exhibits, carnival, and country-and-western entertainers.

LODGING   *Black Oak Motor Lodge,* 1135 24th Street, Paso Robles 93446, 238-4740; $31 (higher during county fair). Area's biggest and best-known motel. Restaurant on premises but not recommended. • *County House Inn,* 91 Main Street, Templeton 93465, 434-1598; $55. Friendly, antique-filled B&B with 5 rooms and 2 baths down the hall. Teatime refreshments and continental breakfast included. No small children, no smoking. • In downtown Paso Robles are two other modest motels to check out personally before checking in: *Paso Robles Inn,* 1103 Spring Street, 238-2660; $32, with nicely landscaped grounds and dining room (see below), and *Melody Ranch Motel,* 939 Spring Street, 238-3911; $28.

DINING   *Joshua's,* 500 13th Street at Vine, Paso Robles, 238-7515. Best restaurant in town. Lunch and dinner daily, also Sunday brunch. • *The Iron Horse,* 508 Main Street, Templeton, 434-1877. Local favorite for dinner nightly except Mondays, in turn-of-the-century surroundings. Open oak-pit barbecue and seafood are specialties. Bar opens at 4 P.M. • *Almond Country Inn,* at Helen Moe's Antique Doll Museum (see above). Family-style breakfasts, lunches, and dinners every day. • *Park Garage Restaurant and Saloon,* 14th and Mission streets, San Miguel 93451, 467-3400. Rustically decorated 1920s garage open daily for lunch and dinner. Popular watering hole, with country-and-western bands on weekend evenings. • *Paso Robles Inn* (see above). Dining room and coffee shop open every day, with all-you-can-eat lunch buffet on Sundays. • Also see dining suggestions for Cambria, page 7.

FOR MORE INFORMATION Contact the Paso Robles Chamber of Commerce, 1113 Spring Street (or P.O. Box 457), Paso Robles 93446, 238-0506.

Flowers and Franciscans at Lompoc

Flower fanciers and mission aficionados will have a field day in Lompoc *(lom-poke)*, a folksy place in scenic Santa Barbara County. Plan your weekend for early summer, as the fields around town become a dazzling rainbow when more than 500 varieties of flowers burst into bloom. During June and July some 2,400 acres blossom like a colorful patchwork quilt, a sight that's unique to Lompoc—the flower-seed center of the nation. And at the edge of town, you'll step back in time with a visit to the most authentically restored of all California missions, La Purisima.

Also return to yesteryear by staying in the Union Hotel, a reborn 1880 Hostelry with a popular family-style dining room that's just over the pastoral hills in tiny Los Alamos. Twelve upstairs rooms have been refurbished for weekend guests—with bathrooms down the hall, of course.

Begin your bucolic escape from Los Angeles by heading north on U.S. 101. Drive past Santa Barbara and the town of Solvang to the Los Alamos exit. Go under the freeway and down Bell Street to the hotel, a rustic two-story building with a false front of weathered barn wood.

Don't waste a trip by arriving during the week, because that's when the Union Hotel's owner locks up the place. "Running a hotel on the weekend is fun," says Dick Langdon, "but after that it becomes work."

This former stagecoach stop has been undergoing restoration since 1972, when Langdon bought the hotel as a business and pleasure venture. He's filled it with hundreds of period pieces and antiques, ranging from a $15,000 Tiffany clock to a pair of burial urns from Egypt. Langdon considers his Union Hotel a working museum and wants to make it the most authentic turn-of-the-century inn in America. He lives there with his wife, Teri, and some of the staff and rents out the dozen tiny rooms only on Friday, Saturday, and Sunday nights.

Those same days they open the dining room to walk-in guests, who sometimes drive the 160 miles from Los Angeles just for the family-style dinner of homemade soup, country-baked chicken, platters of beef, potatoes, fresh vegetables, and corn bread with honey butter.

After the dinner crowd goes home, join the other overnight guests in the hotel's saloon, where the innkeeper likes to have a little songfest. Or go to the old-fashioned upstairs lobby to read, listen to vintage radio programs, or play a little pool. Even more relaxing is to slip into the bubbling Jacuzzi outdoors in the starlit garden.

The next morning after breakfast in the dining room, climb with the other guests into the hotel's former Yellowstone Park touring car for complimentary sightseeing in the countryside. When you return to town, which has a population of less than 800, there are nine antique stores to explore. The largest is Los Alamos Imports, a vast old granary filled with treasures from Holland, especially furniture.

Also be sure to browse in the 100-year-old Los Alamos General Store, which has been restored in nineteenth-century style. You'll see bolts of cloth in the dry goods department, a display of patent medicines, pickles in a counter jar, and even an Indian couple sitting around the potbellied stove.

After spending a lazy day around Los Alamos and another night in the Union Hotel, get up early for a pretty drive over the Purisima Hills to Lompoc. Go south on Drum Canyon Road, then turn right on California 246 to go west and follow the signs to picturesque Mission La Purisima. The setting for its handsome adobe and tile-roof structures is still pastoral—rolling hills, grazing sheep and cattle, and gardens with flowers and fruit-bearing trees. The mission buildings and 980 acres that surround them are now preserved and protected as a state historic park.

La Purisima, midway between missions at Santa Barbara and San Luis Obispo, was founded in 1787 as the eleventh in the chain of California missions that stretched from San Diego to Monterey at intervals of a day's ride on horseback. The original mission buildings, located within the present city limits of Lompoc, were knocked to the ground by an earthquake in 1812. A new site was chosen, and Mission La Purisima was reconstructed four miles northeast in a sheltered valley.

Make a leisurely two-hour self-guided tour of this handsomely restored mission after picking up a descriptive brochure from the park office. Start at the Indian infirmary, which is now a little museum with interesting photos and artifacts. A path leads from there across a wooden and leather-tied footbridge to the mission compound. Along the way, where animals graze in the field, you'll cross a wide dirt track that's the original El Camino Real, the Spanish road that once connected all the missions.

Compared to all the other missions, La Purisima's architecture is especially striking, with a row of long, low buildings that feature distinctive colonnades. Hoping to avoid future damage by earthquakes, the padres built some of the adobe walls four feet thick. When you come to the walled cemetery, look for the tower, with two of the 160-year-old bells that were made in Peru especially for the mission. Go inside the narrow church, which could hold as many as 1,000 Chumash Indians at twice-daily services, to view an altar inlaid with abalone shells.

Another building you can visit served as soldiers' quarters and housed workshops. Exhibits show many of the Indian workers' activities, such as weaving woolen blankets. And nearby the priests' stark residence you'll find the pottery workshop, kitchen, and gristmill. Outside are vats where the Indians made soap and tallow. The mission had an extensive water system, using pipes of ceramic tile to carry spring water to pools for doing laundry and to the garden for irrigation. Go for a stroll in the garden to see hundreds of native California plants that were known to the mission padres and Indians.

You can picnic in a shaded grove near the park office, or head into Lompoc for lunch before driving around the outskirts of town to see its annual floral extravaganza. Taking Purisima Road from the mission into town, you'll spot a few flower fields and the Denholm Seed Company, but the best show is west of Lompoc. Follow Ocean Avenue (California 246) to the other side of town and an observation point that offers an aerial view of the bright fields and Lompoc Valley. Turn left from Ocean Avenue on V Street to Olive Avenue, then go right to Bodger Road. The narrow road is opposite the Bodger Seed Company buildings and goes uphill to the panoramic lookout. To the northwest you'll see the fields of Burpee Seed Company, the valley's pioneer seed grower, which started in the early 1900s with a planting of sweet peas. (Beyond is another big influence on Lompoc's economy, Vandenberg Air Force Base, the West Coast's aerospace center.)

To enjoy the beautiful crop close up, go back down the hill and drive slowly along the side roads that cut through the flower fields stretching from California 246 to the Santa Ynez River. You'll see marigolds, sweet peas, zinnias, asters, petunias, cornflowers, larkspurs, poppies, nasturtiums, calendulas, columbine, lavender, alyssum, lobelia, ageratum, and more.

Sorry, you won't be able to buy any of the beautiful blooms to take home. But their seeds eventually will be for sale in your neighborhood and throughout the world; the Lompoc Valley produces more than half the flower seeds grown around the globe. Back in town at Civic Center Plaza on Ocean Avenue and O Street, you can learn the names of the various flower varieties by visiting a display garden where the plants are labeled.

For extra fun, try to plan your trip for the last weekend in June, when the folks in Lompoc Valley hold their annual flower festival. Highlights are a floral parade, flower show, and tours of the flower fields. And you'll enjoy arts-and-crafts exhibits, outdoor entertainment, a carnival, and plenty to eat.

Return to Los Angeles by driving south from Lompoc on California 1 to join U.S. 101.

Round trip is about 330 miles.

Lompoc/Los Alamos Area Code: 805

SIGHTSEEING   *Mission La Purisima State Historic Park,* Purisima Road (or RFD Box 102), Lompoc 92436, 733-3713. Open 9 A.M. to 5 P.M. daily. Adults 50 cents, children age 6 to 17 and senior citizens 25 cents.

EVENTS   *Lompoc Valley Flower Festival* during the last weekend in June, 736-3100. Festival's activity center is Ryon Park, Ocean Avenue and O Street. From noon until dusk, free bus tours of flower fields and Vandenberg Air Force Base depart hourly from park. Saturday-morning parade of flower floats. Flower show in Veterans' Memorial Building, end of H Street; $1.50 donation, children under age 12 free. One of Southern California's best-known festivals. ● *Mission Fiesta Days,* Mission La Purisima State Historic Park (see above) on the third Sunday in May. Demonstrations of arts and crafts in the Spanish mission era, with free tortillas and beans served to visitors.

LODGING   *Union Hotel,* Bell Street (or P.O. Box 616), Los Alamos 93440, 344-2744. Open Friday, Saturday, Sunday only; no children. 12 rooms, $65 per night, including breakfast; two front rooms with private bath, $75. Reservations a must. Also, delicious bargain-priced dinners in dining room (see below). If the Union Hotel is booked up or outside your budget, stay in one of Lompoc's hotels; be certain to reserve a room months in advance if you're planning to visit during the flower festival. ● *Redwood Motor Lodge,* 1200 North H Street, Lompoc 93436, 735-3737; $40. ● *Flagwaver Motor Hotel,* 937 North H Street, Lompoc 93436, 736-5605; $46. ● *Village Inn,* 3955 Highway S20 (Lompoc–Casmalia Road), Lompoc 93436, 733-3571; $40. Family dining room, coffee shop. North of town in Vandenberg Village. Other accommodations not far away at Solvang (see page 177), Buellton, and Santa Maria.

CAMPING   *River Park,* California 246 at Sweeney Road, Lompoc, 736-6565. 36 sites along Santa Ynez River, $3 per night. No reservations or hookups.

DINING   *Union Hotel,* Los Alamos (see above). Family-style dinner is offered in the antique-decorated dining room to hotel guests and the public beginning at 5 P.M. on Friday and Saturday, noon on Sunday. Adult tab is $8; youngsters step on a scale and pay according to their weight. Good food and fun. ● *The Jetty,* 304 West Ocean Avenue, Lompoc, 736-6969. Locally caught seafood specialties; lunch and dinner daily. ● *Don Pepe's,* 610 North H Street, Lompoc, 736-3202. Fine Mexican fare daily for lunch and dinner; children's menu. ● *Royal Coach Restaurant,* 1501 East Ocean Avenue, Lompoc, 736-3491. Popular for prime ribs, steak, and lobster; reservations preferred. Lunch weekdays, dinner nightly.

FOR MORE INFORMATION   Contact the Lompoc Valley Chamber of Commerce, 119 East Cypress Avenue, Lompoc 93436, 736-4567. Open 9 A.M. to 5 P.M. weekdays.

History and Outdoor Adventure in Kern County and Isabella Lake

The Tehachapi mountain range north of Los Angeles hardly seems like camel country. Nonetheless, anyone traveling through Grapevine Canyon in California's early statehood days could count on seeing those strange beasts of burden. The dromedaries were stationed at Fort Tejon, a military, political, and social center in Southern California during the mid-1800s. The camels, and the U.S. Army's Camel Corps, are only memories today, but you can still visit the important fort. In fact, it's the first stop on a weekend excursion to inland Kern County for a bit of history in Bakersfield and some outdoor adventure at Isabella Lake. The menu of possible activities includes whitewater rafting down the mighty Kern River, as well as fishing, sailing, water skiing, golfing, horseback riding, hunting, hiking, camping, and even downhill skiing in wintertime.

With so much to do and see, it's best to plan a long weekend. At least get an early start in order to visit Fort Tejon on the way to Bakersfield, where you should spend the first night at one of Kern County's most popular resorts, Rio Bravo. With its 19 tennis courts, 18-hole golf course, horse stables, and guest programs that include river rafting, you'll be tempted to stay awhile.

Begin your trip by driving north from Los Angeles on Interstate 5 and go six miles beyond the Tejon Pass summit to the Fort Tejon exit. Cross the freeway to the parking area and visitors center for this 200-acre state historic park. Established in 1854, the fort was regimental headquarters for the First U.S. Dragoons. During the decade they were stationed there, soldiers protected miners and Indians in the area, rounded up stolen horses and cattle, chased bandits, and gave band concerts. By happenstance, it also was a training ground for officers of the Civil War, including Grant and Sherman. In fact, 15 men from Fort Tejon served as generals during the War Between the States.

Today the interstate freeway runs through the old fort's boundaries, but a few of the original adobe brick buildings have been preserved or reconstructed. Interior furnishings and displays with life-size mannequins give you an idea of the frontier soldiers' dress and life-style more than a century ago.

Continue north on Interstate 5 and join California 99 to reach Bakersfield, at the southern end of the San Joaquin Valley. Skirt the city by exiting east on California 58 and follow that freeway to the exit for California 184. Take it north to join California 178 going east toward Lake Isabella, then turn left a mile beyond that intersection and go north on the Alfred Harrell Highway to reach Lake Ming Road and the Rio Bravo Resort.

Check into the lodge, perhaps into one of the suites that features a fireplace and wet bar, then choose dinner from the international menu offered in the resort's excellent dining room. You'll soon discover why this year-round vacation center is a favorite of families who love the outdoor life. Guests can go rafting, tubing, and kayaking with the resort's own Kern River Whitewater Co., and mount up at the Rio Bravo's equestrian center for on-your-own or guided trail rides. You also can play tennis on championship courts (15 are lighted for night play) and try to beat par on the 18-hole golf course. This classy yet comfortable resort even boasts a runway for guests who arrive in their own planes.

If there's another reason besides the Rio Bravo for a visit to Bakersfield, it's to tour Pioneer Village, a 14-acre re-created town of frontier buildings and artifacts gathered from all over the area. You'll see the houses and stores where some of the state's pioneers lived and worked, the clothes they wore, and the tools they used. Visitors can spend an entire day strolling around this rustic Williamsburg of the West.

To get to the Pioneer Village from the resort, continue on the Alfred Harrell Highway as it circles westward back toward town and becomes Panorama Drive. Merge into California 204 (Union Avenue) heading south, then turn right on 34th Street to Chester Avenue. Go right again to the large brick clock tower that marks the museum parking lot.

More than 60 structures and exhibits make up Pioneer Village, an outstanding outdoor museum that's been growing for more than three decades. At the village entrance, pick up a brochure or the illustrated guidebook that identifies the buildings and describes the displays you'll see on a clockwise tour of the town. To get a better idea of life in the Old West, peek in windows and doors as you walk around. Mannequins dressed in period clothes add a real-life look to the exhibits. It's easy to imagine you're in an actual nineteenth-century town, complete with blacksmith shop, general store, newspaper office, undertaking parlor, fraternal lodge hall, railroad station, dressmakers' shop, firehouse, one-room school, and bandstand. Don't be surprised to find a ball and chain in the old jail.

The open-air museum recalls Kern County's importance as an early agricultural center, too. You'll see an intriguing display of branding irons, a harness-making shop, and a quarter-million-dollar collection of vintage horse-drawn vehicles. Notice that even the sheepherder's cabin was built on skids, so it could be pulled from place to place by horses. A group of weathered structures recalls life on the county's early ranches. Look for a cider press and hand-operated washing machine on the back porch of the Weller ranch house. Next to the barn are a wooden windmill, a hay derrick, and a cookwagon that fed the field hands.

After you've toured the village, be certain to visit the adjacent Kern County Museum, where other exhibits will bring back more memories of yesteryear. Handmade quilts are displayed on the second floor, where you can see some of the local women enjoying their weekly quilting bee on Tuesday mornings. The museum's collections of ladies' hats and dresses, fancy lacework, and hand fans will get your attention too.

After you've finished your historical tour, take Chester Avenue south to California 178 and go east to follow the twisting Kern River through Sequoia National Forest to Isabella Lake, a recreational retreat that resembles a mini–Lake Powell. Boating and fishing are its biggest attractions, plus camping and hiking around the 38-mile shoreline.

Before the mid-1950s there wasn't a lake in sight here—only the Kern River, which often became a destructive torrent during the rainy season and when snow melted in the nearby Sierra Nevadas. Then the U.S. Army Corps of Engineers built a pair of earth-fill dams for flood control to protect valuable agriculture and oil fields downstream along the Kern River Valley. The L-shaped lake that resulted has become a favorite destination for folks who enjoy the outdoors. Summer is the busiest season, but wintertime draws a pretty good crowd as well, because snow often decorates the surrounding mountains without reaching the lake below. Most of the campgrounds around the lake are open year round, and there are a number of small and rustic lodgings where you also can spend the night.

Route 178 skirts the southern shore of the lake, but you should exit on California 155 toward Kernville and then take the turnoff to the Corps of Engineers headquarters. From this hilltop location is a pretty panorama of the lake, and from the parking lot on the left you'll also get a bird's-eye look at the main dam.

In the office is a relief map that gives an overview of Isabella Lake and lights up to indicate the recreation areas. You'll be able to locate the lake's three marinas and five public boat ramps, campgrounds, an off-road motorcycle area, wildlife preserve, and entrances to nature trails. Pick up the free maps and brochures, too.

Another good place to get information is in the town of Lake Isabella at Sportsman's Center, the local general store, which is open every day. (Take the California 155 exit right to Isabella Boulevard.) Fishing fans will find rods, tackle, bait, the required state license, and information on where the fish are biting in Isabella Lake and the Kern River. Store personnel also can tell you about campgrounds and places to eat.

Back on California 155, go north along the lake to Kernville. Boats can be rented and launched at Isabella Marina North Fork, and you'll also spot attractive campgrounds flanking the highway. About halfway to Kernville the state highway turns left at Wofford Heights and heads up to Alta Sierra and the scenic Shirley Meadows ski area atop Greenhorn Mountain. In winter, rope tows operate on three hills. Signs are posted when tire chains are required on the steep mountain road (chains can be rented in Lake Isabella).

As you continue on the lakeside Kernville Road to Kernville, look for the Kern Valley Golf and Country Club, which opens its 9-hole course to the public every day. The clubhouse serves refreshments, too. Spend the night in one of the family-run motels in Kernville or northward along the river. Campers can pitch a tent or park an RV in one of the numerous campgrounds by the river or lake.

Kernville itself is a small town with Western-style false-front stores around a little square. Nearby in Riverside Park you'll usually find plenty of people fishing for trout, and it's also a pretty spot to picnic. Upstream the rugged Kern River roars with white water and daredevil rafters in summer. There are some pleasant places to eat in town and up the river, too. Ewings on the Kern, a local favorite for dinner and Sunday brunch, offers a good view of the rafters floating down the river.

When it's time to head home, you can follow Sierra Way along the eastern edge of the lake and rejoin California 178 for the trip back toward Bakersfield. Then turn south at the junction with California 184 and meet Interstate 5 for the return trip to Los Angeles.

An alternate route back to Los Angeles is to turn east from the lake on California 178 and cross 5,250-foot Walker Pass to intersect California 14. Then turn south to go through the Mojave Desert and rejoin Interstate 5.

Round trip is about 322 miles.

Bakersfield Area Code: 805

Lake Isabella/Kernville Area Code: 619

SIGHTSEEING   *Fort Tejon State Historic Park,* off Interstate 5 north of Tejon Pass summit (P.O. Box 895, Lebec 93243), 248-6692. Open 8 A.M. to 5 P.M. daily for self-guided tours. Adults 50 cents, children and senior citizens 25 cents. Members of the Civil War Association from Thousand Oaks stage mock battles in full-dress uniform every third Sunday of the month from May through October. ● *Kern County Museum* *and Pioneer Village,* 3801 Chester Avenue, Bakersfield 93301, 861-2132. Open weekends from 10 A.M. to 5 P.M., weekdays from 8 A.M. Closed holidays. Village admission: adults $1, children 6 to 12 years and senior citizens 75 cents; last tour tickets sold at 3:30 P.M. County Museum free. ● Activities at *Rio Bravo Resort* (see below): one-day river rafting trip, $18 per person; horseback trail rides, $8.50 per hour without guide; 18-hole golf, $15 weekends, $12 weekdays; tennis free to resort guests. ● *U.S. Army Corps of Engineers,* off California 155 at Isabella Lake (or P.O. Box 997), Lake Isabella 93240, 379-2742. Headquarters office open weekdays 8 A.M. to 4:30 P.M., weekends by appointment. Camping, boating, and touring information for Isabella Lake visitors. ● *Isabella Marina North Fork,* off California 155 at Wofford Heights (P.O. Box 808), Wofford Heights 93285, 376-3404. Boat rentals for fishing, water skiing, and touring Isabella Lake. Open daily during daylight hours. ● *Shirley Meadows Ski Area,* off California 155 in Greenhorn Mountains near Alta Sierra (P.O. Box 509, Lake Isabella 93240), 379-2871. Open weekends and holidays Christmas Day through March. Rentals and rope tows; daily lift ticket, $6. ● *Kern Valley Golf and Country Club,* off California 155 south of Kernville (P.O. Box 888), Kernville 93238, 376-2828. 9-hole, 36-par course open daily from daylight to dark. Greens fee $6.50 weekends, $5.50 weekdays. ● *Chuck Richards' Whitewater,* P.O. Box W. W. Whitewater, Lake Isabella 93240, 379-4444. Oldest of several rafting companies that run exciting one- and two-day trips on the upper and lower Kern River. Call or write for current schedule and rates.

EVENTS   *Whiskey Flat Days,* 4-day rip-roaring celebration of the gold rush era, when Kernville was known as Whiskey Flat; held in February on Washington's Birthday weekend. Contact the Kernville Chamber of Commerce (see below) for details.

LODGING   *Rio Bravo Resort,* 11200 Lake Ming Road (or Star Route 4, Box 501), Bakersfield 93306, 872-5000; $83. Fine lodging and all sorts of activities (see "Sightseeing," above). Also an excellent restaurant (see below). Bakersfield hosts a variety of other accommodations, and the Greater Bakersfield Chamber of Commerce (see below) will give you a list. ● *Lazy River Lodge,* on Sierra Way, 2 miles north of Kernville (or Star Route 1, Box 60), Kernville 93238, 376-2242; $36. On 10 acres along Kern River; largest (32 units) and one of the nicest lodgings. Own stable with trail horses, $8 per hour. Small fry can ride Clyde the burro. ● *Pala Ranches Motel,* 11042 Kernville Road, (or P.O. Box 955), Kernville 93238, 376-2222; $27. 25 units in town opposite pretty Riverside Park. ● *McCambridge Lodge,* 13525 Sierra Way, Kernville 93238, 376-2288; $25. 10 rooms overlooking river, 1 mile from town. ● *Hi-Ho*

Resort Lodge, 11901 Sierra Way, Kernville 93238, 376-2671; $34. 8 attractive family units, 1 mile from town near the river.

CAMPING   *Kern River County Park,* off California 178 on Alfred Harrell Highway near Lake Ming, 12 miles east of Bakersfield, 861-2345. 50 RV and tent sites, $6 per night. No reservations. For campers this is a convenient alternate to staying at the Rio Bravo Resort nearby. ● *Isabella Lake* has 9 family campgrounds with hundreds of sites operated by the U.S. Army Corps of Engineers. First come, first served; some sites free, others $4 per night. ● *Kern River* has 18 campgrounds operated along its banks in the Isabella Lake area by the U.S. Forest Service. $3 overnight fee at some sites; no reservations. Call the Forest Service's supervisor's office in Kernville, 376-2294, for more information.

DINING   *Rio Bravo Resort* (see above). Lodge dining room serves breakfast, lunch, and dinner daily; American and French fare. Also popular for Sunday brunch. ● At Isabella Lake, many of the locally popular restaurants only serve dinner and are located at Kernville and northward along the Kern River. A few mom-and-pop cafes offer breakfast and lunch. ● *Ewings on the Kern,* Buena Vista Drive, Kernville, 376-2411. Dinner nightly, plus Sunday brunch. Musical entertainment and dancing. ● *McNally's Fairview Lodge and Restaurant,* 15 miles north of Kernville on the river at Fairview, 376-2430. Great steaks and other dinner fare in cozy Western surroundings. Closed in winter. ● *Paradise Cove Restaurant,* on California 178 overlooking lake, 379-2719. Dinner only, closed Monday and Tuesday. Steak, trout, and seafood, plus prime ribs on weekends.

FOR MORE INFORMATION   Contact the Greater Bakersfield Chamber of Commerce, P.O. Box 1947, Bakersfield 93303, 327-4421. ● Kern County Board of Trade, Tourist Information Office, 2101 Oak Street (or P.O. Box 1312), Bakersfield 93302, 861-2367. Open weekdays 8 A.M. to 5 P.M. ● Kernville Chamber of Commerce, P.O. 397, Kernville 93228, 376-2629. ● Kern River Valley Visitors Council, P.O. Box O, Lake Isabella 93240. ● Sportsman's Center, Lake Isabella Boulevard at California 155, Lake Isabella 93240, 379-2805. Camping, hunting, and fishing information; also tackle, bait, and fishing licenses. Open weekends 6 A.M. to midnight, weekdays to 10 P.M.

Danes, Wines, and Old West in Santa Ynez Valley

When you're yearning for a no-pressure weekend in the countryside, head north to Solvang, the closest thing to a Danish village this side of the North Sea. Windmills dominate the skyline, good-luck storks decorate rooftops, and Carlsberg beer is drawn from cafe spigots. Many of the buildings, even the post office, embody Danish farm-style architecture of brick masonry walls crisscrossed with wooden beams. Danish national flags of red with a white cross fly everywhere, too.

An easy way to get to know the town is to climb aboard the *Honen,* a sightseeing streetcar that's pulled by sturdy shire horses on a 25-minute narrated tour. The driver tells how Solvang was founded as the site for a Danish-type folk school in 1911. The school is gone now, but the 1928 Bethania Lutheran Church on Atterdag Road is worth a visit to see its fourteenth-century Danish style of architecture and the traditional miniature sailing ship suspended from the sanctuary ceiling.

It's easy to reach Southern California's little bit of Denmark. Just drive north from Los Angeles on U.S. 101 and exit east on California 246 to Solvang. Once there, the sight and smell of fresh-baked bread and Danish pastries will entice you into Solvang's many bakeries and cafes. Be sure to sample the aebleskiver, balls of pancake batter cooked until golden brown in a special skillet, turned with a knitting needle instead of a spatula, then served with powdered sugar or fresh jam. Order them any time of the day, with a cup of Danish coffee. Smorrebrod, Denmark's famous open-faced sandwiches, are another tempting treat. And restaurant smorgasbords feature old-country recipes for specialties that range from meatballs and red cabbage to marinated herring.

As you stroll the cobblestone sidewalks beneath old-fashioned gas lamps that once illuminated the streets of Copenhagen, you'll be tempted by gift shops that show off Royal Copenhagen china, crystal, woolen sweaters, and other goods imported from Denmark. Look for the *Little Mermaid,* a duplicate of the famous sculpture in Copenhagen's harbor. And there's a bust of Hans Christian Andersen in the park. Solvang is so Danish that you expect to see Victor Borge peeking around a corner.

About the only reminder that you're still in California is Solvang's Old Mission Santa Ines. It was constructed by Indians from the area as nineteenth in the chain of 21 missions established by the Spanish padres. The restored mission, which still serves as a church, is open daily for self-guided tours.

Solvang certainly is no secret, and visitors often jam its attractive streets. That's especially true during summer, when plays are performed in the outdoor Festival Theater, and in fall during the town's annual Danish Days Celebration, so be certain to have room reservations during those times.

You'll find a number of comfortable motels in Solvang and nearby in Buellton, but an extra-special place to stay is the Alisal Guest Ranch, a deluxe and rather expensive resort on a 10,000-acre working cattle ranch six miles south of town. Horseback riding is a featured attraction at tree-studded Alisal, where trails wind for miles over the scenic ranchland. Wranglers will point out the hilltop hideaway of a neighboring rancher and horseman, Ronald Reagan.

This year-round resort is an especially good choice for a three-day weekend because you'll find plenty to do, like challenging the championship par-72 golf course that's set among clusters of oaks, pines, and sycamores. A PGA professional is on hand to help improve your game. Tennis buffs have seven courts for day play, with a resident pro ready to give lessons. Go swimming in a large pool near the bungalows that accommodate up to 200 guests, or enjoy the fresh air and peaceful surroundings while playing shuffleboard and croquet. When families flock to this ranch in summertime, Alisal's own lake is opened for boating and fishing. And don't be surprised at dinner when a cowboy stops by your table to ask, "How about saddling up in the morning for a trail ride, folks?"

To assure your escape from city life, telephones and television sets are purposely absent from all rooms at the guest ranch. Featured instead are blazing logs crackling in the bungalow fireplaces. Rates at the resort are Modified American Plan (breakfast and dinner included), and excellent meals are served in a dining room reserved for ranch guests only.

Besides enjoying the town and guest ranch, plan a scenic Sunday drive in the Santa Ynez Valley. You'll be charmed by three tiny nineteenth-century towns and some family-run wineries that produce prize-winning vintages.

With its verdant fields, rolling hills, and horses grazing in the pasture, the picturesque Santa Ynez Valley is the prettiest in all of Santa Barbara County. Savor the scenery as you drive east on California 246 to the valley's namesake, Santa Ynez, a town with false-front buildings that give it an Old West flavor. You'll have fun wandering among the memorabilia in the Santa Ynez Valley Historical Society Museum and Parks-Janeway Carriage House; turn north on Edison Street to Saguro Street.

Then follow Edison Street north to Baseline Avenue and turn east to Ballard, the valley's oldest town. The wooden church you'll see at the junction with Alamo Pintado Road was built by volunteers in 1889 and cost only $320 for lumber. Today it's a privately owned chapel and a favorite place for weddings. Another landmark is a century-old little red schoolhouse at the north end of Cottonwood Street that's still attended by kindergarteners through third-graders. Also well known is the Ballard

Store Restaurant on Baseline Avenue, where reservations are a must if you want to dine on fine French cuisine in a country atmosphere. Another popular spot for dinner is Mattei's Tavern, a historic stagecoach inn that's just north of Ballard in Los Olivos; follow Alamo Pintado Road to Grand Avenue. Established by Swiss-born Felix Mattei in 1886, it's now operated by the Chart House restaurant chain. Even if you're not hungry, drop into the fascinating saloon for a drink.

In earlier times Mattei's was across the street from the terminus of the Pacific Coast Railway and also served as a hotel. Los Angeles-to-San Francisco passengers would arrive by stage, have a meal, and spend the night before continuing north by train. Mattei's Tavern is still the main attraction in Los Olivos, but also visit some of the town's other old buildings that have been restored and opened as antique and gift shops and art galleries.

In recent years the Santa Ynez Valley has become Southern California's Napa Valley and it now produces wines that please the wine makers and critics alike. Some already have won gold and silver medals. Make your own judgments and have a good time by visiting a few of the wineries as you tour the valley; pick up a free winery guide map in Solvang.

Most wineries in the Santa Ynez Valley are small operations, so don't expect the fancy tasting rooms or tours offered at many Northern California wineries. Below we mention five of our favorites that will introduce you to a variety of vintages and wine-making operations, as well as some friendly local folks.

On Alamo Pintado Road you'll find J. Carey Cellars, founded in 1978 by the Carey family of physicians. Forty-three acres of grapevines surround a red barn, where visitors can make a little tour and sample some of the Careys' fine wines.

Wine barrels flank the entrance to the Ballard Canyon Winery, home for the Hallock family and 50 acres of grapes. You'll have fun there, because tasting is done in the winery's tiny lab.

On a hilltop along Zaca Station Road, you can't miss the immense modern building erected for the Firestone Vineyard, largest winery in the valley. There you'll be treated to a comprehensive tour, beginning with the grapevines and ending in the handsome tasting room. The 325-acre vineyard is the chosen vocation for Brooks Firestone, who gave up his family's well-known tire business to produce an abundance of excellent wines.

Foxen Canyon Road leads to Zaca Mesa Winery, located in a big cedar barn where several wines are aged and bottled, including the valley's only Zinfandel. Visitors are offered free guided tours, and tasting is done in a handsome visitors center.

Several miles more along Foxen Canyon Road is the modest Rancho Sisquoc Winery, which began as a hobby of Harold Pfeiffer, foreman of the 36,000-acre Sisquoc cattle ranch. He was one of the first to grow grapes in the area and finally built a small winery in 1977.

There are picnic tables at Rancho Sisquoc and a few of the other wineries, but the only thing you can buy is wine, so be sure to bring along some snacks from Solvang to enjoy with the various vintages.

When you're ready to return to Los Angeles, rejoin U.S. 101 by following California 154, a historic inland route that's now designated a state scenic highway. It's the old stagecoach road between Los Olivos and Santa Barbara, once part of a harrowing journey over 2,224-foot San Marcos Pass. As the highway begins to climb you'll pass a vast reservoir and county-run recreation area, Lake Cachuma, a favorite retreat for fishermen, boaters, and campers. Stop to view the man-made lake from an observation point above the dam.

After crossing the modern Cold Spring Arch Bridge, turn right on the old Stagecoach Road, which leads to Cold Spring Tavern, a cluster of rustic log cabins huddled in a tree-shaded glen. If you're hungry, have lunch or dinner at this aged stagecoach stop. A separate saloon, where water from the spring once was bottled, reverberates in the evening with bluegrass, country-western, and rock music. Sunday afternoons the bands play outside.

As you continue on California 154 over the mountain pass and wind through Los Padres National Forest, pause at the roadside turnouts for vistas of the foothills and ocean. Just west of Santa Barbara the road descends to rejoin U.S. 101 for the drive back to Los Angeles.

Round trip is about 334 miles.

Solvang/Santa Ynez Valley Area Code: 805

SIGHTSEEING *Honen,* horse-drawn sightseeing streetcar, departs frequently on Solvang tours from Copenhagen Drive at Alisal Road. Adults $1.50, children under 12 years $1. ● *Old Mission Santa Ines,* 1760 Mission Drive, Solvang, 688-4815. Open daily 9 A.M. to 5 P.M. in summer, 9:30 A.M. to 4:30 P.M. in winter, except Sundays noon to 5 P.M. Adults 50 cents, children under age 16 free. Recorded tape tours available. ● *Santa Ynez Valley Historical Society Museum* and *Parks-Janeway Carriage House,* Sagunto Street, Santa Ynez. Both open 1 to 4 P.M. Friday through Sunday; carriage house also open 9:30 A.M. to 4 P.M. Tuesday through Thursday. Donation. ● *J. Carey Cellars,* 1711 Alamo Pintado Road, 688-8554. Open 10 A.M. to 4 P.M. Tuesday through Sunday; call first. ● *Ballard Canyon Winery,* 1825 Ballard Canyon Road, 688-7585. Open 9 A.M. to 4 P.M. daily; call first. ● *Firestone Vineyard,* Zaca Station Road, 688-3940. Open 10 A.M. to 4 P.M. daily except Sundays. ● *Zaca Mesa Winery,* Foxen Canyon Road, 688-3310. Open 10

A.M. to 4 P.M. daily. ● *Rancho Sisquoc Winery,* Foxen Canyon Road, 937-3616. Open 10 A.M. to 4 P.M. daily except Sundays.

EVENTS *Danish Days,* third weekend in September. Colorful festival with local folks in costume, and featuring a parade, folk dancing and singing, bands, stage plays, aebleskiver breakfasts, smorgasbord, and grand ball. ● *Solvang Theaterfest,* summer-long repertory theater with mix of musicals, classic and modern dramas and comedies performed evenings in open-air theater. Box office at 420 Second Street opens daily at 10 A.M.; tickets $6.50 to $10. Theaterfest hotline 922-8313.

LODGING All accommodations listed are in Solvang; ZIP code 93463. *Alisal Guest Ranch,* Alisal Road, 688-6411, a wonderful self-contained resort that can be a vacation in itself; $110 MAP, with package plans also available. ● *Danish Inn Lodge,* 1455 Mission Drive, 688-4181, newer luxury lodging at edge of town; $44. ● *Svendsgaard's Danish Lodge,* 1711 Mission Drive, 688-3277; $32. ● *Dannebrog Inn,* 1450 Mission Drive, 688-3210; $44. ● *Kronborg Inn,* 1440 Mission Drive, 688-2383; $38. Solvang has 10 other motels, with 8 more nearby in Buellton.

CAMPING *Lake Cachuma County Park,* 12 miles east of Solvang on California 154, 688-4658. 457 sites, $6 per night, $8 with hookup.

DINING *Danish Inn Restaurant,* 1547 Mission Drive, 688-4813. A windmill marks one of Solvang's most popular restaurants, where prize-winning chefs prepare superb smorgasbord and continental cuisine daily. ● *Mollekroen Restaurant,* 435 Alisal Road, Solvang, 688-4555. Daily smorgasbord with 30 dishes, as well as Danish and American lunch and dinner menu. ● *Ballard Store Restaurant,* 2449 Baseline Avenue, Ballard, 688-5319. Unexpected gourmet dinners in renovated country store served Wednesday through Sunday by reservation only. A special treat. ● *Mattei's Tavern,* on California 154, Los Olivos, 688-4820. Delightfully restored stagecoach inn with dinner fare: steak, prime ribs, seafood, salad bar. Opens 5 P.M. weekends, 5:30 P.M. weekdays; no reservations. ● *Cold Spring Tavern,* Stagecoach Road, beneath Cold Spring Arch Bridge off California 154, 967-0066. Very rustic roadhouse open daily with limited menus for lunch (11 A.M. to 4 P.M.) and dinner (5 to 10 P.M.); separate saloon has loud music Sunday afternoon and every evening except Monday and Tuesday.

FOR MORE INFORMATION Contact the Solvang Business Association & Chamber of Commerce, 1623 Mission Drive (or P.O. Box 465), Solvang 93463, 688-3317; open weekdays 9:30 A.M. to 4:30 P.M.

Happy Trails to Apple Valley and Silverwood Lake

Fresh air, warm temperatures, wide-open spaces, and friendly folks make Apple Valley a relaxing vacation oasis in the high desert. The area got its name in the 1890s when a resident planted apple trees in her yard, and in recent years many Apple Valley homeowners have followed suit. Located north of the San Bernardino Mountains, this pleasant residential and resort area offers a nice respite from the city. It's also convenient to one of the Southland's mountain recreation areas, beautiful Silverwood Lake, surrounded by forest scenery at an altitude of 3,380 feet. There you can go for a swim, drop a line to hook some trout, or rent a boat to tour this immense reservoir, part of the state's aqueduct and park systems.

Begin your weekend by driving east from Los Angeles on Interstate 10 or California 60 to join Interstate 15 heading north through the mountains and Cajon Pass. After you descend into the desert and reach Victorville, exit east on California 18 to Apple Valley. Continue on this road through the suburbanized desert and settle in at the informal Apple Valley Inn, a popular resort that's your weekend base for golf, tennis, swimming, horseback riding, or just plain loafing. You'll like the casual Western flavor of this 28-acre retreat.

Have dinner in the Apple Valley Inn's public dining room, a favorite of the local folks. Top off your meal with an appropriate dessert, hot apple pie or apple crisp with brandy sauce. A big draw to this casual resort in summer and fall is the weekly Saturday-night outdoor steak fry, highlighted by singing around the campfire.

Throughout the year the inn's guests enjoy themselves at the swimming pool and on tennis courts that are lighted for cooler play after the sun goes down. Duffers can knock around the resort's putting green, while serious golfers are pleased to have golf privileges at the 18-hole Apple Valley Country Club course next door. For other fun, hop in a saddle and go for a leisurely ride on the valley's myriad trails; the inn's receptionist can direct you to the nearest stables.

To inspire even more memories of the Old West, à la Hollywood, visit the Roy Rogers and Dale Evans Museum sometime on Saturday. Moved in 1980 from its original Apple Valley site to a bigger building in Victorville, the new quarters resemble a Western fort. Inside are exhibits that portray the extraordinary personal lives and professional careers of America's favorite cowboy-and-cowgirl couple. Among the movie stars' mementos are the gun collection and big game animal trophies of the "King of the Cowboys." Even Roy's co-starring horse, Trigger, and dog, Bullet, are there, preserved by a taxidermist.

To reach the museum from the Apple Valley Inn, head back west on California 18, cross over Interstate 15 on Palmdale Road, and turn right on Kentwood Boulevard just past the Holiday Inn. Turn right again on Civic Drive and head for the mock stockade. After your visit, if you don't plan to join in the Apple Valley Inn's steak fry, have dinner at one of Victorville's restaurants. Two good choices near the museum are Cask 'n Cleaver and the Crown 'n Sword Room in the Green Tree Inn.

After brunch at Apple Valley Inn on Sunday, start on a journey along the back roads of San Bernardino County to Silverwood Lake State Recreation Area. If you have enough time, visit another pleasant park that's along the way. Go south on California 18 to Navajo Road, turn right on the Bear Valley Cut-off to Ridge Crest Road, and follow the signs to Mojave Narrows Regional Park.

This 860-acre nature preserve and playground is bordered on the east by the historic Mojave River, long followed as a trail by Indians, Spanish missionaries, soldiers, and settlers. Running along its western boundary are tracks of the Santa Fe Railroad, which opened a route to the West in 1885. Freight trains bound for Los Angeles occasionally rumble past.

You'll enjoy hiking or picnicking among the rocks and trees at the narrows, where Paiute Indians once found shelter for their families. Today's visitors also like to fish in Horseshoe Lake. Or rent a pedal boat and cruise close to the waterfowl that inhabit this picturesque waterway and its island; bird watchers have spotted 200 resident and migratory species. Overnight campers also are welcome.

Continue to Silverwood Lake on the back roads by returning to Bear Valley Cut-off, going left to Peach Avenue and following it south to Main Street. Turn left and then jog right onto Arrowhead Lake Road and keep going south to California 173. Follow it past the dam to California 138 and turn left, skirting southward along Silverwood Lake to the park's main entrance. Get a map of the 2,400-acre recreation area from rangers at the entry station.

Head to Sawpit Canyon, where there's a marina with pontoon boats for touring the lake and outboards for fishing. The lake is stocked with trout, bass, catfish, and bluegill. Nearby is a beach and swimming area (with lifeguards on duty in summer). Buy refreshments at the snack bar or bring a picnic to enjoy at tables under shady ramadas. Despite the lake's altitude, summertime temperatures often range from 90 to 110 degrees during the day, although there's frequently a refreshing breeze.

You'll find another swimming beach with picnic tables and a snack bar in the Cleghorn Area. Paved biking and hiking trails follow the south perimeter of the lake and lead to picnic spots and vista points at more remote Serrano Beach. You also can drive to that especially scenic area of the park along Miller Canyon by returning to California 138, heading east toward Crestline for 4 miles, then going left at the Pilot Rock turnoff. A few picnic areas are accessible only by boat.

Keep an eye and ear open for the park's wildlife, especially birds, including red-shouldered hawks, screech owls, and downy woodpeckers. Chipmunks and gray squirrels are often-seen residents. If you want to spend the night with nature, Mesa Campground has numerous family sites.

When you're ready to return to Los Angeles, go back to California 138 and follow that curvy highway west to Interstate 15, then drive south to join Interstate 10 or California 60 west.

Round trip is about 190 miles.

Apple Valley/Victorville/Lake Silverwood Area Code: 619

SIGHTSEEING *Roy Rogers and Dale Evans Museum,* 15650 Seneca Drive, Victorville 92392, 243-4547. Open daily 9 A.M. to 5 P.M. Adults $2, children 6 to 16 years $1. ● *Mojave Narrows Regional Park,* P.O. Box 361, Victorville 92392, 245-2226. Open daily from 7:30 A.M. until dusk. Day-use entry fee $2 per vehicle. Also overnight camping (see below). Boathouse on Horseshoe Lake rents pedal boats, sells bait and fishing licenses. Nature trail (paved for handicapped visitors), as well as hiking and equestrian trails. ● *Silverwood Lake State Recreation Area,* Star Route Box 7A, Hesperia 92345, 389-2281 or 389-2303. Open daily 6 A.M. to 9 P.M. May through September, 7 A.M. to 7 P.M. rest of the year. Day-use admission $2 per vehicle. Also overnight camping (see below). Marina has pontoon touring boats and fishing boats; phone 389-2320 for rates and reservations.

EVENTS *Apple Valley Powwow* is an annual weekend celebration in mid-September with Indian dances, a parade, rodeo, carnival, pancake breakfast, and plenty of fun.

LODGING *Apple Valley Inn,* on California 18 at No. 20600 (or P.O. Box 5), Apple Valley 92307, 247-7271 or toll-free in California (800) 462-4084; $50, suites and cottages $65. Also, special 2-night packages with room, breakfasts, and dinners with wine, $156 per couple. Dining room (see below) plus lounges with musical entertainment and dancing. ● *Green Tree Inn,* 14173 Green Tree Boulevard, Victorville 92392, 245-3461; $32. One of the alternate accommodations close by Interstate 15 and Roy Rogers and Dale Evans Museum. Dining room (see below) and 24-hour coffee shop.

CAMPING *Mojave Narrows Regional Park* (see above). 87 sites (no hookups) on first come, first served basis; $3 per night. ● *Silverwood Lake State Recreation Area* (see above). Mesa Campground has 136 sites; $5 per night. Reserve through Ticketron.

DINING   *Apple Valley Inn* (see above). Breakfast, lunch, and dinner daily. Saturday-night outdoor steak fry for inn guests and others (June through October); adults $11.95, children 12 years and under (eating hamburgers) $4.95. Big brunch on Sunday from 8 A.M. to 3 P.M.; adults $5.95, children 12 years and under $3.95. ● *Cask 'n Cleaver*, 13885 Park Avenue, Victorville, 245-8427. Popular place for beef and seafood plus salad bar. ● *Green Tree Inn* (see above). Crown 'n Sword Room serves prime ribs and other dinner items nightly.

FOR MORE INFORMATION   Contact the Apple Valley Chamber of Commerce, on California 18 at No. 21812 (or P.O. Box 1073), Apple Valley 92307, 247-3202. Also, the Victorville Chamber of Commerce, in the Green Tree Inn, 14173 Green Tree Boulevard (or P.O. Box 997), Victorville 92392, 245-6506.

Peaceful Pleasures of the Ojai Valley

The Ojai Valley works magic on all its visitors. First to fall under its spell were the Oak Grove Indians and then the Chumash Indians, who called the protected pocket of natural beauty the "nest." Early settlers also were charmed by the secluded valley, 750 feet high in the mountains at the edge of Los Padres National Forest in Ventura County. In 1874 a village named Nordhoff was established, complete with a tourist hotel. Eastern vacationers soon discovered the valley's refreshing climate, and a grand summer hotel, the Foothill, was opened in 1905. One of its guests, millionaire Ohio glass manufacturer Edward Libbey, became mesmerized by the area and took a hand in its future. With Libbey's leadership and financing, Nordhoff's main street of ramshackle false-front buildings was transformed to handsome Spanish mission-style architecture, featuring arcades, a bell tower, and a tree-shaded park framed by arches and arbors. By 1917, even the town's name had been changed to what the Indians had called the valley—Ojai *(o-high)*.

From the earliest days, townsfolk and visitors have enjoyed all sorts of outdoor activities, especially golf and tennis. You can play on the courts in downtown Libbey Park, site of the oldest annual tennis tournament in the U.S., first held in 1899 and now played every April. Ojai's original golf course opened six years earlier, but today golfers challenge the 18-hole Ojai Valley Inn and Country Club course, which had its debut in 1920. Also popular is the city-run par-72 course at Soule Park.

Art and culture are other long-standing traditions in the valley. Besides boasting an array of galleries and studios, Ojai's artists and craftsmen display and sell their creations every Sunday in the parking lot of the Security Pacific Bank. In springtime a fine-arts exhibition is staged in Libbey Park in conjunction with the annual Ojai Music Festival, a well-known event that draws hundreds of concert goers to the valley. The musicians perform amid the oaks and other trees in the park's rustic Festival Bowl. Even when no special events are scheduled, Ojai offers all sorts of divertissements, including excellent restaurants, a riding stable, relaxing hot springs, and even a reducing spa.

Located near the coast but isolated from fog and offshore winds, the peaceful valley also is well known for its stunning scenery. When Hollywood needed a Shangri-La location for the movie *Lost Horizon,* they took their cameras straight to Ojai. To see that beauty for yourself and enjoy the valley's other pleasures during a weekend in Ojai, drive north from Los Angeles on U.S. 101 to Ventura, then continue north on California 33 to join California 150 leading east into the attractive town. On its outskirts you'll come to the area's best-known resort, Ojai Valley Inn, a bucolic retreat where you can settle in the original 1923 two-story lodge or one of the cottages on its country club grounds. Dress is very casual for your Ojai weekend, but male guests at the inn are required to wear coats and ties in the dining room after 7 P.M. Accommodations at the inn are full American plan, so all meals are included. And you'll enjoy the entertainment and dancing in the lodge on Friday and Saturday nights.

In the morning, play a game of tennis or round of golf, then mount up at the inn's own stables for a scenic tour by saddle along woodsy trails in the foothills of Black Mountain. Afterward, drive into town on California 150 and stroll along Ojai Avenue's arcaded sidewalk to browse in the art galleries and antique and gift shops. You'll find more stores behind in a newer courtyard shopping area, which also can be reached from Matilija Street. Be sure to go west on Matilija to Canada Street and an Ojai landmark, Bart's Corner, an open-air bookstore shaded by an ancient oak tree. After business hours you can select books from shelves along the sidewalk and toss the money into the courtyard.

On the opposite side of Ojai Avenue, wander in beautiful Libbey Park, home for the town's music festival and tennis tournament. Its eight courts are open to the public without charge, as are those in Soule Park, a few blocks west. Around the corner from Libbey Park on South Montgomery Street in the old firehouse, visit the Ojai Valley Museum, filled with Indian artifacts, pioneer mementos, and stuffed birds and animals of the area.

If you decide to lunch in town, try the Nest for homemade soups, salads, sandwiches, and sweets, or dine on country French fare in an old house or on its outdoor patio at L'Auberge. It's also a good choice for dinner, as is the popular Firebird across from Soule Park. Another outdoor dining treat awaits you in neighboring Meiners Oaks at the Ranch House, where tables overlook the chef's herb garden. Not far away in Mira Monte the Gaslight Restaurant also draws a crowd. For a refreshment break while poking around town, have coffee and fresh pastries at Bill Baker's Bakery, an Ojai institution since 1896.

Sometime in the afternoon, go west a few miles on California 150 to Lake Casitas, a man-made reservoir that's a favorite of fishermen. The biggest catches are bass and catfish. Rental boats are available at this municipally run recreation area, chosen as the site of canoeing and rowing events for the 1984 Olympics. Since Lake Casitas serves as a domestic water supply, swimming and wading are not allowed, but the park is the focal point in the Ojai Valley for picnickers and campers.

To view more of Ojai's backcountry scenery and enjoy refreshments made from local fruit, turn right from the park on Santa Ana Road and skirt the lake to Santa Ana Boulevard. Go a mile west to rejoin California 33 at the hamlet of Oak View, then head south for another mile and look left for the Rancho Arnaz roadside barn. There you can sample delicious homemade apple cider and bite into fresh apples, dried apple chips, and other snacks produced at the farm. Decorating the barn rafters are county-fair award ribbons that go back to 1930.

If you prefer your fruit drinks fermented, head east on the adjacent Old Creek Road to the very end, where you'll see grape vines planted on the hillside and find the Old Creek Ranch Winery. Its 1981 vintage was the first for Carmel and John Maitland, who resumed the ranch's winemaking tradition, which goes back to the turn of the century. They invite visitors to tour the tiny winery and taste or purchase their current vintages.

Also worth visiting is the Gallery of Historical Figures, a display of remarkable one-quarter-life-size re-creations of famous personalities from important historical eras, ranging from America's founding fathers to the Romanovs of Russia. Ojaian George Stuart has handcrafted and clothed over 100 such figures, and you'll discover how he makes them seem so lifelike. Many of the figures are on permanent display in the county museum in Ventura. Here, George shows off a changing exhibit of a dozen or so in his gallery-workshop. It's east of town off California 150; bear left on Reeves Road to McNell Road.

Then continue beyond that turnoff about a mile along California 150 to visit Dennison Park, near the top of 1,280-foot Dennison Grade, where actor Ronald Colman looked off to Shangri-La in *Lost Horizon*. You'll have the same view of that idyllic paradise, the upper Ojai Valley, and also find tables to spread a picnic beneath the park's pine trees and giant oaks.

On Sunday, plan to explore more of the Ojai Valley area by going north on California 33 into Los Padres National Forest, where mineral hot springs that soothed the Chumash Indians in California's pre-Spanish era still flow. Nowadays the bubbling waters have been captured along

Matilija Creek at two rustic health spas, where visitors are invited to soak away their aches and other troubles. En route to those sylvan hideaways, the scenic canyon road follows above a curvy creek bed flanked by hillside orchards that produce succulent oranges and other fruit. Some of the best are sold at the roadside packinghouse of Friend's Ranch, where there's always fresh orange juice. Stock up on grapefruit, avocados, lemons, limes, and a variety of nuts.

A little farther up the road, look for the turnoff to Matilija Hot Springs, first established as a health center and vacation resort in 1871. Floods destroyed the hotel built for early-day guests, who arrived by stagecoach, but the 100-degree-plus water still flows from the ground and attracts visitors daily. You'll pay a small fee to relax in one of the bathhouse's small or large pools, some with whirlpool features. Make an appointment in advance if you also want a massage. There are tables outdoors for visitors who bring picnics and a swimming pool is open in summer.

Another century-old spa reopened in 1982, Bowmans at Wheeler Hot Springs, one mile farther north along California 33. There you can luxuriate in redwood tubs located in private skylighted rooms that feature both hot and cold mineral baths. Swedish, Shiatsu, and Trager massages can be arranged. An added attraction at this renovated spa is a pleasant dining room with a changing menu of healthful home-cooked meals. The cook describes her dishes as gourmet vegetarian, although the list of entrees includes fresh fish and chicken. You can dine during spa hours or just sit by the fire with a glass of wine, beer, or aromatic water. Cappuccino is also served.

When your peaceful weekend in the Ojai Valley is over, return to Los Angeles by heading east on California 150 to Santa Paula, then take California 129 east to join Interstate 5 going south to the city.

Round trip is about 190 miles.

Ojai Area Code: 805

SIGHTSEEING   *Ojai Valley Museum,* 109 South Montgomery Street, Ojai 92023, 646-2290. Open daily except Tuesday from 1 to 5 P.M. Free; donations accepted. ● *Gallery of Historical Figures,* on McNell Road at Reeves Road (or P.O. Box 508), Ojai 93023, 646-6574. Open weekends only from 1 to 5 P.M.; other days by appointment. Adults 75 cents, children free. ● *Ojai Valley Inn Stables,* Hermosa Road, Ojai 93023, 646-2837. Rental horses for $7 per hour; also guided rides. ● *Libbey Park Tennis Courts,* Libbey Park, Ojai. 8 courts, first come, first served. Free; coin-operated lights for night play. ● *Soule Park Golf Course,* 1033 East Ojai Avenue, Ojai 92023, 646-5633. 18-hole municipal course with putting green and driving range. Pros available for lessons. Greens fee $9 weekends, $6 weekdays. Also public tennis courts. ● *Lake Casitas Rec-*

reation Area, off California 150 at 11311 Santa Ana Road, Ventura 93001, 649-2233. Day-use entry $2 per vehicle. Boat rentals, fishing gear, and license at Boat, Bait and Tackle Shop, 649-2043. Snack bar nearby. Also camping (see below). ● *Rancho Arnaz,* California 33 at Old Creek Road, Oak View 93022, 649-2776. Fresh apple juice and fruit at roadside stand open daily except Monday from 10 A.M. to 5 P.M. ● *Old Creek Ranch Winery,* 10024 Old Creek Road (or P.O. Box 173), Oak View 93022, 649-4132. Open 9 A.M. to 4 P.M. Friday through Sunday. Free. Also, seasonal U-pick berries and other fruit. ● *Friend's Ranch,* 15150 Maricopa Highway (California 33), Ojai 93023, 646-2871. Venerable roadside fruit stand open every day from 8 A.M. to 5 P.M. ● *Matilija Hot Springs,* Maricopa Highway (California 33), Ojai 93023, 646-7667. Open daily 8 A.M. to 9 P.M. Use of baths and whirlpool baths, $5 per person. Massages by appointment, $25. ● *Bowmans at Wheeler Hot Springs,* 16825 Maricopa Highway (California 33), Ojai 93023, 646-8131. Open Thursday from 5 to 9 P.M., Friday through Sunday and Monday holidays from noon to 9 P.M. Use of redwood tub baths, $7.50 per person per half hour. Also Swedish and other massages, one hour $35, including tub. Reservations recommended. Drinks and meals served in comfortable lounge and dining room (closed Thursdays); excellent wine list.

EVENTS   *Ojai Music Festival,* an acclaimed weekend concert series held annually since 1947. A varied repertoire of music and song is performed outdoors in Libbey Park's Festival Bowl in late May or early June. Dress warmly for evening performances. Programs and tickets available from Ojai Festivals, Ltd., P.O. Box 185, Ojai 93023, 646-2094. ● *Ojai Valley Tennis Tournament,* held annually in April with headquarters in Libbey Park. Since the 1960s the busy professional circuit has kept big-name players away, but 1,500 entrants compete in the men's and women's invitational, college, high school, and 12-years-and-under divisions. Contact the Ojai Valley Chamber of Commerce (see below).

LODGING   *Ojai Valley Inn and Country Club,* Country Club Drive off California 150, Ojai 93023, 646-5511; $125 to $175 full American plan. Also golf packages that include greens fees. Country resort with golf, tennis, riding, swimming, and even croquet. Guest dining room open to the public (see below). ● *The Oaks at Ojai,* 12 East Ojai Avenue, Ojai 93023, 646-5573; $65 per person, two-night minimum. No children under 16 years. A veteran hotel in the heart of Ojai that was renovated and reopened in 1977 as a reducing spa. Price includes all low-calorie meals, a dozen daily fitness classes, and use of swimming pool, saunas, exercise equipment, and spas. Also evening workshops, lectures, and craft programs. Special services include massages, facials, cellulite wraps, and a hair salon. • *Casa Ojai,* 1302 East Ojai Avenue, Ojai 93023, 646-8175; $45 weekends, $40 weekdays. • *Los Padres Inn,* 1208 East Ojai Avenue, Ojai 93023, 646-4365; $40 weekends, $32 weekdays.

CAMPING   *Lake Casitas Recreation Area* (see above). 480 sites, no hookups; $6 per night. First come, first served.

DINING   *Ojai Valley Inn* (see above). The public is welcome to join inn guests in the dining room for breakfast and lunch buffets and dinner. Coats and ties for men at dinner. Special Sunday-night buffet features prime ribs; $16 per person. Make reservations for parties of 6 or more. • *The Ranch House,* 102 Besant Road at South Lomita in Meiners Oaks, 646-2360 or 646-4384. Ojai's best-known restaurant, with delightful dining in a garden setting. Dinner served Wednesday through Sunday; two sittings nightly, four on Sunday beginning at 1 P.M. Make reservations well in advance. Price includes full-course meal from appetizer to dessert, with many choices from the continental menu. Chamber music too. Also, the Ranch House's home-baked bread is sold by the loaf to take home. • *L'Auberge,* 314 El Paseo Street, Ojai, 646-2288. French cuisine for dinner nightly except Tuesday. Also weekend luncheons with crepes a specialty. • *The Firebird,* 960 East Ojai Avenue, Ojai, 646-1566. Popular dining and drinking spot open daily for dinner, lunch weekdays, and champagne brunch on Sunday. Nightly entertainment and dancing, too. • *The Gaslight,* 11432 North Ventura Avenue, in Mira Monte, 646-5990. Dinner nightly except Monday. Varied menu; known for veal dishes. • *The Nest,* 108 South Montgomery Street, Ojai, 646-5256. A local favorite for lunch, open Tuesday through Saturday. • *Bill Baker's Bakery,* 457 East Ojai Avenue, Ojai, 646-1558 or 646-1950. Open daily 6:30 A.M. to 6 P.M. A coffee-break spot where you can order fresh-baked pastries, bagels, Chinese eggrolls, and 22 varieties of bread.

FOR MORE INFORMATION   Contact the Ojai Valley Chamber of Commerce, 338 East Ojai Avenue (or P.O. Box 1134), Ojai 93023, 646-3000.

Old-Fashioned Fun in Oak Glen and Redlands

Fruit-filled orchards and stately Victorian homes are highlights of a weekend in the mountain foothills east of San Bernardino. Try to time your excursion in late spring or early summer during the cherry harvest or in the fall at apple-picking time. That's when orchard owners invite visitors to pick their own cherries and apples from the trees, or buy the ripe fruit at roadside stands. Add to that a mission outpost from Spanish days, as well as art and antiques—all part of a relaxing visit to some of the Southland's most scenic countryside.

Another treat is staying at the historic Highland Springs Resort, a favorite of families. The 1,000-acre vacation place first opened as the Highland Home Hotel in 1884. During the resort's summer season, guest activities include hayrides, weiner roasts, morning hikes, card tournaments, and nightly entertainment with comedians, singers, and novelty acts. You'll also enjoy tennis, horseback riding, and swimming. With all kinds of scheduled events and a counseling program for the children, Highland Springs is the West Coast version of a Catskill resort.

Get there from Los Angeles by driving east on Interstate 10 to the Highland Springs Avenue exit just beyond Banning. Follow the road north to the rustic retreat in peaceful wooded surroundings. Dinner and breakfast are included in the lodging price, so enjoy the evening meal and then take an after-dinner stroll around this informal resort.

In the morning dress casually for a circle excursion by car through a picturesque valley and mountain glen that abounds with cherry and apple orchards. Go south on Highland Springs Avenue and turn right on Brookside Avenue to Beaumont Avenue. It runs north and south connecting Beaumont and Cherry Valley, home for 50 or so orchards where ladders and buckets are available so you can pluck your own cherries from the trees. The rewards for such labor are fresh fruit at reasonable prices and plenty of fun. The cherry harvest begins in June, with various varieties ready for picking at different times. The sweet Tartarians usually are ripe first, followed by the much-favored Bings, then the Hardy Giants, Royal Ans, Windsors, and a dozen other kinds. By mid-July most of the cherries have been picked, ending with the luscious Lamperts.

As you drive along, look for U-pick signs that will direct you to the orchards and indicate which varieties of cherries are ripe and ready for plucking from the trees. Turn right on Beaumont Avenue to reach Cherry Valley Boulevard, where you'll find a seasonal cherry-picking-information booth on the northeast corner. Every June Beaumont celebrates the annual harvest with a Cherry Festival, which always draws a crowd for its parade, cherry-pie-eating contests, arts-and-crafts exhibits, and carnival games.

To follow the pretty back road that leads to the Southland's largest apple-growing region, continue north on Beaumont Avenue, which becomes Oak Glen Road. Just beyond Cherry Valley it brings you to Riverside County's art and cultural center, the Edward-Dean Museum of Decorative Arts, an unexpected treasure trove in a bucolic setting. After retirement, two world-traveling interior decorators deeded their 16-acre estate to the county, including a lifetime collection of art and antiques. The interior of the eight-room museum appears more like an eighteenth-century home filled with priceless furniture, paintings, tapestries, and porcelains from Europe and the Orient. Also featured is a gallery with changing art exhibits, as well as art and craft works of local artists that are offered for sale.

Continue north on meandering Oak Glen Road and climb a mile high into the foothills of the San Bernardino Mountains to appleland. Every autumn since 1947 many orchard owners have opened roadside stands to sell their tasty fruit to passersby, and from September through December the Oak Glen area is a favorite destination for folks who savor fresh apples, apple cider, and apple pie. Drive cautiously on the curvy two-lane road as you look for entrances to the orchards that welcome visitors. They include, from south to north, Apple Creek Orchard, Oak Glen Apple Company, Walsh's Apple Orchard, Blackie Wilshire's Ranch, Los Rios Rancho Apple Orchard, Snow Line Apples & Cider, Law's Oak Glen Cider Mill, Parrish Pioneer Ranch, and McFarland's Ranch.

More than half of their annual crop is the Rome Beauty variety, which is best for cooking. Others are great eating varieties, Red and Golden Delicious, as well as McIntosh, Spartan, Winesap, Arkansas Black, and Hoover. Some of the fruit is crushed in cider mills and served hot or cold by the cup and in jugs to take home. Most of the orchards have tree-shaded tables where you can picnic under an umbrella of multicolored leaves that change their hues in the crisp fall weather.

Buy an apple pie for your picnic at the Longbranch Pieloon Restaurant and Bakery, where hot slices of pie also are served. It's in Oak Tree Village, a center of craft and curio shops where you'll find more local fruit creations, such as apple butter, apple jam, apple jelly, apple syrup, and applesauce. Another popular place to stop for apple pie is Law's Oak Glen Coffee Shop, next to the mountain glen's only lodging, Law's Motel.

After spending another night at Highland Springs Resort in the tranquil foothills, return to Interstate 10 and head west to nearby Redlands on Sunday. Dotted with palm trees and circled by snow-capped mountains, the city was founded a century ago and named for its iron-streaked soil. At that time the warm fertile valley was planted with citrus trees, and Redlands called itself the navel orange capital of the world. When the town became a popular winter resort for East Coast folks in the early 1900s, many of them built rather regal homes. Today you can still view a number of those showcase structures during a self-guided drive along the city's wide avenues.

More than 60 historic houses, mostly Victorian, are listed in the *Redlands Turn of the Century Homes* tour booklet produced by the city's chamber of commerce. A map directs you to 19 homes described in detail; two of them are open for afternoon tours the first Sunday of every month. One is the remarkable 20-room Victorian mansion known as the Morey House. To get there from Interstate 10, exit south on Alabama Street to Barton Road, go right to the next street, Terracina Boulevard, and turn left to number 140. Built in 1890 by a retired ship builder, the $20,000 dream house features impressive exterior detail work, including carvings of anchors, flowers, and fruit. The immense house has 96 windows; behind the rounded panes in the onion dome, look for a carved carrousel horse.

Follow the tour map for a circuitous route to several more of Redlands' turn-of-the-century homes, or head directly to the town's other mansion that also is open the first Sunday afternoon of every month, as well as every Thursday afternoon. It's a French château-style home called Kimberly Crest, located on Prospect Drive. From the Morey House, continue on Terracina Boulevard to Cypress Avenue and follow it to Alvarado Street. Turn right to Highland Avenue, then cross that street and go up the narrow unmarked lane that's Prospect Drive. Soon you'll see the three-story mansion built for a wealthy widow from New York State in 1897. When the J. A. Kimberlys of the Kimberly-Clark paper fortune purchased the home in 1905, they had Tiffany's of New York redecorate it. Formal gardens replaced the orange trees that once surrounded the palatial estate.

After viewing the home, go back down the hill as you came, since you'll encounter car-damaging potholes if you continue on Prospect Drive. Recross Highland Avenue back onto Alvarado Street and drive north to Olive Avenue. On the corner is the Holt House, a 13-room Mediterranean home built in 1903 for the developer of the Imperial Valley. There's a full-size bowling lane in the basement. Go right on Olive Avenue, then left on Eureka Street to Vine Street and park where you can to explore pretty Smiley Park, named for the city's founders. There you'll find Redlands' ornate Moorish-style library, which is now a state historic landmark, the octagonal Lincoln Shrine with its collection of Lincolniana, and the Redlands Bowl, an outdoor community amphitheater where free music and dance performances are presented in July and August.

As for the rest of the day's outing in Redlands, you can visit a mission *asistencia* built in 1830 to serve the area's Indians, browse in the modern San Bernardino County Museum, and then enjoy a meal in another of the town's vintage mansions. From Smiley Park and Eureka Street, turn left and go west on Brookside Avenue, which becomes Barton Road and leads to a bell tower that marks the San Bernardino Asistencia. Spanish padres from the San Gabriel mission had established Rancho San Bernardino in 1819 to teach the Indians about agriculture and livestock, and the *asistencia* as built there was a religious center for the natives. Falling into disrepair soon after California's missions were secularized in the 1830s, the *asistencia* was restored by the WPA 100 years later and is now an attractive museum, featuring artifacts and dioramas of the Indian mission and American pioneer periods. It's also a popular place for weddings.

Continue west on Barton Road to California Street and follow it north under the freeway to Orange Tree Lane. At the end is the impressive San Bernardino County Museum with its giant geodesic dome. Inside you'll find splendid displays of land and sea birds, with their varied eggs and recorded calls, as well as a mammal collection, Indian artifacts, and much more. Adjacent and almost hidden in a grove of orange trees is the Edwards Mansion, a restored 1890 residence that's now a popular restaurant serving lunch, dinner, and Sunday brunch. Visitors who aren't hungry are welcome to tour the 14-room home or have a drink in the lounge. And you can stop at the fruit stand nearby for a glass of fresh-squeezed orange juice or oranges and other citrus fruit. When you're ready for the return trip to Los Angeles, rejoin Interstate 10 going west.

Round trip is about 185 miles.

Oak Glen/Redlands Area Code: 714

SIGHTSEEING   *Edward-Dean Museum of Decorative Arts*, 9401Oak Glen Road, Cherry Valley 92223, 845-2626. Open weekends from 10 A.M. to 4:30 P.M., weekdays except Monday from 1 to 4:30 P.M. Admission $1, children under 12 years free. ● *Redlands Turn-of-the-Century Homes*, self-guided-tour booklet, $3 from Redlands Chamber of Commerce (see below). ● *Morey House*, 140 Terracina Boulevard, Redlands. Open from 1 to 4 P.M. on the first Sunday of every month; donations welcome. ● *Kimberly Crest*, 1325 Prospect Drive, Redlands. Open from 1 to 4 P.M. Thursdays and the first Sunday of every month; donations welcome. ● *San Bernardino Asistencia*, 26930 Barton Road, Redlands 92373, 793-5402. Open daily except Monday from 10 A.M. to 5 P.M., Sunday and Tuesday from 1 P.M. Free admission; donations accepted. ● *San Bernardino County Museum*, 2024 Orange Tree Lane, Redlands 92373, 792-1334. Open daily except Monday from 9 A.M. to 5 P.M., Sunday from 1 P.M. Free.

EVENTS   *Cherry Festival*, annual mid-June celebration. Contact the Beaumont Chamber of Commerce (see below).

LODGING   *Highland Springs Resort*, end of Highland Springs Avenue (or P.O. Box 218), Beaumont 92223, 845-1151 or (213) 271-5505; $80, including breakfast and dinner. Also family plans and special packages. Cottage accommodations in woodsy setting. Informal and fun. Great place for the kids, but children under 3 years not accepted. ● *Law's Oak Glen Motel*, 38412 Oak Glen Road, Oak Glen (Yucaipa) 92399, 797-5063; $28. 8 cozy units, most with wood-burning Franklin stove. In the heart of appleland. Coffee shop adjacent (see below).

DINING   *Edwards Mansion*, 2064 Orange Tree Lane, Redlands,

793-2031. Delightful dining in restored Victorian home and greenhouse surrounded by orange trees. Lunch and dinner daily except Monday. Special buffet lunch weekdays in greenhouse. Popular Sunday champagne brunch from 10 A.M. to 2 P.M. Call for reservations. ● *Highland Springs Resort* (see above). Guest dining room open to the public by reservation only. ● *Law's Oak Glen Coffee Shop*, 38412 Oak Glen Road, Oak Glen, 797-1642. Open 9 A.M. to 5 P.M. daily except Monday and Tuesday. In apple season open 8 A.M. to 7 P.M. every day from September until Thanksgiving. ● *Griswold's Smorgasbord*, Ford Street off Interstate 10, Redlands, 793-2158. Popular and inexpensive buffet open daily for all meals.

FOR MORE INFORMATION   Contact the Beaumont–Cherry Valley Cherry Growers Association, info booth (in season) at Cherry Valley Boulevard and Beaumont Avenue (or P.O. Box 1011), Cherry Valley 92223, 845-1525. Also, the Oak Glen Apple Growers Association, P.O. Box 397, Beaumont 92223, 845-1548. Also, the Beaumont Chamber of Commerce, 450 East 4th Street (or P.O. Box 291), Beaumont 92223, 845-1291. Also, the Redlands Chamber of Commerce, 1 East Redlands Boulevard, Redlands 92373, 793-2546.

Orange County's Canyon Country

Burgeoning Orange County has many visitor attractions in its cities and by the sea, but you'll also be delighted by tranquil inland canyons that continue to forestall the bulldozers, housing developments, and high rises. A hundred years ago the people exploring the narrow, twisting canyons that lead into the rugged Santa Ana Mountains were looking for silver and other elusive ore. These days the quiet canyons are destinations for folks seeking a place to relax and savor nature.

During a weekend escape in the foliage-covered foothills only a few miles from the freeway, you'll discover a trio of parks for picnicking, boating, fishing, hiking, and horseback riding, as well as a wildlife sanctuary that's a favorite of bird watchers. Outdoor enthusiasts can settle down in their tents or RVs in a woodsy campground at O'Neill Regional Park or check in nearby at Coto de Caza, a first-class resort with tennis and equestrian activities among its many enticements.

Get to either retreat by driving south from Los Angeles on Interstate 5 beyond Santa Ana to Laguna Hills and then exiting east on El Toro

Road/County Road S18. You'll wind past sprouting subdivisions on this rural road before reaching a roadhouse called Cook's Corner, where you should go right on Live Oak Canyon Road and follow it to the Orange County hideaways. First to be found is O'Neill Park, 670 acres extending along Trabuco Canyon that are popular for overnight camping and daytime picnicking. There's even an equestrian camping area for visitors who bring their horses to explore the oblong park, originally part of a vast Mexican land grant. If you don't cook out on the evening of your arrival, turn right from the park entrance on Trabuco Canyon Road, continue to the next junction, and go left on Trabuco Oaks Drive to the area's best-known dinner spot, the rustic and very informal Trabuco Oaks Steak House. The featured fare is a steak for cowboys that weighs two pounds. For folks who feel like Mexican food, keep going on Trabuco Canyon Road to Rose Canyon Road and turn left to Señor Lico's.

In the morning, get to know more about the canyon's plants and wildlife by following the Edna Spalding Nature Trail in O'Neill Park; borrow a self-guided-trail brochure at the entry station. Across the road from the park are horses and ponies for hire at Live Oak Stables, and you can take a guided trail ride in the hills on weekends and holidays. Families especially will enjoy a horse-drawn hayride through the park that departs weekend afternoons from the O'Neill Park nature center.

If you're not camping for the weekend at O'Neill Park, continue from Live Oak Canyon Road onto Trabuco Canyon Road and follow it to Coto de Caza, a 5,000-acre resort and residential community that you'd hardly expect to find at the end of an isolated canyon. It's not unknown, however, because Coto de Caza is home for the Vic Braden Tennis College, a world-class teaching facility and sports-research center. The impressive resort also was chosen as the site of the 1984 Olympics' modern pentathlon—a five-event men's competition in horseback riding, fencing, pistol shooting, freestyle swimming, and cross-country foot racing.

You'll need a reservation for one of Coto de Caza's 100 condominium-style rooms in order to enter this pastoral property. Once you've checked in, enjoy dinner in the clubhouse restaurant and get rested for all sorts of activities on Saturday. In addition to tennis, you can go horseback riding or bowling, play racquetball, and even try your skill at trap shooting. This former ranchland also has miles of paths for jogging, hiking, and bike riding. Other options are basketball, billiards, and fishing for bass, bluegill, and catfish in well-stocked ponds. And in the tree-shaded youth park, kids and their parents enjoy playing shuffleboard, horseshoes, Ping-Pong, and volleyball. After all this exercise, the saunas and whirlpool baths in ladies' and men's locker rooms are a nice way to ease into the evening. Although the resort's suites include complete kitchens, most guests have their meals in the clubhouse, or you can drive to the Trabuco Oaks Steak House.

On the final day of your getaway weekend, plan to explore more

Orange County canyons. From Coto de Caza or O'Neill Regional Park, go back to Cook's Corner and turn right on Santiago Canyon Road. Go right again on the next paved road, unmarked Modjeska Grade Road, to Modjeska Canyon Road and bear right to reach the Tucker Wildlife Sanctuary. Modjeska Canyon was named for Madame Helena Modjeska, an acclaimed Polish actress who emigrated to the U.S. and later moved to a house in the canyon. A historical marker opposite the fire station describes her home, now hidden by trees. At road's end, park for a visit to the wildlife sanctuary, best known for its abundance of birds. A viewing patio and porch overlook feeders that attract nearly 150 species during the year, especially the hummingbirds that you'll see darting here and there. Also look at the live local rodents and reptiles on display in the nature center, and go for a walk on one of the nature trails in this unique preserve, operated by the Fullerton campus of California State University.

Follow Modjeska Canyon Road out of the canyon and head north (right) on Santiago Canyon Road. Turn right on Silverado Canyon Road, location of abandoned silver and other ore mines. A plaque in the parking lot of the modernistic Silverado Community Church marks the site of Carbondale, a boisterous boom town that developed with the discovery of coal in 1878 but has since disappeared. Now a quiet rural community has become established in rustic homes along peaceful Silverado Canyon. Locals like to gather at the unfancy Pali Cafe, open daily for breakfast, lunch, and dinner. Try the homemade pie.

Return to Santiago Canyon Road and continue north to Irvine Lake, a haven for fishermen. Entry to the private park is a little pricy, but the sprawling Santiago Reservoir is stocked with trout, bass, and crappie, and boats can be rented if you'd like to try your luck. Otherwise, continue north on Santiago Canyon Road and turn right on Chapman Avenue to Irvine Regional Park, another county park on picturesque ranchland. Kids love riding ponies around a ring, petting small animals in the zoo, and boating in a lagoon. There are hiking trails and plenty of picnic spots.

When it's time for your return to Los Angeles, go back on Chapman Avenue and follow it through the city of Orange to rejoin Interstate 5 heading north.

Round trip is about 120 miles.

Orange County Area Code: 714

SIGHTSEEING *O'Neill Regional Park,* 30892 Trabuco Canyon Road, Trabuco Canyon 92678, 586-7962. Open daily from 7:30 A.M. to 10 P.M. from April through September, to sunset the rest of the year. Day-use fee $1 per vehicle. Also overnight camping (see below). ● *Live Oak Stables,* 31101 Live Oak Canyon Road across from O'Neill Regional Park, Trabuco Canyon 92678, 951-9835. Open 8 A.M. to 4 P.M.

weekends and holidays only. One-hour guided trail rides, $8 per person. No reservations. Also weekend hayrides at 2 P.M. from O'Neill Park nature center, $3 per person. • *Tucker Wildlife Sanctuary,* 29322 Modjeska Canyon Road (or Star Route Box 858), Orange 92667, 649-2760. Open daily from 9 A.M. to 4 P.M. Donation 50 cents. Picnic tables. • *Irvine Lake,* off Santiago Canyon Road (or Star Route 38), Orange 92667, 649-2560. Open from 6 A.M. to 5:30 P.M. in summer, to 4:30 P.M. in winter. Adults $8, children under 12 years $6. Fishing for bass, catfish, trout, crappie, and bluegill. License required; sold in the park at Irvine Boat and Tackle Shop, 649-2991. Also rental motorboats and rowboats. • *Irvine Regional Park,* 21501 East Chapman Avenue, Orange 92669, 633-8072. Open daily from 7 A.M. to 10 P.M. from April through September, to sunset the rest of the year. Day-use fee $1 per vehicle. Extra fees for pony rides and rowboats. Petting zoo free. No camping.

LODGING   *Coto de Caza,* end of Trabuco Canyon Road (or P.O. Box 438), Trabuco Canyon 92678, 586-0761; $65, suites from $120. Also Vic Braden Tennis College packages that include use of 16 championship courts, geometric teaching lanes, classroom and on-court instruction, and instant video replay. Guided trail rides Wednesday through Sunday, $12 per hour; boots required. Also reserve for skeet and trap shooting. Supervised all-day youth program for age groups 5 to 8 years and 9 to 12 years in summer. Guests-only restaurant in the clubhouse (see below).

CAMPING   *O'Neill Regional Park* (see above). 300 sites, no hookups. $5 per night. First come, first served. Country store nearby for food and supplies.

DINING   *Trabuco Oaks Steak House,* 20782 Trabuco Oaks Drive, Trabuco Canyon 92678, 586-0722. Open Wednesday through Sunday from 4 P.M. for dinner only. Great beef and fun; don't wear a tie unless you want it cut off. Make reservations. • *Señor Lico's,* 20722 Rose Canyon Road, Trabuco Canyon 92678, 951-2838. Open daily except Monday for lunch and dinner. Mexican plus limited American fare. • *Coto de Caza Clubhouse Restaurant,* at Coto de Caza (see above). Open daily for breakfast, lunch, and dinner for resort guests only. Steak, seafood, and some Mexican dishes. Reservations suggested. Also cocktail lounge and entertainment. • *Pali Cafe,* 28272 Silverado Canyon Road, Silverado, 649-2622. Open daily for all meals. American favorites plus homemade pie.

Boats, Trains, and Planes in Perris Valley

Paris was the focus of attention when Charles Lindbergh landed his *Spirit of St. Louis* after the first solo flight across the Atlantic little more than half a century ago. Nowadays aerial enthusiasts are still talking about Perris—in Riverside County. It's a major center for aerial activities in the Southland. At that rural community's airport you can watch or join in all kinds of airborne events—hot-air ballooning, parachuting, gliding, or even flying a micro-light aircraft. And for visitors who like to travel closer to terra firma, Perris is the home of the Orange Empire Railway Museum, where you can ride old-time trolleys that used to clang through the streets of Los Angeles and San Francisco.

This region also is outstanding for all kinds of outdoor activities, because of the Lake Perris State Recreation Area. It's an inland retreat for boaters, hikers, bicyclists, anglers, picnickers, swimmers, hunters, water skiers, bird watchers, and rock climbers. With 430 RV and tent sites for family camping, the park is the perfect base for a weekend visit to Perris Valley. (Limited lodging also is available at Perris's sole motel, and you'll find a greater choice of accommodations 18 miles northwest in Riverside.)

Get to Lake Perris by driving east on California 60 (Pomona Freeway) past Riverside to the Moreno Beach Road exit. Turn south to the park's 24-hour entrance, then head to the campground and settle in for the evening. Plan to explore and enjoy this pleasure-filled recreation area either Saturday or Sunday and spend the other day of your weekend involved in the aerial and railway activities around Perris.

Like Perrier, the water in Lake Perris is imported to Southern California for your pleasure. No, it's not brought from overseas in bottles. In fact, the journey of Lake Perris water is more fascinating. Beginning as rainfall and melted snow in Northern California, it courses down the state rivers, tunnels, pipelines, and aqueducts to a 2,000-acre reservoir that's the terminus for the 444-mile California Aqueduct bringing water to the Southland from the Sacramento–San Joaquin Delta. Lake Perris, along with 6,000 surrounding acres of rocky hills and rangeland, has subsequently been developed for public recreation. For a panoramic view of the lake and nearby hills, drive or hike to the park's Interpretive Center, which offers an excellent lookout and describes the land in earlier days.

Since it began forming in 1973, Lake Perris has expanded its shoreline to a circumference of 10 miles and is especially popular with boaters. There are two ramps where visitors can launch their own powerboats and sailboats, or you can rent a boat at the marina for some sailing, fishing, or sightseeing. Jet-skis and water skis also can be hired. Boaters can sail to the middle of the lake to swim and picnic on Alessandro Island, named for the Indian hero of Helen Hunt Jackson's well-known novel, *Ramona*. You'll also find sandy beaches for swimming along the lakeshore, as well as numerous picnic sites with tables and grills. Grocery and boat supplies are sold in the small store up the hill from the boat slips, and a coffee shop is adjacent.

Fishing usually is good, especially for channel catfish. Lake Perris is stocked with Alabama spotted bass, Florida bluegill, and rainbow trout, too. You can get the required state fishing license at the boat fuel dock. Another option for anglers is to board a 35-foot pontoon boat for a six-hour fishing trip with a guide. Hooks and bait are provided, so just bring your own pole and line.

For bicyclists and hikers there's a paved path around the lake. A separate equestrian trail also circles the lake, but bring your own horse or bike, because none can be rented in the park. At the south end of the dam visit the Big Rock, a favorite attraction for rock climbers as well as onlookers, who marvel at the human spiders who scale the huge outcropping. Climbers must get a permit from rangers at the park entrance. Scuba divers must also obtain permits from the rangers and be certified divers in order to use the special diving zone, where sections of huge concrete pipe have been placed on the lake bottom. With the proper license, seasonal hunting is allowed in designated sections of the Lake Perris recreation area, too, but only shotguns can be used. Game includes rabbit, quail, dove, and some waterfowl.

Get up early on the day you want some high-flying fun, because the hot-air balloons are launched at sunrise. In the early dawn just south of the Perris Valley Airport, one to two dozen of the colorful air carriers are inflated with heat from roaring propane burners and ascend into the sky, each with a wicker basket carrying a pilot and two or three passengers. These scenic flights, by reservation only, depart from a field at the corner of Goetz and Mapes roads. Get there from the Lake Perris State Recreation Area by taking the Perris Drive exit from the park to the Ramona Expressway. Go right to Perris Boulevard and follow it south through town, jogging left on 11th Street just past the railroad tracks and then turning right to join Goetz Road. Go beyond the airport entrance to Mapes Road to watch or help launch the big balloons. If you go aloft, the cost of the 30- to 90-minute flights includes the traditional champagne to celebrate the completion of your aerial excursion.

Afterward, go back on Goetz Road to the Perris Valley Airport, headquarters for one of the busiest jump centers in the world. In fact, it's popular with sport parachutists from all over the globe. Jumpers float down from the sky every day of the week, but most of the airborne action is on weekends. If you get the urge to parachute instead of just being an observer on the ground, Perris Valley Paracenter offers a training course that takes just 4 to 6 hours and climaxes with your first jump. Folks who are hesitant, or can't afford the enrollment fee, can go along as passengers in the jump plane for a nominal charge.

Nearby is the Orange County Soaring Association, which uses the airfield as its glider port. On weekends you'll see a towplane getting the motorless gliders airborne to begin an exciting yet peaceful ride on the air currents. Members of the glider club are willing to give rides to visitors who sign up on the spot. A small fee for the surprisingly quiet 20- to 30-minute flight gives you a one-day membership in the soaring association to comply with their insurance regulations.

Also in the sky around Perris Valley Airport are micro-lights, one-person aircraft that resemble giant dragonflies. The latest rage in personal air transportation, these micro-lights also are called ultra-lights and often are erroneously referred to as motorized hang gliders. For a close-up look at the fabric-and-aluminum-frame flying machines, walk from the glider club paracenter to the hangar headquarters of the Valley Ultra-lights. If you'd like to be a modern-day Orville Wright, arrange for introductory lessons and an individual flight at the Perris Valley Paracenter.

A short distance from the airport you'll also enjoy the revival of earth-bound transportation aboard an electric railcar. Clickety-clacking joy rides on refurbished trolleys are offered weekends and holidays at the Orange Empire Railway Museum. Get there by returning to Mapes Road and going east to A Street, then turning right to the museum parking area. Walk across the tracks to a world of clanging bells and wheels screeching on the steel rails. Hop aboard one of the vintage vehicles and join the other passengers swaying in their seats as the streetcar circles 2½ miles through the pastureland.

Three or four cars run different routes at varying times. They are selected from the museum's rolling stock, which includes a 1905 Huntington Standard, one of the Los Angeles Railway's Yellow Cars. Another working trolley took commuters around San Francisco in 1925. Rides also are given aboard the newest streetcar, a streamlined version built for L.A.'s Metropolitan Transit Authority 30 years ago. It was retired from city service in 1963. Two other cars that tour the museum grounds are Pacific Electrics (the 1922 model once traveled Hollywood Boulevard). Along the way volunteer conductors and motormen describe the trolley's history and reminisce about city and interurban rail transportation.

Besides taking a nostalgic ride or experiencing a trip by trolley for the first time, you also can browse around the grounds to inspect nonoperating streetcars and train cars from a bygone era. Look for the *Descanso,* a special funeral trolley that transported coffins and mourners to Los Angeles area cemeteries from 1909 to 1939. Another streetcar, No. 913 from New Orleans, should remind you of playwright Tennessee Williams because of the destination on its headsign: Desire Street. Some trolleys are from overseas, including a double-decker that once ran in Dublin. A smaller car, with Japanese lettering, saw service in Tokyo until 1973. There are also open storage and restoration sheds, where volunteers frequently are working to return old and rusted cars to their original condition so visitors can sample electric rail transportation from earlier times. A gift shop sells mementos and books that describe some of the 140 train cars and trolleys at the outdoor museum. There's a tree-shaded picnic area, too, and refreshments are available.

Another item of interest for railroad buffs is back in town, the 1892 Perris train depot with its distinctive Queen Anne-style tower. The red brick building now is home for the Perris Historical Society, with a small museum devoted to railroad and other early-day artifacts from the area. Reach it by going north on A Street to 4th Street and turning right two blocks to the railroad tracks. Just beyond is D Street, the main street of Perris, which leads north to Interstate 215 (formerly I-15E) to rejoin California 60 for the drive back to Los Angeles.

Round trip is about 170 miles.

Perris Area Code: 714

SIGHTSEEING   *Lake Perris State Recreation Area,* 17801 Lake Perris Drive, Perris 92370, 657-0676. Open daily. Day-use fee $2 per vehicle; fee for camping (see below) includes entry. Pick up 50-cent park map at entry gate. Lake Perris Marina open for boat and equipment rentals from 6 A.M. to 8 P.M. in summer, 7 A.M. to 5 P.M. in winter. Call 657-2179 or 657-4080 for current rates. Pontoon boat with fishing-guide service, 8 A.M. to noon, $10 per person; call 653-5869 for reservations. ● *Scorpion Balloons,* 246 Lomita Drive (or P.O. 1147), Perris 92370, 657-6930, offers hot-air balloon rides any day by reservation. One-hour flights $160 per couple, $210 for three passengers. ● *California Balloon Center,* 28630 Goetz Road, Quail Valley 92380, 679-0666, also offers daily flights by reservation. 30- to 45-minute rides cost $55 per person, 60- to 90-minute trips $95 per person. ● *Perris Valley Paracenter,* 2091 South Goetz Road, Perris 92370, 657-3904. Same-day First Jump course costs $125, including equipment, instruction, and airplane flight. Riding in a DC-3 jump plane as an observer costs about $16. ● *Orange County Soaring Association,* P.O. Box 5475, Buena Park 90622. Rides in sailplanes, offered on sign-up basis at Perris Valley Airport, cost $20. No reservations; best to get name on list between 9:30 and 10 A.M. Saturday or Sunday. ● *Valley Ultra-lights,* contact Perris Valley Paracenter (see above) to arrange for a micro-light flight; $250 for anyone without prior aviation experience. ● *Orange Empire Railway Museum,* 2201 South A Street, Perris 92370, 657-2605. Open daily 9 A.M. to 5 P.M., but trolley rides offered only on weekends and holidays from 11 A.M. to 5 P.M. Museum entry free; all-day trolley passes cost $3 for adults, $2.50 for senior citizens and ages 12 through 17, $1.50 for children 6 through 11 years. ● *Perris Historical Society Museum*, in old Perris railroad depot at 120 West 4th Street, Perris 92370. Open Sundays 1 to 4 P.M. Free.

LODGING   *TraveLodge*, 1775 West Perris Boulevard, Perris 92370, 657-1804; $35. The only motel in Perris, 23 rooms; restaurant adjacent. Other accommodations in Riverside.

CAMPING   *Lake Perris State Recreation Area* (see above). Open all year. Sites $6, with hookup $9. Ticketron reservations recommended Memorial Day weekend through Labor Day weekend.

DINING   Perris has few choices for dining out. *La Hacienda*, 502 South D Street, Perris, 657-2636. Mexican fare for lunch and dinner daily. *Spud Cellar*, off Interstate 215 (old I-15E) at Orange Street, Perris, 657-7783. Steak house with lunch and dinner daily except Monday. Fish fry on Friday evening. ● *Louisa's Kitchen*, 140 South D Street, Perris, 657-9001. Family-style meals for breakfast and lunch. ● *Jailhouse Sandwich Shoppe*, 505 South D Street, Perris, 657-8600. Lunch only in onetime jail; closed Sundays.

FOR MORE INFORMATION   Perris Chamber of Commerce, in old railroad depot at 120 West 4th Street, Perris 92370, 657-3555. Open weekdays 10 A.M. to 2 P.M.

Lazy Days at Lake Elsinore and Glen Ivy Hot Springs

When you're eager for a casual outdoor weekend, escape inland to Riverside County and a popular state recreation area, Lake Elsinore, well known for its ups and downs. In the 1950s Lake Elsinore actually disappeared through evaporation and fissures in the lake bed. More than a decade passed before it was refilled with water from the Colorado River and underground springs. Then, in March 1980, the lake overflowed with melting snow and rain water that poured down from the mountains encircling the Elsinore Valley. Some evidence of that devastating flood remains, but the recreational activities in and around the lake are going strong.

Since becoming a state recreation area in 1957, Lake Elsinore has been a favorite destination for boaters, water skiers, and fishermen. Other sportsmen come for the valley's aerial adventures, riding the thermal wind currents with a hang glider or parachuting from the sky to a landing area near the lakeside. Many settle for the weekend or longer in the state park campground at the lake's northwest end. In fact, most of Lake Elsinore's visitors are campers, because lodging in the area is limited to a few unassuming motels.

Reach the park and campground from Los Angeles by driving south on Interstate 5 to California 91, the Riverside Freeway, and following it east just beyond Corona to the exit for Interstate 15. Go south to the California 74/Central Avenue exit and follow that state highway west to Lake Elsinore State Park.

Located at the base of the Elsinore Mountains in a valley that supports some agriculture and a growing number of housing developments, Lake Elsinore boasts a small town of the same name on its northern shore. There you'll find two motels where guests still enjoy soaking in mineral water pumped from the hot springs that originally put Lake Elsinore on the map.

Long ago the Indians knew the area as Etengvo Wumona, "hot springs by the little sea," and they came to soak away their aches and ills. Spanish explorers later named the lake Laguna Grande and it became part of the Rancho La Laguna land grant. A town was started in 1883 and called Laguna, but the state already had a community by that name, so Elsinore was chosen, in honor of the Danish town made famous by Shakespeare's *Hamlet*. Thanks to its warm climate and hot springs, Lake Elsinore soon became a health resort. One of the original spa buildings still stands, the 96-year-old Crescent Bath House, now known as the Chimes and filled with antiques—as well as a resident ghost.

Drive there on Saturday from the state park by going back on California 74/Riverside Drive to Lakeshore Drive and following it east along the water. On the hillside overlooking the lake you'll see streetlights and impressive homes from the town's early days. Out of sight is the Moorish castle home built by world-renowned evangelist Aimee Semple McPherson. When you reach the junior high school, bear left on Graham Avenue to the center of town. Look left for a two-story colonial structure with fancy grillwork on the upper porch. The Chimes, a well-preserved redwood building, has been designated a national historic landmark. The large front rooms of this former bathhouse were the spa's recreation areas. Nowadays they're filled with vintage furniture, china, glassware, clocks, and other collectibles. Go down the long hall to see more antiques and the Roman-style bathtubs, as well the former ladies' and gentlemen's massage rooms. One chamber is a mini-museum of Lake Elsinore memorabilia. Ask the Chimes's owners, Lory and Wilma Watts, about the poltergeist that occupies a room in their fascinating emporium of antiques.

Nearby you'll find a few places to eat and the Jo-Fay and Han's motels, both featuring hot-springs mineral water piped into the guest-room tubs, pools, and Jacuzzis. These are adequate overnight accommodations in case you decide not to camp out.

Enjoy more of the lake and its sporting activities by following Main Street past the town park to return to Lakeshore Drive. Go left and continue to skirt the water on Mission Trail, then turn right on Corydon Street toward the lake's southern end. Look for an unmarked dirt road on your right leading to an airfield and the Elsinore Parachute Center at lakeside. Most weekends you'll see the sky dotted with colorful chutes as expert and novice jumpers float back to earth. Many are first-time parachutists, and you're welcome to watch them pack their chutes and practice for the jump. Or sign up for the jump course yourself—you can dive from the sky the same day.

You also can view hang gliders in action as they soar along the top of the Elsinore Mountains, by continuing on Corydon Street to Grand Avenue. Then turn right to follow that road to California 74 at the Ortega Highway junction, and go left to the open field where the human butterflies make their graceful landings.

Returning to Grand Avenue, continue circling the lake, and bear right on Riverside Drive to come back to the entrance of the state park. If it's summertime, when Elsinore Valley often heats up into the 90s, cool off with a dip in the lake. Or rent a rowboat, kayak, or paddle boat to cruise lazily on the water at twilight.

The next morning after breakfast, take Lakeshore Drive northwest from Riverside Drive and drive a mile to Terra Cotta Road and Torn Ranch, the valley's last remaining walnut grove. Its rustic packing plant has been converted to an old-time general store of gourmet food, wine, and gifts. Then continue north on Lake Street, which becomes Temescal Canyon Road and parallels the freeway before reaching the Glen Ivy Road, marked by a sign to Glen Ivy Recreational Vehicle Resort and Hot Springs Spa. Follow that country road a half mile past the RV camp to one of the Los Angeles area's oldest outdoor spas, Glen Ivy Hot Springs, a popular soaking spot since 1890.

Nestled in the foothills of the Santa Ana Mountains, this venerable health haven is a pleasant surprise for first-time visitors. With such a remote location, you'd hardly expect to find a full-size swimming pool of warm mineral water amid fruit orchards and restful palms. And there's much more: a smaller therapy pool with bubbling 105-degree water straight from the hot springs, a warm wading area for the kids, individual whirlpool baths, an ocher-colored pool where bathers pat on red clay to tone up their skin, and private rooms for massages and wraps.

First to relax at the hot springs were the local Luiseno Indians, who named their valley Temescal after the sweathouses they built by the steaming water source. In the spa's entrance building you'll see photographs of Glen Ivy's early days as a hot-springs resort. One photo dated 1892 advertises a hotel and baths. That lodging has since been converted to apartments, but spa bathing facilities have been expanded considerably. A single admission price lets you enjoy all the pools, including the Southland's only red clay bath, as well as a coed sauna, sunning decks with plenty of lounge chairs, and a picnic area. For additional fees you can get a Swedish-style massage or blanket wrap and be treated by a chiropractor.

With its elevation at 1,200 feet and in the path of ocean breezes, the spa boasts clear and invigorating air most of the year. Bring your own food to the hot springs for a picnic lunch, or order a tasty salad, sandwich, or hot entree at Glen Ivy's cafe. Eat it indoors, poolside, or at a tree-shaded table. Beer, wine, and other beverages are available too. Take towels, or rent them at the spa. Also, it's a good idea to have an old swimsuit for the red clay bath, because it may get stained. And don't forget suntan lotion. If you decide to spend another day at the spa, you'll find lodging a few miles north in Corona; campers can bed down at the adjacent Glen Ivy RV Resort.

On your way home from Glen Ivy Hot Springs, continue north on Temescal Canyon Road, a rural highway that follows a route once used by Indians, pioneers, gold seekers, soldiers, and mail stages traveling between San Diego and Los Angeles. Along the way you can imagine those days of the Old West by renting a horse at Golden West Stables and riding on trails that crisscross the riverbed, hills, and fields in the Temescal Valley. Just beyond the stables, tie up your horse or stop your car at Tom's Farms, an extensive roadside stand filled with fresh produce, dried fruit, nuts, and candies. You'll find plants, pottery, and baskets, too. On weekends the parking lot becomes an outdoor antique mart when Tom sells furniture collected in England, as well as a variety of reproductions from other countries.

Before rejoining the freeway for the journey home, relax with refreshments from an adjacent self-service cafe that has outdoor tables overlooking a duck pond. Then continue north on Interstate 15 to California 91 and go west to pick up Interstate 5 back to Los Angeles.

Round trip is about 180 miles.

Lake Elsinore Area Code: 714

SIGHTSEEING *Lake Elsinore State Park*, 32040 Riverside Drive (off California 74), Lake Elsinore, 674-3177. Day-use fee $2 per vehicle, $4 with boat. Boat and bike rentals. Also camping (see below). ● *The Chimes*, 201 West Graham Avenue, Lake Elsinore, 674-3456. Open weekends only: 10 A.M. to 5 P.M. Saturday, 11 A.M. to 5 P.M. Sunday. ● *Elsinore Parachute Center*, 20701 Cereal Road, Lake Elsinore, 674-2141. Open 8 A.M. to sunset weekends, 9 A.M. to sunset weekdays; Tuesday through Sunday in summer, Thursday through Sunday in winter.

One-day jump course, including first sky dive, $100; ride in jump plane as an observer, $11. • *Torn Ranch,* 31307 Terra Cotta Road, Lake Elsinore, 674-2026. Open 10 A.M. to 5 P.M. daily. • *Glen Ivy Hot Springs,* 25000 Glen Ivy Road, south of Corona, 737-4723. Open 10 A.M. to 6 P.M. daily, and to 10 P.M. Friday and Saturday. Adults $6, children $4. Also cafe (see below). • *Golden West Stables,* 24160 Temescal Canyon Road, near Tom's Farms, 371-0181. Open 7 A.M. to midnight on weekends, 7 A.M. to 9 P.M. weekdays. Rental horses $5.50 per hour; ride two hours Tuesday through Thursday and get an extra hour free. Weekends are first come, first served; on weekdays call for reservations. • *Tom's Farms,* 23900 Temescal Canyon Road, south of Corona, 735-0092. Open from 8 A.M. to dusk daily; antique mart on weekends. Cafe adjacent (see below).

LODGING *Han's Motel & Mineral Spa,* 215 West Graham Avenue, Lake Elsinore 92330, 674-3551, $26. • *Jo-Fay Motel & Health Spa,* 316 North Main Street, Lake Elsinore 92330, 674-9997, $29. • *Sahara Dunes Motel,* 20930 Malaga Road, Lake Elsinore 92330, 674-3101, $33. • *King's Inn,* 1084 Pomona Road, Corona 91720, 734-4241, $40; special rates for Glen Ivy Hot Springs guests. • *Travelodge,* 1701 West 6th Street, Corona 91720, 735-5500, $31.

CAMPING *Lake Elsinore State Park,* 32040 Riverside Drive (off California 74), Lake Elsinore, 674-3177. 242 sites, $6.50 per night, $9 with electrical hookup. • *Glen Ivy Recreational Vehicle Resort,* 24601 Glen Ivy Road, south of Corona, 737-4261. 350 sites, full hookup, $12.50 per night. Swimming pool, tennis courts.

DINING *Rainbow Gardens Restaurant,* 111 West Graham Avenue, Lake Elsinore, 674-3047. • *The Lakehouse Restaurant & Coffee Shop,* 123 North Main Street, Lake Elsinore. • *Ambassador Villa & Restaurant,* 164 South Main Street, Lake Elsinore, 674-9904. • *Sahara Dunes Casino Restaurant & Coffee Shop,* 20930 Malaga Road, Lake Elsinore, 674-3101. • *Park Plaza Family Restaurant,* 31731 Riverside Drive, Lake Elsinore, 674-5744. • *Glen Ivy Hot Springs Cafe,* at spa, 25000 Glen Ivy Road, south of Corona, 737-4723. • *Knowl-Wood Cafe,* at Tom's Farms, 23900 Temescal Canyon Road, south of Corona, 735-5110.

FOR MORE INFORMATION Contact the Lake Elsinore Valley Chamber of Commerce, 132 West Graham Avenue (in the old train depot), Lake Elsinore 92330, 674-2577.

Historic Riverside, the "Inn" Place

The Mission Inn made Riverside the "in" spot for discriminating travelers half a century ago. In its heyday the imposing hotel welcomed six U.S. Presidents, assorted royalty, stars of stage and screen, and business tycoons such as Henry Ford and John D. Rockefeller. Now designated both a state and national historic landmark, the inn is still reason enough for a visit to Riverside, where the townsfolk are credited with saving this incomparable hostelry from the wrecker's ball. Covering an entire city block, the born-again hotel is the keystone of Riverside's rejuvenated downtown. More than 70 of the guest rooms have been refurbished, so you can spend the night as did Theodore Roosevelt, Grand Duke Alexander of Russia, Sarah Bernhardt, and other well-known visitors several decades ago.

Riverside's roots go back more than two centuries; explorer Juan Bautista de Anza camped there in 1774 on his first overland expedition in California. Founded as an agricultural colony, the town began to flourish at the side of the Santa Ana River and was incorporated in 1883. Riverside soon became one of the most prosperous places in the Southland, thanks to the navel orange from Bahia, Brazil, that was introduced a decade earlier.

Opulent Victorian homes and grand public buildings were erected amid acres of citrus groves, reflecting the city's status as the center of the Orange Empire. While many of those orchards have been lost to urban and industrial encroachment, much of historic Riverside remains and makes an enjoyable weekend. Get there from Los Angeles by driving east on California 60 to Riverside and exiting south on Market Street. Turn left at Seventh Street and go a block to the Mission Inn, marked by a bell tower seven stories high.

Born as the Glenwood Cottage in 1876, the inn began as a two-story adobe boardinghouse run by the C. C. Miller family. Soon it was expanded to a 12-room hotel and managed by the eldest son, Frank. He devoted his life to the inn, eventually building the mission-style structure that Will Rogers once described as the most unique hotel in America. To decorate his inn, Frank traveled the world to gather antiques and other treasures, including a novel collection of bells and crosses. And he staged art exhibits, music recitals, and other cultural events that made the hotel a Southern California social center.

The Mission Inn's guest registers read like a *Who's Who* until the owner's death in 1935, and by the end of World War II the hotel had slipped from prominence and fell into disrepair. It was saved from demolition in 1976 by a determined citizen's group and $2 million in city funds to purchase the property. Restoration work continues, although much of the historic hostelry already has been returned to its former glory. You'll have fun exploring the vast hotel on your own, but be sure to join a guided tour to learn all about its fascinating past.

Have dinner in the inn's Spanish Patio amid orange trees, statuary, and fountains, or in the adjacent dining room. If a dinner show is scheduled the weekend of your visit, enjoy music with your meal by reserving a table in the impressive Cloister Music Room, where Frank Miller once held free Sunday-afternoon organ concerts. For daytime cocktails or after-dinner drinks head for the intimate Presidential Lounge just off the lobby. And sometime during your stay drop into Glenwood Tavern, a pleasant pub on the hotel's lower level.

Begin Saturday with a leisurely breakfast and perhaps have a dip in the hotel pool before taking the morning guided tour of the Mission Inn. Small groups are led by Friends of the Mission Inn volunteers, and the token tour fees go toward additional hotel restoration, as well as the re-purchase of original artifacts and furnishings that were auctioned off by the inn's interim owners. A highlight of the tour is the impressive St. Francis Chapel, which was the marriage site for a number of Hollywood stars, such as Bette Davis and Humphrey Bogart, and is still popular for weddings. Its Tiffany stained-glass windows and eighteenth-century gold-leaf altar from Mexico are outstanding. Next door is the Galeria Museum, with much of Frank Miller's worldwide collection, which was first put on public view in 1983. In the chapel courtyard, don't miss the Famous Flyers Wall, with plaques that honor and record the visits of prominent aviators, including Amelia Earhart and Orville Wright.

From the balcony overlooking the dining patio you'll see three domes that are replicas from the missions at Carmel, San Juan Capistrano, and Santa Barbara. Also watch carved figures move on the half hour in the giant German glockenspiel that dates to 1709. During the tour you'll also get a peek into some of the inn's refurbished suites and special rooms and view the impressive Rotunda with its spiral staircase that leads to shops and offices. If you decide to make a self-guided tour, buy a *History of the Mission Inn* pamphlet at the lobby gift shop. It's opposite the immense chair that was specially built for 340-pound President Taft when he at-tended a banquet at the hotel in 1909.

Leave your car parked at the inn and spend the afternoon browsing in the downtown shops and viewing more of the regal edifices that were erected earlier in this century with income from Riverside's orange groves. Much of the city's arresting architecture is concentrated in two blocks along 7th Street. Begin by looking across from the Mission Inn for wrought-iron balconies and a tile roof that mark the old Spanish-style city hall, now home for an antique mart with 21 dealers of vintage goods. On the opposite corner, explore the marble-decorated Riverside Museum, built in 1912 as a post office. You'll find exhibits about area Indians, natural science, and local history, including the citrus industry.

At the corner with Lemon Street, two other eye-catching buildings along 7th Street are the First Unitarian Church, built of red sandstone brought from Arizona, and the Mission-style Municipal Auditorium, crowned by a Moorish dome. Next door is the Riverside Art Center, designed as a YWCA in 1929 by Julia Morgan, who gained fame as the architect of Hearst Castle at San Simeon. Drop in to view the permanent collection of artwork and buy some originals in the gallery shop.

Also be certain to stroll in another direction from the Mission Inn along the five-block Main Street pedestrian shopping mall. Capping one end is the new city hall, designed with a modern version of the Spanish arch. On weekdays from its sixth-floor rooftop patio you can survey the thousands of ornamental trees that decorate this sprawling city. Walk another block to a beaux arts beauty, the Riverside County Courthouse, built in 1903 and modeled after the Grand Palace of Fine Arts in Paris. You can't miss its Ionic columns and classic statuary.

The next day you'll need your car to see more of historic and scenic Riverside. After Sunday brunch at the Mission Inn, check out and head to a natural lookout in the heart of town, Mount Rubidoux, a city park on a bouldered mountain that rises to nearly 1,400 feet. Follow 7th Street several blocks northwest to Mount Rubidoux Drive, a narrow one-way road that spirals to a summit parking area near the World Peace Tower, dedicated to Frank Miller. In 1909 the Mission Inn owner initiated an Easter sunrise service on the mountaintop, now an annual Riverside event held at the huge concrete cross that was erected two years earlier as a monument to the founder of California's famed missions, Father Junipero Serra.

After enjoying a bird's-eye view of the Riverside area, especially worthwhile on a clear winter's day, descend carefully via the twisting road that joins Glenwood Drive and leads to 14th Street. Head east to the intersection of Market Street and Magnolia Avenue and turn right to go south on Magnolia. It leads to another busy intersection with Arlington Avenue, where you'll spot a tiny triangle of citrus trees behind a wrought-iron fence. Park where you can to have a close-up view of the Parent Navel Orange Tree, sole survivor of the original seedless orange stock planted in Riverside in 1873. This living historical landmark, which still bears fruit, is the ancestor of the thousands of trees that created the area's multi-million-dollar citrus industry. Also growing there is another honored fruit tree, the grapefruit, introduced to the Southland from Florida.

Continue south on Magnolia Avenue, which widens into a divided boulevard bordered by fan palms, eucalyptus, and pepper trees and brings you to the Heritage House, a restored Victorian mansion built in 1891. See its exquisite period decorations by taking a guided tour of that elegant home, now part of the Riverside Museum. Besides a beautiful staircase, tile-faced fireplaces, and gas-lamp fixtures, you'll like the Oriental rugs, oil paintings, clocks, and antique furniture.

A trio of schools line the left side of Magnolia Avenue as the boulevard continues southwest, beginning with the Spanish-style buildings of California Baptist College. After passing a public school, circle back at Jackson Street on the other side of the avenue to Sherman Indian High School, a federally run boarding school that opened in 1902 to educate young native Americans from the area. One of the original buildings on this now-modernized campus is a museum of Indian artifacts. You'll see some wonderful beadwork, baskets, pottery, dolls, and other handicrafts, as well as dioramas that portray the California, Plains, Hopi, and Cherokee Indian cultures.

Heading southwest again on Magnolia Avenue, turn left on Van Buren Boulevard to join California 91 and then Interstate 5 back to Los Angeles.

Round trip is about 120 miles.

Riverside Area Code: 714

SIGHTSEEING   *Mission Inn,* 3649 7th Street, Riverside 92501, 784-0300. Hour-long guided tours daily at 11:30 A.M. and 2:30 P.M. Adults $2, children 5 through 11 years 75 cents. Half-hour mini-tour on Sundays only at 1:15 P.M. Adults $1.50, children 75 cents. Also lodgings and dining (see below). ● *Old City Hall Antique Mart,* 7th Street at Orange Street, Riverside 92501, 788-8191. Open daily except Tuesday from 11 A.M. to 5:30 P.M. ● *Riverside Museum,* 7th Street at Orange Street, Riverside 92501, 787-7273. Open weekends from 1 to 5 P.M., weekdays except Monday from 9 A.M. to 5 P.M. Free. ● *Riverside Art Center,* 3425 7th Street, Riverside 92501, 684-7111. Open daily except Sunday and Monday from 10 A.M. to 4:30 P.M. Free. ● *Mount Rubidoux Memorial Park,* via Mount Rubidoux Drive from 7th Street, Riverside, 787-7301. Road open to cars only (no Rvs or trailers) Sunday through Wednesday from 9 A.M. to 7 P.M. In summer, to 5 P.M. in winter. Closed to vehicles Thursday through Saturday; hikers and joggers welcome every day. Free. Pilgrimage to the summit for sunrise service on Easter Sunday. ● *Heritage House,* 8193 Magnolia Avenue, Riverside 92503, 689-1333. Guided tours on Sundays from 12 to 3:30 P.M., Tuesday and Thursday from 12 to 2:30 P.M. Donation $1 adults, 50 cents children and senior citizens. ● *Sherman Indian Museum,* 9010 Magnolia Avenue at Sherman Indian High School, Riverside 92503, 359-9434. Open weekends by appointment, weekdays from 1 to 4 P.M. Free; donations appreciated.

LODGING   *Mission Inn* (see above), 784-0300; $40 to $60. Also summertime packages including guided tour and some meals. Some suites available. ● Other accommodations are west of downtown along University Drive, Riverside's motel row.

DINING   *Mission Inn* (see above). Breakfast, buffet lunch, and dinner served daily in the Spanish Dining Room and on the Patio (weather permitting). Also Sunday brunch. Dinner in the Squire Arms in winter. American and continental fare. Cocktails daily from 11 A.M. in the Presidential Lounge, with entertainment most evenings. Also hors d'oeuvres and drinks from late afternoon in the Glenwood Tavern. Dinner theater and musical shows are staged in the Cloister Music Room at various times during the year; call the hotel for current schedule. ● Other popular Riverside dining spots are west of downtown along University Avenue.

FOR MORE INFORMATION   Contact the Riverside Visitors and Convention Bureau, 3443 Orange Street (at Raincross Square Convention Center), Riverside 92501, 787-7950.

Fallbrook and Temecula for Antiques and a Taste of the Grape

You'll rekindle lots of childhood memories with a visit to rural Fallbrook. Not only is the village reminiscent of a small Midwestern town, it's home for a number of antique shops brimming with memorabilia. And Fallbrook's fertile rolling countryside abounds with avocados, a prized taste treat that's featured in the town's restaurants and sold at roadside stands with all kinds of other homegrown fruit. This northern San Diego County region is rich in gemstones, too, especially tourmalines, and visitors can search for some at one of the world's most productive mines.

Not far away is another old-time town, Temecula, that's also popular with antique seekers. It's becoming known for quality wines as well, and you'll have fun on a tasting tour of the area's wineries.

Embark on a relaxing rural weekend by driving south from Los Angeles on Interstate 5 to join California 91 (the Riverside Freeway) heading west, then turn south on Interstate 15. Pass the Temecula/Rancho California exits and continue about 12 miles to the Pala Mesa Resort, just off the freeway at the eastern edge of Fallbrook. With an 18-hole championship course, that attractive retreat is a favorite of golfers. Other pleasant places to headquarter for the weekend are the Rainbow Canyon Golf Resort and Rancho California Inn near Temecula.

In the morning continue south on Interstate 15 or old Highway 395 to California 76 and exit west toward Oceanside to begin an antiquing escapade. Drive about 8 miles, and just before crossing the San Luis Rey River, look right for the Bonsall Antique Collective. In the large historic building, once a dance hall and restaurant, you can browse through the Americana collections of 30 antique dealers. It's like being in Grandmother's attic. Among the treasures are Depression glass, fine china, grandfather clocks, solid oak furniture, vintage kitchenware, and even presidential campaign buttons and baseball cards. You'll also find dozens of nickel-plated coal- and wood-burning stoves, some dating to the 1880s. Back rooms are filled with copperware and farm implements. And don't miss the collection of antique jewelry.

Go back on California 76 through Bonsall, then bear left on San Diego County Road S13/Mission Road to find more antique shops and reach Fallbrook's friendly downtown with its delightful restaurants. Along Mission Road, pull in at the Fallbrook Stage Stop, where three shops are filled with collectibles. Antique hunters also should stop at Thomas Antiques and Jane's Junk.

Once in town, don't miss Kirk's Antiques on North Orange Avenue, occupying one of Fallbrook's oldest homes. It's also the residence of the dealer, Kirk Kirkeeng, who will show you around. Weddings often take place in his lush garden beneath a 200-year-old pepper tree, where he also holds occasional luncheon fashion shows of vintage clothes.

Other shops with mementos of the past include Village Antiques and Fallbrook Trading Company on South Main Street, the Candy Cottage on North Main Street, and the Iron Kettle and the Classical Collection on East Mission Road. To the right off East Mission on North Brandon Road is an arts-and-crafts complex called the Cultural Village, where there are more antiques at Rainbow's End.

Besides antiquing, eating out is a treat in Fallbrook. At the top of the list for old-fashioned fun is Grandma's House Restaurant, which occupies an 1878 home that's set back from South Main Street on Elder Street. Patrons wash up in tin buckets, and one of the advertised entrees is a mini-chicken dinner for 25 cents (you get a hard-boiled egg). The menu offers hearty fare for lunch and dinner daily, as well as country-style breakfasts on weekends. Also popular and on South Main Street is the Packing House, built in 1930 as a meat market, where meals are now served in a cozy book-lined dining room. Tucked upstairs in a building on North Main Street is the Cauldron, praised for its homemade soups, salads, and sandwiches.

If you'd rather picnic, take Stage Coach Lane from Mission Road to Reche Road and head east to Live Oak Park, a favorite spot for family outings in Fallbrook. After your lunch in the park, go back on Reche

Road and bear right on Live Oak Park Road to The Collector, at number 912. Behind its unassuming facade is an elegant shop that's also a museum of gemstones from all over the globe. Tourmaline, opal, topaz, garnet, quartz, and other gems are displayed in rough and polished forms, and you'll be tempted by the exquisite handcrafted jewelry sparkling with the colored stones. If you'd like to find tourmalines yourself, reserve a place on the weekend midday treasure hunts offered at Stewart Lithia Mine. The excursions include a mine tour and a chance to dig for your own specimens in the tailings outside.

For the final day of your weekend, head north from Fallbrook on Interstate 15 to the Rancho California Road exit that leads under the freeway to Temecula. It's not quite St. Helena or Calistoga or one of the other quaint wine towns of the Napa Valley, but the tiny and easygoing frontier town of Temecula has become the focal point of Riverside County's nouveau wine country. Test vineyards in Temecula Valley were planted in 1966, and now the area boasts 8 wineries, plus more on the way. Visitors are welcome at a half dozen of them, as well as other Temecula attractions that include 10 antique shops and an Old West museum.

Temecula first flourished as a stop on the Butterfield Stage run and then was the trading center for the vast Vail cattle ranch that surrounded the town. In the mid-1960s the Kaiser Alumium corporation acquired 90,000 acres of the ranchland to establish a sprawling planned community, Rancho California. Currently, 3,000 acres are covered with orderly rows of grapes watered by drip irrigation. The vineyards and wineries begin about four miles east of Temecula, and you can embark on a circular wine tour by going east on Rancho California Road. Start early if you'd like to see them all.

Make your first stop the Hart Winery, marked by a small sign on the left side of the highway. Drive up the dirt road to the brown hilltop building that houses the one-man operation of Joe Hart, a former junior high school teacher. He's usually around on weekends; look for his pickup truck. If the bearded wine maker isn't too busy, he'll show you the winery and let you sample his Gamay Beaujolais and other wines.

The adjacent winery along Rancho California Road is the Temecula area's biggest and best-known, Callaway. Stop here first if you only have time to visit one or two wineries. Retired businessman Ely Callaway, who planted his first grapes little more than a decade ago, sold Callaway Vineyards and Winery in 1981 to Canadian liquor giant Hiram Walker in a multi-million-dollar deal. Praised for its Chenin Blanc and other whites, Callaway offers daily tours of the modern winery, where annual production has reached more than a million bottles. There's wine tasting (for a fee), and if you've brought a picnic lunch, buy a bottle to have with your alfresco meal at tables shaded by a grape arbor. Small signs near the picnic area identify the different varieties of grapevines, and you can climb a platform for a view of the vineyards and rolling countryside.

Almost next door and hidden among the grapevines is the area's other best-known winery, Mount Palomar. Look for the entrance marked by a wooden wine cask on Rancho California Road. John Poole, who once owned L.A.'s KBIG radio station, opened the winery in 1975 and now has nine varietals for sale, including a Riesling that won a gold medal at the Orange County Fair. John or wine maker Joe Cherpin takes visitors on tours, and you're welcome to sample Mount Palomar wines in the tasting room. There also are deli goods to buy for a picnic at shaded tables outside.

If you have time to continue your wine tour, keep going east on Rancho California Road, turn right at the sign to the Cilurzo Winery, and go up the dirt Calle Contento Road. On weekends you're likely to meet Vince Cilurzo, lighting director for the Merv Griffin TV show. He started the family-run winery in 1978, 10 years after planting the area's first commercial vineyard. Vince and his wife, Audrey, offer visitors informal tours and tasting. Cilurzo has several red wines for sale, some of them medal winners at the L.A. and Orange County fairs.

Farther along Rancho California Road you'll spot the entrance to Mesa Verde Winery, the pride of Keith Kaarup, a former L.A. County fireman. The highlight is a connoisseurs' wine shop of special varieties from all over the state. Keith also offers informal tasting of his winery's current vintage and a few from Hugo's Cellar, a neighboring winery that is not open to the public.

To complete your circle winery tour, turn right from Rancho California Road onto Glenoaks Road before reaching Lake Skinner. When Glenoaks Road dead-ends, turn right on DePortola Road and follow it to the Filsinger Winery. Operated by Anaheim pediatrician Bill Filsinger and his wife, Kathy, the small winery has won medals at the L.A. County Fair for its Chardonnay and Fumé Blanc. You can taste them and other white wines on a weekend tour.

Return to Temecula by going right on DePortola Road past country ranch estates, then left on Anza Road and right on California 79. It goes north under the freeway, becomes Front Street, and leads you to the center of the older part of town. Turn left on Main Street to a historical building, the 1891 Temecula Mercantile, where 20 antique dealers display and sell their nostalgic collections. Across the street you'll see the two-story Temecula Hotel, rebuilt 90 years ago after a fire destroyed the original 1882 hostelry. Today the building is a private residence and home for two antique shops. The Emporium, also on Main Street, is another haven for antique hunters, and more vintage goods are for sale in Butterfield Square and two other stores on Front Street.

On the corner at Front and Main streets you'll spot a brick building that was built as a bank in 1912, with a second story that once saw duty as the community's dance hall. The Bank is now a Mexican restaurant, and the most private tables are in the vault. Another restaurant about two miles farther north on Front Street is a treat for Temecula. Waiters in tuxedos serve French and Rumanian cuisine at the Bucharest, where women who want to remove their shoes are offered foot pillows.

On the way to that restaurant, signs on Front Street will lead you to Temecula's newest attraction, the $5-million Frontier Museum Historical Center. That's where you'll encounter an assortment of gunfighters— both outlaws and lawmen—who became legendary figures in the days of cowboys and six-guns. Lifelike wax images bring you face to face with the likes of Jesse James, Billy the Kid, and Wyatt Earp. As you'll discover, this impressive museum is much more than Madame Tussaud-type mannequins dressed in gun belts. Inside the modern building you'll be taken back to the small Western towns of a century ago.

A stroll along old wooden sidewalks brings you to the Wells Fargo office, a boot shop, and a knife maker. Drop into the marshal's office, or push back the saloon's swinging doors for a drink at the bar (sorry, nothing stronger than coffee is served). The Arizona town of Tombstone is re-created as it was in the 1880s, and you'll meet the participants in its famous shootout at the O.K. Corral. Watch the 15-minute film that shows what happened during that violent event. Over 60 wax figures, in original or duplicated clothing, add realism to the displays of Old West memorabilia that are mostly the personal collection of the museum's founder, John Bianchi, also owner of the adjoining Bianchi Corporation, the world's largest manufacturer of gun leather products. His array of mementos includes an impressive collection of more than 1,000 firearms, notably Colts and Winchesters.

When it's time to return to Los Angeles, follow Interstate 15 and Interstate 215 (formerly Interstate 15E) north to join California 60 (Pomona Freeway) and head west.

Round trip is about 248 miles.

Fallbrook Area Code: 619

Temecula Area Code: 714

SIGHTSEEING   *Bonsall Antique Collective,* off California 76, Bonsall 92003, 758-0363. 30 shops open 10 A.M. to 5 P.M. daily. ● Note: Fallbrook's antique shops usually open at 10 or 11 A.M. and close at 4 or 5 P.M.; most are closed Monday and Tuesday. ● *Kirk's Antiques,* 321 North Orange Avenue, Fallbrook 92028, 728-6333. ● *Fallbrook Stage Stop,* 3137 South Mission Road, Fallbrook 92028, has three shops: Don Antonio's Antiques, the Tin Barn, and Doc's Antiques. ● *Thomas Antiques,* 2809 South Mission Road, Fallbrook 92028, 728-5156. ● *Jane's Junk,* 2633 South Mission Road, Fallbrook 92028, 728-1600. ● *Village*

Antiques, 339 South Main Street, Fallbrook 92028, 728-6213. • *Fallbrook Trading Co.,* 1019 South Main Street, Fallbrook 92028, 723-1991. • *Candy Cottage,* 109 North Main Street, Fallbrook 92028, 728-0685. • *Classical Collection,* 837 East Mission Road, Fallbrook 92028, 728-4695. • *Rainbow's End,* 300 North Brandon Road, Fallbrook 92028, 433-3532. • *The Collector,* 912 South Live Oak Park Road, Fallbrook 92028, 728-9121. Precious gems, fine jewelry, minerals, shells, and fossils. Open daily from 10 A.M. to 5 P.M. • *Tourmaline Gem Mine Tour* at Stewart Lithia Mine near Pala. Sightseeing and digging from 10 A.M. to 2 P.M. every Saturday and Sunday, weather permitting. Bring sack lunch. Adults $8.50, children 15 years and under $4. Make reservations and get map to tour meeting site by contacting Jeanette ("Johnny") Springer, P.O. Box 23, Bonsall 92003, 722-2783; call from 8 to 10 A.M. • *Temecula Mercantile,* Main Street, Temecula 92390, 676-2722. Vintage furniture and other goods from 20 dealers. Open daily 10 A.M. to 5 P.M. except Tuesdays. • *The Emporium,* Main Street, Temecula 92390, 676-2002. A trio of antique shops; look for the early-day slot machines. • *Frontier Museum Historical Center,* 27999 Front Street, Temecula 92390, 676-2260. Open daily from 9:30 A.M. to 5 P.M. Closed on major holidays. Adults $4.95, children 5 through 11 years and senior citizens $3.95. • *Hart Winery,* 31500 Rancho California Road, Temecula 92390, 676-6300. Open 10 A.M. to 4 P.M. weekends. • *Callaway Vineyard and Winery,* 32720 Rancho California Road, Temecula 92390, 676-4001. Open daily 10 A.M. to 5 P.M., with tours on the hour. Free; optional tasting at end of the tour costs $1. Bring your own picnic. • *Mount Palomar Winery,* 33820 Rancho California Road, Temecula 92390, 676-5047. Open daily from 9 A.M. to 5 P.M., with tours at 1:30 and 3:30 P.M., plus 11:30 A.M. on weekends. • *Cilurzo Vineyards and Winery,* 41220 Calle Contento (off Rancho California Road), Temecula 92390, 676-5250. Open 9 A.M. to 5 P.M. weekends, weekdays by appointment. • *Mesa Verde Winery,* 34565 Rancho California Road, Temecula 92390, 676-2370. Shop open daily from 9 A.M. to 5 P.M. with wines from 120 wineries statewide. • *Filsinger Vineyards and Winery,* 39050 De Portola Road, Temecula 92390, 676-4594. Open 11 A.M. to 5 P.M. weekends, weekdays by appointment.

LODGING *Pala Mesa Resort,* 2001 South Highway 395, Fallbrook 92028, 728-5881 or (213) 688-7377; $79, with condominium suites from $140. Golf and tennis package plans. Par-72 golf course, putting green and driving range; 4 tennis courts. Also dining room (see below). • *Rainbow Canyon Golf Resort,* Rainbow Canyon Road via Pala Road from California 79 (or P.O. Box 129), Temecula 92390, 676-5631; $50. Overlooking 18-hole golf course. Also 2 tennis courts and dining room. • *Rancho California Inn,* 28235 Ynez Road in Rancho California Plaza off Rancho California Road (or P.O. Box 776), Temecula 92390, 676-5656;

$39. 37 motel units around a pair of duck ponds. Food and drink available at Homestead Restaurant in the Plaza.

DINING   *Pala Mesa Resort* (see above). Breakfast, lunch, and dinner in lodge dining room. Prime ribs on Friday nights. Entertainment in the lounge. ● *Grandma's House Restaurant,* 127 West Elder Street, Fallbrook 92028, 728-9595. Varied menus featuring old-time favorites like chicken and dumplings to special creations like shrimp jambalaya. Also sandwiches and salads. Try grandma's baked apple dumpling for dessert. ● *The Packing House,* 125 South Main Street, Fallbrook, 728-5458. Seafood and beef dishes for lunch and dinner daily, plus buffet-style brunch on Sunday. ● *The Cauldron,* 119 North Main Street, Fallbrook, 728-1505. Lunch and dinner daily except Sunday, when champagne brunch is served. ● *The Bank of Mexican Food,* 28645 Front Street, Temecula, 676-6160. Lunch and dinner daily, except dinner only on Sunday. ● *The Bucharest,* 27780 Front Street, Temecula, 676-5311. Lunch and dinner daily except Monday. Champagne brunch on Sunday. Jackets required for men at dinner. Make reservations.

FOR MORE INFORMATION   Contact the Fallbrook Chamber of Commerce, 300 North Main Street (or P.O. Box 671), Fallbrook 92028, 728-5845. Also, the Temecula Valley Chamber of Commerce, 27585 Ynez Road in Rancho California Plaza (or P.O. Box 264), Temecula 92390, 676-5090.

Wild Animals and Wunnerful Music Near Escondido

You don't have to leave the U.S. to find out what it's like to go on a safari. Just head to the Wild Animal Park, a vast preserve that's home for more than 3,200 mammals, reptiles, and birds. One of the most exciting ways to see and photograph the wildlife is to hop in the back of an open flatbed truck and be driven inside the 1,800-acre enclosure for a close-up view of its exotic residents.

That novel safari will be a highlight of a delightful weekend exploring along San Diego County back roads through the rocky countryside and fertile valleys that surround Escondido. Along with the wild animals, this wunnerful trip includes a museum honoring one of America's best-known bandleaders, Lawrence Welk. You also can tour two of the county's oldest and newest wineries and visit the only early California mission that continues to serve the Indians.

Make your headquarters at the Rancho Bernardo Inn, a well-known golf and tennis resort that lately has expanded its facilities to the tune of $10 million. Overnight guests and day visitors are welcome to play on the resort's 18-hole golf course and dine in the inn's excellent El Bizcocho restaurant. You'll need to dress for dinner, when some of the area's finest continental cuisine is served by candlelight. Casual attire is okay for other meals in the hotel's restaurants, including Sunday brunch, and you'll notice that some guests never change from their tennis togs; the resort features 12 courts and a full-fledged tennis college.

Get to the Rancho Bernardo Inn by driving south from Los Angeles on Interstate 5 and turning inland beyond Oceanside on California 78. Just before reaching Escondido, join Interstate 15 going south and then exit east on Rancho Bernardo Road. Follow it through ever-growing suburbia to Bernardo Oaks Drive and turn left to the entrance of the impressive resort.

In the morning after breakfast at the inn, dress casually for a day at the wild-animal preserve. Head back north on Interstate 15 to the Via Rancho Parkway exit and go east to join Bear Valley Parkway to California 78 (San Pasqual Valley Road). Turn right and continue east a few miles through the countryside to the San Diego Wild Animal Park.

The reserve was established in 1972 to help scientists learn about breeding in captivity in order to save many species of animals from extinction. Among the animals on the endangered list that have given birth in the park are the rare Indian one-horned rhinoceros, lowland gorillas, South African cheetahs, Arabian oryx, addax, slender-horned gazelles, and Przewalski's wild horses. A major objective of the nonprofit park, which is operated by the Zoological Society of San Diego, is to provide living conditions similar to the animals' native homelands while allowing visitors to observe the wild creatures.

The most popular way to view them is aboard the Wgasa Bush Line Monorail, which makes a five-mile circle tour through the animals' varied habitats in the vast parkland. Bring binoculars and a telephoto camera lens for even closer views. A guide on the silent tour train identifies the different species and describes their living habits as you glide along. In the hotter months of summer and fall, the monorail also runs with searchlights at night so you can watch the animals when they become more active after the sun goes down.

For closer encounters, reserve in advance for one of the special Caravan Tours that take you in the back of a truck to see the animals. Because food is brought to them in white trucks like those used for these safari tours, you'll have some thrilling moments when the more fearless animals come right up to your vehicle in hopes of a handout. For views of species like lions, Bengal tigers, and cheetahs, which are kept segregated in other natural enclosures, you can stroll along the Kilimanjaro Hiking Trail, a 1¼-mile path with observation points and places to picnic.

Visitors to the park also get to enjoy various wildlife exhibits, including an immense aviary that's home for 100 different species of birds. Another enclosed area re-creates a tropical rain forest where monkeys, deer, and exotic birds can be easily observed, while snakes and other reptiles are on view at an adjacent herpetarium. Through windows of the nursery you can watch newborn animals being cared for by park attendants acting as substitute mothers. And children like the kraal, where they can pet and feed gazelle, deer, and antelope. It's also fun to observe the family of gorillas cavorting on the grassy terrace of their special grotto.

Be sure to attend the shows that reveal the natural behavior and intelligence of animals, including some wonderfully trained canines—a wolf, a coyote, and a variety of dogs. Trained birds of prey also take the stage daily in the outdoor amphitheater, and you can watch elephants perform at other times during the day and evening. The Wild Animal Park is a botanical reserve, too, with a million-dollar collection of flowers, plants, trees, and shrubs. You'll enjoy them in the Tropical American Rain Forest display, along the Kilimanjaro Trail, and in Nairobi Village, the park's exhibit and entertainment area, where meals and snacks also are available.

If it's not too late when you leave the park, plan to stop at a winery or two on your way back to the Rancho Bernardo Inn. Return west on California 78 and turn left on Old San Pasqual Road at the sign to San Diego. Drive through the scenic San Pasqual Valley, an agricultural preserve, until you see rows of grapevines and the entrance to San Pasqual Vineyards. This modern hilltop winery opened in 1977 and visitors are welcome for informal touring and tasting. Several San Pasqual wines already have won high praise from wine critics, and the winery plans to make champagne as well.

Continue on San Pasqual Road, then go left on Bear Valley and Via Rancho Parkways to join Interstate 15. Head south and take the first exit, Pomerado Road, toward Rancho Bernardo. Turn left on Paseo Verano Norte and drive a mile through the housing developments to Bernardo Winery, established in 1889. You're welcome to look around this old-fashioned winery and sample its products. Added attractions are several gift shops on the vineyard grounds, including one specializing in old books, magazines, and postcards. Return to the inn by going back to Pomerado Road, turning left to Rancho Bernardo Road and then right to Bernardo Oaks Drive.

Enjoy the resort's evening entertainment and dance music, and in the morning lounge by the pool or have a game of tennis or round of golf topped off by Sunday brunch. Then check out and go north on Interstate 15 to the Valley Parkway/S6 exit to downtown Escondido. Head east via one-way 2nd Avenue and turn left on Broadway to Grape Day Park.

Escondido means "hidden" in Spanish, but nowadays the burgeoning city isn't hard to find. Freeways lead from four directions to this once-remote agricultural center, which was especially well known for grapes. Escondido's Grape Day, an annual festival to celebrate the September grape harvest, was one of the Southland's biggest events from 1908 to 1950, surpassed only by Pasadena's Rose Parade. Avocados and citrus have replaced grapes as the area's prize produce, but there are reminders of the time when grapes were king, such as the two wineries on your previous day's itinerary. Another is Grape Day Park, site of the early grape harvest celebrations. A few of the city's old buildings have been preserved there along Heritage Walk, including Escondido's first library, built in 1894. Today it's a historical museum with vintage photographs of the area, books, and a display of glassware. Next door you'll see a Victorian-style country house with enclosed water tower, and a turn-of-the-century barn with farm implements from the past.

Continue north on Broadway, then go left on California 78 to rejoin Interstate 15 north. Exit at Deer Springs Road and turn left immediately on Champagne Boulevard. It parallels the freeway north to Lawrence Welk Drive and Lawrence Welk Village, an attractive mobile-home community that also has become a vacation resort since the bandleader began developing it in the 1960s.

Many visitors come to see the theater-museum that traces the accordion squeezer's life from a North Dakota farm boy to headliner on the longest running weekly musical show in television history, 27 consecutive years. During the multiprojector show you'll watch Welk's bands progress from the Hotsy Totsy Boys and Honolulu Fruit & Gum Orchestra to his famous Champagne Musicmakers. Stand by a life-size cutout photo of the maestro and see yourself on television with Lawrence Welk.

The Lawrence Welk Village Theater also presents live musical productions of hit Broadway musicals, such as *Fiddler on the Roof, The Music Man,* and *Hello, Dolly*. There are daily matinees, or choose an evening show preceded by a buffet meal and cocktails served in the Village Restaurant. Day-long Sunday brunch and other meals also are available in that dining room, where choice tables overlook the village's verdant par-3 golf course. (Adjacent is a 95-room inn that's a less expensive alternative to weekending at Rancho Bernardo.) Nearby at the Village Center you'll also find a variety of shops, including one that sells Christmas ornaments throughout the year.

For the drive back to Los Angeles, take Champagne Boulevard to rejoin Interstate 5 north, then exit east on California 76 and go about five miles past dairy farms and fields to San Diego County S16, Pala Mission Road. Turn left and continue a mile more to Mission San Antonio de Pala on the Pala Indian Reservation. It was built in 1816 as an *asistencia*, a branch of the San Luis Rey mission for Indians living inland. Of all the missions established by the Spanish padres, only Pala continues to serve the Indians today, providing both a chapel and school for the people at Pala and other reservations in the area. Notice that the bell tower, modeled after one in Juarez, Mexico, is separate from the main building. Behind this campanile you'll find the old cemetery where hundreds of Indians and pioneers are buried beneath a pair of ancient pepper trees. Walk into the long, dark chapel that was constructed and decorated by the Indians, where worship services are still conducted daily. The mission building's history and its unusual altar statues are described in a display case outside.

Also in the main building is a mini-museum with the original Indian-carved religious statues and other mission relics. There you also can buy silk-screened Christmas cards made from drawings by the mission school children. After your visit, return to Los Angeles by going back to Interstate 15 and driving north to join California 91 (Riverside Freeway) and then Interstate 5.

Round trip is about 250 miles.

Escondido Area Code: 619

SIGHTSEEING   *San Diego Wild Animal Park,* 6 miles east of Escondido on California 78 (or P.O. Box 551, San Diego 92112), 234-6541. Opens daily 9 A.M., closes 9 P.M. mid-June through Labor Day, 5 P.M. post–Labor Day through October, 4 P.M. November to mid-June. Adults $5.75, children 3 through 15 years $3.95. Admission, including Wgasa Bush Line Monorail ride, $8.50 adults, $6.20 children. Kids age 2 and under free. Animal shows and other entertainment included in all entry tickets. Caravan Tours through the reserve in a truck operate May through September by reservation only, with departures Saturday and Wednesday. Shorter 1¾-hour tours at 2:30 and 4:30 P.M. cost adults $30, children 12 through 15 years $20. Longer 3½-hour tour at 2:30 P.M. costs adults $50, children $35. No children under age 12 allowed on Caravan Tours. Buy food and drink in the park, or bring a picnic. ● *San Pasqual Vineyards,* 13455 San Pasqual Road, Escondido 92025, 741-0855. Tasting room open Thursday through Sunday from 11 A.M. to 5 P.M. Free. ● *Bernardo Winery,* 13330 Paseo del Verano Norte, Rancho Bernardo 92128, 487-1866. Open daily 9 A.M. to 5 P.M. Free. Gift shops open Wednesday through Sunday from 11 A.M. to 5 P.M. ● *Grape Day Park* on Broadway in Escondido. Heritage Walk historical buildings can be viewed anytime during daylight hours. Museum in the 1894 library, Escondido Historical Society's headquarters, is open 1 to 4 P.M. daily except Monday. Free. ● *Lawrence Welk Village Theater-Museum,* 8845 Lawrence Welk Drive, Escondido 92026, 749-3448. Free museum open daily from 9 A.M. to 7 P.M. (to 5 P.M. Monday, Wednesday, and Sunday). Closed from 1 to 4:30 P.M. on musical theater matinee days. 30-

minute film, *The Lawrence Welk Story,* shown hourly on weekends from 9:15 A.M. through 12:15 P.M. Also, Broadway musicals staged daily except Mónday at 1:45 P.M. or 8 P.M. Tickets $12.50 to $16.50; with pre-show buffet lunch or dinner $19.50 to $24.50. Call for show schedule and reservations. ● *Mission San Antonio de Pala,* Pala Mission Road (or P.O. Box 70), Pala 92059, 742-3317. Mission chapel open daily. Museum open daily except Monday from 10:30 A.M. to 3 P.M. Admission $1, children under 12 years free.

LODGING *Rancho Bernardo Inn,* 17550 Bernardo Oaks Drive, Rancho Bernardo 92128, 487-1611, or California toll-free (800) 542-6096; $75 to $105 seasonally, suites from $135. Golf and tennis packages available. Casual dining in the Veranda Room or outside on the terrace. Music and dancing evenings in the adjacent La Bodega Lounge. Gourmet meals and Sunday brunch served in El Bizcocho (see below). ● *Lawrence Welk Village Inn,* 8860 Lawrence Welk Drive, Escondido 92026, 749-3000, or outside (619) Southern California toll-free (800) 962-2270; $54. Also theater package. A favorite of the senior set. Par-3 golf, tennis, and popular restaurant (see below). Adjacent Village Center has gift shops and Lawrence Welk Village Theater-Museum (see above).

DINING *El Bizcocho* in Rancho Bernardo Inn (see above). French cuisine for dinner in an award-winning restaurant. Try salmon specialties or duck Normande. Popular for Sunday brunch ($8, children $7). Reservations required for all meals; jackets for men after 6 P.M. ● *Village Restaurant* at Lawrence Welk Village Inn (see above). Hearty fare for breakfast, lunch, and dinner. A favorite is Lawrence's own chicken and dumplings. Sunday buffet served from 11:30 A.M. to 8 P.M. ($11 adults, $5.50 children). Also, daily lunch and dinner buffets for theatergoers.

FOR MORE INFORMATION Contact the Escondido Visitors and Information Bureau, 720 North Broadway (or P.O. Box C), Escondido 92025, 745-4741. Open Monday through Saturday and holidays from 8:30 A.M. to 5 P.M.

Retreating to Rancho Santa Fe and Lake San Marcos

A blunder by the Atcheson, Topeka and Santa Fe Railroad has become a benefit for the fortunate folks who live in one of Southern California's most exclusive enclaves, Rancho Santa Fe. The setting for that private community of elegant estates is a forest of eucalyptus trees that were planted for railroad ties. Spend a relaxing weekend there and in a newer residential retreat, Lake San Marcos, to sample their leisurely life-styles. Both are located in San Diego's bucolic north county area, only a few miles inland from the freeway and encroaching urbanization.

Drive south from Los Angeles on Interstate 5 and exit east on Lomas Santa Fe Drive at Solana Beach. This also is San Diego County road S8 and becomes Linea del Cielo as it winds past expansive ranch-style manors and leads to the tranquil village center of Rancho Santa Fe. The area originally was covered with scrub brush at the time a Mexican land grant gave the terrain to an early mayor of San Diego, Juan Maria Osuna. He named his 8,800 acres Rancho San Dieguito and used it to graze cattle. After Osuna's heirs sold the land to the Santa Fe railway in 1906, more than three million eucalyptus seeds were imported from Australia and planted. Lumber was needed to make ties for the booming railroad, and it was reported that eucalyptus grew quickly in such an arid environment. Unfortunately, no one had checked to see if the wood would splinter when driven with spikes. The forest was a failure for the railroad, but a blessing for future homeowners.

Today the lofty eucalyptus offer dignity, shade, and fragrance to handsome country estates, which also are adorned with fruit orchards and riding horses. Residents of The Ranch, as they affectionately call their community, gather to gossip, shop, and dine in the minuscule business area that extends from the village's sole hostelry, the Inn at Rancho Santa Fe. This rambling public showplace was the keystone of the planned community that the railroad's land-development subsidiary began more than 60 years ago. Nowadays the 20-acre resort allows visitors to slip into the easy yet swank life-style that is a main attraction for the Ranch's 4,500 residents. Check into one of the Inn's lodge rooms or garden cottages, then dress up for dinner in its Garden Room or Vintage Room restaurant. Have after-dinner drinks in the lounge, filled with the innkeeper's family heirlooms.

In the morning you can volley tennis balls on the resort's own trio of courts, play a quiet game of American six-wicket croquet on the front lawn, or swim and lounge at the heated pool. For a substantial greens fee, guests at the family-run Inn also have privileges at Rancho Santa Fe's 18-hole country-club golf course in the afternoon.

Stroll through the village's 2½-block-long business district and you'll discover some lovely stores, such as the Country Friends Shop. Although appearing to be an antique store, it's actually Rancho Santa Fe's secondhand thrift shop, and all proceeds go to charity. You'll also enjoy browsing in Toy Village and the Two Goats, a fashionable clothing store.

The Ranch has some delightful places to eat, including the well-known and very expensive Mille Fleurs, where the menu features French cuisine. Much more casual is Quimby's, which has a delicatessen, too. For picnic treats you can shop with the local gentry at Ashley's Market, but only on weekdays.

After another night at the Inn, go west from Rancho Santa Fe on La Granada, which is county road S9 and becomes La Bajada and then Encinitas Boulevard. When you reach Rancho Santa Fe Road, which is county road S10, turn right and go north into Olivenhain, a peaceful colony established by German families in the past century to raise olives. Look in a grove of eucalyptus trees on your right for the shuttered community meeting hall they built of redwood in 1895.

Continue north on Rancho Santa Fe Road/S10 through farm country and home developments to a private community that has a country-resort flavor, Lake San Marcos. Go right on Lake San Marcos Drive, then left on San Marino Drive, and right at the shopping plaza to Quails Inn. Join the crowd for a Sunday-brunch buffet in the inn's adjacent restaurant. It overlooks a quiet lake bordered by homes and dotted with waterfowl and occasional fishermen. An added attraction is a lakeside art show on the Quails Inn lawn the second and the last Sunday of every month. Overnight guests at this popular getaway spot can play golf at the private country club nearby, and also rent boats for a cruise around the lake.

Afterward, drive north through agricultural land that's being transformed by light industry and housing developments. Just beyond Vista you'll find Guajome Regional Park, 600 pastoral acres of a Mexican land grant that are being preserved for future generations. Get there from Lake San Marcos by continuing on Rancho Santa Fe Road/S10 to join county road S14 and turn left to follow it north. The road becomes Santa Fe Avenue and leads to the Guajome *(guah-homey)* Adobe, a historic ranch house from California's early days. Go up the entry drive just beyond a roadside park information signboard at number 2210.

Built nearly 130 years ago, the old hacienda remained in the same family until acquired by San Diego County's park department in 1973. The rancho comes to life on weekends, when rangers escort visitors on guided tours of the 20-room adobe that Colonel Cave Couts constructed for his wife, Ysidora Bandini, after they were married in 1851. Ysidora received the ranchland as a wedding gift from her prominent brother-in-law, a wealthy Los Angeles merchant who had purchased the land grant for $550 from two Indians. On the informal tour you can see the painstaking work that's being done to restore the ranch house to its former grandeur. You'll start in the courtyard, where carriages were received with Rancho Guajome's frequent visitors. One was Ulysses S. Grant, who had known Couts earlier when the ranch owner served in the U.S. Army. During one visit the hard-drinking general is reported to have ridden his horse into the hacienda's parlor. You'll also hear from the rangers that Helen Hunt Jackson based the Indian heroine of her novel *Ramona* on a servant at the ranch.

Around the carriage courtyard visitors will see a blacksmith shop, the ranch's own jailroom, majordomo's quarters, and a huge pepper tree planted as a seedling from nearby Mission San Luis Rey. A doorway leads to the garden courtyard, surrounded by rooms that include everything from a bakery and kitchen to a schoolroom for the family's children, servants' quarters, and a general store. A second-story sewing room was added later.

At the end of your rancho visit and weekend in the countryside, continue north on Santa Fe Avenue/S14 to join California 76 and drive west toward Oceanside to pick up Interstate 5 back to Los Angeles.

Round trip is about 250 miles.

Rancho Santa Fe/Lake San Marcos Area Code: 619

SIGHTSEEING   *Guajome Regional Park,* with Guajome Adobe at 2210 North Santa Fe Road, Vista 92083, 565-3600 (county park office phone weekdays only). 45-minute guided tours offered weekends at 2 P.M. Meet at historical marker by the old hacienda near the more modern family chapel at end of the parking area. Free; donations welcome.

LODGING   *The Inn at Rancho Santa Fe,* Linea del Cielo at Paseo Delicias (or P.O. Box 869), Rancho Santa Fe 92067, 756-1131; $45. Also suites with fireplace. Classic country inn with 75 varied accommodations amid beautifully landscaped grounds. Ocean beach house nearby at Del Mar for guests' use in summertime. Also two dining rooms in the inn (see below). ● *Quails Inn,* 1025 La Bonita Drive, San Marcos 92069, 744-0120; $55, two-night minimum on weekends. 80-room motel at the edge of Lake San Marcos. Also lakeview dinner house (see below).

DINING   *The Inn at Rancho Santa Fe* (see above). Garden Room serves American favorites daily for breakfast, lunch, and dinner, including chef's chicken pot pie. Vintage Room offers lunch and dinner daily, with dancing on the patio Friday and Saturday evenings in summer. Dinner reservations a must; jackets required for men after 6:30 P.M. ● *Mille Fleurs,* 6009 Paseo Delicias, Rancho Santa Fe, 756-3085. Dinner nightly except Monday. Lunch daily, with buffet brunch on Sunday. Fine French fare served with European elegance in romantic surroundings; outdoor dining, weather permitting. Seafood, lamb, and duck specialties. Make reservations. ● *Quimby's,* La Granada at Paseo Delicias, Rancho Santa Fe, 744-2445. Open daily for breakfast, lunch, and dinner, plus Sunday brunch. Country-kitchen decor and cozy bar with American and continental menu. Omelettes are excellent. ● *Quails Inn* (see above), 744-2445. Two-level lakeside restaurant and lounge open daily for lunch, dinner, and Sunday brunch. Salad bar and seafood specialties.

High and Low Desert Destinations

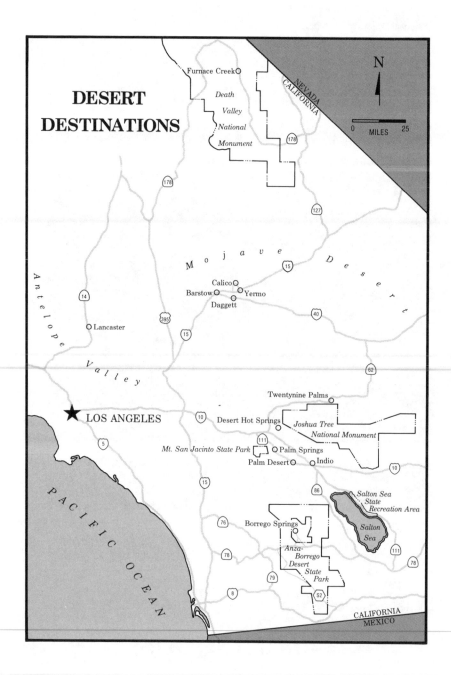

Overleaf: Death Valley National Monument

The Delights of Death Valley

Rushing to the California gold fields in 1849 seemed like a profitable idea to a group of Midwestern emigrants, but in their hurry to reach Mother Lode country, they made a mistake. The would-be miners decided to take a shortcut through a scorching, desolate valley. Suffering thirst and starvation, they gave the arid expanse an appropriate name—Death Valley.

With a name like that, you'd figure it's a good place to avoid. And there are places in the valley that sound equally foreboding: Hell's Gate, Devil's Hole, Dante's View, Furnace Creek, Badwater. Despite the names (or because of them), Death Valley is one of America's most popular national monuments. Ringed by a barrier of mountains, the vast valley of sand dunes and salt flats annually attracts thousands of fascinated visitors, who now drive on paved roads to the chief attractions.

Before the turn of the century, tales of gold and other precious metals drew prospectors year round to the Death Valley region, and towns like Rhyolite, Bullfrog, Panamint City, and Skidoo sprang up. Borax was discovered soon after, bring 20-mule teams and more people to the valley.

A luxury-class hotel, the Furnace Creek Inn, was built for winter vacationers in 1927. Six years later the Death Valley area was declared a national monument by President Hoover. Today it covers two million acres in southeastern California and a bit of Nevada.

There are enough natural wonders in Death Valley National Monument to keep you sightseeing for several days; at least a weekend is needed for the highlights. Plan to come in winter, when daytime temperatures average 75 degrees. During the unmerciful summer months, the thermometer often rises to 120 degrees.

Make your headquarters at the elegant Furnace Creek Inn, its more rustic sister, Furnace Creek Ranch, or the motel complex at Stovepipe Wells. In addition, there are over 1,600 campsites in Death Valley. Reserve rooms well in advance of your visit to Death Valley, especially for holiday weekends. And try to avoid the Easter school vacation, when the park is especially crowded. (Campsites are on a first come, first served basis.)

To reach this vast desert playground from Los Angeles, drive east and north on Interstates 10 and 15 to Baker in the Mojave Desert, then continue north on California 127. Just past Shoshone, go west on California 178 and follow it over the Black Mountains into Death Valley.

After the road descends below sea level, you'll pass the ruins of Ashford Mill, where ore from nearby mines was processed during the valley's gold rush days. At Badwater, look out to the lowest spot in the U.S., 282 feet beneath sea level.

Just beyond, take the short side road to view the jagged pinnacles of rock salt spreading over an area called the Devil's Golf Course. Then continue north and make the loop trip on Artists Drive through some colorful badlands and canyons.

With this introduction to Death Valley's varied terrain, settle into the centrally located and surprisingly sophisticated Furnace Creek Inn. Pack something dressy for this extraordinary and rather expensive resort, where one of the treats for guests is a supper club with nightly entertainment.

You'll enjoy suntanning at the palm-fringed swimming pool, a cool game of night tennis on lighted tennis courts, and golf privileges at the 18-hole course nearby at Furnace Creek Ranch. The Ranch is the central gathering spot for visitors in Death Valley because of its less-expensive lodgings, several places to eat, grocery store, gas station, and trio of campgrounds. Another attraction at Furnace Creek Ranch is a stable where you can mount up for guided horseback rides.

Park visitors also overnight 28 miles north of Furnace Creek at Stovepipe Wells, the only other location in the park with lodging, cafe, store, and gas station. There's a big (but barren) campground, too.

Plan to make several excursions, starting with an orientation visit to Death Valley Museum at Furnace Creek. This is the visitors center, where you'll find out about all the things to see and do in the vast park. Also inquire about the enjoyable ranger talks and programs. Close by Furnace Creek, make another stop at the Harmony Borax Works ruins to take pictures of the family in front of the enormous 20-mule-team wagons that carried borax to the railhead at Mojave.

To view more of the park's unusual scenery, head south of Furnace Creek to Zabriskie Point, the best spot to photograph the valley's forlorn badlands. Farther along is Dante's View, a spectacular panorama that includes (on clear winter days) the continental United States' highest point, 14,494-foot Mount Whitney, as well as its lowest spot, Badwater.

Near Stovepipe Wells, go for a hike over the undulating sand dunes, especially picturesque in the late afternoon. Take off your shoes to make footprints that will soon be erased by the desert breeze, then sit for a while to watch the drama as the spectacular dunes change color with the setting sun.

Your weekend won't be complete without visiting Scotty's Castle, a 1920s vacation home that's a desert showplace. It was named for one of the real characters of the Old West, Death Valley Scotty.

Kentucky-born Walter Scott had been a trick rider with Buffalo Bill's Wild West Show prior to talking a wealthy Chicago insurance executive into giving him a grubstake to prospect for gold in California. Eventually Scott's benefactor, Albert Johnson, headed west to inspect the prospecting scene for himself, and he fell in love with the desert. Johnson brought his wife to Death Valley for yearly vacations, and they decided to build a retreat. With the help of Scott, who had become known as Death Valley Scotty, Johnson found a suitable location for his elaborate vacation home. Construction in the desert was a challenge, and workmen were busy for nine years.

As the consummate storyteller, Scotty spread the word that the project was financed by gold from his own secret mine. Johnson, who put more than $2 million into Death Valley Ranch, went along with the myth. As Johnson said later, Scotty repaid him with laughter and friendship.

With the stock-market crash and subsequent Depression, Johnson didn't have the funds to complete the elaborate swimming pool, landscaping, and other finishing touches. But the handsomely furnished 18-room hacienda is just as it was in its heyday, when the Johnsons and Scotty lived there.

The National Park Service acquired the house and 15 acres of Johnson ranchland a few years ago. Besides making a self-guided tour of the grounds, pay the small fee to follow a park ranger on a one-hour narrated tour of the home's Spanish-style interior. Redwood-beam ceilings, red tile floors, heavy wooden furniture, and wrought-iron chandeliers and decorations set the mood. You're certain to notice the handwoven carpets from Majorca and drapes made of sheepskin leather. The regally decorated music room houses a theater-size organ with 1,100 pipes. Guides play their own tunes or set an automatic player in motion to give an unexpected mini-concert in the desert.

If you have more time, plan a side trip to Death Valley Junction to enjoy the ballet and pantomime of Marta Becket in her famed Amargosa Opera House. She and husband Tom Williams converted the former Death Valley Junction movie theater into a playhouse for her one-woman show.

Marta painted an audience of 260 on the walls so she'd never have to play to an empty theater, but now the intimate opera house is such an attraction that you need reservations for her three weekly performances. Also book in advance for a pre-show dinner in the Amargosa Hotel, next door.

When it's time to return to Los Angeles, explore more of Death Valley National Monument by following California 190 south from Stovepipe Wells through Emigrant Pass in the Panamint Mountains (look for wild burros). Then pick up U.S. 395 beyond Trona and continue south to rejoin Interstates 15 and 10 back to Los Angeles.

Round trip is about 595 miles.

Death Valley Area Code: 619

SIGHTSEEING *Monument Headquarters, Visitors Center & Museum,* Furnace Creek, 786-2331. Open November through April 8 A.M.

to 9 P.M. daily, other months 8 A.M. to 5 P.M. Free. ● *Scotty's Castle,* 35 miles northeast of Furnace Creek. Grounds hours 7 A.M. to 7 P.M. daily. Free. Ranch house open 9 A.M. to 5 P.M. daily; by guided tour only. Adults $4, children age 6 to 11 $2. ● *Amargosa Opera House,* Death Valley Junction, ask operator for Death Valley Junction toll station number 8. Performances 8:15 P.M., Monday, Friday, Saturday from October 15–April 30, Saturday only in May and October 1–14. Reservations required; all tickets $5.

EVENTS   *Death Valley 49ers Encampment* in November. Features fiddlers' contest, burro flapjack race, square dancing, special tours, Western art show, golf tournament. Contact park office for details, 786-2331.

LODGING   *Furnace Creek Ranch,* Furnace Creek, Death Valley 92328, 786-2345; $44, June through September $38. Cottages and motel units. ● *Furnace Creek Inn,* Furnace Creek, Death Valley 92328, 786-2345; $130 MAP. Luxurious desert resort open mid-October to June. ● *Stove Pipe Wells Village,* Stovepipe Wells, Death Valley 92328, ask operator for Stovepipe Wells toll station number 1; $42, June through August $35. Motel-type rooms. ● *Amargosa Hotel,* Death Valley Junction 92328, ask operator for Death Valley Junction toll station number 1; $26.50. Restored 20-room hotel adjoining Amargosa Opera House.

CAMPING   Nine National Park Service campgrounds within the monument, 786-2331. At Furnace Creek, *Furnace Creek* (open all year), *Sunset,* and *Texas Spring* (open November to April), $3 per night. Near Scotty's Castle, *Mesquite Springs* (open all year), $4 per night. Also Stovepipe Wells (open November to April), $3 per night. No reservations; first come, first served.

DINING   *Furnace Creek Ranch* (see above), coffee shop, cafeteria, steak house (steak house closed in summer). ● *Furnace Creek Inn* (see above), open mid-October to June. Excellent Dining Room, Oasis Supper Club; dress code; non-Inn guests by reservation only. ● *Stove Pipe Wells Village* (see above), restaurant open at meal hours from mid-October to May. ● *La Casa Maria* in Amargosa Hotel (see above), home-cooked Mexican fare; open 11 A.M. to 10 P.M. on Amargosa Opera House performance days (see above), 5 to 10 P.M. other days; closed Tuesdays. Make reservations for pre-show dinner on opera nights, dessert afterward.

FOR MORE INFORMATION   Contact Superintendent, Death Valley National Monument, P.O. Box 157, Death Valley 92328, 786-2331.

Beyond Barstow: Fun for All Ages Around Calico

You don't have to go north to the Mother Lode region to visit California's famed ghost towns. The Southland boasts one of its own, Calico, a century-old mining camp that boomed between 1881 and 1896. More than $86 million in silver was hauled from mines that honeycomb the colorful Calico Mountains behind the town, which grew from one prospector's shack to a bustling community of 4,100 residents. Besides homes, hotels, mine offices, and quarters for Chinese laborers, there were 22 saloons and a schoolhouse. But the ore played out before the turn of the century, and Calico quickly became a ghost town. Happily, it's now back in business, saved from obliteration by Walter Knott, founder of the famed berry farm in Buena Park.

Best of all, Calico is a "living" ghost town, a unique county park that's open to visitors year round. As in Calico's heyday, Lil's Saloon is packed with thirsty customers, the general store and other shops are open for business, music and laughter spill from the playhouse, and gunslingers still settle their disputes in the street. It's no wonder Calico Ghost Town has become a favorite family outing, despite its isolated location in the desert.

A visit to the Calico area in San Bernardino County is like opening a time capsule. Few places can match its range of historical sites—from the earliest man in North America to the latest in solar power.

For this enjoyable and educational weekend, make your tour base nearby in Barstow. Get there from Los Angeles by driving east on Interstate 10 toward San Bernardino and joining Interstate 15 north. Exit at East Main Street and check into one of the motels lining that highway. Although it's the hub of the high desert, few travelers ever consider Barstow a getaway destination. Most folks rush through town en route to the high life in Las Vegas or some sun and fun on the Colorado River. However, as the central city of the Mojave Desert, Barstow has several nice overnight accommodations and good places to eat. For a hearty meal, have dinner at the Steak Eaters Inn or Idle Spurs Steak House.

In the morning, head east again on Interstate 15 to the exit for Ghost Town Road. Follow it toward the mountains, where you'll see Calico nestled in a quiet canyon. Nowadays it's hard to imagine the town was in such ruin that it took 15 years of careful research and rebuilding to bring Calico back to life. Walter Knott began restoration in 1951 in memory of his uncle, John C. King, a San Bernardino County sheriff who grubstaked the prospectors whose silver discovery gave birth to Calico.

Take a short ride aboard the Calico & Odessa Railroad, a former mine train, while the engineer describes the town's boom days. Tour the tunnels in the Maggie Mine, and peer into the Glory Hole, which yielded silver worth $65,000. For other Old West action, join in the melodrama shows presented in the Calikage Playhouse. Musicians and actors also offer entertainment along the main street on weekends. Don't be surprised if you find yourself in the middle of a shootout.

Drop into Lil's Saloon to see paintings that depict the town in the good ol' days, when Wyatt Earp was a regular visitor. You'll find food and drink at Lil's, too. Meals also are served in the Silver Queen Restaurant. For dessert, head uptown to the Top of the Hill Cafe & Ice Cream Parlor.

As you stroll along the wooden sidewalks, be sure to visit the gem shop, where a window is constructed of translucent rocks. Another eye-catcher is the house made of bottles. Visitors always have fun poking around the general store, and the Mystery Shack and Western museum also are worth a peek. Be sure to watch the craftsmen at work in the pottery and leather shops.

After your visit to Calico, return to Barstow to explore that city and spend another night. Two diverse museums recall the area's early days and show off the natural attractions that make the region a popular place for outdoor recreation. Also, because it's the converging point for the Santa Fe and Union Pacific railways, Barstow is a special delight for train buffs.

As the desert junction for overland wagon trains in the 1860s, the Barstow area was first known as Fishpond. It became a railroad community called Waterman when the Southern Pacific laid tracks through the desolate terrain a century ago. When the Atchison, Topeka and Santa Fe arrived in 1886, the growing desert crossroads was renamed in honor of William Barstow Strong, tenth president of that railroad.

You'll discover more historical lore by visiting the Mojave River Valley Museum, just off Barstow Road on Virginia Way. Barstow's heritage is revealed through an assortment of exhibits that range from artifacts taken from the Calico Early Man site to models of space tracking devices at nearby Goldstone station. Also included are arrowheads, baskets, pottery, petroglyph replicas, and other reminders of the area's Indian days.

A little farther north on Barstow Road, look right for an adobelike building called the Barstow Way Station. It's the modern visitors facility of the Bureau of Land Management and features a number of displays about the natural history of the high desert. You can even sample native plants once used by the Indians for food and medicine. Exhibits emphasize desert ecology, recreation sites, and hazards for travelers. Visitors also are advised of desert road conditions and given free guide maps.

If you want to glimpse a bit of Barstow's role as a rail center for Southern California, continue north on Barstow Road, turn left on Main Street, then go right on First Street and over the railroad tracks to the now-abandoned Harvey House. Built in 1910, it was one of 75 restaurants and lodgings that once served Santa Fe passengers. Harvey Houses were best known because of a 1946 movie, *Harvey Girls,* that starred Judy Garland and featured Johnny Mercer's hit song "On the Atchison, Topeka and Santa Fe." One wing of the old hotel, named Casa del Desierto, still serves Barstow train passengers as the Amtrak depot.

Returning to Main Street, turn right to H Street, then go right again to reach a sprawling classification yard. From a visitors parking area you can view this impressive Santa Fe facility where hundreds of railroad cars are sorted out and switched to trains bound for destinations nationwide.

Go back east along Main Street to the interchange with Interstate 15 and a favorite travelers' stop called Barstow Station, a collection of railroad cars converted to souvenir stores and snack shops. The Bakery has tasty breakfast pastries, and you can stock up on refreshments for your next day's outing to other attractions in the surrounding desert.

Begin that excursion in the morning by following Main Street to join Interstate 40 and taking it east about 6½ miles to the Daggett exit. Turn left to cross over the freeway, then go right at the solar-information-center sign for 2½ miles. On the horizon you'll see Solar One, the world's largest solar power plant. As the nation's first major solar generating station, its central tower receives the sun's heat reflected from hundreds of computer-controlled mirrors to produce up to 10,000 kilowatts of electricity. Push-button exhibits in the visitors center explain not only solar thermal power production but also how energy is created from coal, oil, natural gas, and other sources such as geothermal and wind power. Outside from a shaded picnic area you'll have a distant view of the pilot solar plant.

Also pick up a leaflet to Daggett's historic landmarks, keyed to numbered signs in the shape of covered wagons. Go back to the 1860s town, turn right across the railroad tracks and right again on Santa Fe Street to Scott's Market, where area miners often exchanged their gold and silver for cash. Next door is the turn-of-the-century Stone Hotel and a general store, which are planned for restoration as a local museum. Turn back to Mill Street and look for huge ore wagons at Alf's blacksmith shop, a relic dating to 1884.

Continue north on the Daggett–Yermo Road past the U.S. Marine Corps supply depot to join Interstate 15 east toward Baker. Go about 6½ miles to the Minneola exit, cross over the freeway, and follow signs to the Calico Early Man site. This is the spot that famed anthropologist Dr. Louis Leakey and others believed to be the earliest trace of man in the Western Hemisphere, an ancient workshop for making stone tools. The site was excavated extensively from 1964 until Leakey's death in 1972. These days volunteers, including college students from as far away as Maryland, continue the painstaking work that you'll see on a guided tour. Controversy surrounds the archaeological dig because previous evidence put the first humans in the Americas around 20,000 years ago, but the

Calico site recently has been dated at about 200,000 years old. On the second weekend of every month you're welcome to attend lessons in archaeological digging. Look for some of the early-man discoveries, or their replicas, in an old miner's shack that's site headquarters.

Then return to the freeway for the drive back west to Los Angeles via Interstates 15 and 10.

Round trip is about 320 miles.

Special note: Be aware that temperatures in the Mojave Desert can soar in summertime, often exceeding 100 degrees during daytime. Take some drinking water in your car. The air is usually dry, but there are occasional breezes. Summer evening temperatures range in the 70s.

Barstow/Calico Area Code: 619

SIGHTSEEING   *Calico Ghost Town Regional Park,* Ghost Town Road or Calico Road exit from Interstate 15, 10 miles east of Barstow (or P.O. Box 638, Yermo 92398), 254-2122. Townsite open every day from 7 A.M. to dusk, shops from 9 A.M. to 5 P.M. Free admission; parking $2 per vehicle. Small extra fees for train ride, mine tour, and some other attractions. Also camping (see below). Annual Calico Days celebration in October. ● *Mojave River Valley Museum,* 270 East Virginia Way, Barstow 92311, 256-5452. Open 11 A.M. to 4 P.M. weekends, 8 A.M. to 4 P.M. weekdays. Donations appreciated. ● *Barstow Way Station,* 831 Barstow Road, Barstow 92311, 256-3591. Open 9 A.M. to 5 P.M. Saturdays and holidays, 1 to 5 P.M. Sundays, 8 A.M. to 5 P.M. weekdays. Free. ● *Solar One,* 3502 National Trails Highway, Daggett 92327, 254-2941. Open every day from 9 A.M. to 5 P.M. Exhibits and movies. Free. ● *Calico Early Man Site,* east of Barstow at Minneola Road exit from Interstate 15, no phone. Open 8 A.M. to 4:30 P.M. Wednesday through Sunday; guided tours 8:30 A.M. to 3:30 P.M. on the same days beginning on the half hour (except at 12:30 P.M.). Donation appreciated in lieu of tour fee. Archaeological dig on hillside site; wear comfortable walking shoes.

LODGING   Accommodations listed are in Barstow (ZIP code 92311). Catering to cross-desert travelers rather than weekend visitors, they are not resorts, but all have swimming pools and standard motel amenities. ● *Desert Inn,* 1100 East Main Street, 256-2146, $30. ● *Town & Country,* 1230 East Main Street, 256-2133, $42. ● *Vagabond,* 1243 East Main Street, 256-5601, $42. ● *Travelodge,* 1261 West Main Street, 256-8936, $34. ● *Howard Johnson's,* 1431 East Main Street, 256-0661, $40. ● *Holiday Inn,* 1520 East Main Street, 256-6891, $39.

CAMPING   *Calico Ghost Town Regional Park* (see above). County-run campground with 110 sites (no hookups); $4 per night.

DINING   Calico Ghost Town Regional Park (see above) offers *Silver Queen Restaurant, Lil's Saloon,* and *Top of the Hill Cafe & Ice Cream Parlor.* All other dining spots are in Barstow. • *Steak Eaters Inn,* 1050 East Main Street, 256-2334. Local favorite for family dining in the Crown Room. Also farm-style breakfasts and other meals in the coffee shop. Cocktail lounge, plus music and dancing nightly. • *Idle Spurs Steak House,* north of town at 29557 West Highway 58, 256-8888. Lunch and dinner daily (no lunch Saturdays) and Sunday champagne brunch. • *Canton Restaurant,* 1300 West Main Street, 256-9565, and *Palm Cafe,* 930 West Main Street, 256-2032, offer Chinese/American fare. • *La Scala,* 513 East Main Street, 256-3989, has Italian dishes. • *Rosita's,* 540 West Main Street, 256-9218, features home-style Mexican cooking.

FOR MORE INFORMATION   Contact the Barstow Area Chamber of Commerce, 270 East Virginia Way (or P.O. Box 698), Barstow 92311, 256-8617. Office located at the Mojave River Valley Museum.

Desert on Display at Joshua Tree National Monument

Mormon pioneers would rather have avoided the desert when they came overland to settle in California a century ago. These days travelers deliberately set out to see the same terrain. Instead of a hot and hostile wasteland, the desert is now considered a unique natural attraction that should be preserved and enjoyed. An 870-square-mile area, noted for its rich and diverse vegetation, was given permanent protection as Joshua Tree National Monument in 1936.

Spanning both high and low deserts—the Mojave and the Colorado—the monument is host to hundreds of species of plants, birds, and animals. Best known is its namesake, the Joshua tree, a tall and grotesque plant that's actually a member of the lily family. It grows to heights of 40 feet and is believed to have been named by the Mormons, who imagined that its branches resembled the upraised arms of Joshua leading the Israelites into the promised land. Joshua trees, which are found mostly above 3,000 feet on the western side of the monument, often are confused with the Mojave yucca, which grows at lower elevations. You'll discover the difference and learn more of the desert's delights by getting away for a weekend in Joshua Tree National Monument.

To reach the park from Los Angeles, drive east on Interstate 10 and choose either the park's north or south entrance. Its southern gateway is just off the freeway 25 miles beyond Indio at the Cottonwood Springs exit. Or you can turn north earlier from Interstate 10 onto California 62, which goes through the Morongo Valley to Twentynine Palms and the monument's northern entry road, Utah Trail, where you'll find the main visitors center. (There's a western entrance 15 miles sooner at the town of Joshua Tree, but it's worthwhile to begin at the visitors center down the road.)

Within the monument you'll find quiet places to picnic and rustic campsites for spending a couple of peaceful nights under the stars. Camping in Joshua Tree is first come, first served. You'll pay an overnight fee at only the two most developed campgrounds; seven other camping areas are free. Before entering the park, stock up on water or other beverages and any food you might like during your visit; no refreshment facilities are located within the national monument. There are major grocery stores in shopping centers along California 62 in Yucca Valley, where you'll also find a few restaurants. Other places to eat are in two neighboring high-desert towns, Twentynine Palms and Joshua Tree, where you'll also find inexpensive lodgings if camping doesn't suit your fancy. If you arrive or leave the park via its southern entrance, the nearest food stores, restaurants, and accommodations are 25 miles west off Interstate 10 in Indio or a few miles beyond in Palm Springs.

Start your exploration of the park at the main Oasis Visitors Center, where displays will give you an idea of the varied flora, fauna, and geology in this rare desert sanctuary. The terrain ranges from mountains of twisted rock and granite monoliths that are a favorite of rock climbers to the flat Pinto Basin, where primitive man once roamed. Ask the rangers for a park map and the schedule of guided walks and campfire talks that are offered every weekend from October through May. They also will advise you of the location of the wildflowers that pop up in profusion in the springtime.

On Saturday, you can make a leisurely loop by car to see most of Joshua Tree's points of interest. Also take the side road to the scenic lookout called Keys View for a panorama of Southern California mountain peaks, including 11,500-foot San Gorgonio and its slightly shorter brother, San Jacinto. In the central and western sections of the monument, growing at 3,000- to 5,000-foot elevations, you'll be surrounded by the wild-looking Joshua trees. Nicknamed the praying plant because of their upstretched arms, Joshua trees bloom with creamy white blossoms in March and April.

Some of the monument's most fascinating landscape can be seen on a winding dirt road that is an 18-mile motor nature route. The *Geology*

Tour Road brochure describes its highlights. As you drive or walk among the massive boulders that give special character to this desert monument, look for dangling ropes and weekend climbers carefully making their way up and down the rocks. If you or the children decide to scramble over some of the boulders, beware of their slippery surfaces.

Very special attractions in the park are five oases of stately California fan palms. A self-guided nature trail from the main visitors center leads to one of the shady palm clusters that were discovered by a government survey party in 1855. If you have time, also follow the southern park road to the Cholla Cactus Garden for a walk along the short nature trail. On the way the road passes through an ecological transition zone where the high and low deserts meet.

Cattlemen and miners were part of the desert scene before Joshua Tree was declared a national monument and protected wilderness area. You can see how they lived by joining a ranger-led tour on Sunday to the Desert Queen Ranch, also known as Keys Ranch. Almost like a mini-ghost town, the homestead of the William Keys family includes a derelict ranch house, guest cabins, a tiny schoolhouse, and quarters for the teacher. An assortment of weathered machinery, including a stamp mill from the mine, decorates the landscape. Meet at the ranch gate near the Hidden Valley campground, where the one- to two-hour guided ranch tour departs weekend mornings from October until May.

By leaving the park early to return to Los Angeles via California 62, you can visit two other high-desert attractions in Yucca Valley. First along the highway as you drive west is the Hi-Desert Nature Museum in the town's community center. Nature lovers will be intrigued by its attractive and diverse displays, which include butterflies and other insects, birds' nests and eggs, fossils, and even live reptiles. A colorful collection of rocks and minerals glows under special fluorescent light. In springtime look for an extensive array of wildflowers gathered in the area and labeled with both their common and scientific names.

A few blocks away on a hillside along Sunnyslope Drive you'll discover Desert Christ Park, with an unusual display of Biblical statuary. Thirty-three larger-than-life statues are scattered in a desert landscape that's reminiscent of the Holy Land. They're dedicated as a world peace shrine and are the work of one man, Antone Martin, a retired aircraft worker who devoted the final years of his life to creating the statuary in solid concrete molded around steel support rods. Each of the remarkable figures weighs from 4 to 16 tons. Near the parking area, a statue that was unfinished at the time of Martin's death in 1961 reveals his sculpting techniques. Don't miss the Sermon on the Mount scene, featuring 13 figures, or the massive Last Supper bas-relief, standing three stories high. There are tables where you can picnic in solitude in this one-of-a-kind public park or eat in one of Yucca Valley's restaurants before continuing your trip back to Los Angeles on Interstate 10.

Round trip is about 295 miles.

Joshua Tree Area Code: 619

SIGHTSEEING *Joshua Tree National Monument,* 74485 National Monument Drive, Twentynine Palms 92277, 367-7511. Headquarters and main visitors center at northern entrance near Twentynine Palms open daily from 8 A.M. to 5 P.M. Visitors center at Cottonwood Springs southern entrance open same hours from mid-October through May. Nightly camping fee $4 per site at Black Rock Canyon and Cottonwood Springs campgrounds only. ● *Hi-Desert Nature Museum,* 57117 Twentynine Palms Highway (California 62), Yucca Valley 92284, 365-9814. Open from 1 to 5 P.M. Wednesday through Sunday. Free. ● *Desert Christ Park,* north of Twentynine Palms Highway (California 62), Yucca Valley. Open 24 hours daily. Free.

EVENTS *Grubstake Days,* annual high-desert high jinks in Yucca Valley during Memorial Day weekend. Details from Yucca Valley Chamber of Commerce (see below). ● *Pioneer Days,* annual weekend community celebration during October. Details from Twentynine Palms Chamber of Commerce (see below).

LODGING *The Gardens Motel,* 71487 29 Palms Highway, Twentynine Palms 92277, 367-9141; $40. The area's newest and nicest accommodations. 41 rooms, 8 suites with kitchens. ● *Twentynine Palms Inn,* 73950 Inn Avenue, Twentynine Palms 92277, 367-3505; $27. 12 bungalows with fireplaces amid palm tree oasis that's close to park entrance. Also restaurant (see below). ● *Yucca Inn,* 7500 Camino del Cielo, Yucca Valley 92284, 365-3311; $28. 18-hole golf course nearby.

DINING *Twentynine Palms Inn* (see above). Lunch daily except Saturday, dinner nightly, with prime ribs on weekends. Also Sunday brunch. ● *Reflections,* 56193 Twentynine Palms Highway, Yucca Valley, 365-3810. Dinner nightly, also lunch on weekdays and Sunday brunch. Dancing Friday evenings. ● *Scenic Mountain Dinner Club,* 8100 Evers Lane, Yucca Valley, 365-9383. Hillside restaurant south of town with a view of Yucca Valley. Lunch and dinner daily except Monday, plus Sunday brunch buffet. All-you-can-eat prime ribs every Saturday night. Music and dancing on weekends. Reservations required; also ask for driving directions.

FOR MORE INFORMATION Contact the Twentynine Palms Chamber of Commerce, 6476 Adobe Road, Suite 9 (or P.O. Box 1164), Twentynine Palms 92277, 367-3445. Also, the Yucca Valley Chamber of

Commerce, 56020 Santa Fe Trail, Suite K, Yucca Valley 92284, 365-6323.

Sunning and Soaking at Desert Hot Springs

Southern California has its own Baden-Baden, but unlike that renowned German health resort in the lush Black Forest, the Southland's spa town sits smack-dab in the desert. At Desert Hot Springs you bask in Ol' Sol's rays as well as the mineral water that bubbles up from the earth. Nearly 50 hostelries welcome soakers and sunbathers to a spa-filled oasis only a dozen miles from Palm Springs. Get there from Los Angeles by heading east on Interstate 10 to the exit for Palm Drive. Follow it up the slope to Desert Hot Springs, at the base of the Little San Bernardino Mountains.

Spread along a gentle slope of the foothills at 1,200 feet, the unpretentious town presents wonderful panoramas of the desert valley and snow-topped Mount San Jacinto. At that elevation, winter sunshine lasts longer in the late afternoon, and summertime temperatures are often cooler too. Since its incorporation, little more than two decades ago, Desert Hot Springs has been one of the state's fastest-growing communities. About 6,500 soakers and sun seekers currently call it home, plus hundreds of others who escape there for a weekend or the winter.

Of course, Desert Hot Springs's main drawing card is its steaming mineral water, which has been touted as beneficial for arthritis, rheumatism, neuralgia, and gout. However, most visitors have no medical reason for soaking or swimming in the clear, odorless water—they just enjoy it. A half dozen of the town's motel resorts open their spas to the public for a daily fee, including the popular Desert Hot Springs Spa, which has six hot pools of varying temperatures and a cooler Olympic-size swimming pool. For more privacy while enjoying Desert Hot Springs's warm waters and sunshine, stay at a spa where the pools and other facilities are reserved exclusively for its overnight guests.

Topping the list of such resorts is Two Bunch Palms, named early in this century by a survey party of the U.S. Army Camel Corps. The pair of palm tree clusters noted on their maps still stand, thanks to the natural springs, which also nourish willowy tamarisk trees and other vegetation that create a secluded desert oasis. In the early 1930s it reportedly became the hideaway of Chicago mobster Al Capone. You can stay in his rock-hewn bungalow, complete with a private rooftop sunning area that once

served as a lookout for Big Al's bodyguards. That bygone era is re-created in Suite 14, with overstuffed velvet chairs, handcrafted stained-glass
windows, an antique bar, and a bullet hole in the bedroom mirror. Two
Bunch became a playground for Mafia bosses and movie stars, who enjoyed its hot-spring pools and private casino. More rooms were built for
Capone's guests, and the 105-acre compound later became a public resort
after the mobster went to the penitentiary.

In 1978 Two Bunch was saved from a rather run-down state by a Reno-
based entrepreneur who's spruced it up to the tune of several million
dollars. The 40 bungalow and villa rooms have been redecorated with
antique furniture and art deco accessories, while the casino has become a
gourmet dining room. Beneath the restaurant is a full-service spa offering
a sauna, Swedish and Shiatsu massages, salt and herbal steam baths,
facials, and hair treatments. Outside at this very friendly and informal
resort you can relax in palm-shaded pools of steaming mineral water.
Guests who want an all-over tan are welcome to stretch out nude in secluded sun bins.

The town has several other private and pleasant spa accommodations,
such as the 11-room Lido Palms Spa Motel on Tamar Drive. Get a complete list of lodgings from the Desert Hot Springs Chamber of Commerce.

Although Indians had long enjoyed its soothing natural springs, no one
settled at Desert Hot Springs until Cabot Yerxa arrived as a homesteader
in 1913. He left the town a landmark, Cabot's Old Indian Pueblo, a four-
story adobe home hand-built in pseudo-Hopi style. Visitors can explore
the uncompleted structure, which has 35 rooms and forgoes the traditional exterior Indian ladders for inside stairs.

Take an informal guided tour on Saturday, to learn about the colorful
Yerxa, who was a miner during Alaska's 1898 gold rush before spending
more than two decades constructing his remarkable pueblo. The rustic
residence also is a museum of pioneer mementos, Indian relics, and artifacts of the Alaskan Eskimos that he collected. You'll find Cabot's Old
Indian Pueblo about a mile east of Palm Drive on East Desert View Avenue. Look for a towering Indian head, a recent monument carved from
redwood and cedar trees by Hungarian-born sculptor Peter Toth.

Another Desert Hot Springs attraction will please hobby-minded visitors, the Kingdom of the Dolls. For a quarter of a century Betty Hamilton
has created doll-filled dioramas of the highlights of world and Old West
history. In the winter and spring months she shows off her unusual hobby
in a small building a few blocks west of Palm Drive on Pierson Boulevard.

Happily, you'll also find some good places to eat in the spa town. Very
popular for lunch and dinner is the Garden Restaurant. Another local
favorite for dinner is the Capri, serving Italian fare, and Johnny Costa's
always draws a crowd in the evenings for its fresh seafood.

On Sunday golfers will enjoy playing the 18-hole course at Mission

Lakes Country Club or go to the Desert Crest Country Club, where a 9-hole course is open to the public as well. For more outdoor enjoyment, leave Desert Hot Springs by midday on your way back to Los Angeles in order to detour from Interstate 10 at the Whitewater exit (just before the California 111 junction to Palm Springs). Drive north on the winding Whitewater Canyon Road, which follows a river and heads into the hills to the Whitewater Trout Company.

Even if you've never fished before, you'll be catching rainbows like a veteran angler at this picturesque trout farm, established in 1939. The frantic fish literally race to take the bait. Just squeeze the doughy fish food around the hook, drop in the line, wait for a tug, and then reel in your trout. It's not much sport, but a lot of fun. You'll find fisherpersons of all ages encircling the two freshwater pools that teem with trout. For a couple of bucks you get a rod and reel, bait, and a bucket for your catch. The kids or a few friends can share your equipment without extra charge. No license is required. Fish are weighed and sold to you at a bargain price per pound, and the Whitewater trout farm staff will clean them if you ask. Adjacent to the fish ponds is a 10-acre private picnic area, where you can cook your catch on an outdoor barbecue. Charcoal and beer are available, but bring the other picnic supplies.

To continue your return trip to Los Angeles, go back on the same canyon road to Interstate 10 and head west.

Round trip is about 236 miles.

Desert Hot Springs Area Code: 619

SIGHTSEEING   *Cabot's Old Indian Pueblo Museum,* 67616 East Desert View Avenue, Desert Hot Springs 92240, 329-7610. Open September through June from 9:30 A.M. to 4:30 P.M. daily except Tuesday; in July and August 10 A.M. to 4 P.M. Friday through Monday. Adults $2, senior citizens $1.50, children 5 to 16 years $1. Includes 20-minute guided tour. • *Kingdom of the Dolls,* 66071 Pierson Boulevard, Desert Hot Springs 92240, 329-5137. Usually open December through May from 12 to 5 P.M. daily except Monday. Adults $2, children 50 cents. • *Whitewater Trout Company,* at end of Whitewater Canyon Road (or P.O. Box 131), Whitewater 92282, 325-5570. Open daily except Mondays from 9 A.M. to 5 P.M. (to 6 P.M. on weekends in summer). Fee for tackle, bait, bucket, and towel is $1.50, with up to three people permitted to use the same pole. Fish you catch are charged at $2.25 per pound; no limit or extra fee for cleaning and packing. Additional charge for use of picnic area. • *Mission Lakes Country Club Golf Course,* 8484 Clubhouse Drive, Desert Hot Springs 92240, 329-8061. 18-hole par-71 championship course; $22 greens fee. • *Desert Crest Country Club Golf Course,* 69400

Country Club Drive, Desert Hot Springs 92240, 329-8711. 9 holes; $4 greens fee.

LODGING   *Two Bunch Palms Spa and Resort,* 67425 Two Bunch Palms Trail, Desert Hot Springs 92240, 329-8791; $75, continental breakfast included. Villa suites with living room and kitchen $125, Capone Suite $225 with two bedrooms. Repeat guests often fill the resort's 40 units, so book weeks in advance; 2-night minimum. No one under age 18. Full spa services with expert staff; one-hour massages or facials, $35. Tasty gourmet dinners served nightly to resort guests in former casino; ever-changing menu with seafood specialties. ● *Lido Palms Spa Motel,* 12801 Tamar Drive, Desert Hot Springs 92240, 329-6033; $40. Small, attractive family-run spa with hot pools and sauna. No children. ● *Ponce de Leon Spa Hotel,* 11000 Palm Drive, Desert Hot Springs 92240, 329-6484; $58 winter, $44 summer. 108 rooms, a few with private hot mineral pool. Massages available; sauna. Also coffee shop. ● *Desert Hot Springs Spa,* 10805 Palm Drive, Desert Hot Springs 92240, 329-6495; $66 summer, $42 winter. Also spa and golf packages that include breakfast and dinner in hotel restaurant. Six hot pools, sauna. Massages available.

DINING   *Garden Restaurant,* 66121 Pierson Boulevard, Desert Hot Springs, 329-6825. Popular dinner house; chateaubriand a specialty. Entertainment and dancing nightly; closed Mondays. ● *Capri Restaurant,* 12260 Palm Drive, Desert Hot Springs, 329-6833. Dinner daily except Monday; closed in August. Local favorite for Italian fare. ● *Johnny Costa's Seafood House,* 66540 8th Street, Desert Hot Springs, 329-0155. Dinner daily except Monday. Fresh fish and Italian dishes. Reservations suggested.

FOR MORE INFORMATION   Contact the Desert Hot Springs Chamber of Commerce, Palm Drive at Desert View Avenue (or P.O. Box 848), Desert Hot Springs 92240, 329-6403.

Palm Springs
Part 1: Touring the Southland's Premier Resort

Where do you go for the best tour of celebrity and movie star homes? Not Beverly Hills, where the city fathers have outlawed tour buses from most residential streets. Make your destination Palm Springs, the affluent desert resort that's also home for many folks of television and film fame. While you probably won't see them in person, the stars are brought to mind as you drive around the area on streets such as Bob Hope Drive and Frank Sinatra Drive. Among many others with celebrity namesakes are (John) Wayne Road, (Bette) Davis Way, (Spencer) Tracy Drive, Rock (Hudson) Circle, and (Ginger) Rogers Road.

As you'll discover during a weekend escape to the Southland's premier desert destination, Palm Springs is unique in more ways than its street names. With about 1,200 palms lining the main thoroughfare, Palm Canyon Drive, the town's own name is well deserved. And there are springs, too, one still bubbling where the Cahuilla Indians first came to relax and find healing powers in its hot mineral waters. The Spa Hotel occupies that site now, but the land still belongs to the Indians. In fact, Palm Springs looks like a checkerboard in the real estate plat books, because every other square mile is owned by the Agua Caliente band of the Cahuilla Indians. They lease out their land in this prime recreational oasis and share in the revenue, making the tribe's 180 members the city's largest collective landowners and some of the wealthiest Indians in the nation. A pristine section of their 32,000-acre reservation is open to visitors, rocky canyons with picturesque palm groves and bedrock mortar holes for grinding grain that recall the simple life of the Agua Caliente's ancestors.

Since beginning as a winter haven for Hollywood's elite in the 1930s, Palm Springs is now a bona fide year-round playground for folks of all occupations and incomes. Although helter-skelter development is evident in a few neighboring communities that sprouted later in the Coachella Valley, Palm Springs has preserved its dignity and maintains a style that's unique to Southland vacation spots. Consider the city's strict ordinance that forbids flashing, rotating, neon or garish signs, which means McDonald's may be in town but its golden arches aren't. Likewise, building codes prohibit new homes from casting a shadow on neighbors' houses. The tallest commercial structure in town, the Spa Hotel, rises only five stories.

Palm Springs has accommodations galore—more than 6,500 rooms—but don't look for a "motel." That word is banned, even for the nationwide Motel 6 chain, whose Palm Springs' property is called *H*otel 6 Palms. Lodgings also can be named inns, resorts, lodges, and manors. Others are called villas, like La Mancha and Sundance, where some of the posh accommodations feature your own private swimming pool. Certainly you'll have no problem taking a dip in Palm Springs; the last census of swimming pools tallied 7,000! And while recreational outlets are being counted, the city and adjacent Coachella Valley communities can boast more than 300 tennis courts and 40 golf courses. No wonder golf carts have the right-of-way when crossing Palm Springs streets.

On some of the fairways or greens you might catch a glimpse of Gerald Ford and other well-known resident golfers; or come to town during the Bob Hope Desert Classic or Dinah Shore Invitational to see an array of famous folk. If you're star-struck, another idea is to make your weekend headquarters where Hollywood's gadabouts often gather, the Ingleside

Inn, or soak up movie-star nostalgia by checking into Harlow Haven, the onetime estate of Jean Harlow.

For those on a budget who like the hot and very dry desert air, summer is a good time to visit Palm Springs, because lower room rates are in effect at nearly one-third of the resort town's 200 lodgings. (Of course, some of the larger hotels are open only during the winter season, which generally runs from October through May.) All lodgings, restaurants, and shops are air-conditioned, so you'll stay comfortable even when the mid-day summer temperatures top 100 degrees. A cooling alternative is to rise from the desert floor to the slopes of Mount San Jacinto aboard the Palm Springs Aerial Tramway, a dramatic cable-car excursion that is another delight of this uncommon resort.

With so much to see and do—including nothing but lounging at poolside while Ol' Sol gives you a tan—Palm Springs will fill up at least two weekends. To capture its flavor, plan to take an orientation tour of the town on your first trip, and also go aboard the tram for a ride up the mountain. Come back another time to discover more about the Indians and cowboys of Palm Springs's past and to become more familiar with the desert's amazing plant and animal life.

Get to this world-famous vacation retreat from Los Angeles by heading east on Interstate 10 and joining California 111 into the heart of Palm Springs. When checking into your hotel, name your favorite food and you'll be directed to the area's wonderful collection of dining spots, where the fare ranges from fresh fish to homemade pasta, barbecued ribs to Kobe steak, moo goo gai pan to duck à l'orange. Supper shows, comedy clubs, and discothèques offer other evening diversions.

The following day join one of the guided tours that provide an extensive look at Palm Springs and adjoining resort communities, featuring the past or present homes of many Hollywood stars and other notables. Along the way you'll see elegant country clubs, designer boutiques, and impressive shopping centers, and also make a refreshment stop. Especially recommended are the trips offered daily by Gray Line Tours in large buses and by Celebrity Tours in 14-passenger vans.

Although many of the celebrity homes are hidden behind walls or landscaping to preserve the owners' privacy, from the tour vehicles you can peek at Frank Sinatra's estate and glimpse the train caboose next to his lighted tennis court that serves as a bar, barbershop, and sauna. The tours also cruise by Liberace's abode, easily recognized by a huge candelabrum in his front yard, and you'll pass Elvis Presley's former desert home as well as the longtime residence of Red Skelton.

Your driver-guide will point out Bob Hope's multi-million-dollar mansion, which dominates a hillside like a mini-Superdome and has a dining room large enough to seat 300 guests. The comedian has deeded his home to Palm Springs for a museum after he passes to that great stage in the sky. Along with Hope, the list of current or former celebrity homeowners in Palm Springs includes Lucille Ball, Danny Thomas, Debbie Reynolds, Paul Newman, Lena Horne, Jack Benny, Mary Martin, Kirk Douglas, Mary Pickford, George Burns, Zsa Zsa Gabor, Edward G. Robinson, William Holden, Gene Autry, George Hamilton, Peter Lawford, and Danny Kaye.

For a do-it-yourself tour of the town, go by bicycle. Palm Springs has 35 miles of bike paths, marked by blue-and-white signs that guide you to many of the city's sights. Hire any type of bike you like, including a side-by-side three-wheeler or a tandem bicycle built-for-two, from Burnett's Bicycle Barn or Mac's Bike Rental. Ask for a bikeway map, too.

Whatever season you go to Palm Springs, be sure to pack a sweater. That may sound like foolish advice for a trip to the desert, but temperatures cool down considerably at night, even during the summer. Besides, on Sunday you'll want to take the thrilling ride on the aerial tramway, and thermometer readings at its mountain station often are 40 degrees cooler than those on the desert floor. Get to the cable car from downtown Palm Springs by driving north on California 111 and turning left at the tramway sign. Follow the four-mile access road up Chino Canyon to parking areas at the desert valley station.

Initially the Palm Springs Aerial Tramway was conceived as just a quick way for desert residents to escape to the cooler mountains during the summer. The father of the tramway, Francis Crocker, had that dream one scorching day in 1934, but nearly three decades passed before it came true. Eventually men and material made 23,000 helicopter flights without mishap to create the longest single-span passenger tramway in the world. The cost of construction exceeded $8 million. Since its inaugural run in 1963, the tram's twin 80-passenger cable cars have carried several million people from desert palms to towering pines at the 8,516-foot mountain station.

As the enclosed gondola travels at 18 miles per hour on its breathtaking journey, a taped commentary tells you about the unique tramway and the sights you pass. Variations in temperatures, geological formations, and vegetation during the trip are comparable to what you'd encounter on a drive from Mexico to Alaska. Awaiting you at the mountain station is a visitors facility with food and drink and a 25-minute movie about building the tramway. Observation decks and telescopes present inspiring views of Palm Springs and the Coachella Valley, as well as the Colorado Desert and the surrounding mountains.

After the easy 18-minute aerial ascent, energetic folks also will like hiking on trails behind the tramway station in forested Long Valley. It's part of Mount San Jacinto (hah-sin-toe) State Park, where rangers often conduct nature walks and summer campfire programs. And they issue wilderness permits in case you'd like to explore more of the park's 54 miles of marked trails or spend a night at one of its primitive campgrounds.

If nature's sights aren't enough, plan your tramway trip for early July, when a beauty pageant is held at the mountain station to select the year's Miss Tramway. Or go in January for the annual sled-dog races. Visitors always can enjoy a variety of activities on Mount San Jacinto, including Nordic cross-country skiing in wintertime. In summer you might wear a pair of jeans, because surefooted mules are waiting to take you on a short trail ride in the scenic mountain valley at the top of the tramway. Visitors also can enjoy a Western cookout at sunset while watching the desert change colors in the evening's afterglow.

After becoming acquainted with Palm Springs and its enchanting surroundings, you'll be looking forward to another weekend at the enticing desert resort. Meanwhile, return to Los Angeles by heading north on California 111 to rejoin Interstate 10 west.

Round trip is about 210 miles.

Palm Springs Area Code: 619

SIGHTSEEING   *Gray Line Tours,* 1090 North Palm Canyon Drive, Palm Springs 92262, 325-0974. 2½-hour Palm Springs Celebrity Home Tour departs daily except holidays at 1 P.M. year round. Adults $8, children 5 through 11 years $3.80. Pickup at most major Palm Springs hotels; reservations required. ● *Celebrity Tours,* 454 North Indian Avenue, Suite 43, Palm Springs 92262, 325-2682. 2-hour Palm Springs and Country Club Tour departs daily at 10:30 A.M. and 2 P.M. in winter, 9 A.M. in summer. Adults $12, senior citizens $9, children 5 through 11 years $6. Pickup at any hotel in Palm Springs; reservations required. ● *Burnett's Bicycle Barn,* 429 South Sunrise Way at Ramon Road, Palm Springs 92262, 325-7844. Open year round Thursday through Monday from 8 A.M. to 5 P.M. Bike rentals by the hour or day. ● *Mac's Bike Rental,* 700 East Palm Canyon Drive, Palm Springs 92262, 327-5721. Open from 9 A.M. to 4 P.M. during winter season only. ● *Palm Springs Aerial Tramway,* off California 111 via Chino Canyon Road (or P.O. Drawer FF), Palm Springs 92262, 325-1391. Open daily year round except for one month after Labor Day for annual maintenance. First car up at 8 A.M. weekends, 10 A.M. weekdays; last car down at 9:15 P.M. Adults $8.95 round trip, children 3 through 12 years $4.95. After 4 P.M. Ride 'n' Dine combination tickets include tram fare and buffet dinner or barbecue cookout at mountain station. Adults $12.95, children $8.50; no reservations required. ● *Mount San Jacinto State Park,* Long Valley Ranger Station atop Palm Springs Aerial Tramway, Palm Springs (or P.O. Box 308, Idyllwild 92349), 327-0222. Free 45-minute guided nature walks in Long Valley offered weekends in summer by park rangers. Also in summer, daily 20-minute trail rides on mules in Long Valley available from 10:30 A.M. until dusk. Adults $4, children 12 years and under $3. In winter, Nordic Ski Center open for cross-country ski and snowshoe rentals.

LODGING *La Mancha Private Villas and Court Club,* 444 North Avenida Caballeros, Palm Springs 92262, 323-1773 or (213) 275-7962; $200 with private pool in winter season; less in summer. Also year-round packages. Non–club members limited to 3 visits. 45 Mediterranean-style accommodations, most with private swimming pool and/or Jacuzzi. A home away from home offering full kitchens, wide-screen television, video-disk players, and fireplaces, plus tennis and gourmet dining at the club's restaurant. • *Sundance Villas,* 378 Cabrillo Road, Palm Springs 92262, 320-6007 or toll-free (800) 367-5124; $150 in winter season, $85 in summer, including continental breakfast and happy hour. Deluxe resort of 19 spacious villas with private pools and Jacuzzis, kitchens and fireplaces. Also lighted tennis courts. • *Ingleside Inn,* 200 West Ramon Road, Palm Springs 92262, 325-0046; from $75 October through May, $65 in summer, including continental breakfast. Classic hacienda-style inn with 28 antique-decorated rooms and personalized service. Some fireplaces and private patios. Also a popular restaurant (see below). • *Harlow Haven,* 175 East El Alameda, Palm Springs 92262, 325-0943; from $70 October through mid-July, less in summer, continental breakfast included. Fully renovated 1930s movie-star estate with 12 bungalow rooms around the swimming pool in lush and very private grounds.

DINING *Melvyn's Restaurant* in the Ingleside Inn (see above), 325-2323. Continental cuisine daily for lunch and dinner. Popular for patio brunch on weekends. Make reservations and dress up; valet parking. Also piano bar. • *Las Casuelas Terraza,* 222 South Palm Canyon Drive, Palm Springs, 325-2794. Lunch and dinner daily. Lovely Mexican restaurant with patio dining in the heart of town. Try the chimichanga or tostado suprema. One of three Las Casuelas restaurants; others at 368 North Palm Canyon Drive, Palm Springs, and 70-050 Highway 111, Rancho Mirage. • *Tony Roma's,* 450 South Palm Canyon Drive, Palm Springs, 320-4297. Open from 11 A.M. to 1:30 A.M. daily. No reservations, but worth the wait for barbecued baby back ribs or chicken; split a loaf of onion rings. • *Gaston's,* 777 East Tahquitz-McCallum Way, Palm Springs, 320-7750. Classic French cuisine for dinner, lighter fare for lunch served daily except Sunday. • *Paul DiAmico's Steak House,* 1180 South Palm Canyon Drive, Palm Springs, 325-9191. Prime beef for lunch and dinner daily; also fish and chicken. • *Louise's Pantry,* 124 South Palm Canyon Drive, Palm Springs, 325-5124. Tiny 1940s counter-and-booth diner with home-style cooking and delicious pies and pastry. A downtown landmark open daily for all meals.

FOR MORE INFORMATION Contact the Palm Springs Convention and Visitors Bureau, Airport Park Plaza, 255 North El Cielo Road, Suite 315, Palm Springs 92262, 327-8411.

Palm Springs
Part 2: Cowboys, Indians, and Desert Lore

How did folks get around Palm Springs in the days before Cadillacs and golf carts? By horse, of course. A cadre of local equestrians still take to outlying trails on their trusty steeds, and visitors to this fashionable desert resort can do the same by mounting up at Palm Springs's first rental stable, Smoke Tree. It opened its corral gates to would-be cowboys and cowgirls in 1929, and later other stables did the same, but nowadays Smoke Tree is the only place in Palm Springs with horses for hire. Best of all, the horse trails take you to unspoiled canyons on the Agua Caliente Indian reservation, some of the most pristine places in this popular vacation spot. Although one of those hideaways, Palm Canyon, can be reached by car, making the trip on horseback takes you back to the era of the Old West.

During a wonderful weekend on the trail of history and nature in Palm Springs and environs, you'll become immersed in the area's early days with a visit to the Village Green Heritage Center, and discover all about the desert's animals, birds, and plants by touring Moorten's Botanical Garden and the Living Desert Reserve. In the hot summer months the stable, desert reserve, heritage center, and Indian canyons are closed, so take this trip anytime from September through May.

Get to Palm Springs from Los Angeles by driving east on Interstate 10, then following California 111 along the base of the San Jacinto Mountains into town. Check into one of Palm Springs's resort lodgings that might be appropriate for your Old West weekend, such as the Gene Autry Hotel, where the movie cowboy's memorabilia are displayed in the lobby, or the Spa Hotel, on the site of the hot springs that first attracted Indians to the area. Other convenient choices are the Canyon Hotel Racquet and Golf Resort close by Smoke Tree Stables and the Indian canyons, and the Sheraton Plaza and Sheraton Oasis hotels in the heart of town.

In the morning, continue on California 111, also called Palm Canyon Drive, as it goes through town and swings east. At the crossroad marked Sunrise Way, turn right and take La Verne Way to Toledo Avenue, then go left and continue to the Smoke Tree Stables entrance. (Don't turn in at Smoke Tree Ranch.)

Over 100 miles of horse and hiking trails meander throughout the Palm Springs area, giving you close-up looks at desert plants and wildlife, as well as beautiful views. Many of the trails are located in the southeastern Palm Hills section of the city, with convenient access from Smoke Tree Stables. Easy hour-long rides can be made along Palm Canyon Wash, a wide stretch of sand between a flood-control dike and Smoke Tree Mountain. Look for jackrabbits, quail, and roadrunners darting among the hardy desert willows and smoke trees.

A longer ride brings you to the Indian reservation, where all visitors pay an entry fee before proceeding to the picturesque canyons. Popular for two-hour trail trips is Andreas Canyon, which reopened to the public in 1982 after being closed by fire two years before. Besides Indian caves and grinding rocks, you'll ride past sycamores, willows, alders, and stately palms growing along the banks of an icy stream.

Also reopened is Murray Canyon, a three-hour round trip on horseback. The trail winds back and forth by a creek that nourishes an oasis of palms and other trees in the canyon. Or plan to spend four hours in the saddle for the round trip to Palm Canyon and its most scenic section, where lofty palms have lined the stream bed for at least two centuries. Nearby you'll find an Indian trading post with welcome refreshments.

Before you mount up for a trail ride, be honest when the wranglers inquire about your experience in the saddle. The stable has over 75 horses, and they want riders and mounts to be matched for an enjoyable trail trip. All ages are welcome; parents are permitted to ride with a small child under 3 years in the same saddle. Experienced riders can take to the trails on their own, but novices should pay the extra fee to hire a wrangler as a guide. You'll pick up some riding tips and learn more about the arid landscape from your cowboy or cowgirl escort.

If you'd rather not see the Indian canyons from a saddle, you can drive into the reservation and then explore the canyons on foot. Get there from town by following Palm Canyon Drive south to the Agua Caliente reservation (don't turn onto East Palm Canyon Drive). Visitors are welcome every day from September through May. Stop to pay the admission charge at the toll booth, then head three miles beyond to the Hermit's Bench parking area at the trading post that overlooks Palm Canyon; drive carefully on the narrow and winding road. A trail leads down to the lush grove of 3,000 Washingtonia palms.

Afterward, drive to another place that proves the desert is much more than sand and cactus, Moorten's Botanical Garden. Get there from the Indian canyons by going back north on Palm Canyon Drive to number 1701, two blocks before the junction with California 111. The unique garden was begun in 1938 by Pat Moorten and her late husband, Cactus Slim, who collected more than 2,000 desert plants from all over the world. Most are identified by their popular and scientific names. As you wander through this plant showplace and nursery, you'll notice that it's also become a home for many species of birds and small desert wildlife.

Return to your hotel to relax and get ready for a night on the town at any of the Palm Springs area's excellent restaurants and entertainment spots. Don't sleep too late in the morning, because you'll want to visit the Living Desert Reserve, a botanical and wildlife sanctuary located at the base of the Santa Rosa Mountains in Palm Desert. Get there by following Palm Canyon Drive/California 111 southeast through Cathedral City and Rancho Mirage to Palm Desert, then turn right on Portola Avenue and drive up the hill to the reserve's parking lot. Established in 1970 as a branch of the Palm Springs Desert Museum, the Living Desert Reserve is a 1,200-acre area protected from development so that people will always have a place to observe the desert in its natural state.

Although most desert animals hide out during the day to escape the heat and conserve body moisture, you can view some of them at the visitors center. You'll see kangaroo rats, sidewinder snakes, fringe-toed lizards, great hairy scorpions, tarantulas, and 20 other desert inhabitants. Some 200 species of birds make the area either their permanent or winter home, and an outdoor aviary has been constructed so they can be observed more closely.

Also walk to a rocky hillside that's the fenced-in home for a family of desert bighorn sheep. They're under study by scientists who hope to learn the environmental needs of this rare breed and prevent its extinction. The sheep blend perfectly with the chalk-colored rock, so look carefully. You'll need a telephoto lens if you want to photograph these impressive animals.

Stroll through the unusual exhibit gardens that re-create small portions of six North American deserts. The Mojave section has intriguing varieties of cactus—pancake, beavertail, barrel, calico, foxtail, and grizzly bear. Don't miss the ethnobotanical garden, a fascinating display of desert plants that the Indians of the Coachella Valley used for food, medicine, and building materials.

There are six miles of nature trails in the Living Desert Reserve, and a self-guided tour booklet available at the entrance identifies plants and points of interest along the way. It also describes the destructive 1976 flood that roared through the reserve, and tells how the desert is making a slow but certain comeback.

You're bound to notice the contrast between the untouched desert and man's intrusion as you drive back to Palm Springs. It's another world entirely that you see along California 111, a busy highway bordered by stores, offices, residential enclaves, golf courses, restaurants, and resort hotels. There's no question that many of the lodgings in Palm Springs are pretty plush, a far cry from the desert resort's early days, when visitors slept in tents. Even the town's leading citizens had rustic living quarters, such as adobes and a house made of railroad ties.

To glimpse some of Palm Springs's pioneer era, visit the Village Green Heritage Center in the heart of town. It's just beyond the corner of South Palm Canyon Drive/California 111 and Arenas Road. On a bit of land amid downtown shops, you'll find a pair of restored desert homes from the previous century. One is considered the city's oldest building, an adobe built in 1884 by "Judge" John McCallum, Palm Springs's first permanent settler. It's now the main museum of the Palm Springs Historical Society. Among its exhibits is a re-creation of an early Palm Springs hotel lobby, with guests in long high-collared dresses. Another shows artifacts and photos of Cahuilla Indians, the area's earliest residents. Also look for the display of sun-tinted lavender glass.

Next door, with more memorabilia donated by local folks, you can tour the home of another Palm Springs pioneer, Cornelia White. She arrived in 1912 and bought the cottage from the town's first hotel proprietor, Dr. Welwood Murray. He had constructed the home 19 years earlier with railroad ties taken from a defunct spur line that real estate speculators ran to town from the Southern Pacific tracks. Mounted on one wall is Palm Springs's first telephone, complete with crank. Beneath the hand-carved rosewood bed, look for Miss White's fancy slippers made by the Agua Caliente Indians. Above the fireplace is a mantel clock with wooden works.

While you're in town, also be sure to tour the multi-million-dollar Palm Springs Desert Museum, the community's cultural center dedicated to art, natural science, and the performing arts. Visitors often spend several hours viewing the permanent art exhibits and traveling shows, as well as interpretive displays of the desert environment. There are Sunday-afternoon concerts in the winter season, too.

When your weekend with history and nature in Palm Springs is over, return to Los Angeles by retracing your route on California 111 and Interstate 10.

Round trip is about 230 miles.

Palm Springs Area Code: 619

SIGHTSEEING *Smoke Tree Stables,* 2500 Toledo Avenue, Palm Springs 92262, 327-1372. Open daily Labor Day weekend through mid-June from 8 A.M. to dusk; closed in summer. $10 per person per hour. Wrangler-guide $10 more for 1 to 10 riders. First come, first served; no reservations. ● *Moorten's Botanical Garden,* 1701 South Canyon Drive, Palm Springs 92262, 327-6555. Open daily from 9 A.M. to 5 P.M. year round. Adults $1, children 7 through 16 years 50 cents. Self-guided tours. ● *Indian Canyons,* end of South Palm Canyon Drive on the Agua Caliente Indian Reservation, Palm Springs, 325-2086. Open daily from 9 A.M. to 4 P.M. September through May; closed in summer. Adults $3.50, children 6 through 11 years 50 cents. Admission includes Palm, Andreas, and Murray canyons. Picturesque picnic spots. ● *Living Desert Reserve,* 47-900 Portola Avenue, Palm Desert 92260, 346-5694. Open daily September through May from 9 A.M. to 5 P.M.; closed in summer. Adults $3, children under 17 years free. Self-guided tours. ● *Village Green Heritage Center,* 221 South Palm Canyon Drive, Palm Springs 92262, 323-8297. Open Sunday from 2 to 4 P.M., Wednesday through Saturday from 10 A.M. to 4 P.M. from mid-October through May; closed in summer. Adults 50 cents per house, students and children free. Docents of the Palm Springs Historical Society will answer questions during your self-guided tour of two nineteenth-century homes. ● *Palm Springs Desert Museum,* 101 Museum Drive, Palm Springs 92262, 325-7186. Open mid-September through May from 10 A.M. to 5 P.M. on weekends, and 10 A.M. to 4 P.M. weekdays except Monday. Adults $2.50, students and children 8 through 16 years $1.25.

LODGING   *Canyon Hotel Racquet and Golf Resort,* 2850 South Palm Canyon Drive, Palm Springs 92262, 323-5656; from $150 in high season, $95 at other times; closed from mid-June until early September. Sprawling resort with 470 units amid lushly landscaped grounds. 18-hole golf course and 10 tennis courts with resident pros, plus health club. Also two restaurants (see below). ● *Sheraton Plaza,* 400 East Tahquitz-Mc-Callum Way, Palm Springs 92262, 320-6868; from $145 high season, $65 in summer. Classy new downtown resort. Tennis, health club, 24-hour room service, and two fine dining rooms (see below). ● *Spa Hotel & Mineral Springs,* 100 North Indian Avenue, Palm Springs 92262, 325-1461 or California toll-free (800) 472-4371; from $105 in winter season, $50 in summer. Landmark downtown hotel with outdoor hot mineral pools. Also complete health spa: infrared inhalation room, rock steam sauna, Roman swirlpool baths, massages, complete gymnasium; spa facilities closed mid-June until Labor Day. Excellent dining room (see below). ● *Sheraton Oasis Hotel,* 156 South Belardo Road, Palm Springs 92262, 325-1301; from $75 high season, $40 in summer. Older and smaller Sheraton on lovely grounds in town. Also popular dining room (see below). ● *Gene Autry Hotel,* 4200 East Palm Canyon Drive, Palm Springs 92262, 328-1171 or toll-free (800) 472-1264; from $95 in winter season, $60 in low season; closed from mid-June to mid-September. Two-story motor hotel with some suites and bungalows, tennis courts, and 3 swimming pools. Dining in the Sombrero Room; champagne buffet on Sunday.

DINING   *Tapestry Room* in the Sheraton Plaza (see above). Gourmet continental fare served nightly beneath Venetian crystal chandeliers. Also the plant-filled *Terrace Cafe* opens on the pool courtyard with fresh air and tasty dishes for breakfast, lunch, dinner, and Sunday brunch. ● *Agua Room* in the Spa Hotel (see above). Open daily for breakfast, lunch, and continental cuisine presented with flair in the evening, when veal and lamb are the favorites; closed for dinner from July to September. ● *Hank's Cafe Americain* in the Sheraton Oasis Hotel (see above). Moroccan decor complete with ceiling fans, but the fare is all-American for breakfast, lunch, dinner, and Sunday-brunch buffet. ● *Perry's* in the Canyon Hotel (see above). Fine French cuisine for dinner; closed in summer. Also *Bogie's*, 325-1463, serves breakfast, lunch, and dinner daily across the street from the main Canyon Hotel lobby; closed in summer.

FOR MORE INFORMATION   Contact the Palm Springs Convention and Visitors Bureau, Airport Park Plaza, 255 North El Cielo Road, Suite 315, Palm Springs 92262, 327-8411.

A Date in Indio and at the Salton Sea

Indio is worth a trip just to enjoy its famous dates—Medjool, Halaway, Khadrawy, Barhee, Deglet Noor, and Zahidi. In addition to that delectable fruit, there's another date to remember—mid-February. That's when the desert city hosts a lively exposition to celebrate the end of the date harvest in the Coachella Valley. Even if you can't time your weekend getaway for the colorful National Date Festival, make a journey to Indio to enjoy the desert and devour the delicious, freshly picked dates. At least a dozen date garden shops along the main highways invite you to sample different varieties and learn about the exotic fruit, long favored by Arabian royalty. All have date gift packs ready for shipping and will be happy to mail them to your friends.

With Indio as your headquarters, an outing to the date gardens will show you how irrigation has turned this part of the desert into a fruit and bread basket for the Southland. It's also a vacation playground, with abundant sunshine, golf courses, tennis courts, and swimming pools. Check into a deluxe resort just west of Indio, La Quinta Hotel or Indian Wells Racquet Club, or stay in one of the pleasant motels in the town itself.

Plan to spend one day of your weekend discovering a vast desert lake called the Salton Sea, located south of Indio in an arid area that some visitors describe as "Death Valley with water." The below-sea-level lake was created by accident in the early 1900s and has since become a state recreation area and national wildlife refuge.

Less known than its western neighbor, Palm Springs, Indio is located in the heart of Riverside County's fertile Coachella Valley in the midst of the Colorado Desert. It's the hub of a vast agricultural area that produces scores of crops, including 95 percent of all American-grown dates. Date palms from North Africa and the Middle East were planted in the Indio area early in this century, the beginning of an unusual crop that now yields 20,000 tons of fruit and $18 million annually. The Coachella Valley, nicknamed the Date Capital of the United States, is second only to Iraq in world date production.

If you've been indifferent about dates, don't judge them from the machine-processed dry type sold in supermarkets. The best dates are soft and rather delicate, picked and sorted by hand, and unpitted. These you'll discover in the roadside date garden shops clustered around Indio. Besides the naturally sweet fruit itself, look for all kinds of date products: the popular date shake, date nut bread, date butter, date cookies, and date candy. Most date shops also sell seasonal citrus, some from trees that are planted beneath the tall date palms.

Begin your trip by driving east from Los Angeles on Interstate 10 to Indio, exiting on California 86/Business I-80. (If you're staying in one of the resorts west of town, take the prior exit, Washington Street, south.) In the morning, when you're ready to embark on a sampler of date gardens, head west from Indio on California 111 until you see Jensen's. Long known as Sniff's before being sold a few years ago, it's one of the oldest and most interesting gardens. Stroll around this botanical showplace, which is planted with dozens of different trees, including one that has produced 14 varieties of fruit.

Almost next door is another of the area's earliest date gardens, Shields. Established in 1924, it now suffers from being the biggest and most commercial shop. Shields does not offer date samples to visitors, having given up the tradition carried on at most of the other date garden shops. If you don't mind faded photographs, watch its much-advertised but outdated audiovisual show, *The Romance and Sex Life of the Date*. Farther west along California 111 in Indian Wells are the vintage Eldorado and Indian Wells date garden shops, adjacent to some stately palms. Take a close look at clusters of dates in their protective paper covers, which are cut from a palm tree for display at the Eldorado shop.

You'll see more extensive date gardens and can visit a few other shops south of Indio. Reverse your route and go back eastward on California 111. On the way you'll pass the Moorish-looking Riverside County fairgrounds between Arabia and Oasis streets in Indio. It's home for the National Date Festival, a 10-day event every February that includes comic camel races in the afternoon. The unpredictable dromedaries and their jouncing jockeys lead off the daily grandstand shows featuring musical and variety entertainment. Also staged nightly is the traditional *Arabian Nights Pageant,* a melodramatic musical fantasy with a cast of 75 singers, dancers, and actors from the community. The production is performed outdoors and is free to all fairgoers. Besides the shows, there are carnival rides, a mini-circus, visitor contests, marionette performances, 4H and FFA livestock judging, and all sorts of exhibits, including a display of the festival's namesakes—119 varieties of dates grown in the Indio area.

To sample more fresh dates and see groves of the stately palm trees, continue on California 111 south to the city of Coachella. Bear right on California 86 to Lee Anderson's Colvalda Date Company (at 6th Street) to watch the fancy fruit being graded and packed by hand. Seven miles farther south on California 86 is the Valerie Jean Date Shop, where you'll get a tasty date milk shake for a reasonable price. Or go left on Avenue 52 in Coachella to rejoin California 111, then turn right and continue south to the family-run Laflin Date Gardens just beyond Thermal. Undoubtedly you're all dated up by now and ready for a relaxing evening at your resort hotel.

On Sunday morning return to California 111 and keep driving south through Coachella and Thermal to reach an unexpected body of water that's 235 feet below sea level, the Salton Sea, which proves that accidents aren't always bad. If a dam diverting the Colorado River for irrigation in the Imperial Valley hadn't broken in 1905, there wouldn't be a huge lake for recreation in the desert today. Floodwaters tore through a makeshift levee near Yuma, dumping the river into a desolate salt basin that once was filled with ocean water from the Gulf of California. When the mighty Colorado was finally forced back to its original course, a vast lake had been created.

Nowadays the Salton Sea is especially popular with boaters, fishermen, and campers. At several spots around its perimeter you'll find marinas and private and state-run campgrounds and RV parks, as well as a motel or two. The weather is most pleasant in the winter season, with daytime temperatures rising regularly into the 70s and 80s. Desert nights can be cold, however, so bring warm clothing if you linger after sunset.

Most visitors head to the Salton Sea State Recreation Area, an 18,000-acre park along the lake's northeast shore. To learn about the varied desert flora that surround the lake, stroll through the native-plant garden adjacent to the park's entrance station. Signs identify numerous cacti, shrubs, and trees, but borrow a plant-description folder from the ranger for detailed information. Also look for the rare desert pupfish in a special pond. Continue your tour by car to the interpretive visitors center to discover more about the Salton Sea's formation and fishing, as well as the desert area's history and wildlife. Be sure to watch the excellent slide presentation about the unusual lake. From January through March during the migratory bird season, a slide show about the birds is shown at noon on weekends.

Although created with fresh water, the lake has leached salt from the desert floor—once a prehistoric seabed—and it is now slightly saltier than the ocean. That's the reason the Salton Sea has been planted with ocean fish, especially Gulf croaker, orangemouth corvina, and perchlike sargo. In addition to fishermen, boaters and water skiers enjoy the big lake, which is about 35 miles long and 15 miles wide. Boats can be launched in the park at Varner Harbor. The southern end of Salton Sea is a national wildlife refuge, and patient boaters should be able to glimpse many bird species during their winter migrations. Be on the lookout for Canadian honkers and snow geese. Swimmers will find beachfront areas designated by buoys at two park campgrounds; no lifeguards are on duty, so keep an eye on the kids. Hikers can take to the Ironwood Trail, a nature path that introduces you to the ecology of the desert during a two-mile round trip.

Just outside park boundaries in Imperial County, not far from Bombay Beach, you might enjoy soaking in a hot mineral pool. Head into the foothills of the Chocolate Mountains, where you'll find a few spas, including one known as the Fountain of Youth. Surrounded by RV and trailer parks, their therapeutic pools are fed by underground hot springs. Take Hot Mineral Spa Road north from California 111 and follow the signs to reach them.

For a novel experience, go back on California 111 just beyond the park headquarters entrance to North Shore Beach and Yacht Club, where Salton Sea Air Service operates a seaplane for pilot training and sightseeing. If the one-passenger floatplane is at the boat ramp, go aboard for a short flight to survey the lake, its wildlife refuge, an earthquake fault, and agricultural fields with their cornucopia of crops.

Be certain to pack a picnic for your Salton Sea outing; a cafe in North Shore serves meals, but in the park itself there are no restaurants, snack bars, or food stores. On the opposite side of the lake you find a few places to eat, as well as motels, RV parks, campgrounds, and marinas. Get to them from the state recreation area by going north on California 111, west (left) on Avenue 66 at Mecca to California 195, then south to join California 86 leading to rather desolate sea-view developments at Desert Shores, Salton Sea Beach, and Salton City.

Return to Los Angeles via California 86 and 111 north to Interstate 10. Round trip is about 318 miles.

Indio Area Code: 619

SIGHTSEEING *Jensen's Date and Citrus Gardens,* 80-653 Highway 111, Indio 92201, 347-3897. Open 9 A.M. to 5 P.M. daily. • *Shields Date*

Gardens, 80-225 Highway 111, Indio 92201, 347-0996. Open 9 A.M. to 6 P.M. daily. ● *Eldorado Date Gardens,* 75-291 Highway 111, Indian Wells 92260, 346-6263. Open September through May. ● *Indian Wells Date Gardens,* 74-774 Highway 111, Indian Wells 92260, 346-2914. Open 9 A.M. to 5 P.M. daily. ● *Lee Anderson's Colvada Date Co.,* 51-392 Highway 86 (near Bagdad Ave.), Coachella 92236, 398-3551. Open daily except Sundays from 9 A.M. to 4:30 P.M. ● *Valerie Jean Date Shop,* 66-021 Highway 86 at Avenue 66, Thermal 92274, 397-4159. Open 8 A.M. to 5 P.M. daily (to 6 P.M. in summer). ● *Laflin Date Gardens,* 59-111 Highway 111, Thermal 92274, 399-5665. Open 8:30 A.M. to 5 P.M. daily; closed Sundays September and October, closed weekends July and August. ● *Salton Sea State Recreation Area,* off California 111 (or P.O. Box 5002), North Shore 92254, 393-3052. Day-use admission $2 per vehicle. Overnight camping (see below). ● *Fountain of Youth Spa,* Spa Road off California 111 (or Route 1, Box 12), Niland 92257, 348-1340. Hot mineral pools and swimming pools surrounded by 1,100 RV sites. Guest bathers $2. ● *Salton Sea Air Service,* at North Shore Yacht Club (or P.O. Box 4009), North Shore 92254, 393-3994. 15-minute seaplane sightseeing flights, $20.

EVENTS *National Date Festival,* Riverside County Fairgrounds, Highway 111 at Arabia Street (or P.O. Box NNNN), Indio 92201, 342-8247. Annual Coachella Valley celebration beginning mid-February for 10 days. Hours 10 A.M. to 10 P.M. Admission $4, children 5 through 11 years $2, including all stage and arena events. All-day parking $2, RVs $5. Hometown fun for everyone.

LODGING *La Quinta Hotel,* 49-499 Eisenhower Drive, La Quinta 92253, 564-4111 or California toll-free (800) 472-4316; $95. Open October to mid-May. Classy resort with accommodations in Spanish-style adobe cottages spread among date groves and formal gardens. Lighted tennis courts, three 9-hole golf courses. Also restaurant (see below). ● *Indian Wells Racquet Club Resort,* 46-765 Bay Club Drive, Indian Wells 92260, 345-2811 or toll-free in Southern California (800) 472-4391; $95 winter/spring, $60 summer. Also 2- and 4-day tennis packages. Lodging in attractive townhouses. 10 championship tennis courts with instructors available. Golfing at adjacent Indian Palms Country Club. Casual dining in clubhouse. ● *Indian Palms Country Club,* 48-630 Monroe Street, Indio 92201, 347-0688; $45 winter, $35 summer. Motor inn and condominiums adjacent to Indian Palms Country Club golf course. Golf and tennis available. Also dining in clubhouse, with popular Sunday brunch. ● *Date Tree Motor Hotel,* 81-909 Indio Boulevard, Indio 92201, 347-3421; $38. Pleasant motel in landscaped setting. Restaurant adjacent. ● *Royal National Nine Motel,* 82-347 Highway 111, Indio 92201, 347-0911; $44. Coffee shop and restaurant on premises. ● *El Morocco Motor Hotel,*

82-645 Miles Avenue, Indio 92260, 347-2306; $38. Also restaurant (see below).

CAMPING *Salton Sea State Recreation Area* (see above). 135 developed sites but no hookups at Viejo (headquarters) and Mecca campgrounds; $6 per night. Primitive campsites at 3 other park locations; $3 per night. Reserve through Ticketron, except summer first come, first served.

DINING *El Morocco,* in El Morocco Motor Hotel (see above). Three meals served daily; rack of lamb a specialty. Evening entertainment and dancing. ● *El Portal Restaurant,* 47-735 Towne Avenue, Indio, 345-4560. Mexican fare for lunch and dinner daily; also seafood and steaks. ● *La Quinta Hotel* (see above). Three meals daily in Mirage dining room. Jackets for men at dinner. Reservations required. Continental cuisine with veal specialties. Super Sunday brunch, $15 per person, $8.50 for children 12 years and under.

FOR MORE INFORMATION Contact the Indio Chamber of Commerce, 82-503 Highway 111 (or P.O. Box TTT), Indio 92201, 347-0676.

Adventures in Anza-Borrego Desert State Park

The folks in San Francisco were cheering 125 years ago when the Butterfield Overland Mail stage rolled into town with its first passenger and pouch of letters. It heralded the beginning of regular overland transportation and mail service to and from the West Coast. Today's travelers might not be so enthusiastic. The bone-jarring journey from Missouri in a crowded stagecoach took 24 days and nights. Passengers paid $150 for a one-way ticket and were encouraged to bring blankets, a revolver or knife, and extra food for the desert crossing. Those who made it through the 2,600-mile trip lost an average of 23 pounds.

Reminders of those early days of travel can be glimpsed by driving along San Diego County Road S2 on the fringe of the Colorado Desert. It closely follows the first overland route to California, the Southern Emigrant Trail, which was used initially by trappers, then soldiers and gold seekers, and finally the stage coach lines.

That quiet backroad also cuts across the spectacular Anza-Borrego Desert State Park, the nation's largest state park. One of California's first frontiers, the half-million-acre preserve is now one of the state's last remaining undisturbed areas. For visitors from the city there's the promise of smog-free days and star-filled nights, wide-open spaces and wonderful serenity. And you'll see that despite its foreboding reputation, the desert has not been abandoned by Mother Nature. Plants and trees color the landscape, especially when a profusion of wildflowers bursts into bloom after the winter rains. Birds and animals add other enjoyment, like the comical roadrunners and quick cottontails that scurry across your path.

With only a weekend and the family car, you'll just be able to glimpse the natural attractions in this vast, unspoiled land. While many desert devotees come with 4-wheel-drive vehicles and plenty of time to explore along the hundreds of miles of paved and primitive roads, you'll become well acquainted with Anza-Borrego's wildlife, geology, and history by following a few of the park's self-guiding nature trails and auto tours. Park rangers also lead special tours by car and foot on weekends in the winter season, which is the most popular time to enjoy the desert.

In the midst of this immense park is the hospitable little community of Borrego Springs and an outstanding hostelry, La Casa del Zorro, another of the desert's unexpected delights. A treat for campers is the freedom to select a site anywhere along the road; no other California state park permits such unrestricted camping.

Get to Anza-Borrego Desert State Park from Los Angeles by taking California 60 (Pomona Freeway) east past Riverside and joining Interstate 215 and then Interstate 15 south toward San Diego. Just beyond Temecula, exit east on California 79 to Warner Springs. En route, at Oak Grove, six miles past the Riverside–San Diego county line, a historical marker points out one of the original adobe stage stations on the Butterfield Overland Mail route. After only 30 months of service, the cross-country stages stopped running when the Civil War began in 1861. Continue on California 79 beyond Warner Springs and turn left on San Diego County Road S2. A half mile beyond is the Warner Ranch House, also a stage stop. U.S. troops fighting in the Mexican War of 1846–1848 were billeted in this old adobe, which now shows the toll of time and is protected by a fence until it can be restored. Continue east about four miles to join S22, a road that winds down the mountainside to the vast Colorado Desert.

Appearing as an oasis is the resort and retirement community of Borrego Springs, your base for exploration of the desert park that's two-thirds the size of Rhode Island. The flat arid land of Borrego Springs has been made green by irrigation, with majestic mountains for a backdrop. There you'll find warm sun, blue skies, pure air, and evidence of the good life—swimming pools, golf courses, tennis courts.

This is a friendly place, where the year-round townsfolk—numbering 2,200 at last count—gather weekdays at the post office to gossip and get their mail. Outside, a community bulletin board also keeps them abreast of the latest happenings. Many residents are retired, happy with the desert's peace and quiet, opportunities for outdoor recreation, and low property taxes.

Unless you camp in the park, bed down in Borrego Springs at La Casa del Zorro, the area's best and best-known lodging. It has grown around an adobe ranch house built in 1937 and is now Anza-Borrego's premier resort. Nestled in a grove of willowy tamarisk trees are a number of comfortable cottages and a trio of modern buildings with studio rooms and suites. Guests enjoy a swimming pool, putting green, and tennis court, along with privileges on the 18-hole public golf course close by at the new Rams Hill Country Club. If this popular resort is filled, Borrego Springs also has six modest motels and a number of condominium apartments for rent.

You'll probably eat most of your meals at La Casa del Zorro, which has the best food in town. Guests and drop-ins dine in the Presidio and Butterfield rooms amid paintings of stagecoaches and early California scenes. The surroundings may be Western, but don't show up for dinner in blue jeans; the resort has an evening dress code in its restaurant. For more informal dining, local folks like the Rawhide Restaurant and Saloon out by the Borrego Valley Airport and Young China Cafe, a landmark eatery in old World War II Quonset huts near the center of town.

You'll quickly discover that enjoyment of the desert itself is a significant part of the relaxed life-style in Borrego Springs. At the western edge of town is the Anza-Borrego park headquarters and a new million-dollar visitors center. Like the shelters of desert animals, it's built underground and topped with displays of native plants and rocks. Exhibits inside explain more about the desert's history, geology, wildlife, and weather. Be sure to watch the outstanding slide show about desert life. For your weekend excursions in the park, ask at the visitors' center for a map, self-guided-tour leaflets, and current road conditions. The rangers will tell you the subjects and times of their weekend naturalist programs, too.

By hiking the nearby Borrego Palm Canyon nature trail, you'll find out that the desert is more beautiful and alive than it sometimes seems. Take your time ambling along this path, which offers a close-up look at 15 desert plants once used by the Cahuilla *(ka-WE-ya)* Indians for food, medicine, and shelter. You'll see buckhorn cholla, creosote bush, honey mesquite, white sage, California fan palms, and more. Continue up the canyon to view a scenic grove of those native palms, officially named *Washingtonia filifera* in honor of the first U.S. President. The Cahuilla ate the palm's dried fruit and used its fronds to make baskets, sandal-like footwear, and even houses.

Afterward, follow the park's auto-tour brochures and drive east on S22 beyond Borrego Springs to witness more of the desert's varied geography. If the dirt side road is open, take the 4½-mile trip to Font's Point for a view of the multicolored Borrego Badlands, a maze of barren, steep-sided ravines. They were carved through the centuries by water erosion during the desert's infrequent thunderstorms. Farther along S22 are faults and fractures created by earthquakes.

An alternative to exploring the park on your own is to arrange an outing with 4-Wheel Drive Desert Tours. For years Dick Linkroum has been escorting visitors in his Jeep all over Anza-Borrego. He shares his intimate desert knowledge with up to four passengers on all-day itineraries that are designed according to what you especially want to see and experience. Book well in advance for this adventurous personalized outing, especially during the wildflower season.

There's not much in the way of evening entertainment in Borrego Springs, except for looking at the star-filled sky or attending a park campfire program at the Borrego Palm Canyon campground. La Casa del Zorro usually draws a crowd on Saturday night for its bountiful buffet, which alternates weekly with theme dinners and dance music during the winter season. Before turning in for a peaceful night's sleep, arrange at the hotel reception desk to have a picnic lunch ready for the next day's excursion to the southern part of the park.

You'll relive the travels of Old West pioneers by driving south from Borrego Springs on S3 and California 78 to rejoin S2, the county road that parallels the historic Southern Emigrant Trail. At Scissors Crossing, where the highways intersect, a marker recalls the location of the San Felipe Stage Station. Farther along S2, turn left at the sign to the Little Pass Campground and follow campground roads on the left side until you spot a canyonlike cleft in the hills. Walk to the marker that describes the Foot and Walker Pass, a place where stage passengers got out so the horses could climb the steep hill. Then stroll up to the high point, where you can look down on wagon-wheel tracks, traces of the original route that ran through the desert.

After driving south three more miles to Box Canyon, also take the walkway down to the spot where Lieutenant Colonel Cooke and his Mormon Battalion widened the trail through the gorge with picks and shovels in 1847, thus opening the first road into southern California wide enough for wagons. As S2 descends to the western limits of the great Colorado Desert, you'll find the Vallecito Stage Station in a green oasis. Built in 1835 and first used as a stop on the San Antonio–San Diego "Jackass" Mail Line, the adobe was authentically reconstructed in 1934 and is now part of a San Diego county park. The Vallecito station was a welcome sight to westbound stage passengers, because it marked the end of their desert crossing. Read the plaques that tell about important events at this historic outpost.

Continue a few miles more for a refreshing finish to your weekend in the Anza-Borrego desert, a relaxing dip in the therapeutic mineral pools at Agua Caliente Hot Springs, also a county park. Beyond are the sites of two more way stations on the Butterfield Stage route, at Palm Springs and

Carrizo Marsh, but these can be reached only by vehicles with 4-wheel drive.

Return to Los Angeles by following S2 northwest to join California 79 near Warner Springs and continue home the way you came. For an alternate route, you can make a longer circle trip back to Los Angeles by continuing southeast on S2 to join Interstate 8 at Ocotillo. Then go west toward San Diego and pick up Interstate 15 or 5 for the drive north.

Round trip is about 360 miles.

Borrego Springs Area Code: 619

SIGHTSEEING   *Anza-Borrego Desert State Park,* headquarters and visitors center located at west end of Palm Canyon Road (P.O. 428), Borrego Springs 92004, 767-5311. Visitors center open every day from 9 A.M. to 5 P.M., except June through August from 10 A.M. to 3 P.M. on weekends. Desert exhibits; also 25-minute slide show presented on the hour. Naturalist programs offered weekends and holidays except in summer. ● *4-Wheel Drive Desert Tours,* P.O. Box 511, Borrego Springs 92004, 767-5707. All-day explorations via specially equipped Jeep anywhere in Anza-Borrego park; $80 per couple or $35 per person for 4 passengers. A rewarding experience. ● *Rams Hill Country Club,* 1881 Rams Hill Road (near La Casa del Zorro Resort), Borrego Springs 92004, 767-5125. New 18-hole public golf course; $25 weekends, $20 weekdays, plus mandatory cart rental. ● *Agua Caliente County Park,* 1 mile south of Agua Caliente Springs off S2, 565-3600. Popular since Indian days for therapeutic hot springs. Features mineral pools, bathhouse, recreation building, general store, and gas station, plus camping (see below) and picnicking.

LODGING   *La Casa del Zorro,* Borrego Springs and Yaqui Pass Road (or P.O. Box 127), Borrego Springs 92004, 767-5323; $50, casitas (cottages) from $75, October through May. Rates considerably lower during hot summer months. Also excellent restaurant (see below). Two-night minimum stay on weekends. ● *Club Circle Resort,* 3134 Club Circle East (or P.O. Box 338), Borrego Springs 92004, 767-5944; $50. Fully furnished condominium apartments surrounded by 9-hole, 3-par golf course. Two-night minimum. ● *Villas Borrego Resort,* 533 Palm Canyon Drive (or P.O. Box 1077), Borrego Springs 92004, 767-5371; $60. Condominium apartments with kitchens. Two-night minimum. ● Borrego Springs also has a half dozen modest motels with 7 to 21 rooms and rates from $28; a list is available from the chamber of commerce (see below).

CAMPING   Anza-Borrego Desert State Park (see above) has three main fee campgrounds, and visitors may also camp anywhere along park roads without charge. *Borrego Palm Canyon,* near park headquarters and Borrego Springs off S2, 52 RV sites with hookups and 65 tent sites; $6 per night. *Tamarisk Grove,* 12 miles south of Borrego Springs on S3, 25 sites, $6 nightly. *Bow Willow,* 12 miles south of Agua Caliente Springs off S2, 10 sites, $3 per night. Reservations through Ticketron advised in winter and spring wildflower season. ● *Vallecito County Park,* 4 miles north of Agua Caliente Springs on S2, 565-3600. 50 sites, $5 per night. ● *Agua Caliente County Park* (see above). 140 sites, many with hookups. $9 nightly. Bathing in natural hot springs.

DINING   *La Casa Del Zorro* (see above). Breakfast, lunch, and dinner daily; coats required at dinner. Delicious steak, lobster, and continental cuisine. ● *Rawhide Restaurant and Salon,* 1886 East Palm Canyon Drive, Borrego Springs, 767-5222. 3 miles east of town at Borrego Valley Airport. Sunday champagne brunch, dinner nightly, lunch daily except Monday, breakfast on Saturday. Popular place with good food. ● *Young China Cafe,* east of Christmas Circle on Palm Canyon Drive, Borrego Springs, 767-5502. Venerable Chinese eatery in converted Quonset huts. Lunch and dinner daily except Wednesdays.

FOR MORE INFORMATION   Contact the Borrego Springs Chamber of Commerce, 622 Palm Canyon Drive (or P.O. Box 66), Borrego Springs 92004, 767-5555. Hours: 10 A.M. to 4 P.M. Wednesday through Sunday. Lists of lodgings and restaurants. ● Also, Anza-Borrego Desert State Park (see above) for touring and camping information.

Springtime Spectacular: Viewing the Wildflowers

Springtime brings a profusion of color to the Southern California scene as wildflowers awake across the countryside. Winter rain, spring sunshine, and the altitude determine the extent of the annual floral extravaganza, but you're certain to find a good show somewhere in the Southland from mid-March through May.

Easter week traditionally is an excellent time to view the bright blossoms that are scattered like a patchwork quilt, first in the lower Colorado Desert regions and later in the higher Mojave Desert areas. Of course, Mother Nature can change her fickle mind and cancel the show. Too many overcast days or strong winds will fold up the flower petals and ruin the dazzling display.

With any luck, you'll see a colorful array on any weekend excursion during the wildflower season. The blossoms pop open in more shades than a rainbow, notably yellow, orange, pink, purple, and blue, as well as white. Easy to spot from your car is the brilliant golden California poppy, the official state flower. California lilac, lupine, and wild mustard also are obvious to passing motorists. However, many wildflowers are so small that you need to get on hands and knees to see their tiny petals. Some are so minute and close to the ground that veteran viewers have nicknamed them "belly flowers." For the most enjoyment, buy an illustrated wild-flower book to take on your outing. Then be on the lookout for plants like fiddleneck, sand verbena, coreopsis, desert dandelion, blazing star, sand mat, woolly marigold, evening primrose, and dozens more.

To help you locate the best of the blooms, here are some suggestions for wildflower excursions in springtime. Before taking off, avoid disappointment by calling the flower folks at your destination for an up-to-the-minute blossom report; phone numbers are given for those local contacts.

What follows is a county-by-county report on wildflower viewing around the Los Angeles area, starting to the south in the low Colorado Desert areas of San Diego County, where the flowers often bloom the earliest. Be aware that many wildflower fanciers are on the road from March through May, so be sure to reserve accommodations before you take off for the weekend, especially in those desert areas where lodging is limited.

For specific places to shelter overnight and dine out, as well as driving instructions, refer to the trips that include the wildflower areas described below.

If you'd rather not worry where to look for the flowers, hire a wild-flower guide. Pat Flanagan, whose tour service goes by the novel name of Rent-a-Naturalist, will hop in your car and direct you to San Diego County's best floral displays, especially in Anza-Borrego Desert State Park. (See "Adventures in Anza-Borrego Desert State Park," page 256.) She'll guide a carload around for $15 per hour, with a four-hour minimum. Call her at (619) 765-1066 or write Box 301 BSR, Julian 92036.

Wildflower outings in that vast park also can be arranged with 4-Wheel Drive Desert Tours, operated by Dick Linkroum. He'll escort you to Anza-Borrego's blossoms in his specially equipped Jeep. An all-day excursion costs $80 per couple or $35 per person for 4 passengers. Call (619) 767-5707 or write P.O. Box 511, Borrego Springs 92004.

Park rangers will help you find the flowers too, including blooming ocotillo and cactus. Pick up the brochure, which is updated every two weeks with the sites currently in blossom, and ask about the ranger-led wildflower tours by foot and car. Also inquire which evening campfire programs feature talks about wildflowers and desert plants. Stop by the Anza-Borrego Desert State Park visitors center at the west end of Palm

Canyon Road in Borrego Springs (P.O. Box 428, ZIP 92004) or call (619) 767-5311.

You also can make your park wildflower excursion headquarters at the attractive town of Julian. (See "Escape to Old-Time Julian and Heavenly Palomar Mountain," page 153.) It's a few miles southwest of Borrego Springs in San Diego's hilly backcountry. You might want to time your visit to Julian for its annual wildflower show in early May, when the flowers are blooming at higher elevations around that area. The local townsfolk collect several hundred varieties each day of the week-long show and display them in the town hall from 9 A.M. to 5 P.M.

The low Colorado Desert extends north into Riverside County, and so does a splendid assortment of wildflowers. In the Palm Springs area you'll see purple sand verbena, yellow-flowered desert gourd vines, wild daisies, buttercups, and many more types. (See "Palm Springs: Part 1," page 240, and "Part 2," page 246.)

Visit Moorten's Botanical Garden at 1701 South Palm Canyon Drive to view 30 varieties of wildflowers that usually are in full bloom. They're part of a collection of nearly 2,000 desert plants that Pat Moorten and her husband began in 1937. She'll give you a free map to show you where to look for wildflowers in the Coachella Valley. Hours are 9 A.M. to 5 P.M. daily; adult admission costs $1, children 50 cents. You also can phone for wildflower information, (619) 327-6555.

Continue on South Palm Canyon Drive to the peaceful canyons in the Agua Caliente Indian Reservation to view more flowering desert plants. Daily hours are 9 A.M. to 4 P.M., through May. Entry is $3.50 per adult, 50 cents for children. Also explore for other bright blossoms in Chino Canyon along the road that leads to the desert station of Palm Springs Aerial Tramway.

Nearby in Palm Desert, head for the Living Desert Reserve, 47-900 Portola Avenue, where a sand dune is seeded annually with wildflowers and should be ablaze with color. The 1,200-acre wildlife preserve has many more desert plants and animals on display. It's open 9 A.M. to 5 P.M., through May. Admission costs $2.50; children 16 years and under enter free with an adult. The Living Desert Reserve also sponsors an annual all-day wildflower tour by air-conditioned bus in March or April. Phone (619) 346-5694 for details.

Northeast of Palm Springs is a very popular destination for folks in search of wildflowers, Joshua Tree National Monument. It spans the Riverside–San Bernardino county line, as well as high and low deserts, the Mojave and the Colorado. (See "Desert on Display at Joshua Tree National Monument," page 233.) Rangers at the visitors centers near Twentynine Palms and at the southern Cottonwood entrance will mark park maps directing you to the flowering areas. Buy the informative wildflower brochure, *Pollen on Your Nose,* to identify what you see. Or join the rangers for escorted wildflower tours by car and foot during Easter week and April weekends. Phone (619) 367-7511 for meeting times and places. During April and May you also can count on the Joshua trees and other yuccas being in flower, although the abundance of their impressive creamy white blossoms is difficult to predict.

On the way to or from Joshua Tree National Monument, you'll find wildflower specimens that are collected daily and put on display at the Hi-Desert Nature Museum in Yucca Valley. Each plant is labeled by its common and scientific names to help you identify the flowers you see in the wild. Go through the town of Yucca Valley on California 62 (Twentynine Palms Highway) and turn left on Dumosa Drive to reach the museum. This annual wildflower exhibit is scheduled in April, Wednesdays through Sundays from 1 to 5 P.M., but call in advance to be sure, (619) 365-9814.

North of Joshua Tree National Monument in the Mojave you can join Desert Trails for wildflower tours from Barstow. Harvey Walker runs all-day bus and 4-wheel-drive trips to high-desert areas that are in bloom. Call (619) 256-3430 for tour dates and rates. (See "Beyond Barstow: Fun for All Ages Around Calico," page 229.) Also, the staff at the Bureau of Land Management's Barstow Way Station will give you a high-desert map and can point out good viewing areas. Located at 831 Barstow Road in Barstow, the visitors center is open weekdays from 8 A.M. to 4:30 P.M. and Saturday 9 A.M. to 5 P.M.; closed Sunday. Phone (619) 256-3591.

Closer to Los Angeles, the Antelope Valley always draws a caravan of wildflower fans. Get there by going north on Interstate 5 and California 14 to Lancaster, where the accommodating local folks even open a Wildflower Center during the month of April to guide you to the best viewing spots. It's at 841 West Avenue J and open from 9 A.M. to 4 P.M. daily except Mondays. Pick up a map to the areas currently in bloom, and buy some seeds to try your luck growing flowers at home. The center's phone is (805) 945-5055.

Be sure to see the floral fantasy at the Antelope Valley Poppy Reserve, 15 miles west of town via Avenue I/Lancaster Road. Dedicated to preserving the Golden State flower, this 1,760-acre state park also features a hillside interpretive center with desert displays and paintings. During April, the poppy's top flowering time, it's usually open daily from 9 A.M. to 4 P.M. weekends and 10 A.M. to 3 P.M. weekdays. Entry is $2 per car. Phone (805) 942-0662.

If you decide to stay overnight in the area to spend more time in search of wildflowers, Lancaster has a number of lodgings, including the Antelope Valley Inn (telephone 948-4651), the Desert Inn (942-8401), and the Essex House (948-0961)—all in area code 805. Contact the Lancaster Chamber of Commerce, 44943 North 10th Street West (ZIP 93534), for a list of accommodations and restaurants. The phone is (805) 948-4518.

Wildflowers abound in Kern County as well, and its Board of Trade will help you find them. Bulletins noting the latest blooming areas are posted at the visitors information center, 2101 Oak Street in Bakersfield. On weekdays you can call (805) 861-2367. (See "History and Outdoor Adventure in Kern County and Isabella Lake," page 167.)

Travelers in the valley, mountain, and coastal areas of Santa Barbara, Ventura, and San Luis Obispo counties also are likely to see wildflowers during April and May. In fact, if you're enjoying a getaway weekend anywhere in Southern California from March through May, ask the local folks where the flowers might be blooming.

Finally, here's a plea from fellow nature lovers: please leave the wildflowers for everyone to enjoy. If you're tempted to take some of their pretty blossoms home, take color pictures instead.

Index

A

Aerospace Historical Center, 112, 113
Agua Caliente County Park, 259, 260, 261
Agua Caliente Hot Springs, 259, 260
Agua Caliente Indian Reservation, 241, 242, 247, 250, 263
Agua Caliente Racetrack, 124, 127
Agua Hedionda Lagoon, 87
Ah Louis Store, 14, 16
Ahwahnee Hotel, 139, 140, 142, 143
Airport-in-the-Sky, 48
Alessandro Island, 196
Alisal Guest Ranch, 174, 177
Aliso Beach Park, 66, 67
Alt Karlsbad, 86, 89
Alta Sierra, 170
Altmans RV Center, xii
Amargosa Opera House, 227, 228
Amtrak, xii
Anacapa Island, 35, 37–39
Anaheim, 74–80
Anaheim Convention Center, 75, 79
Anaheim Stadium, 75, 79
Andreas Canyon, 247
Andree Clark Bird Refuge, 20
Annual Events, x
Antelope Valley Poppy Reserve, 264
Antelope Valley Wildflower Center, 264
Anza-Borrego Desert State Park, 256, 261, 262
Apple Valley, 178–181
Apple Valley Inn, 178, 180, 181
Apple Valley Pow Wow, 180
Arabian Nights Pageant, 253

Arch Rock, 38
Armacost and Royston, 33
Art-a-Fair, 67
Atascadero State Beach, 16, 17
Automobile Club of Southern California, xi
Avalon, 47–52
Avalon Casino, 49, 51
Avenida Revolucion, 123–124
Avila Beach, 8–9, 11, 12
Avila Hot Springs, 9, 11

B

Badger Pass, 141–142
Badger Pass Ski Area, 141–142, 143
Badwater, 225
Bahia de Todos Santos, 128
Baja California, 123–131, 135
Bakersfield, 168, 170–171, 265
Balboa, 60, 61–62
Balboa Ferry, 60, 62
Balboa Park, 108–113
Balboa Pavilion, 60, 61, 62
Balboa Pier, 60
Ballard, 174, 177
Ballard Canyon Winery, 175, 176
Banning, 187
Barston, 229–233, 264
Barstow Way Station, 230, 232, 264
Barton Flats, 150
Batequitas Lagoon, 87
Bernardo Winery, 216, 218
Big Bear Lake, 148–153
Black Mountain, 15, 161, 182

Black Mountains, 225
Blue Jay, 149
Bodegas de Santo Thomas, 128, 130
Bonsall Antique Collective, 209, 212
Borrego Badlands, 258
Borrego Palm Canyon Nature Trail, 258
Borrego Springs, 251–258, 260, 262, 263
Bowmans at Wheeler Hot Springs, 184, 185
Bridalveil Fall, 140
Brinkerhoff Avenue, 26, 27
Broadway Pier, 104
Brooks Institute of Photography, 31
Buellton, 174
Buena Park, 74–80
Buena Vista Lagoon, 87

C
Cabot's Old Indian Pueblo, 238, 239
Cabrillo Beach, 20
Cabrillo Festival, 107
Cabrillo Marine Museum, 133, 135
Cabrillo National Monument, 103, 105, 106, 107
Cajon Pass, 178
Cal Poly State University, 15
Calico, 229–230, 232–233
Calico Early Man Site, 231–232
Calico Ghost Town Regional Park, 229–230, 232, 233
Calico Mountains, 229
California Alligator Farm, 74, 79
California Challenge Fire Muster, 17
Callaway Vineyard and Winery, 210, 213
Cambria, 4–7, 161
Camp Joseph H. Pendleton, 83–84
Camping, x, xii
Cannery Village, 59, 63
Capistrano Depot, 71, 73
Carlsbad, 85–87, 89–90
Carlsbad Spring Fair, 86
Carlsbad State Beach, 87
Carnegie Cultural Arts Center, 42, 43
Carpinteria, 32, 33
Casa Sirena Marina Hotel, 40, 43
Catalina Cruises, 49, 50, 51, 133
Catalina Island Museum, 49, 51
Catalina Sightseeing Tours, 48–49, 50
Cathedral City, 248

Cayucos, 6
Cedar Grove, 146, 147
Chambers of Commerce, x
Channel Islands Harbor, 40–44
Channel Islands National Park, 37–39
Cherry Festival, 190
Cherry Valley, 187, 191
Chino Canyon, 243, 263
Chocolate Mountains, 254
Cilurzo Vineyards and Winery, 211, 213
Cleveland National Forest, 72, 153
Coachella, 253, 255
Coachella Valley, 241, 243, 251, 263
Cold Spring Tavern, 176, 177
Colorado Desert, 233, 243, 252, 256, 259, 262, 263
Corona, 200, 203
Corona del Mar, 60, 61, 62
Corona del Mar State and City Beach, 60, 62, 63
Coronado, 119–122
Coronado Bay Bridge, 119, 121
Coto de Caza, 192, 194
Crestline, 148
Crystal Cave, 145, 146
Curry Village, 139, 142, 143
Cuyamaca Rancho State Park, 154–155, 156, 157

D
Daggett, 231
Dallidet Adobe, 14, 16
Dana Point, 69–74
Dana Point Harbor, 69–74, 133
Danish Days Celebration, 174, 177
Dante's View, 226
Death Valley, 225–228
Death Valley Junction, 227, 228
Death Valley Museum, 226
Death Valley National Monument, 225–228
Del Mar, 93–96
Del Mar National Horse Show, 95
Del Mar Thoroughbred Club, 95
Dennison Park, 183
Desert Christ Park, 235, 236
Desert Hot Springs, 237–240
Devil's Hole, 225
Dining, x

Disneyland, 74–80
Disneyland Hotel, 75–76, 79
Doheny State Beach, 69, 73
Doll and Toy Museum, 74, 79

E
Eagle Mine, 154, 156
Edward-Dean Museum of Decorative Arts,
    187, 190
Edwards Mansion, 190
El Camino Real, 158, 164
El Capitan, 140
El Encanto Hotel, 31, 34
El Paseo, 24, 27
El Presidio de Santa Barbara State Historic
    Park, 24, 27
El Rancho Escondido, 48
El Toreo Bullring, 126
El Toro, 191
Eldorado Date Gardens, 252, 255
Elsinore Mountains, 200, 201
Elsinore Parachute Center, 201, 202
Elsinore Valley, 199
Embarcadero Marine Park, 105
Emigrant Pass, 227
Emigrant Trail, 256, 259
Encinitas, 88–89
Ensenada, 128–131
Escondido, 216–217, 218–219
Estrella Adobe Church, 160
Estrella River Winery, 160, 162

F
Fallbrook, 208–210, 212–214
Fashion Island, 58
Fernald House, 26, 27
Festival of Arts, 64, 66, 67
Festival of Lights Boat Parade, 62
Festival of the Whales, 72
Fiesta de Las Golondrinas, 73
Filsinger Vineyards and Winery, 211, 213
Firestone Vineyard, 175, 176
Fisherman's Wharf Village, 41
Fishing, xii
Font's Point, 258
Fort Tejon State Historic Park, 167, 170
Forty-Niners Encampment, 228
Freeways, xi
Fresno, 139, 145

Frontier Museum Historical Center, 212,
    213
Fronton Palacio, 123, 126
Furnace Creek, 225, 226, 227, 228
Furnace Creek Inn, 225, 226, 228
Furnace Creek Ranch, 225, 226, 228

G
Gallery of Historical Figures, 183, 184
Giant Forest, 144, 145, 146, 147
Glacier Point, 140, 142
Glen Ivy Hot Springs, 201–203
Glorietta Bay Marina, 120, 121
Gold Fever Trail, 150
Goldmine Ski Area, 150, 151
Goleta, 31–32
Good Old Days Museum, 10, 11
Grant Grove, 144, 145, 146, 147
Grape Day Park, 216–217, 218
Grapevine Canyon, 167
Great American Melodrama and Vaude-
    ville Theater, 10, 11
Greenhorn Mountain, 170
Greyhound Bus, xii
Grover City, 10, 12
Grubstake Days, 236
Guajome Adobe, 221–222
Guajome Regional Park, 221, 222

H
Half Dome, 140
Hall of Champions, 111, 112
Harbor Island, 103, 105
Harmony, 6, 7
Harmony Borax Works, 226
Hart Winery, 210
Harvey House, 230–231
Hearst Castle, 3–7, 161
Hearst San Simeon State Historical Monu-
    ment, 3–7, 161
Heisler Park, 65
Helen Moe's Antique Doll Museum, 159,
    161
Hell's Gate, 255
Heritage House, 206, 207
Heritage Park, 99, 101
Hi-Desert Nature Museum, 235, 236, 264
Highland Springs Resort, 187, 190, 191
Historical Museum of Old California, 99

Hobby City, 74, 79
Holcomb Valley, 150
Hortense Miller Garden, 65, 67
Hotel del Coronado, 119–120, 121
Hotel Riviera del Pacifico, 129
Hotel La Valencia, 91, 95
House of Hospitality, 111, 112
House of Pacific Relations, 111, 113
Hughes Flying Boat Expo, 53, 54–55, 56
Hussong's Cantina, 128, 130

I
Imperial Beach, 121
Indian Wells, 252
Indian Wells Date Gardens, 252, 255
Indio, 251–252, 254–256
Inn at Rancho Santa Fe, 220, 222
Irvine Bowl, 66
Irvine Lake, 193, 194
Irvine Regional Park, 193, 194
Isabella Lake, 169–172

J
J. Carey Cellars, 175, 176
Jensen's Date and Citrus Gardens, 252
Joshua Tree National Monument, 233–236, 263–264
Julian, 153–158, 263
Julian Fall Harvest and Apple Days Celebration, 153, 157
Julian Memorial Museum, 154, 156
Junipero Serra Museum, 98, 101

K
Kern County Museum and Pioneer Village, 168–169, 170–171
Kern River, 168, 169, 170, 171, 172
Kern River County Park, 172
Kernville, 169, 170, 171
Keys View, 234
Kilimanjaro Hiking Trail, 216
Kimberly Crest, 189, 190
Kingdom of the Dancing Stallions, 74, 79
Kingdom of the Dolls, 238, 239
Kings Canyon National Park, 144–147
Kings River, 146
Kings River Canyon, 146
Knott's Berry Farm, 74–80

L
La Bufadora, 129
La Casa del Zorro, 257, 258, 259, 260, 261
La Costa Hotel and Spa, 86, 90
La Jolla, 91–92, 94–96
La Jolla Cave and Shell Shop, 92, 94
La Jolla Museum of Contemporary Art, 92, 94
La Quinta, 255, 266
Laflin Date Gardens, 253, 255
Laguna Beach, 64–68
Laguna Beach Museum of Art, 65, 67
Laguna Hills, 191
Lake Arrowhead, 148–153
Lake Cachuma, 176
Lake Cachuma County Park, 177
Lake Casitas, 183, 184
Lake Elsinore, 199–203
Lake Elsinore State Park, 200, 202, 203
Lake Henshaw, 155
Lake Isabella, 169, 171
Lake Perris, 195–196
Lake Perris State Recreation Area, 195–196, 198, 199
Lake San Marcos, 221, 222
Lancaster, 264
Las Flores Adobe, 84
Las Tablas Winery, 161, 162
Lawrence Welk Village Theater-Museum, 217, 218
Lee Anderson's Colvalda Date Company, 253, 255
Leucadia, 88, 89
Libbey Park, 181, 182, 184
Lido Marina Village, 59, 63
Little San Bernardino Mountains, 237
Live Oak Park, 209
Living Desert Reserve, 248, 250, 263
Lodging, x
Lompoc, 163–167
Lompoc Valley, 165
Lompoc Valley Flower Festival, 165, 166
Long Beach, 50, 52–57, 133
Los Alamos, 163–164, 166
Los Angeles, ix
Los Olivos, 175, 176, 177
Los Padres National Forest, 29, 176, 181, 183

M
Machado-Steward Adobe, 99
Madonna Inn, 13, 17
Magee House, 87
Main Beach Park, 65
Maps, xi
Marina del Rey, 133
Mariposa Grove, 140, 142
Marriott's Santa Barbara Biltmore, 19, 22
Matilija Creek, 184
Matilija Hot Springs, 184, 185
Mattei's Tavern, 175, 177
Merced, 142
Merced River, 140
Mesa Verde Winery, 211, 213
Mirror Lake, 140
Mission Archaeological Museum, 36, 39
Mission Bay Park, 114–118
Mission Beach, 114
Mission Fiesta Days, 166
Mission Inn, 204–205, 207–208
Mission La Purisima State Historic Park, 164–165, 166
Mission San Antonio de Pala, 217–218, 219
Mission San Buenaventura, 35, 36, 39
Mission San Diego de Alcala, 97, 101
Mission San Juan Capistrano, 70–71, 72
Mission San Luis Obispo de Tolosa, 14, 16
Mission San Luis Rey de Francia, 82, 84
Mission San Miguel Arcangel, 159, 161
Mission Santa Barbara, 30–31, 33
Mission Santa Ines, 173, 176
Mission Santa Ysabel, 155, 156
Mission Valley, 97
Modjeska Canyon, 193, 194
Mojave Desert, 141, 170, 225, 229, 232, 233, 261, 264
Mojave Narrows Regional Park, 179, 180
Mojave River, 179
Mojave River Valley Museum, 230, 232
Montana de Oro State Park, 16, 17
Montecito, 29, 34
Moonridge Animal Park, 150, 151
Moortens Botanical Garden, 247–248, 249, 263
Morey House, 188, 190
Morongo Valley, 239
Morro Bay, 13, 15

Morro Bay Aquarium, 15, 17
Morro Bay State Park, 15, 17
Morro Rock, 13, 15
Morro Strand State Beach, 16
Mount Ada, 49
Mount Palomar Winery, 211, 213
Mount Rubidoux, 206, 207
Mount Rubidoux Memorial Park, 206, 207
Mount San Gorgonio, 234
Mount San Jacinto, 234, 237, 242
Mount San Jacinto State Park, 243, 244
Mount Whitney, 144
Movieland, 74, 79
Mozart Festival, 17
Murray Adobe, 14, 16
Murray Canyon, 247
Museum of Man, 111, 112
Museum of Natural History-Morro Bay State Park, 15, 16
Museum of World Wars, 75, 79

N
National Date Festival, 251, 252–253, 255
National Shakespeare Festival, 111, 113
Nevada Falls, 141
Newport Beach, 58–63, 133
Newport Center, 58
Newport Harbor, 59
Newport Pier, 59
North Island Naval Air Station, 103

O
O'Neill Museum, 71, 72
O'Neill Regional Park, 192, 193
Oak Glenn, 188, 190, 191
Oak Grove, 257
Oak Tree Village, 188
Oceano, 10, 11, 12
Oceanside, 81–85
Oceanside Harbor, 81, 133
Ojai Music Festival, 182, 185
Ojai Valley, 181–186
Ojai Valley Inn and Country Club, 182, 185, 186
Ojai Valley Museum, 182, 184
Ojai Valley Tennis Tournament, 181, 185
Oktoberfest, 151
Old Creek Ranch Winery, 183, 185
Old Globe Theater, 111

Old Miners' Days, 151
Old Spanish Days Carriage Museum, 26, 27
Old Spanish Days Fiesta, 24, 27
Old Town Opera House, 99, 101
Old Town San Diego State Historic Park, 98, 101
Olivas Adobe, 37, 39
Olivehain, 221
Orange County Marine Institute, 70, 72
Orange Empire Railway Museum, 197, 198
Ortega Adobe, 37, 39
Ortega Highway, 71, 201
Owens Valley, 141
Oxnard, 40–44, 134

P
Pageant of the Masters, 64, 66, 67
Palm Canyon, 246, 247
Palm Desert, 248, 263
Palm Park, 20
Palm Springs, 240–251, 263
Palm Springs Aerial Tramway, 242, 243, 244
Palm Springs Desert Museum, 249, 250
Palomar Mountain, 153, 155–156
Palomar Mountain State Park, 156, 157
Palomar Observatory, 153, 155–156
Panamint Mountains, 227
Parent Navel Orange Tree, 206
Parks-Janeway Carriage House, 174, 176
Paso Robles, 158–163
Path of History, 13–14
Penguin Encounter, 115
Perris, 195–199
Perris Historical Society Museum, 198, 199
Perris Valley Airport, 196, 198
Perris Valley Paracenter, 196, 197, 198
Pesenti Winery, 160, 162
Pine Hills, 155, 157
Pioneer Days, 236
Pioneer Yosemite History Center, 140
Pismo Beach, 7–12
Pismo Beach Mardi Gras, 8, 11
Pismo State Beach, 9–10, 12
Playas de Tijuana Beach, 126
Plaza de Monumental Bullring, 126

Plaza Park, 42
Plaza Rio Tijuana, 124
Point Loma, 103, 105
Point Loma Lighthouse, 105, 106
Point Mugu, 41
Port Hueneme, 40, 42, 43
Port San Luis, 9, 11
Presidio Park, 98
Public Transportation, xii
Puerto Nuevo, 125, 127
Purisima Hills, 164

Q
Quail Botanic Gardens, 88, 89
Queen Mary, 52–57
Queen Mary Hotel, 52–54, 56, 57
Quivira Basin, 116

R
Rancho Bernardo Inn, 215, 216, 219
Rancho California, 209, 210, 213
Rancho Los Alamitos, 55, 56
Rancho Los Cerritos, 55, 56
Rancho Mirage, 248
Rancho Santa Fe, 219–220, 222
Rancho Sisquoc Winery, 175–176, 177
Recreational Vehicles, xii
Red Tile Walking Tour, 24–27
Redlands, 150, 188–191
Redondo Beach, 133
Reuben H. Fleet Space Theater and Science Center, 111, 112
Ribbon Falls, 141
Rim of the World Drive, 148
Rio Bravo Resort, 167–168, 171, 172
Rios Adobe, 71
Rios-Caledonia Adobe, 159, 162
River Park, 166
Riverside, 204–208
Riverside Art Center, 206, 207
Riverside County Courthouse, 206
Riverside Museum, 205–206, 207
Riverside Park, 170
Rogers Gardens, 61, 62
Rosarito, 125–127
Rosarito Beach Hotel, 125
Roy Rogers and Dale Evans Museum, 178, 180
Running Springs, 149

S
Salton Sea, 251–252, 253–254
Salton Sea State Recreational Area, 253–254, 255, 256
San Bernardino, 186
San Bernardino Asistencia, 189, 190
San Bernardino County Museum, 190
San Bernardino Mountains, 148, 178, 188
San Bernardino National Forest, 148
San Buenaventura State Beach, 35
San Clemente, 84, 85
San Clemente Island, 37
San Diego, 96–118
San Diego Bay, 103, 120
San Diego Harbor, 103, 106, 134
San Diego Maritime Museum Association, 104, 107
San Diego Museum of Art, 111, 112
San Diego Natural History Museum, 111, 112
San Diego Scenic Drive, 103, 105
San Diego Wild Animal Park, 214–216, 218
San Diego Zoo, 109–110, 112
San Elijo State Beach, 90
San Ignacio Lagoon, 135
San Joaquin Valley, 142, 168
San Juan Capistrano, 69–74
San Juan Capistrano Hot Springs, 72
San Luis Bay Inn, 8, 11, 12
San Luis County Fair, 162
San Luis Obispo, 12–18
San Luis Obispo Art Center, 14, 16
San Luis Obispo County Historical Museum, 14, 16
San Luis Rey River, 81, 209
San Marcos Pass, 176
San Miguel, 160, 161–162
San Miguel Island, 37
San Nicholas Island, 37
San Pasqual Vineyards, 216, 218
San Pedro, 50, 132–133
San Simeon, 3–6, 7
San Simeon State Beach, 4, 7
San Ysidro Guest Ranch, 29, 34
Santa Ana, 191
Santa Ana Mountains, 191, 201
Santa Ana River, 204
Santa Barbara, 19–34, 135

Santa Barbara Biltmore, 19, 22
Santa Barbara Botanic Garden, 30, 33
Santa Barbara County Courthouse, 23, 24–25, 27
Santa Barbara Historical Society Museum, 24, 27
Santa Barbara International Orchid Show, 33
Santa Barbara Island, 37
Santa Barbara Museum of Art, 25, 27
Santa Barbara Museum of Natural History, 30, 33
Santa Barbara National Horse and Flower Show, 34
Santa Barbara Orchid Estate, 32, 33
Santa Barbara Polo and Racquet Club, 32, 33
Santa Barbara Scenic Drive, 30–32
Santa Barbara Zoological Gardens, 20, 22
Santa Catalina Island, 47, 52
Santa Catalina Island Conservancy, 48
Santa Clara River, 37
Santa Cruz Island, 37
Santa Lucia Mountains, 3, 12, 158, 160
Santa Margarita Mountains, 83
Santa Monica, 41
Santa Paula, 184
Santa Rosa Creek, 37, 161
Santa Rosa Island, 37, 89, 93
Santa Rosa Mountains, 248
Santa Ynez, 174, 176
Santa Ynez Mountains, 19
Santa Ynez Valley, 173–177
Santa Ynez Valley Historical Society Museum, 174, 176
Santa Ysabel, 155, 156
Santiago Canyon, 193
Sawdust Festival, 66, 67
Scammons Lagoon, 135
Scotty's Castle, 226–227, 228
Scripps Aquarium-Museum, 92, 94
Sea World, 114–116, 117
Seabee Museum, 42, 43
Seaport Village, 104–105, 107
Self-Realization Fellowship, 89, 90
Sequoia National Park, 144–147, 169
Shell Beach, 12
Shelter Island, 103, 105
Sherman Indian High School, 207

Sherman Indian Museum, 207
Sherman Library and Gardens, 61, 62
Shield's Date Gardens, 252, 254
Shirley Meadows Ski Area, 170, 171
Shoreline Village, 55, 56
Shoshone, 225
Sierra Nevada Mountains, 139, 141, 144
Sightseeing, v
Silver Strand, 119
Silver Strand County Beach, 42
Silverado Canyon, 193, 194
Silverwood Lake, 178, 179
Silverwood Lake State Recreation Area, 179, 180
Smiley Park, 189
Smoke Tree Stables, 247, 249
Snow Forest Ski Area, 150
Snow Summit Ski Area, 149, 150, 151
Solana Beach, 220
Solar One, 231, 232
Solvang, 173–174, 176–177
Solvang Theaterfest, 173, 177
South Carlsbad State Beach, 87, 88, 90
Southern California Automobile Club, xi
Southern California Exposition, 95
Spanish Village Art Center, 111, 112
Spreckels Organ Pavilion, 111
Spreckels Park, 121
Spruce Goose, 53, 54–55, 56
S.S. *Azure Seas,* 128, 130
Star of India, 104
Stearns Wharf, 20, 22
Stonewall Mine, 154
Stovepipe Wells, 225, 226, 228
Stow House, 32, 33
Stubbs Fuschia Nursery, 88, 89
Summerland, 33
Sycamore Mineral Springs, 9, 11

T
Tejon Pass, 167–168, 170
Temecula, 210–214
Temecula Valley, 210–211
Temescal Valley, 201, 202
Templeton, 159, 162
The Stack, xi
Thermal, 253, 255
Ticketron, xii
Tijuana, 123–124, 126–127

Tijuana Cultural Center, 124, 126
Timken Art Gallery, 111, 112
Tioga Pass, 141
Torrey Pines City Park, 93
Torrey Pines State Reserve, 93, 94
Tourmaline Gem Mine, 210, 213
Trabuco Canyon, 192, 193
Trailways Bus, xii
Trona, 227
Trussell-Winchester Adobe, 26, 27
Tucker Wildlife Sanctuary, 193, 194
Tulare, 145
Tuolomne Meadows, 141, 142
Twentynine Palms, 234, 236, 263
Twin Inns, 87, 90
Two Bunch Palms Spa and Resort, 237–238, 240

U
Union Hotel, 163–164, 166
University of California San Diego, 92
Upper Newport Bay, 58

V
Valerie Jean Date Shop, 253, 255
Vallecito County Park, 259, 261
Vallecito Stage Station, 259
Vandenberg Air Force Base, 165
Ventura, 35–37, 39–40, 134
Ventura County Court House, 36
Ventura County Historical Society Museum, 36, 39
Ventura Harbor, 38, 39
Vernal Falls, 141
Victorville, 178, 179, 180
Villa Montezuma, 100, 101
Village Green Heritage Center, 249, 250
Vincent Thomas Bridge, 50
Visalia, 145
Visitors Bureaus, x

W
Walker Pass, 170
Warner Ranch House, 257
Warner Springs, 257
Wawona Hotel, 139, 142, 143
Weidner's Begonia Gardens, 88, 89
Western States Museum of Photography, 31, 33

Wgasa Bush Line Monorail, 215, 218
Whale Watching, 131–135
Whaley House, 99, 101
Wheeler Hot Springs, 184, 185
Whiskey Flat Days, 171
Whitewater Trout Farm, 239
Wildflowers, 261–265
William Heise County Park, 155, 157
Windansea Beach, 92
Wolverton Ski Bowl, 146, 147
World Peace Tower, 206
Wrigley Memorial and Botanical Garden, 51

Y
York Mountain Winery, 161, 162
Yosemite Falls, 140
Yosemite Ice Rink, 143
Yosemite National Park, 139–144
Yosemite Valley, 139–144
Yucca Valley, 234, 235, 236, 264

Z
Zabriskie Point, 236
Zaca Mesa Winery, 175, 176